D1116783

The Theory of
MACROECONOMIC POLICY

Nancy Smith Barrett

Associate Professor of Economics, The American University

Prentice-Hall, Inc., Englewood Cliffs, New Jersey

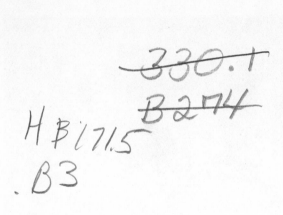
© 1972 by Prentice-Hall, Inc.
Englewood Cliffs, New Jersey.
All rights reserved.
No part of this book may be reproduced
in any form without permission
in writing from the publisher.
Library of Congress Catalog No. 79-1711842.
Printed in the United States of America.

10 9 8 7 6 5 4 3 2 1

ISBN: 0-13-913848-X

PRENTICE-HALL INTERNATIONAL, INC., London
PRENTICE-HALL OF AUSTRALIA, PTY. LTD., Sydney
PRENTICE-HALL OF CANADA, LTD., Toronto
PRENTICE-HALL OF INDIA PRIVATE LIMITED, New Delhi
PRENTICE-HALL OF JAPAN, INC., Tokyo

FOR HARRY, CLARK, AND CHRISTOPHER

. . . the ideas of economists and political philosophers, both when they are right and when they are wrong, are more powerful than is commonly understood. Indeed, the world is ruled by little else. Practical men, who believe themselves to be quite exempt from any intellectual influences, are usually the slaves of some defunct economist. Madmen in authority, who hear voices in the air, are distilling their frenzy from some academic scribbler of a few years back. I am sure that the power of vested interests is vastly exaggerated compared with gradual encroachment of ideas.

John Maynard Keynes
The General Theory of Employment, Interest, and Money

Contents

Preface
The Theory of Macroeconomic Policy

A major contribution of Keynesian economics has been to show the need for well-planned intervention in the economy by government and monetary authorities. Far from being an apologist of state socialism, Keynes believed that wise governmental control of the level of aggregate demand is the key to the long-run survival of free-enterprise capitalism.

In demonstrating the need for active government intervention, modern macroeconomic theory requires a complementary theory of economic policy. This text shows how economic policy can be designed by placing it in a theoretical framework and demonstrates how a theoretical Keynesian system can be adapted into a policy-planning or forecasting model.

The limitations of Keynesian economics for dealing with some of the problems facing policy planners are also pinpointed, and new models and programs for dealing with these problems are discussed. Alternative approaches to the theory of inflation are introduced early in the exposition, and the determination of the price level is incorporated into the general theory of income and employment rather than treated as a "special topic" late in the text. In keeping with this approach, the variables are treated in money rather than real terms in the early chapters.

Non-Keynesian models often suggest the applicability of non-Keynesian policy instruments. In developing anti-inflation policy, for instance, such programs as wage–price guidelines, investment tax credits, and depreciation policy are introduced and analyzed in terms of their efficacy in reaching the objectives of the model.

The importance of empirical specification of macroeconomic policy models is emphasized. The treatment of consumption and investment introduces the possibility of alternative *a priori* hypotheses about behavior and their implications for forecasting and policy design. An appendix on the

ix

construction and use of econometric models for forecasting and policy planning is also provided.

Departing from the traditional format, the national accounts are treated in Appendix B. To be useful for policy design, the data of the national accounts must be defined in the same terms as the economic theory on which the planning model is based. Thus, an understanding of the theory of macroeconomic policy must precede a discussion of the sources and appropriate definitions of the data used for economic forecasting and policy planning.

This text is designed for use in a one-semester course in macroeconomics beyond the introductory level. Furthermore, it should be of use to anyone who questions the relevance of economic theory to practical economic policy. No advanced mathematics beyond simple algebra is required.

I owe a great debt of gratitude to my teachers who first stimulated my interest in macroeconomics; in particular, to Robert Dorfman, James Duesenberry, and Arthur Smithies of Harvard University, and Frederick G. Reuss of Goucher College, from whom I first learned not to accept Keynesianism uncritically. Professor A. M. Agapos of Louisiana State University (New Orleans), Norman F. Keiser of San Jose College, and David J. Smyth of State University of New York at Buffalo all read the manuscript at various stages. Their suggestions enhanced the finished product (although I, alone, of course am responsible for any errors). My colleagues at The American University, Gail Ellis Huh and Richard D. Morgenstern, helped me over many difficulties.

The production of the book was directed skillfully by Jim Bacci at Prentice-Hall, under whose supervision the manuscript was miraculously turned into a book. Judy Hushbeck, Ruthann Alfred Müller, Janice L. Robinson, and Kathy Smith provided expert and cheerful editorial and typing assistance.

Finally, I would like to acknowledge the great influence that my students at The American University have had on this book. Not only did they encourage me to write it, but the book reflects many hours of discussion and debate which they initiated.

N. S. B.

Washington, D.C.
August, 1971

1

The Method
and Scope
of Economic
Theory

John Kenneth Galbraith once remarked that the bumblebee does indeed fly, defying those laws of aerodynamics which would conclude that he cannot.[1] The success of mature or industrially developed economies in maintaining high levels of production and employment in the face of affluence is similarly in contradiction to the conclusions of the "dismal" economists of the nineteenth century who foresaw overproduction, falling profit rates, and stagnation as the inevitable result of the process of economic development. To some extent, Keynes echoed the teachings of economists such as Ricardo, Malthus, and even Marx in his speculation that private demand in a mature economy would generally be inadequate to warrant full employment of the labor force. He showed, however, that the public sector, with appropriate policy planning, can maintain full employment and rising incomes indefinitely within the institutional framework of a capitalistic or free-enterprise economic system. In the Keynesian model, public policy is the key to the maintenance of affluence.

The basic theoretical analysis introduced by Keynes is readily adaptable into a model for practical policy design. This text shows how the theory of the impact of economic policy can be used for designing a policy-planning model. Implicit in the theory, therefore, is the role of economic policy as a society seeks to attain its economic goals.

1-1 The Methodology of Economic Theory

This text is concerned with how economic policy can be used to reach certain economic goals or objectives. The approach will be theoretical rather than descriptive.

Methodologically, economic theory consists of

1. describing and formulating hypotheses about economic behavior,
2. recognizing interrelationships among various aspects of economic activity,
3. analyzing, or deducing the implications of, the various hypotheses and interrelationships.

A descriptive hypothesis may have more than historical interest. Suppose the policy planner wants to know whether a transfer of income from high-income to low-income families will stimulate total spending. He wishes to test the hypothesis that the proportion of an additional dollar of income which will be spent by low-income families will exceed the percent-

---

[1] John Kenneth Galbraith, *American Capitalism: The Concept of Countervailing Power* (Boston: Houghton Mifflin Company, 1962), p. 1.

age decrease in spending by high-income families per dollar of tax collected. While the hypothesis is purely descriptive, it must be tested to gauge the impact of a potential economic program.

Some hypotheses are part of a larger analytical framework. The hypothesis that consumption increases with disposable income, together with the recognition that aggregate demand is composed of consumption and investment, leads ultimately to the conclusion that an increase in investment, by increasing income, will stimulate additional consumption and result in an increase in national income that is greater than the original change in investment. This result, known as the *multiplier effect*, is derived from the formulation of a behavioral hypothesis about consumption, the recognition of the interrelationship between aggregate demand, income, consumption, and investment, and the deduction of its implications. This approach to economic theory also yields fruitful insights for forecasting and policy planning.

Both deductive and inductive reasoning is important in the construction of useful hypotheses. A hypothesis is useful if it provides a reasonably accurate description of reality, particularly when predicting future events on the basis of past information. The observation that, in the past, consumption has been closely related to disposable income is useful to the forecaster only if the relationship is expected to continue into the future. A hypothesis based on past experience alone reflects an inductive, *a posteriori*, relationship. Unless a hypothesis also has some deductive, *a priori*, basis, its reliability as a predictor of future events is questionable. The hypothesis that consumption is related to disposable income is reasonable, *a priori*, that is, on a logical basis in the absence of empirical confirmation. Since this particular relationship has considerable *a priori* appeal, and since it has stood up well to *a posteriori* testing, that is, data on past consumption and income reflect the relationship, it has become a useful forecasting tool.

Suppose a study in a small town showed that, over a period of five years, consumption was closely related to the number of high school dropouts. Since the hypothesis that an increase in the dropout rate stimulates consumption has little to recommend it *a priori*, it would be inadvisable for a policy planner to use the dropout rate as an indicator of future consumption, especially when generalizing from the sample to the economy as a whole. Instead, he might suspect that the observed relationship for the particular sample studied was a coincidence rather than a reliable behavioral relationship.

A posteriori testing of *a priori* relationships is important for policy planning, however. The theorist may deduce that consumption is a function of disposable income, but the policy planner wants to know exactly how much consumption spending will increase in response to a tax cut or an income transfer. The exact magnitude of the response to be expected cannot always be determined on the basis of *a priori* or deductive reasoning alone. Instead, past experience must be examined.

ECONOMIC MODELS

The hypotheses and interrelationships of economic theory can be used to construct a model of economic behavior. The scope of the model depends upon the particular aspect of economic activity being examined. If the economist is concerned with the behavior of a particular commodity price, for instance, he will develop a market model. The model will consist of hypotheses about behavior in the market, or *behavioral relationships*, as well as other interrelationships such as *technological relationships*, definitions or *identities*, and *equilibrium conditions*.

A market model might be based on the following *a priori* hypotheses:

1. The quantity of the good demanded is a linear function of its price, or algebraically,

$$q_D = a_1 + a_2 p$$

2. The quantity of the good supplied is also a linear function of its price, or

$$q_S = b_1 + b_2 p$$

3. Market prices will fluctuate until the market is cleared, that is, until quantity demanded equals quantity supplied, or

$$q_D = q_S$$

The first two equations are behavioral relationships; the third is an equilibrium condition.

The complete model:
$$q_D = a_1 + a_2 p$$
$$q_S = b_1 + b_2 p$$
$$q_D = q_S$$

is consistent. Since there are three equations and three unknowns, the equilibrium market price can be determined (except in special cases). Algebraically, in equilibrium

$$q_D = q_S$$

Substituting the behavioral relationships for q_D and q_S, the equilibrium condition can be expressed as

$$a_1 + a_2 p = b_1 + b_2 p$$

Solving for p, the price in equilibrium is found to be

$$p = \frac{b_1 - a_1}{a_2 - b_2}$$

The behavioral coefficients, or *parameters*, a_2 and b_2 reflect the response of quantity demanded and quantity supplied, respectively, to changes in market price. The parameters a_1 and b_1 measure that amount of the commodity demanded and supplied, respectively, that is independent of the influence of market price. The behavioral coefficients can be estimated by examining past experience in this market. If they are known, the equilibrium market price can be determined.[2]

Macroeconomics is concerned with the study of national income aggregates. Consequently, the models studied in this book will contain hypotheses about aggregate behavior (such as the consumption function), aggregate technological relationships (such as the aggregate production function), and national income identities and equilibrium conditions. John Maynard Keynes, in his 1935 classic, *The General Theory of Employment, Interest, and Money*, was one of the first modern economists to formulate hypotheses about aggregate behavior and to pinpoint relationships between various macroeconomic variables. Consequently, modern macroeconomic models are often referred to as *Keynesian models*. Although many of Keynes' original hypotheses have been revised in the light of *a posteriori* or empirical information, the framework of the Keynesian system remains as the basis for most of today's policy-planning and forecasting models.

1-2 Economic Theory and the Keynesian Revolution

An economic theory is distinguished by the particular activities or variables it selects for study. Economists before Keynes had traditionally ignored national income and other aggregate concepts, such as employment, output, and prices, and had concentrated their attention instead on the markets for

---

[2] A forecasting model would have to consider the possibility of dynamic instability in this market, in which case the price may never reach equilibrium. A *dynamic* model examines the *movement* of the variables over time, whether or not the system is in equilibrium. This is a *static* model which examines only the equilibrium itself.

individual goods and services.[3] Price fluctuations within these markets served to clear them, that is, to equate supply and demand. Only monopoly influences or market imperfections which promoted price rigidity could produce excess supply in any particular market.

Thus, traditional (or classical) economic theory concluded that, if prices were permitted to fluctuate freely, particularly in the downward direction, and if monopoly influences were eliminated, there would be no excess supply in any commodity or factor market. If wages were to fall sufficiently, then there would be no unemployment. Since the notion did not arise that what was true for individual markets might not be valid for the economy as a whole (in the aggregate), the economists of the 1930's urged a policy of wage and price deflation as the best remedy for the Great Depression.

A theory which left the job of clearing all markets to a freely fluctuating price system was ill-equipped to handle a depression such as the world faced in the 1930's. There was a substantial excess supply of labor—over 25 percent of the labor force was unemployed in most industrial countries. Classical theory, based on extrapolation from the model of a single market, implied that a decline in the general wage level would solve the problem. All one had to do to get a job was to offer to work for a lower wage. Practical policy makers intuitively felt that the heart of the difficulty was an inadequate demand for goods. Wage cuts, in the face of insufficient demand, would reduce purchasing power and, therefore, would only aggravate the situation.

Even before the publication of *The General Theory*, Keynes appeared before national radio audiences in Britain advocating public works programs and deficit spending. Economic policy makers agreed with these recommendations, and all but the most orthodox economists had to admit that intuitively his suggestions made sense. *The General Theory* presented a theoretical model which corroborated the Keynesian policy prescriptions. The theoretical model served two purposes. First, it gave respectability to the measures designed by the policy planners to reduce the unemployment rate. These measures attempted to stimulate demand without reducing prices and wages. Although few people actually read *The General Theory*, the very fact of its publication made everyone feel more comfortable about what they were doing. In addition, the theoretical analysis, including hypotheses about aggregate behavior as well as the specification of key macroeconomic identities and equilibrium conditions, provided the basis for the development

---

[3]This is not true of economists of the late eighteenth and early nineteenth centuries, such as Hume, Ricardo, and Malthus. While there are some marked similarities in the Keynesian and Malthusian analyses, the passage of over a century between them represented enough of a discontinuity in the tradition that it is legitimate to refer to the Keynesian contribution as a revolution in the development of economic theory.

of a macroeconomic model for policy planning and forecasting. If the relationships specified *a priori* in *The General Theory* could actually be determined from historical data, then policy decisions would not have to be made on an *ad hoc* basis.

One of the major contributions of Keynesian analysis was to show that a flexible price system alone does not necessarily ensure that all resources will be fully employed. Indeed, his demonstration that government intervention in the economy may be required to engineer full employment implied a new role for economic policy and for the economist as well. In justifying *laissez-faire* capitalism as the ideal form of economic organization, pre-Keynesian theory established no role for economic policy or for the economist other than to advocate free trade and to oppose all forms of monopoly. In fact, the idea of policy planning suggested interference with the free-market system and was consequently something to be discouraged. On the other hand, Keynes believed that wise governmental control of aggregate spending or demand was the key to the long-run survival of free-enterprise capitalism. When the government decides to step in, however, it is clear that programs must be designed carefully. The amount of government spending required to achieve full employment is not arbitrary: too much spending will be inflationary; too little will not provide jobs for everyone wishing to work.

Keynesian economics implied an active role for public policy. The economist of today is far different from the armchair sage of the nineteenth century, who was concerned with proving theorems about optimal resource allocation in a market system. Instead, the large majority of economists are found outside the university, and many of these are concerned with the day-to-day business of planning practical ways to achieve the economic goals society has put before them.

1-3 The Goals of Economic Policy

The Employment Act of 1946 reflected the official acceptance of Keynesian economics in the United States. Based on the recognition that full employment must be a concern of public policy, it admitted that a free-market system might not automatically generate enough jobs to employ the entire labor force and implicitly rejected wage deflation as a policy to promote full employment. The Act reads in part:

> The Congress declares that it is the continuing responsibility of the Federal Government to use all practicable means . . . to promote maximum employment, production and purchasing power.

Besides the goal of full employment, macroeconomic policy is concerned with controlling inflation, avoiding unmanageable balance-of-payments deficits, and promoting growth. Each of these goals will be considered briefly.

FULL EMPLOYMENT

Goods are scarce because resources are scarce. If economic welfare can be increased by reducing the scarcity of goods, then policies designed to provide jobs to individuals who wish to work will increase the amount of goods available and, hence, the general welfare. Unemployment, defined as a situation in which people are seeking jobs but cannot find them, may be undesirable for social and psychological reasons as well. Unemployment, so defined, recognizes the value of leisure and the right of an individual not to work if this is his preference.

PRICE STABILITY

Price stability is important in an economy which uses money as a store of value. Since prices seem to drift upward more easily than downward, inflation is a primary target of remedial government policy.

Inflation has serious distributive consequences. It penalizes those whose incomes are fixed in money terms. Workers whose wage contracts contain cost-of-living escalator clauses will receive money increases when prices rise, but this is not true of individuals relying on pensions and annuities. Inflation hurts creditors and reduces the real obligations of debtors.

Aside from its impact on income distribution (which could be remedied by appropriate redistributive policies), the primary concern is that inflation not become so rampant that the currency becomes unacceptable. If prices are rising and consumers and investors expect the trend to continue, they may be encouraged to spend immediately, exchanging money for goods, driving prices up still further. Such an occurrence would lead to breakdown or panic in financial markets which would have a deleterious effect on investment, the basis for growth. It would also have a disastrous impact on the balance of international payments and the international acceptability of the currency. In a rare instance, such as the runaway inflation in Germany in the 1920's, the economic fabric of the society may be destroyed, with dire political and social consequences.

While it is unlikely that the events in post-World War I Germany will be repeated often, inflation does tend to reinforce itself. Unless it is controlled, the uncertainty it generates may result in recession and concomitant unemployment.

AVOIDING EXCESSIVE
BALANCE-OF-PAYMENTS DEFICITS

In the United States, the foreign sector comprises less than 5 percent of national income. However, as long as the international gold standard is in effect and the dollar is to maintain its position as a reserve currency, the United States must maintain confidence in the value of the dollar abroad by preventing large outflows of dollars and gold.[4] A loss of confidence in the dollar, given current international monetary arrangements, would have considerable destabilizing effects on world markets.

For countries which transact a larger part of their business in world markets, balance-of-payments equilibrium is a more important national goal. This is particularly true for countries that are dependent upon imports for food, capital equipment, and other essential items. If their currency becomes unacceptable or if creditors doubt their ability to pay because of excessive payments deficits, these countries may have difficulty finding import sources.

ECONOMIC GROWTH

Growth of productivity, or output per worker, is generally considered to be an improvement in economic well-being. If productivity increases are matched by increases in wages, workers can realize either an increase in real income or in leisure. It is not always true, however, that economic growth reflects an increase in welfare, particularly if that growth is accompanied by undesirable changes in the distribution of income. Nevertheless, if economic growth can be achieved, a redistributive income policy could ensure that it represents an increase in national economic welfare.

CONFLICTS IN ECONOMIC GOALS

The goals of economic policy may be conflicting. It is not always possible to achieve all our goals simultaneously. This being the case, it is necessary to accept a trade-off between them. Figure 1-1 shows the relationship between increases in the price level and the unemployment rate for the United States over the period 1935–1960. This downward-sloping curve, often called a "modified Phillips curve,"[5] indicates that periods of low

---

[4]Many economists argue that maintenance of a gold standard and the dollar's position as a reserve currency is not a desirable policy objective. Currently, however, it is a stated national goal.

[5]A "modified Phillips curve" relates price increases to the unemployment rate, while a "Phillips curve" relates wage increases to the unemployment rate. For the original derivation, see A. W. Phillips, "The Relation Between Unemployment and the Rate of Change of Money Wage Rates in the United Kingdom, 1861–1957," *Economica* (n.s.), XXV (November, 1958), 283–299.

unemployment are associated with rising prices. In a period of rising demand and employment, labor markets tighten, wage increases are demanded and achieved, and prices drift upward. Experience has shown that as the unemployment rate approaches 3.5 percent, sharp price increases are expected. Recently, inflation has been associated with even higher rates of unemployment.

Many economists would argue that an unemployment rate of 3.5 percent is the lowest rate consistent with price stability. At this level, unemployment is due primarily to structural influences such as rapid tech-

Figure 1-1   Relationship Between Increases in the Price Level
and the Unemployment Rate

Source: Paul A. Samuelson and Robert M. Solow, "Analytical Aspects of Anti-
Inflation Policy," *The American Economic Review*, L (May, 1960), 177–194.

nological change and shifts in demand, which provide new jobs requiring special skills in some areas while rendering other skills obsolete. It is generally recognized that macroeconomic measures to stimulate aggregate demand will not eliminate structural unemployment. New jobs may be created, increasing the demand for labor in some occupations. As money wages increase in these markets, unions in the declining sectors demand and achieve wage increases, thus reducing the quantity of labor demanded and accentuating the problem of structural unemployment. Furthermore, firms may respond to the wage increases by raising product prices. In this instance a policy which stimulates aggregate demand could have the disastrous effect of increasing the rate of inflation *and* the unemployment rate at the same time.

A policy which stimulates demand may reduce the unemployment rate at the expense of the goal of price stability. It may also increase the rate of economic growth. Whether or not this represents an improvement in the economic welfare of the community depends upon the output mix and how it is distributed. A reduction in taxes at all income levels by a fixed percentage of income, for instance, will increase disposable income for all tax payers without affecting income distribution. This might be compared with an increase in military spending for materials of war. In both cases, spending increases will stimulate employment and growth of output; however, it will be distributed differently among the various sectors. In one case, the demand and output will increase in the consumer goods industries, while in the other, more war materials will be produced. Some people feel that the production of more war materials does not constitute an improvement in social welfare.

Macroeconomic policy to stimulate growth may also conflict with the goal of balance-of-payments equilibrium. As demand increases, imports rise, while rising prices at home discourage exports and further encourage imports.

Thus, macroeconomic policy is framed in large measure in terms of trade-offs between the various goals. In some cases the planner may be able to reduce the rate of the trade-off. For instance, training programs which increase labor mobility may reduce the rate of structural unemployment and consequently lower the rate of inflation associated with expansionary public policy. This would, in effect, shift the Phillips curve leftward, or make it more L-shaped. Policies to stimulate investment during boom periods enable supply to increase with demand, again serving to promote price stability.

INSTRUMENTS OF ECONOMIC POLICY

An economic model essentially pinpoints the relationship between policy targets, or goals, and the policy instruments at the disposal of the planner.

Suppose each target is represented as a variable in a linear model.[6] Further-more, for each target there is an equation which specifies its relationship to the policy instruments. For instance, employment, N, and prices, p, might be related to government spending, G, and interest rates, i. The relationship can be represented algebraically:

$$a_1 G + a_2 i = N$$
$$b_1 G + b_2 i = p$$

Suppose target values for N and p are specified so that
$$N^* = 75 \text{ million}$$
$$p^* = 100$$

where p is a price index. Then the system becomes
$$a_1 G + a_2 i = 75$$
$$b_1 G + b_2 i = 100$$

and, generally, a solution can be found. Note that two instrumental variables are required if two targets are to be fulfilled. Since there must be as many equations as there are unknowns to determine a solution to a linear system, there must be as many instruments as targets in the planning of practical policy.

While the equality between instruments and targets is a necessary precondition for successful planning, it is not sufficient. As we have seen, some targets are inconsistent. Furthermore, there are often political or economic constraints on our instruments. Suppose, for example, the solution of the model requires a negative rate of interest. This would mean sub-sidizing borrowers and extracting an interest payment from lenders, a practice which is quite alien to established financial practice. Furthermore, it would not be behaviorally feasible, since it is unlikely that lenders would be willing to pay borrowers to take their money. There may also be political constraints on economic policy. For instance, it may not be politically feasible to cut government spending in certain areas, such as national defense or social development programs. Policy instruments are generally assumed to be economic activities or parameters which planners can manipulate at will, at least within certain boundaries. However, even presidential advisors have found it nearly impossible to predict the level of federal spending, taxes, or interest rates within a planning period. In the last year of the Johnson administration, with the Vietnam War a hot political issue, the President's

---

[6]Policy planners prefer to work with linear models because they are easier to estimate and solve than nonlinear models.

Council of Economic Advisors was criticized for its apparent underestimate of aggregate demand and their failure to recommend measures which would have prevented the economy from "overheating". Much of the difficulty, however, was due to the fact that the administration consistently underestimated defense spending. In this instance the planners found it easier to forecast spending by the private sector than to forecast public spending, which was theoretically a "known" parameter in their model.

Thus, to achieve policy targets, planners must have sufficient policy instruments at their disposal. More policy instruments than targets may be required if the instruments are not flexible or if they are constrained by political and economic influences. Generally, the planner is faced with too many objectives and too few flexible policy instruments.

1-4 Toward a Theory of Macroeconomic Policy

The distinguishing feature of Keynesian theory is that the particular variables it studies are those of most concern to economic policy planners. Income and employment are both policy targets. The analyses of price level and growth rate can be incorporated in the Keynesian system. Consequently, macroeconomic policy-planning and forecasting models consist of the relationships specified by Keynes in *The General Theory*. The actual parameters of the model are, of course, derived from historically generated information using the techniques of statistical inference.

For example, Keynes suggested that consumption is primarily a function of disposable income. Algebraically,

$$C = a + bY$$

where C is aggregate consumption and Y is aggregate disposable income. A policy planner, using the basic Keynesian hypothesis about consumption, will examine actual data measuring income and consumption.

Figure 1-2 is a scatter diagram of consumption and income data such as a planner might use in attempting to specify a consumption function for his model. Each point in the scatter represents a pair of observations on consumption and income at a particular point in time. Approximating the scatter with a straight line, the actual values for the constant a (the intercept) and b (the slope) of the relationship can be identified.

If public policy is to be used to achieve economic goals, it must be planned. Economists are not omniscient, however, and their models are not perfect. Consequently, their forecasts are not always accurate and public policy may be of the too-much-too-soon or too-little-too-late variety.

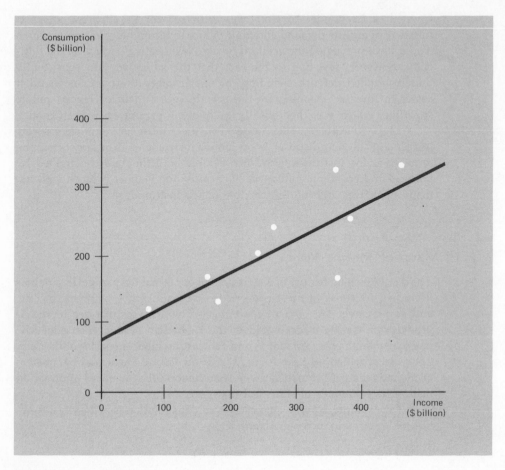

Figure 1-2 Scatter Diagram of Consumption
and Income Data

Inaccurate forecasts and inappropriate policy recommendations may
be due to

1. poor theoretical construction, inconsistency, or error in the logical basis
   of the forecasting and planning model,
2. incorrect *a posteriori* specification of the model due to poor data or
   inappropriate statistical procedure,
3. random, unexpected, or unknown events or behavior,
4. political or institutional constraints on the policy instruments.

When all the potential sources of error are considered, however, the record of policy planning since the Keynesian revolution has been remarkable. Since World War II, there has been no serious depression or financial panic. While recent attempts at achieving price stability have not been as successful as those used to promote full employment, the economy has managed to support two wars in Asia without general price controls.

One reason that macroeconomic policy has been more successfully applied to the full-employment goal than the price stability goal is that Keynesian theory is concerned primarily with the causes of unemployment rather than inflation. There is no general theory of inflation which guides policy planning, and consequently, anti-inflation policy in this country has been framed on an *ad hoc* basis, changing dramatically with each administration. On the other hand, most economists essentially agree on the appropriate remedies for unemployment of the nonstructural variety.

Another factor in the traditional emphasis on the full-employment goal in the United States is the experience of the Great Depression of the 1930's. While this country has experienced the trials of a large unemployed labor force, it has not had to cope in this century with the ravages of runaway inflation. Less fortunate countries such as Germany and many Latin American nations are willing to accept a relatively high unemployment rate as a safeguard against the potential runaway inflations that they remember from recent experience.

A theory of inflation will be developed in the text along with the traditional Keynesian model. This approach will be useful in evaluating various economic programs in terms of all the targets of economic policy. After developing the complete model, we shall return to a consideration of policy planning in the final chapter. Appendix A, on the construction and use of macroeconomic models, ties the policy-planning approach to the development of the model in each of its phases.

Questions for Study and Review

1. "Economic planning is not inconsistent with a free-enterprise economy; indeed, it is the key to its long-run survival. The main problem with 'automatic mechanisms' is that they are insufficient in perspective." Discuss.

2. What is an *economic model?* Discuss some of the advantages and limitations of using economic models in the planning of national economic policy.

3. The hypothesis that consumption is a function of income is central to the Keynesian theory. If you were developing a model of the economy

16

to be used for forecasting and policy planning, how would you test the validity of the hypothesis? What problems would you expect to encounter in your effort to achieve realistic specification of the consumption equation?

4. "An effective economic policy program must contain at least as many policy instruments as there are goals to be attained. With enough instruments, any targets can be reached." Discuss the validity of each of these statements.

Additional Reading

Beach, E. F., *Economic Models*. New York: John Wiley & Sons, Inc., 1957, Part I.

"The Employment Act: Twenty Years of Policy Experience," *Economic Report of the President*. Washington, D.C.: Government Printing Office, January, 1966, Chapter 7.

Smithies, Arthur, "Reflections on the Work and Influence of John Maynard Keynes," *The Quarterly Journal of Economics*, LXV (November, 1951), 578–601.

2

The Analytics
of Income Determination:
Aggregate Supply
and Aggregate Demand

To achieve the goals of full employment and stable prices, the policy maker must have a clear understanding of macroeconomic relationships. Two variables, employment and the level of prices, require consideration. Both are linked directly to output. Employment is tied to output through the production function, while prices and output are simultaneously determined in product markets. Because of its connection with employment and the price level, the value of output or, equivalently, of income becomes the focal point of macroeconomic analysis. In equilibrium, when the plans of firms and households are realized, the level of money income is determined by aggregate demand. Employment, in turn, depends upon the equilibrium relationship between aggregate demand and aggregate supply.

In Chapters 2 and 3 the basic model of income and employment will be developed. After a preliminary discussion of the aggregate supply and aggregate demand functions in this chapter, the equilibrium model will be presented in Chapter 3. Although these chapters are concerned primarily with the relationship between income and employment, the foundation is laid for an analysis of the price level in Chapter 10.

2-1 The Output–Income Identity

As goods are produced, factor services are performed, and income, in the form of wages, rent, interest, and profits, is earned. Part of income is the return to factors, labor, land, and capital, in the form of wages, rent, and interest for services rendered in the process of production. The remaining part of income, profits, is the residual between the value of output and payments to factors. Thus, when profits are included in income, income will always be exactly, or *identically*, equal to the value of output.

THE ACCOUNTING FRAMEWORK

Consider the following example: A farmer produces 100 bushels of wheat with his own labor on an acre of land belonging to a landlord. He sells the wheat to a miller for $100, paying the landlord a rent of $50, and earning a profit of $50. The farmer's accounts are shown in Table 2-1. Sales, or the value of output, is exactly equal to total income in the form of profits and rent.

The miller who buys the wheat produces 500 pounds of flour which he sells to a baker for $300. The miller's accounts are shown in Table 2-2. The value of output of the miller is $300 and total income earned (wages, $100; overhead, $50; profits, $50) is $200. Does this violate the output–income identity? Not if we remember that part of the value of the flour

Table 2-1   Accounts of the Farmer

Sales		Expenses and Profit	
100 bushels of wheat	$100	Expenses:	
		Rent	$ 50
		Profit:	$ 50
Total sales	$100	Total expenses and profit	$100

is derived from the value of the wheat. As shown in Table 2-3, income earned in the total process, including wheat production, is $300, which is exactly equal to the value of the flour.

In actual practice, it would be difficult to account for all income earned in the intermediate stages of the production process. Instead, keeping in mind that the value of output is always equal to income, the accounts can be balanced by subtracting the value of intermediate products from the value of the final product to obtain *value added* at each stage. Value added will exactly equal income for each stage of production, as seen in Table 2-4.

The sum of the value added at each stage is equal to the value of total output which is equal to the total income earned. The value-added approach is used to avoid "double counting" of intermediate outputs while still accounting for all income earned at all stages of production.

Table 2-2   Accounts of the Miller

Sales		Expenses and Profits	
500 pounds of flour	$300	Expenses:	
		100 bushels of wheat	$100
		Wages	$100
		Overhead (interest and rent)	$ 50
		Total expenses	$250
		Profit:	$ 50
Total sales	$300	Total expenses and profit	$300

Table 2-3 Income Earned in the Production of Flour

Wheat production:	
Rent	$ 50
Profits	$ 50
Total income	$100
Milling process:	
Wages	$100
Overhead (interest and rent)	$ 50
Profits	$ 50
Total income	$200
Total income earned in flour production	$300
Total value of flour	$300

Table 2-4 Value Added and Income in the Production of Flour and Wheat

Flour			
Value of Output		**Income**	
Flour	$300	Wages	$100
		Overhead	$ 50
Wheat	−$100	Profits	$ 50
Value added	$200	Total income	$200
Wheat			
Value of Output		**Income**	
Wheat	$100	Rent	$ 50
		Profits	$ 50
Value added	$100	Total income	$100

Table 2-5   Accounts of the Baker

Sales		Expenses and Profit	
1000 loaves of bread	$500	Expenses:	
		500 pounds of flour	$300
		Wages	$ 75
		Overhead (interest and rent)	$ 40
		Total expenses	$415
		Profit:	$ 85
Total sales	$500	Total expenses and profit	$500

The baker who buys the flour sells 1000 loaves of bread for $500. His accounts are shown in Table 2-5. Value added in this stage of production is $200 and income earned is $200. As shown in Table 2-6, the value of the bread, $500, is equal to the sum of the value added at each stage which is equal to total income earned.[1]

Table 2-6   Value Added and Income in All Stages of Bread Production

Value of Final Product		Value Added		Income	
Bread	$500	Wheat	$100	Wheat	$100
		Flour	$200	Flour	$200
		Bread	$200	Bread	$200
Value of output	$500	Total value added	$500	Total income	$500

ANALYTICAL USE
OF THE OUTPUT—INCOME IDENTITY

In the study of macroeconomic relationships it is sometimes convenient to use income rather than output value as a variable. Since income and output

[1] Appendix B contains a detailed discussion of national income accounting techniques.

22

values are identical within a given time period, it will not matter which variable is considered.

Analytically, the output–income identity is represented by means of a 45° line which bisects the positive quadrant of a graph with output on one axis and income on the other. Since income and output never take on negative values, only the positive quadrant is of interest. In Figure 2-1, any point on the 45° line is equidistant from the two axes. If income is known to be Y_0, the corresponding level of output, Q_0, can immediately be determined from the graph.

In the discussion which follows, it is convenient to treat the aggregate

Figure 2-1 The Output–Income Identity

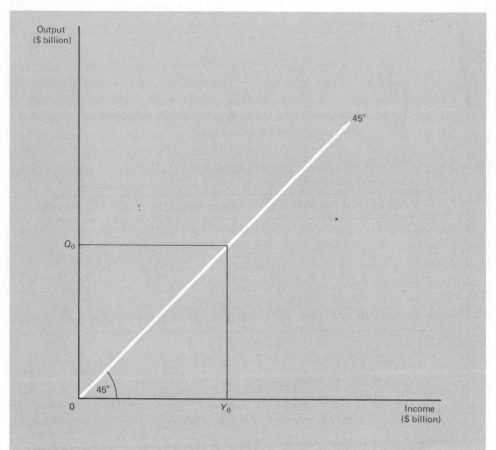

demand for goods and services as a function of income and to treat the supply in terms of output value. This will pose no analytical difficulties if the output–income identity is kept in mind.

2-2   Aggregate Supply and Employment

To produce a given output, a firm will require a certain amount of factor services. The demand for any factor of production will depend upon the cost of that factor per unit of output as well as upon the price at which the product is sold. Consequently, it is the expected value of sales that determines the amount of a factor a firm will hire when the factor cost is known.

Suppose the capital stock is fixed so that the firm can vary the amount of goods it produces and sells only by varying the number of workers it employs. The *aggregate supply function* relates the number of workers that firms wish to hire and the amount of total revenue firms expect to receive from sales. For any level of expected sales, or total spending, the aggregate supply function provides an estimate of the number of workers that will be employed.

The shape of the aggregate supply function will be of interest. If entrepreneurs become pessimistic about the prospects for total sales in the next quarter, how will their pessimism affect employment?

Assuming that the firm will attempt to maximize profits, it will hire additional workers only if the expected contribution of those workers to total revenue exceeds their addition to the total wage bill. This suggests that firms will hire additional workers only if they expect sales revenue to increase. Consequently, we expect the aggregate supply curve to be upward sloping as in Figure 2-2.

In constructing our complete model of income and employment in Chapter 8 and in our analysis of price level changes in Chapter 10, we will need to know more about the shape of the aggregate supply function. Will changes in employment be proportional to expected changes in total revenue or will the demand for labor in response to a given change in expected sales depend upon how much labor is already employed? The possibilities are indicated in Figure 2-3.

Changes in employment will be proportional to changes in total revenue only if the aggregate supply function is a straight line, such as Z_2 in Figure 2-3. In this case the change in employment associated with any given change in product demand is independent of the number of workers already employed. If the aggregate supply function is convex to the employment axis, such as Z_3, for a given change in expected total revenue (product

24

Figure 2-2   The Aggregate Supply Function

demand), the demand for additional workers will be smaller the more labor is already employed. If the function is concave, such as Z_1, the opposite will be the case.

DERIVATION
OF THE AGGREGATE SUPPLY FUNCTION

A firm will continue to hire additional workers until the contribution of the last worker to total revenue is just equal to his cost, or wage. Let us assume that the firm is a perfect competitor in both the product market and the labor market. This means that he can sell all his output at some

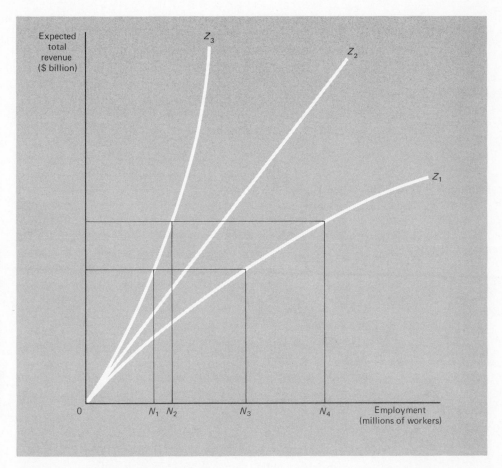

Figure 2-3   Alternative Specifications
of the Aggregate Supply Function

constant price, p, and hire all his labor at a constant wage, w. Given these
assumptions, the contribution to total revenue of the last worker hired is
equal to the added output resulting from his employment, or the marginal
product, MP, multiplied by price of the output. The profit-maximizing firm
will hire workers up to the point at which the value of the marginal product
is just equal to the wage, or algebraically,

$$p \times MP = w$$

for the last worker hired.

To derive the shape of the aggregate supply function, something must be known about the relationship between employment and marginal productivity. Since the capital stock is assumed to be fixed, the *law of diminishing returns* should take effect as more workers are employed. In other words we would expect output to increase with employment, but at a decreasing rate. The marginal contribution of each additional worker, although positive, will decrease as employment increases. Figure 2-4 represents a typical production function (the relationship between input and output) displaying

Figure 2-4   Typical Production Function for a Firm with a Fixed Stock of Capital diminishing returns to employment. The decreasing marginal product per worker associated with this production function is shown in Figure 2-5.[2]

Given these relationships, the aggregate supply function can be derived. We shall begin the analysis by examining the relationship between expected total revenue (product demand) and employment for the firm. This relationship is the *expected total revenue function*.

From the production function of the firm we can determine the level of output associated with each level of employment. From the marginal productivity schedule we can find the price at which the output will be sold at any level of employment.

The firm in perfect competition will hire workers until, for the last worker,

$$p \times MP = w$$

This implies that, for any level of employment, the price at which the firm expects to sell its output is equal to the cost of producing the last unit, which is the wage divided by the marginal product of labor, or

$$p = \frac{w}{MP}$$

If we assume that the wage which the firm must pay is uniform for all workers (since the firm is a perfect competitor in the labor market), we can find the expected supply price at any level of employment from the marginal productivity schedule.

With our knowledge of the firm's production function and the assumption that the firm is a perfect competitor, attempting to maximize profits, we can now proceed to derive the firm's expected total revenue function. Figure 2-6 shows the production function, the relationship between output and employment, as well as the relationship between expected supply price and employment. Since output multiplied by expected supply

---

[2]The marginal product is the change in total product associated with a change in employment. Algebraically,

$$MP = \frac{\Delta TP}{\Delta N}$$

where ΔTP is the change in total product and ΔN is the change in employment. Thus, the marginal product for any level of employment, N, is the slope of the total product function there, and the marginal product function can be derived from the production function. Notice that if the production function displays diminishing returns, its slope is constantly falling, and the marginal product function will be downward sloping.

Figure 2-5   Marginal Productivity
of an Additional Worker

price is equal to expected total revenue, we have all the information required to derive the expected total revenue function.

The production function relating labor input to output is shown in Figure 2-6(A). When N_0 workers are employed, output will be q_0, read from the production function. Figure 2-6(B) shows the marginal product, also as a function of employment. The marginal product function is derived from the production function. At N_0, the marginal product is MP_0. Remember that the firm will employ workers until the value of the marginal product just equals the wage. If the wage is known, and since for any level of employment the marginal product is also known, then for any level of

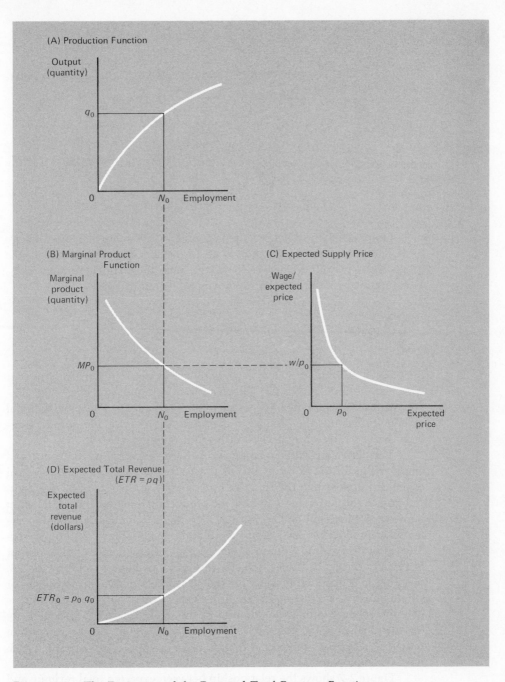

(A) Production Function

Output
(quantity)

q_0

0   N_0 Employment

(B) Marginal Product
Function

Marginal
product
(quantity)

MP_0

0   N_0 Employment

(C) Expected Supply Price

Wage/
expected
price

w/p_0

0   p_0 Expected
price

(D) Expected Total Revenue
$(ETR = pq)$

Expected
total
revenue
(dollars)

$ETR_0 = p_0 q_0$

0   N_0 Employment

Figure 2-6   The Derivation of the Expected Total Revenue Function
from the Production Function for a Firm

employment the price at which the firm expected to sell its output is determined. Algebraically,

$$p_0 = \frac{w}{MP_0}$$

which implies

$$MP_0 = \frac{w}{p_0}$$

Graphically the relationship is found in the following way. Figure 2-6(C) shows the ratio w/p_0 plotted as a function of p_0. This is simply the graph of a hyperbola when w is a constant. Since the marginal product, MP_0, is determined by the level of employment, N_0, in (B), and

$$MP_0 = \frac{w}{p_0}$$

the price p_0 at which the firm expects to sell its output when employment is N_0 can be found from (C). Expected total revenue associated with employment of N_0 workers is $p_0 q_0$ as seen in Figure 2-6(D). The expected total revenue function is the product of expected supply price and output, similarly derived for each hypothetical level of employment.

The derivation of the relationship between expected total revenue and employment for the firm can also be illustrated by means of a hypothetical example. Suppose that the firm can hire workers at the rate of $2 per hour. Columns 1 and 2 of Table 2-7 show the production function, the relationship between employment and output per man-hour. From this information the marginal product for each group of 10 additional workers can be derived. The result is shown in column 3. For example, if employment is 20, output is 190. By hiring 10 more workers, the firm can increase output to 270, resulting in a marginal product for the 10 workers of 80. For each level of employment, the price at which firms expect their output to be sold is determined by dividing the addition to the total wage cost, column 4, by the marginal product, column 3. Then, expected total revenue in column 6 can be calculated as expected market price multiplied by output for each level of employment.

Figure 2-7 shows the relationship between expected total revenue and employment for our hypothetical firm. An increase in expected total revenue from $67.50 to $98.60 per hour, for example, would induce the firm to hire 10 additional workers. As employment increases, the firm requires successively greater increments to expected total revenue to induce it to hire 10

Table 2-7 The Derivation of Expected Total Revenue
as a Function of Employment for a Firm

(1) Employment	(2) Output (per hour)	(3) Marginal Product (for each 10 addi- tional workers)	(4) Addition to Wage Cost (for each 10 additional workers)	(5) Expected Market Price = (4)/(3)	(6) Expected Total Revenue = (2) × (5)
0	0	0	$ 0.00	$0.00	$ 0.00
10	100	100	$20.00	$0.20	$ 20.00
20	190	90	$20.00	$0.22	$ 41.80
30	270	80	$20.00	$0.25	$ 67.50
40	340	70	$20.00	$0.29	$ 98.60
50	400	60	$20.00	$0.33	$132.00

additional workers. Therefore, the expected total revenue function firm is convex to the employment axis, as seen in Figure 2-7.

The aggregate supply function can be derived from the expected total revenue functions of the individual firms in the economy. An aggregate supply function, such as that shown in Figure 2-8, is obtained by aggregating the expected total revenue functions of the individual firms.

THE SHAPE
OF THE AGGREGATE SUPPLY FUNCTION

Although we know *a priori* that the aggregate supply function is upward sloping, its actual shape will be determined by the aggregate production function of all the firms in the economy and the money wage.[3] Assuming again that our firms are perfect competitors maximizing profits, price will be equal to the cost of the last unit produced,[4] or

$$p = \frac{w}{MP}$$

[3]The derivation which follows is taken from Paul Davidson and Eugene Smolensky, *Aggregate Supply and Demand Analysis* (New York: Harper & Row, Publishers, 1964), pp. 125–128.

[4]If the capital stock is fixed, the wage divided by the marginal product of labor represents the cost of the last unit, or the marginal cost, *MC*. Thus, in perfect competition, firms will produce until price is equal to marginal cost or

$$p = \frac{w}{MP} = MC$$

Figure 2-7   Relationship Between Expected Total Revenue
and Employment for a Hypothetical Firm

Multiplying both sides of the profit maximizing equation by output, q, the
value of output, pq, will be equal to the cost of the last unit multiplied by
the number of units, or

$$pq = \frac{wq}{MP}$$

Figure 2-8   An Aggregate Supply Function

Since output per worker, q/N, is called the average product of labor, AP, or

$$AP = \frac{q}{N}$$

the relationship can be expressed as

$$pq = \frac{wq}{MP}\frac{N}{N} = \frac{w}{MP}\left(\frac{q}{N}\right)N = w\left(\frac{AP}{MP}\right)N$$

The expression $w(AP/MP)$ represents the slope of the aggregate supply function. It indicates the change in employment which will occur in response to expected changes in total revenue or sales. The slope depends upon the money wage, w, as well as the ratio AP/MP. The behavior of the ratio AP/MP as employment changes depends upon the production function and reflects the importance of diminishing returns to labor as employment increases with a fixed capital stock.

If the money wage is assumed to be fixed, the aggregate supply function will be a straight line (having a constant slope) only if the AP/MP ratio is constant for all levels of employment. This property characterizes certain special types of production functions, including the Cobb–Douglas production function which is extensively used in empirical research.[5]

If the slope increases with employment, the aggregate supply function will be convex to the employment axis. If the money wage is fixed, this will be the case if the ratio AP/MP rises as employment increases. The ratio will rise if diminishing returns become more important as successive increments of labor are added to a fixed capital stock. In our hypothetical example, marginal productivity decreases faster than average productivity as employment increases, and the expected total revenue function is convex to the employment axis. The slope will also increase with employment if money wages tend to rise as labor markets tighten.

It is unlikely that the slope of the aggregate supply function will decrease with employment, making it concave to the employment axis. This implies that diminishing returns become less important as more and more labor is added to a fixed capital stock, making AP/MP a decreasing function of employment. Alternatively, it suggests that money wages tend to fall as labor markets tighten, an unlikely occurrence.

Assuming a fixed money wage, the relationship between the aggregate production function and the aggregate supply function is shown in Figure 2-9. The slope Z_3, derived from a production function in which diminishing returns become progressively more important as employment increases, implies that successively greater increments in expected total revenue will be necessary to induce firms to hire additional workers. The slope Z_2 implies that diminishing returns are of equal importance at all levels of employment. Firms will always employ the same number of additional workers for equal increments in expected total revenue at all levels of employment. Both Z_3 and Z_2 are likely shapes that an actual aggregate supply function might take.

The function Z_1, based on a production function displaying diminishing returns that become less important as employment increases, implies

---

[5] A Cobb–Douglas production function is of the form

$$q = A x_1^\alpha x_2^{1-\alpha}$$

where x_1 and x_2 are factor inputs, A is a constant which reflects the general efficiency of the technology and α is a constant which reflects relative factor shares in the total product.

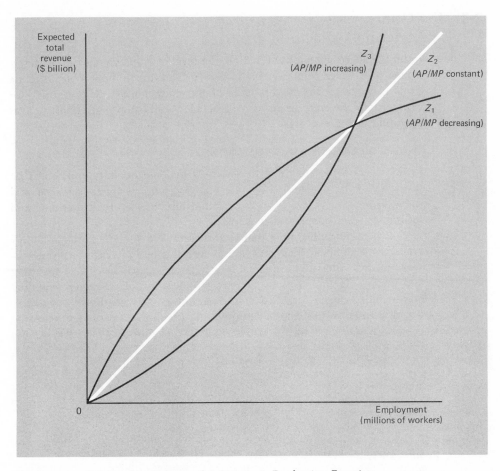

Figure 2-9   Relationship Between the Aggregate Production Function
and the Aggregate Supply Function

that firms require successively smaller increments in expected total revenue
to induce them to hire additional workers. This is not likely on an *a priori*
basis, and consequently, we shall generally reject the notion of a concave
aggregate supply function, unless, of course, an empirical investigation
should demonstrate otherwise.

While the exact shape of the aggregate supply function must be
determined empirically, *a priori* reasoning suggests that it will be positively
sloped, originating from the origin and either linear or convex to the employment axis.

2-3 The Components
of Aggregate Demand

From the aggregate supply function, the level of employment can be determined if expected total revenue is known. To estimate how much revenue firms can expect, the buyers' side of the market must be examined. Of course, total revenue of firms will be identically (always) equal to total spending of buyers.

THE AGGREGATE DEMAND FUNCTION

In this section the spending decisions of major economic groups will be investigated. Total spending by all economic groups is *aggregate demand,* and the *aggregate demand function* is the relationship between total spending and income for the economy as a whole.

It is important to note that total income and spending are *functionally* related, not identical. This means that spending and income are not necessarily always equal, but are equal only at some particular level of spending and income. In the Keynesian model, the relationship between spending and income is behavioral. Total income, however, is identically, or definitionally, equal to the value of output, and this implies that total spending is not always equal to the value of output. Therefore, all goods will not be purchased at all levels of output.

Denoting an identity relationship by the symbol $\equiv$, then

$$\text{Income} \equiv \text{Value of output}$$

and

$$\text{Total spending} \equiv \text{Total revenue}$$

Therefore, if

$$\text{Income} \not\equiv \text{Total spending}$$

then

$$\text{Total revenue} \not\equiv \text{Value of total output}$$

It is the aggregate demand *function* of the Keynesian analysis that represents the basic departure from the classical point of view. By stating that total income is equal to total spending only at a single level of income, Keynes was in effect denying the validity of Say's Law on which classical macroeconomics was based. Say's Law, held by classical economists to be a basic macroeconomic principle, asserted that "supply creates its own demand." This was interpreted to mean that spending is *identically,* not functionally, related to income, or that all goods produced will be purchased regardless of the level of output and income.

SPENDING UNITS IN THE ECONOMY

It is convenient to divide buyers into four categories, since the spending decisions of economic units within each of the four groups are based upon similar factors. The consumer sector, or household units, purchases consumption goods; the business sector purchases capital, or investment goods; economic units abroad, the foreign sector, purchase our exports; and the government, or public sector, purchases "public goods." Total spending, or aggregate demand, D, can be treated as the sum of consumption, C, investment, I, net exports, X_n[6], and government spending, G:

$$D = C + I + X_n + G$$

Since each spending group is motivated by different factors, the analysis of aggregate demand will involve the consideration of each of its components separately. Chapters 5 and 6 will look at factors affecting consumption and investment in some detail. However, to develop the preliminary model of income determination in the next chapter, something about the shape of the aggregate demand function must be known. Government spending will be treated as a policy variable that can be controlled by a central authority. It will be apparent that one goal of government expenditure policy will be to control the level of aggregate demand. The remainder of this chapter will take a preliminary look at factors affecting spending in the consumer and business sectors.

THE CONSUMPTION FUNCTION

Expenditures by the consumer sector represent the largest component of aggregate demand in most economies. Empirically the *consumption function*, or the relationship between aggregate consumption and aggregate income, is one of the most stable or reliable of all macroeconomic relationships. Consequently, if the amount of income earned in a particular period is known, a forecaster can predict consumption, the major component of total spending, with a fair amount of accuracy.[7]

[6]Only *net* exports, that is, total exports minus imports should be included in aggregate demand. Since some of the demand in the domestic sectors, C, I, and G, is met by imports, spending on imports must be subtracted from total aggregate demand to obtain domestic aggregate demand. Treating exports as net exports, that is,

$$X_n = \text{total exports} - \text{total imports}$$

does, in effect, reduce the aggregate demand equation by the amount spent on imports.

[7]One reason that such good estimates of consumption can be obtained when income is known is that consumption itself represents a high percentage of income. In most years, consumption represents over 90 percent of the after-tax income of households in the United States. It is more difficult to predict *changes* in consumption where a change in income is expected.

Keynes postulated that consumption is a function of income. He believed that, barring sudden changes in tastes and institutions, consumption could be expected to increase as income increased.

A consumption function such as Keynes suggested is shown in Figure 2-10. The consumption function intersects the consumption axis above the origin and has a slope that is less than 1. (The 45° line has a slope equal to 1.)

Keynes reasoned that while people with high incomes consume more than people with low incomes, high-income families consume a smaller proportion of their income than low-income families. He believed that the same type of behavior would characterize whole economies. The higher the level of aggregate income, the greater would be the proportion saved, in

Figure 2-10   The Keynesian Consumption Function

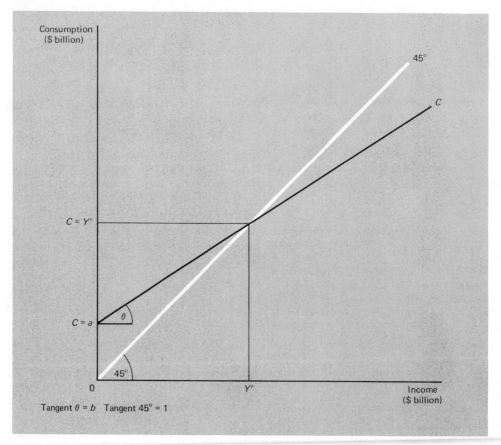

the aggregate. A poor society might actually consume more than its current income by borrowing from abroad. A rich economy, on the other hand, would not spend all of its income on consumption goods.

In Figure 2-10, if aggregate income is less than Y', consumption will be greater than income and must be financed by borrowing or utilizing accumulated assets. If income is above Y', it is not all spent. A moment of reflection will reveal that the vertical distance between the consumption function and the 45° line measures saving when income is above Y' and dissaving or borrowing when income is below Y'. Only when income is Y' will income and consumption be equal.

Keynes labeled the proportion of income consumed at any income level the *average propensity to consume*, APC. Since saving is defined as income not consumed, the reader should verify that

$$APC + APS = 1$$

where APS is the *average propensity to save*, defined as the proportion of income saved. In Figure 2-10 the APC is a decreasing function of income. This implies that the APS increases with income.

The *marginal propensity to consume*, MPC, is the proportion of an increment of income spent on consumption. If a family receives an extra dollar of income (e.g., in the form of a tax rebate), the proportion of the *additional* dollar spent on consumption is the MPC. The MPC is of particular interest to forecasters and policy planners who are concerned with the effect of tax cuts and changes in government spending on consumption. Since the APC decreases with income, the MPC will be less than the APC. Defining the *marginal propensity to save*, MPS, as the proportion of an increment of income saved, it is clear that

$$MPC + MPS = 1$$

For a linear or straight-line consumption function the MPC will be constant and equal to its slope.

Consider the algebraic representation of Figure 2-10:

$$C = a + bY$$

The constant, a, represents the point of intersection with the consumption axis and indicates the amount of consumption that would take place even if no income were earned. The slope of the function, b, represents the ratio of vertical to horizontal change along the function.[8] Notice that b is the MPC, since

$$MPC = \frac{\Delta C}{\Delta Y} = b$$

where ΔC and ΔY signify change in C and Y, respectively. The expression $(1 - b)$ is the MPS, since

$$MPS = 1 - MPC = 1 - b$$

Along this function the APC, C/Y, declines with income since

$$APC = \frac{C}{Y} = \frac{a + bY}{Y} = \frac{a}{Y} + b$$

and the expression $(a/Y) + b$ declines with income if a and b are positive.

A linear consumption function with a positive intercept and positive slope less than 1 reflects Keynes' postulates about consumption behavior. It is realistic to assume that there will be some positive consumption forthcoming even if there is no current income, at least in the short run, so that

$$0 < a$$

It is also reasonable to assume that

$$0 < MPC = b < 1$$

That is, some of an increment to income is always saved even if the APC is greater than 1. Given such a consumption function, the APC will decline with income and the MPC will be constant. As discussed in Chapter 5, there is empirical evidence in support of such a linear consumption function for many economies, particularly for short-run situations in which practical policy planning and forecasting take place.

THE INVESTMENT DECISION

Investment, or expenditure on capital equipment and inventories, is undertaken for the purpose of producing other goods and services rather than for directly satisfying human wants. Although smaller in magnitude than

---

[8]The slope of the function is the tangent of the angle of inclination.

consumption spending, investment presents more difficult problems to the forecaster because its relationship to income is more complicated and less reliable. It is financed by depreciation allowances, profits, and borrowing. *A priori* reasoning suggests that investment will increase with rising sales and profits, making more funds available. Consequently, investment will be an increasing function of income. Since some expenditure on capital equipment is financed by borrowing, investment should also be sensitive to credit conditions, reflected in the market rate of interest. Investment should be a decreasing function of the rate of interest, since as the interest rate rises, firms will be discouraged from borrowing and consequently will invest less. Furthermore, some additional investment may be forthcoming that is independent of the level of sales or credit conditions. This may occur as old machines wear out or become obsolete, or when firms undertake innovative investment to capture a larger market share.

These considerations are reflected in a hypothetical *investment function* which relates aggregate investment with aggregate income and the interest rate. Algebraically,

$$I = g + dY + ei$$

where g, the constant term, represents investment taking place independently of income and the interest rate, and i is the market rate of interest. We expect the constant d to be positive and less than 1; that is,

$$0 < d < 1$$

since firms will most likely invest some, but not all, of an increment in national income. While firms may invest all or more of their own income, the share of national income at their disposal is relatively small, generally not exceeding 15 percent.[9] The term e should be negative, reflecting the hypothesized inverse relationship between investment and the interest rate.

To portray the investment function graphically, the equation must be reduced to two variables. For any given interest rate, the investment represented by the expression ei can be combined with g, and the investment function can be written as

$$I = (g + ei) + dY$$
$$= h + dY$$

where

$$h = g + ei$$

[9] See Appendix A (Section A-4) for a discussion of the relationship between income shares and the marginal propensity to spend out of national income.

In this way investment is broken down into a function of income as well as a component which is independent of income.

This investment function is shown in Figure 2-11. The slope of the investment function, *d*, is the *marginal propensity to invest* or the proportion of an increment of income invested by firms. This will be positive, and unless firms invest all of the increment of national income (an unlikely event), it will be less than 1.

If the rate of interest were to fall, we would expect the constant term in the investment function to increase (since *e* is negative), shifting the investment function upward. In fact, we can conceive of a *family* of parallel

Figure 2-11   An Investment Function for a Stipulated
                   Rate of Interest

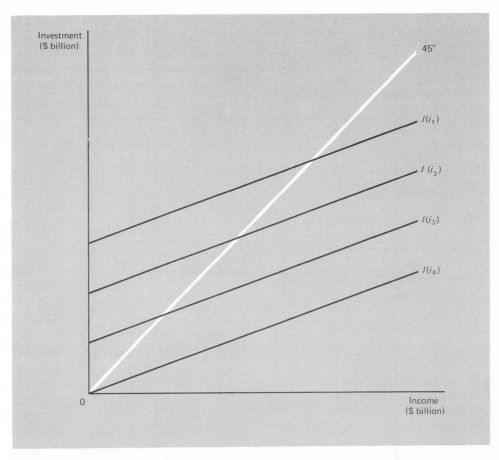

Figure 2-12   A Family of Investment Functions
Associated with Different Rates of Interest

investment functions, each associated with a different rate of interest but having the same slope. Such a family of investment functions is shown in Figure 2-12. As the interest rate rises from i_1 to i_4, the investment function shifts downward, indicating the inverse relationship between investment and the rate of interest. The lowest interest rate, i_1, is associated with the highest investment function in the family.

THE FOREIGN SECTOR

Demand from abroad, exports, is also included in aggregate demand. Imports, or purchases of foreign goods, should be subtracted from consumption, investment, and government spending to determine domestic aggregate demand.

Factors governing export demand are complex and are linked only in an indirect way to the level of domestic income. Consequently, we shall treat them as *exogenous*, that is, determined independently of income.

Imports, on the other hand, are determined by the same factors that affect the demand for domestic goods. In particular, imports are directly related to the level of income.[10] Algebraically,

$$M = mY$$

where

M = imports
Y = income
m = marginal propensity to import[11]

and

$$0 < m < 1$$

While the marginal propensity to import is greater than 0, it will be smaller in magnitude than the marginal propensity to consume.

Since imports, M, are a function of income, net exports, X_n, will also be a function of income, even though total exports, E, are exogenous. Algebraically,

$$X_n = E - mY$$

Graphically, the net export function is shown in Figure 2-13. Since exports, E, are fixed at E_0, and imports, M, increase with income at a rate m, then net exports decline with income. Notice that net exports become zero at income Y_0, where the import function equals total exports. When income is greater than Y_0, the trade balance is in deficit, while at lower income levels the balance is in surplus.[12] Note that when exports are treated as fixed, the trade deficit increases as national income increases, as long as the marginal propensity to import is positive.

[10] Imports can also be affected by credit conditions at home, reflected in the interest rate. The impact of the domestic interest rate on import demand is likely to be small, however, and we shall ignore it in this model for simplicity. The interest rate can be introduced, however, in a more complete model, with no loss of generality.

[11] Since there is no constant term, the marginal propensity to import equals the average propensity to import. This is not necessarily true for all models.

[12] The balance of trade is not to be confused with the balance of payments, which includes financial transactions, transfers, and gold flows.

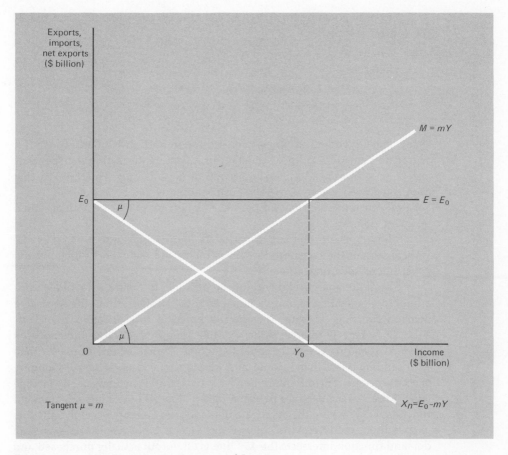

Figure 2-13   Net Exports as a Function of Income

THE SHAPE
OF THE AGGREGATE DEMAND FUNCTION

We are now prepared to consider the shape of the aggregate demand function. Aggregate demand is equal to the sum of its components:

$$D = C + I + X_n + G$$

The aggregate consumption, investment, and net export functions have been specified:

$$C = a + bY$$
$$I = h + dY$$
$$X_n = E_0 - mY$$

Suppose government spending can take on any value, G_0, selected by the central authorities:

$$G = G_0$$

Therefore,

$$
\begin{aligned}
D &= C + I + X_n + G \\
&= (a + bY) + (h + dY) + (E_0 - mY) + G_0 \\
&= (a + h + E_0 + G_0) + (b + d - m)Y
\end{aligned}
$$

Using our hypothetical linear consumption and investment functions, aggregate demand is a linear function of income, intersecting the spending axis at $(a + h + E_0 + G_0)$, with a slope of $(b + d - m)$. This implies that even if income were zero, the level of spending would be $a + h + E_0 + G_0$. For every increment of income, $b + d - m$ percent of that increment would be spent domestically.

The aggregate demand function is shown in Figure 2-14. It is the vertical sum of the consumption, investment, and net export functions and government spending.

Recall the analytical device of the 45° line. In Figure 2-14, along such a line, total spending is always equal to total income. Along the aggregate demand function, D, total spending is equal to total income, Y, only at $Y_E = D_E$ where D intersects the 45° line. There is no other income level at which spending is exactly equal to income. When income is greater than Y_E, spending is less than income, and when income is less than Y_E, spending exceeds income. The difference between income and spending at any income level is the vertical distance between the 45° line and the aggregate demand function. Only where the aggregate demand function intersects the 45° line is spending exactly equal to income or output. Only where the aggregate demand function intersects the 45° line is all output actually purchased and no orders left unfilled. At all other income levels, Say's Law is invalid.

In this chapter the aggregate supply and demand functions have been defined and analyzed. Chapter 3 will show how the macroeconomic equilibrium between aggregate supply and demand determines the level of income and employment. Once the theory of income determination is thoroughly developed, we shall see how macroeconomic policy can be used to manipulate the level of income and employment.

Questions for Study and Review

1. (a) Suppose the baker in the text example found that he could sell only 800 loaves of bread for $400. Then he would be left with an inventory of 200 loaves of bread valued at $100. How would this affect his accounts?

(b) Because he has accumulated unplanned inventory valued at $100, the baker expects that his future sales will amount to only $400 in each production period. Consequently, he decides to produce only 800 loaves of bread,

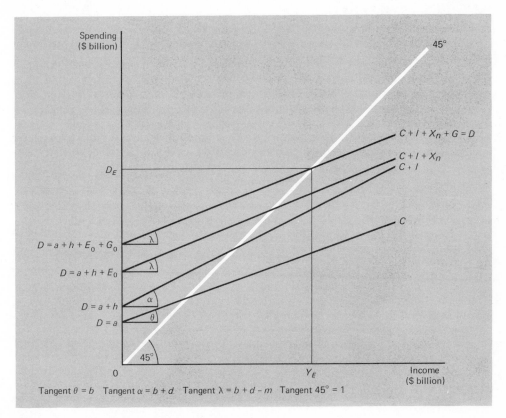

Figure 2-14 The Aggregate Demand Function

valued at $400. Show how his decision to produce less bread will affect the accounts of the miller and the farmer, as well as his own.

When the value of output falls to $400, total income must also fall to $400. Be sure your revised accounts reflect the output–income identity.

2. A production function for a firm in perfect competition is shown below:

Labor Input (per hour)	Output (per hour)
0	0
1	10
2	17
3	22
4	26
5	27

(a) If the hourly wage is $1.00, derive and graph the expected total revenue function for the firm.

(b) Suppose minimum wage legislation goes into effect and the firm must now pay an hourly wage of $1.50. How will this affect the expected total revenue function of the firm? Show the new expected total revenue function in the same graph with the old one.

(c) Suppose the firm undertakes a program which trains labor to produce output more efficiently. If man-hour productivity is doubled, so that

Labor Input (per hour)	Output (per hour)
0	0
1	20
2	34
3	44
4	52
5	54

and the hourly wage is $1.50, how will this affect the firm's expected total revenue function?

3. Consider the aggregate demand function

$$D = C + I + X_n + G$$

for a hypothetical economy for which

$$C = 200 + 0.6Y$$
$$I = 100 + 0.3Y$$
$$X_n = E - 0.1Y$$
$$E = 150$$
$$G = 150$$

(a) Find the level of aggregate demand in this economy when total income, Y, equals total spending, D.

(b) Suppose the government increases spending by 50. What will be the effect on aggregate demand? (*Hint:* Aggregate demand will increase by *more* than 50.)

(c) Suppose the government wants to effectuate an increase in aggregate demand of 500. How much will the government need to increase its spending to achieve this goal? (*Hint:* Government spending will have to increase by *less* than 500.)

(d) It is possible that the government may wish to use monetary policy rather than fiscal policy to increase the level of aggregate demand. Suppose the interest rate is reduced and the investment function becomes

$$I = 150 + 0.3Y$$

What will be the effect on aggregate demand?

4. We have defined a consumption function which relates total consumption and total income:

$$C = a + bY$$

Household spending on some types of durable consumption goods, however, may be a function of the interest rate. Can you derive a *family* of consumption functions, each associated with a *different* rate of interest? (*Hint:* Remember how we derived the family of investment functions.)

Additional Reading

Davidson, Paul and Eugene Smolensky, *Aggregate Supply and Demand Analysis.* New York: Harper & Row, Publishers, 1964, Chapters 9 and 10.
Hansen, Alvin H., *A Guide to Keynes.* New York: McGraw-Hill Book Company, Inc., 1953, Chapter 1.
Keynes, John Maynard, *The General Theory of Employment, Interest, and Money.* New York: Harcourt Brace Jovanovich, Inc., 1965, Chapter 3; originally published by Macmillan & Co., Ltd., 1936.

3

The Analytics
of Income Determination:
National Income
and Employment Equilibrium

Having examined the output–income identity and the aggregate supply and demand functions, we shall consider how the interaction of aggregate supply and demand determines a unique level of national income and employment. The analysis of this chapter represents the framework of Keynesian economics.

3-1 The Theory of Income Determination

THE CONCEPT OF ECONOMIC EQUILIBRIUM

Equilibrium in economics refers to the attainment of a position from which there is no tendency to move because that position is preferred by the economic units involved. Equilibrium reflects only the preferences of economic units, households, and firms, acting independently of each other, not social or aggregate preferences. Consequently, an equilibrium position is not necessarily socially desirable. The preferred position will depend upon certain underlying conditions or *parameters*.

For example, recalling the analysis of aggregate supply, a firm will employ N workers on the basis of some expected total revenue—for example, $1000. These workers will produce output valued at $1000. The firm's expected total revenue function, based on the assumption that the firm wishes to maximize profits at each level of sales, is shown in Figure 3-1.

The desire to hire N workers, however, is contingent upon receipts or sales actually totaling $1000. If total sales fall short of $1000, the firm will regret hiring N workers since profits will be less than they could have been, had a smaller wage cost been incurred and had less output been produced. If sales fall short of expectations, the firm will most likely revise its estimates of future sales receipts. Suppose expected total revenue is revised to $900 and the firm hires M workers. If actual sales receipts are now $900, as shown in Figure 3-1, the firm will be at its maximum profit position for that level of sales. The firm is said to be in equilibrium, given the underlying condition, or parameter, that actual sales are $900.

In Figure 3-1, point E on the expected total revenue function represents an equilibrium, or preferred, position for the firm when actual sales are $900. Actual total revenue is $900, and the firm maximizes profits by hiring M workers. Point D is a disequilibrium position, since expectations are not fulfilled and the firm can increase profits by reducing its labor force and moving to point E. There will be a movement from D to E, from a disequilibrium to an equilibrium position.

Suppose actual sales increase to $1000. This represents a change in

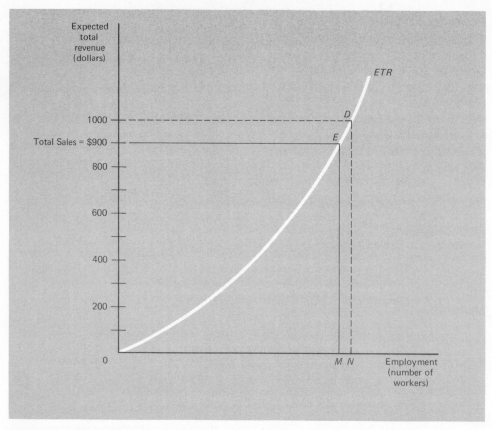

Figure 3-1   Equilibrium and Disequilibrium Positions for a Profit-Maximizing Firm
When Total Sales Are $900

the underlying conditions, or parameters, for the firm. Now the firm maximizes profits by hiring N workers, and D is the new preferred, or equilibrium, position. The examination of the various equilibrium positions associated with different underlying conditions, or parameters, is called *comparative statics*.

THE ATTAINMENT
OF MACROECONOMIC EQUILIBRIUM

For the production sector, income and employment equilibrium occurs when actual revenue is equal to expected total revenue for all firms. The attainment of macroeconomic equilibrium, therefore, implies that total spending equals expected total revenue or, alternatively, that aggregate demand equals aggregate supply.

Keeping in mind the various national income identities, the macroeconomic equilibrium condition can be expressed in a number of ways. By definition, it is clear that

$$\text{Total income} \equiv \text{Value of output} \equiv \text{Expected total revenue}$$

and

$$\text{Total spending} \equiv \text{Total revenue}$$

Furthermore, the firm is in a preferred, or equilibrium, position when

$$\text{Total revenue} = \text{Expected total revenue}$$

Given these relationships, the equilibrium condition can be expressed in several alternative ways:

$$\text{Expected total revenue} = \text{Total revenue}$$

or

$$\text{Expected total revenue} = \text{Total spending}$$

or

$$\text{Total income} = \text{Total spending}$$

It is important to keep in mind that all these relationships reflect essentially the same equilibrium condition; that is, the firms' expectations are realized. Keynes used the same reasoning presented here in his criticism of Say's Law. The equality between income and spending, he pointed out, is an equilibrium condition, not an identity. Expectations of firms are not necessarily realized at all levels of employment.

The reader will recall the relationship between income and spending, the aggregate demand function. Equilibrium is attained when income is equal to spending. This is shown in Figure 3-2. Equilibrium income occurs at the point where the aggregate demand function intersects a 45° line from the origin, point P in Figure 3-2.

At all points on the 45° line, spending is equal to income, but only at income E, where the aggregate demand function, D, is coincident with the 45° line, will spending units decide to spend exactly E, in the aggregate. If income is greater than E, spending will fall short of income. At income F, for example, income exceeds spending by the amount AB, the vertical distance between the aggregate demand function and the 45° line at income

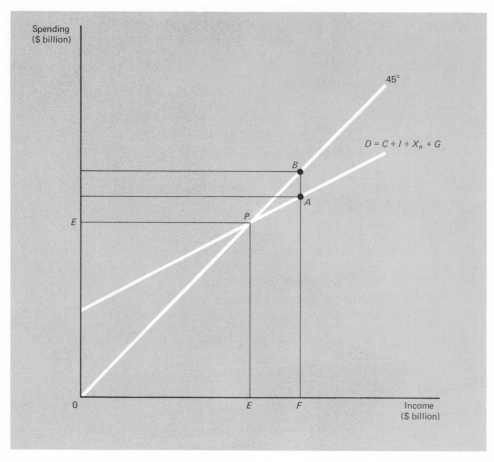

Figure 3-2   National Income Equilibrium

F. If income is less than *E*, spending will exceed income. The difference between income and spending at any level of income is the vertical distance between the aggregate demand function and the 45° line at that income level.

If all income is not spent, all output will not be purchased and total revenue of the firm will fall short of expectations. Aggregate supply will exceed aggregate demand, and a preferred, or equilibrium, position will not have been attained. Employment and income will fall until equilibrium is reached. If, on the other hand, spending units wish to spend more than their income, in the aggregate, firms will not be able to fill all orders. Aggregate demand will exceed aggregate supply, and consequently, firms will employ more workers, thereby increasing the level of aggregate income until an equilibrium is attained. The relationship between aggregate supply and aggregate demand is shown in Figure 3-3.

Suppose firms expect total revenue to be at level Q and so employ R workers. Total output and income is Q and total spending is S. If total spending is S, total revenue is also S, since

$$\text{Total spending} \equiv \text{Total revenue}$$

Since total revenue has fallen short of expectations by SQ, the firms will revise estimates of total revenue. Employment and income will fall until income and spending reach point E and employment falls to T. At this point

$$\text{Total income} = \text{Total spending} = \text{Expected total revenue}$$

Consumers and producers have reached a preferred, or equilibrium, position from which there is no tendency to move.

Figure 3-3   The Relationship Between Aggregate Demand
and Aggregate Supply

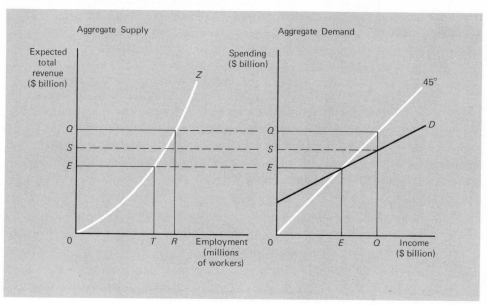

3-2 The Classical Theory of Income and Employment

SAY'S LAW

Pre-Keynesian macroeconomics was based upon Say's Law. Say's Law implied that firms' total revenue expectations would always be realized since all income earned would always be spent. Income, it was postulated, is identical to spending for all levels of income. The analysis of macroeconomic equilibrium which we have just developed was unnecessary, because the assumption was made that aggregate demand always equals aggregate supply. Everyone who wanted to work would be employed since all output could always be sold, no matter how much was produced, and any amount of expected total revenue could be realized.

Say's Law was based on the assumption that all income not spent on consumption or by the government would be channeled to firms through the credit market and ultimately spent on investment. If this were true, then aggregate demand would always lie on the 45° line from the origin of the income–spending graph. Ignoring the foreign sector for simplicity, as shown in Figure 3-4, Say's Law implied that investment would always be equal to the gap between the $C + G$ portion of the aggregate demand function and the 45° line.

Classical macroeconomics, relying on Say's Law, was obviously not adequate for analyzing the Great Depression in which 25 percent of the industrial labor force was unemployed. Economists could not recommend appropriate government action when they were guided by a theory which said that a full-employment level of income would always be maintained, regardless of the level of government spending. Any deviation from full employment was viewed as only a short-run phenomenon which would be corrected automatically by free-market adjustments. Such a wait-and-see attitude was difficult to maintain politically as pressure from the jobless mounted.

THE KEYNESIAN APPROACH

The innovation of Keynesian analysis was the notion that equality of aggregate demand and supply is an equilibrium condition, not an identity. The problem with the classical approach should be clear from the analysis which has preceded. Spending decisions and output–employment decisions are made by different economic units with different motives. There is no reason to expect that spending units will decide to buy exactly as much as firms can produce at all levels of employment.

We have seen that consumption is a function of income. Saving is the

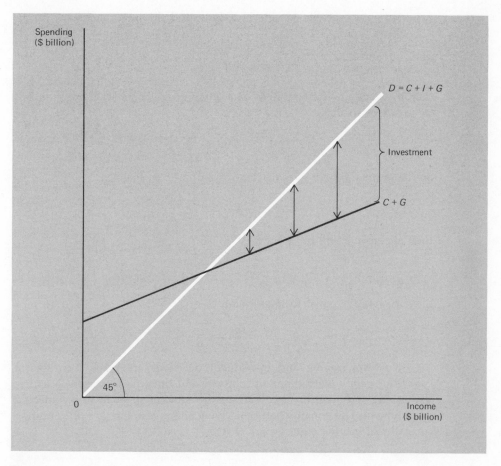

Figure 3-4   The Classical Aggregate Demand Function

residual left over from income after consumption expenditures are made and taxes are paid:

$$Y = C + T + S$$

Therefore,

$$S = Y - C - T$$

The decision to save, therefore, is made by households.

The decision to invest is made by business firms. As we shall see in Chapter 6, the investment decision is based upon many factors, including

expected future profits, credit conditions, and the internal flow of funds.
Since

$$D = C + I + X_n + G$$

then if we assume for simplicity that government finances all expenditures
by taxation, so that

$$G = T$$

and assuming exports are matched by imports, so that

$$X_n = 0$$

then all income will be spent; that is,

$$Y = D$$

only if saving is equal to investment, or

$$S = I$$

However, saving and investment decisions are made by different
groups of people with different motives, and there is no reason to expect
that saving and investment will always be equal at all levels of income and
employment. The equality between saving and investment is a precondition
for national income equilibrium; that is,

$$S = I$$

is not an identity.

Say's law implied that the saving–investment relationship is an identity
rather than an equilibrium condition; that is,

$$S \equiv I$$

or, in other words, firms will always decide to invest exactly what households
decide to save. The Keynesian approach, on the other hand, asserted that
saving and investment decisions are independent, and therefore, saving and
investment are equal only in equilibrium. Figure 3-5 shows the relationship
between saving and income.

Saving at any level of income is equal to the distance between the

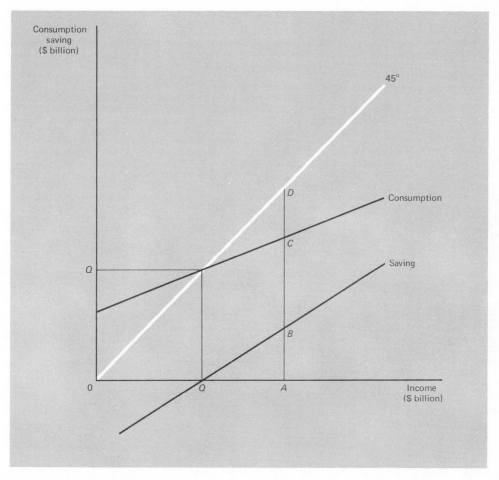

Figure 3-5   The Saving Function

consumption function and a 45° line on the income–spending graph. At income A, for example, saving is AB, consumption is AC, and the difference between consumption and income is $CD = AB$. At income Q, the consumption function intersects the 45° line, consumption is equal to income, and saving is zero.

Figure 3-6 shows a Keynesian income equilibrium, ignoring the public and foreign sectors. Since investment and saving are independent linear functions of income, equilibrium occurs at a unique level of income. Equilibrium is at E, where saving is equal to investment and where the aggregate demand function crosses the 45° line. Both investment and saving represent

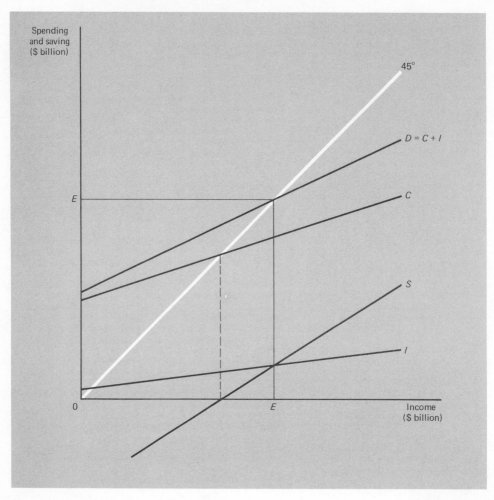

Figure 3-6 A Keynesian Income Equilibrium

the distance between the consumption function and the 45° line at equilibrium.

Critics of the Keynesian approach were quick to suggest an inconsistency in his thinking. Consider the possible uses to which income can be put. It can be spent on consumption goods, C, imports, M, or taxes, T, or it can be saved, S:

$$\text{Income} \equiv C + S + T + M$$

Output produced is either consumed by households, C, foreigners, E, or government, G. Any output not consumed is invested in plant and equipment or inventories. Therefore,

$$\text{Output} \equiv C + I + E + G$$

Since

$$\text{Income} \equiv \text{Output}$$

then

$$C + S + M + T \equiv C + I + E + G$$

If the government budget is balanced, so that

$$G = T$$

and the net trade surplus is zero, so that

$$E = M$$

then investment will be identical to saving,

$$I \equiv S$$

since

$$C \equiv C$$

Does the output–income identity imply an investment–saving identity? Is Say's Law vindicated after all? Keynes pointed out that two different concepts of saving and investment are involved in the discussion.

Returning to the question of the disposition of output,

$$\text{Output} \equiv C + I + E + G$$

we recall that investment was defined as any output not purchased by households, governments, and foreigners. This is an *ex post* concept of investment and includes unplanned or unexpected inventories of goods not purchased by the spending units as well as planned inventories and capital goods. Firms will not be in equilibrium if unplanned inventory is accumulated.

On the other hand, investment in the aggregate demand function is an *ex ante* concept. *Ex ante* investment is the amount all firms plan to spend on capital goods and inventories. Only when *ex post* (actual investment) and *ex ante* (planned) investment are equal will firms be in a preferred position and hence in equilibrium.

While *ex post* investment, a residual component of output, is identical to saving, that is,

$$I_{ex\ post} \equiv S$$

ex ante investment is equal to saving only *in equilibrium*. Indeed, the equalities

$$I_{ex\ ante} = S$$

and

$$I_{ex\ ante} = I_{ex\ post}$$

are alternative statements of the macroeconomic equilibrium condition that aggregate demand be equal to aggregate supply. Thus, in answering his critics Keynes clarified the relationship between the saving–investment equality and macroeconomic equilibrium.

To summarize the results, consider the aggregate supply and demand schedules in Figure 3-7. Point *B* represents a disequilibrium level of income.

Figure 3-7 Aggregate Supply and Aggregate Demand

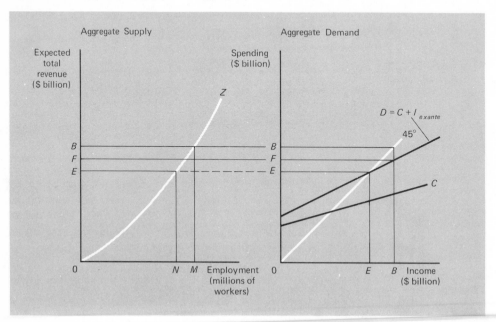

At income B, expected total revenue is B, the value of output is B, and employment is M. However, spending is equal to F. Since B is produced and F is purchased, then FB is unplanned inventory investment:

$$I_{ex\ post} = I_{ex\ ante} + FB$$

Now it is clear that

$$S = I_{ex\ ante} + FB$$

since saving is measured by the distance between the 45° line and the consumption function is measured on the income–spending graph.

Therefore,

$$I_{ex\ post} = S$$

and

$$I_{ex\ ante} \neq S$$

This analysis holds for any disequilibrium point, so that

$$I_{ex\ post} \equiv S$$

Only in equilibrium, at an income level of E and employment of N, will

$$I_{ex\ ante} = S \equiv I_{ex\ post}$$

3-3   Conclusions of the Equilibrium Analysis

THE POSSIBILITY OF AN UNDEREMPLOYMENT EQUILIBRIUM

The equilibrium level of income is determined by the level of aggregate demand. The equilibrium level of employment associated with that income in turn is determined by the aggregate supply function.

Aggregate demand, which determines the level of employment, is a function of income and other economic variables. Since equilibrium does not occur at all levels of income and employment, everyone looking for work will not necessarily find jobs. Spending decisions of the major spending groups are not guided by considerations of the economy's full-employment goal.

64

Thus, Keynes, writing in the midst of the worst economic depression the world has ever known, envisioned the possibility of a macroeconomic equilibrium persisting at less than full employment:

> In particular, it is an outstanding characteristic of the economic system in which we live that, whilst it is subject to severe fluctuations in respect of output and employment, it is not violently unstable. Indeed it seems capable of remaining in a chronic condition of sub-normal activity for a considerable period without any marked tendency either toward recovery or collapse. Moreover, the evidence indicates that full, or even approximately full, employment is of rare and short-lived occurrence.[1]

Suppose, for example, in Figure 3-8, full employment is at F. When F workers are employed, the value of aggregate output and income is G, and at an income level of G, aggregate supply will exceed aggregate demand by the amount KG. In equilibrium, firms will hire fewer than F workers to produce less output. Output and income in equilibrium will be H, and employment will be E. Consequently, EF workers will be unemployed in

[1]John Maynard Keynes, *The General Theory of Employment, Interest, and Money,* (New York: Harcourt Brace Jovanovich, Inc., 1965), pp. 249–250; originally published by Macmillan & Co., Ltd., 1936.

Figure 3-8   An Underemployment Equilibrium

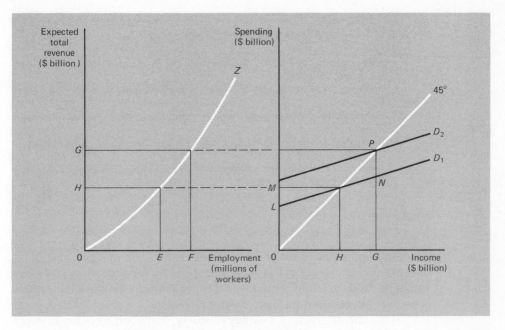

Figure 3-9   Attainment of a Full-Employment Equilibrium
by a Shift of the Aggregate Demand Function

equilibrium; that is, *EF* workers will be looking for work and unable to find jobs.

Full employment in equilibrium can be achieved by an upward vertical shift of the aggregate demand schedule from D_1 to D_2 as shown in Figure 3-9. An upward shift of $LM = ND$ is required to bring the economy to full employment.

What factors might cause the aggregate demand function to shift from D_1 to D_2? Recalling that

$$D = C + I + X_n + G$$

and assuming that all the spending units are at equilibrium at D_1, then the central authority can take measures to shift aggregate demand to D_2.[2]

---

[2] A shift in aggregate demand can also occur as a result of changes in certain underlying conditions or parameters which we have assumed to be constant. For instance, an advance in technology might affect investment by increasing the rate of replacement for obsolete machines, thus causing the investment function to shift upward. We shall consider such possibilities in Chapter 6. However, in general, economic policy makers cannot rely upon chance events for maintaining full-employment income equilibrium.

66

The most obvious measure is to increase government expenditure by the amount *LM*. Other possibilities include

1. reducing personal taxes, thereby causing households to increase consumption spending,
2. reducing corporate income taxes, thereby encouraging investment spending by firms,
3. reducing the interest rate, thereby stimulating both consumption and investment,
4. increasing tariffs to discourage imports and stimulate consumption of domestic goods,[3]
5. reducing taxes and the interest rate for exporters, thereby stimulating demand in the foreign sector.

UNEMPLOYMENT
AS A MONETARY PHENOMENON

A second important result of our analysis is the notion that income is not always equal to spending. If income and spending were identical, Say's Law would be valid, and equilibrium would occur at any level of income without conscious intervention by the central government.

It is a characteristic of a money economy, that is, an economy in which goods and factor services are exchanged for money rather than for goods and factor services, that units receiving income can choose not to expend their income. In a nonmoney (or barter) economy, income is received in kind, all goods produced are received as income, and

Aggregate demand $\equiv C + I + X_n + G \equiv$ Income $\equiv$ Aggregate supply

at all levels of income.

In a money economy we can conceive of income and output as a circular flow, as illustrated in Figure 3-10. Income earned in the form of money represents claims on goods produced. Therefore, money functions as a *store of value*. Since income earned is identical to the value of output, that is,

Income $\equiv$ Value of output

the value of claims, or money, in the hands of spending units is exactly equal to the value of output. If all the claims are not exercised, that is, if aggregate demand is less than income, the spending loop will be smaller

[3]Such a policy may be unsuccessful if foreign countries respond by increasing their tariffs and discouraging your exports. It proved to be self-defeating during the depression of the 1930's.

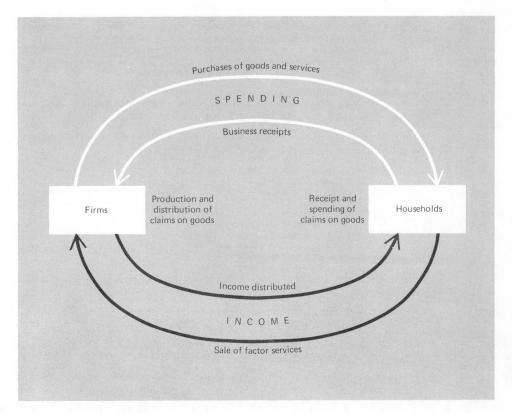

Figure 3-10   The Circular Flow of Income

than the income loop and all output will not be purchased. Unplanned inventory investment will result, and firms will produce less and employ fewer people, distributing fewer claims in the form of income. The circular flow shrinks until the equilibrium position has been reached. Equilibrium occurs when all claims generated in the circular flow are exercised, when the spending loop is the same size as the income loop, or in other words, when all goods produced are purchased. Government, of course, through its power not only to reduce taxes but also to increase the supply of money, or claims on goods, can prevent the spending loop from shrinking and can even cause it to expand. When the spending loop expands, firms will produce more and employ more people, distributing more claims in the form of income, and consequently, both loops of the circular flow will expand until they are of equal size.

It is important to keep in mind that unemployment, except for the structural and frictional varieties, is basically a monetary phenomenon. Because money serves as a store of value, the equilibrium condition

$$Income = Spending$$

is not an identity and holds for a single value of income and employment, not necessarily at full employment. In a barter economy, on the other hand, Say's Law is an identity and equilibrium can occur at any value of income and employment, including, of course, full employment.

3-4 The Multiplier Analysis

FULL EMPLOYMENT
THROUGH POLICY PLANNING

Although equilibrium occurs in a money economy only at a single value of income and employment, we need not worry about being trapped in a permanent underemployment equilibrium. Keynes was overly pessimistic in *The General Theory* when he wrote of full employment as a "rare and short-lived occurrence." As long as the central government can manipulate the aggregate demand function through appropriate fiscal and monetary policies, equilibrium can be effectuated at many levels of income and employment. The ultimate objective is to design government policies that will always fill the gap between spending and income at all levels of income up to full employment. As illustrated in Figure 3-4, classical economic theory suggested that the gap between consumption spending and income will always be filled by investment. Keynes asserted that if investment does not fill the gap, it can be filled by expenditure stimulated or initiated by government action.

Under these circumstances a new kind of aggregate demand function can be envisioned. Government policies will always ensure that the gap between income and consumption spending is filled at all levels of income, up to the level of full employment. This gap can be filled in a variety of ways: by stimulating additional consumption and investment through tax and monetary policies or by increasing government expenditure.

The aggregate demand function, embodying this principle, is shown in Figure 3-11. Full-employment income is at F. By stimulating or initiating expenditures in the amount AB, government policy enables the economy to achieve its goal of full employment.

This is the principle difference between classical and Keynesian macroeconomics. The classical approach asserted that full employment could

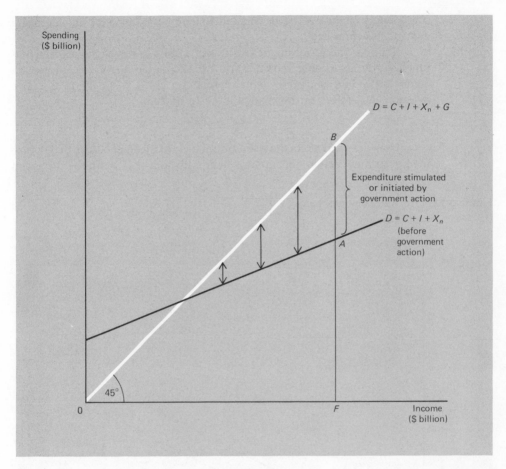

Figure 3-11   Aggregate Demand with Government
Intervention

be achieved automatically through the market mechanism. Recognizing the possibility of an underemployment equilibrium resulting from the independent spending decisions of households and firms, Keynesian theory implied an active role for government. To attain the full-employment goal, the government must manipulate the level of aggregate demand.

AUTONOMOUS AND INDUCED EXPENDITURES

There are many ways in which the government can affect the level of aggregate demand. All of these involve vertical shifts in one or more of the components of the aggregate demand function and hence of the aggregate demand function itself.

Suppose the government effectuates a shift in the aggregate demand function by increasing expenditure by the amount AB, as shown in Figure 3-12. The aggregate demand function shifts from D_1 to D_2. The notation, ΔG, refers to the change in G. In this case

$$\Delta G = AB$$

How does this affect the equilibrium level of income? Notice that before the government action, income was in equilibrium at C. With the increased

Figure 3-12   An Autonomous Change
in Spending

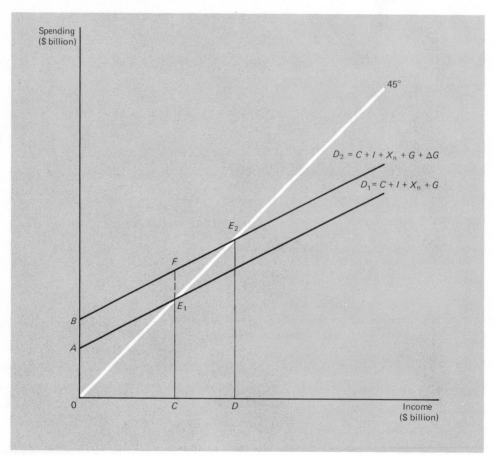

expenditure of $AB = E_1F$, equilibrium income increases from C to D. The change in the equilibrium level of income, CD, is greater than the initial change in spending, AB. The relationship between the change in equilibrium income and the initial change in spending depends upon the slope of the aggregate demand function. For any initial change in spending, the ultimate change in equilibrium income is greater, the steeper is the slope of the aggregate demand function.[4]

Why does the ultimate change in income and spending exceed the initial change in spending? The *autonomous* increase in government expenditure *induces* spending in other sectors. A change in spending is said to be *autonomous* if it is initiated by factors other than income variation. It is represented by a *shift* in the aggregate demand function. A change in autonomous spending can originate in any sector. A change in spending is said to be *induced* if it is initiated by income variation. Induced expenditure changes are represented by a *movement along* the aggregate demand function. A change in induced spending can occur in any sector in which spending is a function of income.

How does an autonomous change in spending induce additional spending? Remember that in both the household and business sectors spending is partly a function of income. Since autonomous spending by the government sector raises income in the private sectors, further spending by households and businesses is induced. Since an initial autonomous expenditure induces further spending, the ultimate change in equilibrium income is greater than the initial expenditure.[5]

Autonomous changes in spending can occur in any sector. For instance, technological changes in several important industries can cause firms to replace obsolete machinery more rapidly than usual, thus increasing invest-

---

[4]Consider, for example, the case in which the aggregate demand function is horizontal. The change in income will exactly equal the initial change in spending. See the figure below.

[5]For a horizontal aggregate demand function there are no induced effects since spending is not a function of income in any sector. Consequently, the total change in spending is equal to the initial change.

ment demand. This increase in investment demand will generate increased income in the investment goods industries, inducing further investment and consumption. Now the increase in demand has spread to consumer goods industries and other investment goods industries throughout the economy, generating further increases in income and inducing still more spending.

A DYNAMIC MULTIPLIER ANALYSIS

Our model of national income equilibrium can be used to forecast the ultimate impact of an autonomous change in spending on national income. We shall ignore the foreign sector for simplicity. Suppose the consumption function in an economy is

$$C = 100 + 0.6Y$$

and the investment function is

$$I = 200 + 0.2Y$$

Table 3-1 traces the time path of income in this economy when government spending increases by $100 million.[6] The initial increase in government expenditure of $100 million generates additional income of $100 million. This added income induces additional consumption expenditure of $60 million and investment expenditure of $20 million, generating $80 million of income in addition to the $100 million generated by the government expenditure. This increased income induces even further spending. The process continues, with total expenditure increasing at a decreasing rate, until a new equilibrium is reached at a level of income $500 million greater than at the previous equilibrium. At the new equilibrium, the change in income becomes approximately zero, so that no further spending is induced. Thus, the initial increase in autonomous expenditure is multiplied five times before a new equilibrium is reached. The ratio between the total change in spending and the initial or autonomous change in spending is called the *income multiplier*. In this example, the multiplier is 5.

The process of adjustment to equilibrium is shown in Figure 3-13. With aggregate demand at D_1, the economy is at equilibrium at E_1, at an income level of C. An autonomous increase in spending shifts the aggregate demand schedule from D_1 to D_2 by the amount AB. The initial change in

---

[6]The time path presented in this example is based on the assumption that it takes a single period for consumption and investment to respond to changes in income. Also, the possibility of a lag in output in response to changes in demand is ignored. If the response lag is different, then the time path will also be different.

Table 3-1 Time Path of Income for a Continuous Increase
in Government Expenditure

Period	Increase in Government Expenditure + (in millions of dollars)	Increase in Consumption Expenditure + (in millions of dollars)	Increase in Investment Expenditure = (in millions of dollars)	Total Increase in Expenditure and Income (in millions of dollars)
1	100	0	0	100
2	100	60	20	180
3	100	108	36	244
4	100	146	49	295
5	100	177	59	336
6	100	220	67	387
7	100	232	77	409
8	100	245	82	427
9	100	256	85	441
10	100	265	88	453
11	100	272	91	463
12	100	278	93	471
	–	–	–	–
	–	–	–	–
	–	–	–	–
	100	300	100	500

spending is E_1F which is equal to AB. This spending generates additional
income $CH = FG = E_1F = AB$. The change in income, CH, induces increased
spending of the amount GI. Algebraically,

$$GI = (b + d)CH$$

where $b + d$ is the sum of the marginal propensities to consume and invest
or, geometrically, the slope of the aggregate demand function. The process
continues with income and spending increasing at a decreasing rate until
the new equilibrium E_2 is reached at an income level of D. As a result of
the shift in the aggregate demand function from D_1 to D_2, the total change
in equilibrium income is CD. The equality $CH = AB$ is generated by the

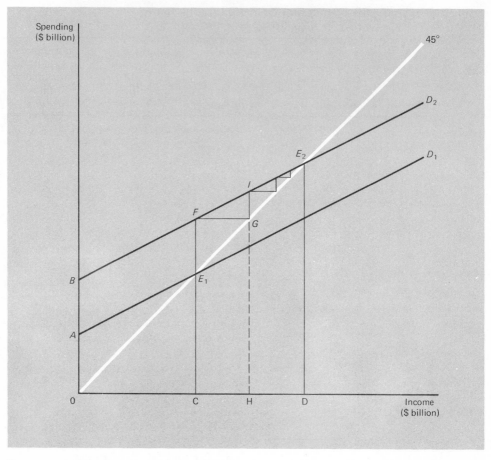

Figure 3-13   The Dynamics of Equilibrium
Adjustment

change in autonomous spending; *HD* is induced. The multiplier is the ratio *CD/CH.*

There are other ways in which the government can control aggregate demand besides varying its own expenditure. Tax and monetary policy can be employed to increase aggregate demand without increasing the size of the public sector. One important result should be clear, however. The equilibrium level of income will change only when the aggregate demand function shifts. And shifts in the aggregate demand function occur only when there are autonomous changes in spending.

DERIVATION OF THE MULTIPLIER

We saw on page 71 that, for any initial change in spending, the ultimate change in equilibrium income is greater when the slope of the aggregate demand function is steeper. Recalling that the slope of the aggregate demand function is equal to the sum of the marginal propensity to consume and the marginal propensity to invest minus the marginal propensity to import, we can derive the relationship algebraically.[7]

Algebraically, the multiplier can be derived from the national income model,

$$
Y = C + I + X_n + G
$$
$$
C = a + bY
$$
$$
I = h + dY
$$
$$
X_n = E_0 - mY
$$
$$
G = G_0
$$

where C, I, X_n, and G represent spending on consumption, investment, net exports, and public goods, respectively, and Y represents total income. The first equation represents the equilibrium condition:

Total income = Total spending

The next three equations are the consumption, investment, and net export functions, and the last equation indicates that government spending is being treated as predetermined, or exogenous.

Since *changes* in spending are the primary concern, the model should be expressed in terms of changes or deviations from the previous equilibrium[8]:

$$
\Delta Y = \Delta C + \Delta I + \Delta X_n + \Delta G
$$
$$
\Delta C = \Delta a + \Delta bY = \Delta a + b\Delta Y
$$
$$
\Delta I = \Delta h + \Delta dY = \Delta h + d\Delta Y
$$
$$
\Delta X_n = \Delta E - \Delta mY = \Delta E - m\Delta Y
$$
$$
\Delta G = \Delta G
$$

The secret in calculating multipliers is to *reduce* the aggregate demand function to its autonomous components. That is, since the multiplier reflects

---

[7] This section and the section to follow will develop the analysis algebraically. The reader should test his understanding by providing a graphical interpretation. The graphical analysis can be developed in the framework of Figure 3-13.

[8] These changes can be either negative or positive. An autonomous *decline* in spending of $100 will cause a multiplied *decline* in income.

the total impact on income of a change in any of its autonomous components, ΔY must be expressed in terms of Δa, Δh, ΔG, and ΔE only.

Performing the appropriate substitutions,

$$\Delta Y = \Delta a + b\Delta Y + \Delta h + d\Delta Y + \Delta E - m\Delta Y + \Delta G$$
$$\Delta Y - b\Delta Y - d\Delta Y + m\Delta Y = \Delta a + \Delta h + \Delta E + \Delta G$$
$$\Delta Y = \frac{1}{1 - b - d + m}(\Delta a + \Delta h + \Delta E + \Delta G)$$

In this model, any change in autonomous spending, ΔD, will change total spending or income by

$$\Delta Y = \frac{1}{1 - b - d + m}\Delta D$$

In our previous example,

$$\Delta G = \$100 \text{ million}$$
$$b = 0.6$$
$$d = 0.2$$
$$m = 0$$

and the change in the other autonomous components, Δa, Δh, and ΔE, was zero. Consequently,

$$\frac{1}{1 - b - d + m} = \frac{1}{1 - 0.8} = 5$$

and

$$\Delta Y = \frac{\Delta G}{1 - b - d + m} = \frac{\$100 \text{ million}}{1 - 0.8} = \$500 \text{ million}$$

This is the same result we found in tracing the time path of income through all its stages. Obviously, this method of determining the multiplier is less tedious.

Suppose the foreign sector had been included in the dynamic multiplier analysis. Let us assume that the marginal propensity to import is 0.1, so that

$$M = 0.1Y$$

When import demand is induced by changes in income, the multiplier effect of an increase in spending is less than if the foreign sector had been ignored, since

$$\frac{\Delta Y}{\Delta G} = \frac{1}{1 - b - d + m} = \frac{1}{1 - 0.7} = 3.3$$

Import demand represents a "leakage" from the circular flow of income and spending which reduces the impact of changes in income on domestic spending.

The value of the multiplier will depend upon the induced components of aggregate demand. In particular, the multiplier will always equal the reciprocal of 1 minus the slope of the aggregate demand function:

$$\text{Multiplier} = \frac{1}{1 - \text{slope of } D}$$

The steeper the slope, the greater is the multiplier. This is the same result we obtained by graphical analysis.

The slope of the aggregate demand function will equal the sum of the *marginal induced effects* on expenditure. Marginal induced effects include the marginal propensity to consume, the marginal propensity to invest, and the marginal relationship between any component of spending and income. The marginal propensity to import has a negative impact on domestic spending, and, since it represents a leakage, it must be subtracted from the other marginal induced effects to estimate the overall impact of a change in income. Whether or not expenditure in a particular sector is autonomous or induced must be determined empirically. The equations in the model which describe the behavior of the various economic groups, the consumption function, investment function, and the like, will specify the values of the marginal induced components such as the marginal propensity to consume, the marginal propensity to invest, and the marginal propensity to import. In general, the degree to which expenditure is induced will vary from model to model, depending on the behavioral specification. Since the multiplier is a *forecasting* tool, it is obvious that accurate *behavioral* specification based on careful and critical analysis of empirical data is a crucial aspect of building a good forecasting model.

Complete behavioral specification of a forecasting model is also important since some components may be indirectly induced. Suppose, for example, the autonomous component of investment is a function of the rate of interest, i. The rate of interest may itself rise and fall with income. In this case an autonomous change in spending will induce a change in the interest rate which will indirectly induce a change in investment spending. Examining the complete investment model

$$I = dY - ei$$
$$i = g + fY$$

we can see that part of the "autonomous" component of I is indirectly induced. By performing the appropriate substitutions,

$$I = dY - e(g + fY)$$
$$= dY - eg - efY$$
$$= (d - ef)Y - eg$$

the reader should verify that the new multiplier is now

$$\frac{\Delta Y}{\Delta D} = \frac{1}{1 - b - d + ef + m}$$

where ΔD represents changes in autonomous components.[9] Note that the complete multiplier, taking account of the interest rate effect, is smaller than the multiplier which ignored the effect of the income change on credit conditions. As income rises in this model, tighter money discourages investment, thereby depressing demand and reducing the expansionary effect of the initial spending increase.

In addition to its usefulness as a forecasting tool, multiplier analysis is also helpful for policy planning. In the next chapter we shall see how the multiplier can be used for evaluating various fiscal and monetary programs.

Questions for Study and Review

1. Keynes had two different concepts of investment in mind in *The General Theory*. On the one hand, he said that saving is necessarily always equal to investment, while on the other, he said that the multiplier makes saving and investment equal.

Explain the difference between these two concepts of investment, and as an application, show which concept is of significance in defining equilibrium.

[9] An obvious restriction on the multiplier is that it does not become infinite. Furthermore, to be theoretically meaningful, it should not take on negative values. This implies that the sum of the marginal induced effects must be less than unity. This will be ensured if the marginal propensity to invest is less than the marginal propensity to save.

2. Keynes believed that, aside from structural and frictional unemployment, general unemployment is basically a characteristic of a money economy and would not occur in a barter economy. Explain Keynes' position as you think he would have justified it to a classical economist.

3. Return to the dynamic multiplier analysis in Table 3-1. Suppose the net export function is

$$X_n = 50 - 0.1Y$$

(a) How will this affect the time path of income in this economy?

(b) By completing the table in accordance with the new specification, show that the ultimate impact on national income of an increase in G of $100 will approach $333.

4. Consider an economy represented by the following macroeconomic model:

$$D = C + I + X_n + G$$
$$C = 200 + 0.6Y$$
$$I = 0.3Y - 15i$$
$$X_n = 50 - 0.1Y$$
$$G = 100$$
$$i = 4$$

(a) Find the equilibrium level of income.

(b) Calculate the multiplier.

(c) What will be the impact on national income of the following policies:

(i) increasing government spending by 25
(ii) reducing the interest rate to 3
(iii) imposing an import tariff (tax) which reduces the marginal propensity to import by 50 percent?

(d) Suppose the government undertakes policy (iii) in part (c) and foreign governments reciprocate by raising their tariffs with the result that exports are reduced by 50 percent. What will be the impact on

(i) national income,
(ii) the balance of trade (net exports)?

Additional Reading

Keynes, J. M., Ohlin, B., and Hawtrey, R. G., *The Economic Journal*, XLVII (June, September, and December, 1937), 221–252, 423–443, 663–669.

Lutz, Friedrich A., "The Outcome of the Saving-Investment Discussion," *The Quarterly Journal of Economics*, LII (August, 1938), 588–614.

Samuelson, Paul A., "The Simple Mathematics of Income Determination," in *Income, Employment, and Public Policy: Essays in Honor of Alvin Hansen,* ed. L. A. Metzler et al., New York: W. W. Norton and Company, 1948.

4

Evaluating
the Impact
of Public
Policy

The analysis of national income equilibrium showed that public policy for manipulating the level of aggregate income and employment will have indirect effects which must be accounted for in the formulation of policies to achieve the full-employment goal. In this chapter we shall develop a framework for analyzing the effectiveness of alternative monetary and fiscal programs in closing the gap between actual employment and full employment.

4-1 The Use of Multiplier Analysis in Evaluating Government Programs

The policy planner must consider the multiplier effects of fiscal or monetary programs. Suppose he must evaluate a variety of alternative government actions that might be used to manipulate the level of aggregate demand.

Consider a variant of the original model introduced in Chapter 3:

$$Y = C + I + X_n + G$$
$$C = a + bY$$
$$I = dY - hi$$
$$X_n = E_0 - mY$$
$$G = G_0$$
$$i = i_0$$

In this formulation of the model the rate of interest, i, is a policy parameter, subject to autonomous change at the discretion of the central authority.[1]

Any change in G will shift the aggregate demand function by an amount $\Delta D = \Delta G$ which represents the autonomous change in spending measured along the spending (vertical) axis and will result in an ultimate change in expenditure and income of

$$\Delta Y = \frac{1}{1 - b - d + m} \Delta G$$

where

$$\frac{\Delta Y}{\Delta G} = \frac{1}{1 - b - d + m}$$

is the *expenditure multiplier*.

---

[1] In more sophisticated treatments, the rate of interest is not viewed as a policy parameter but is determined within the context of a model of the monetary sector. In technical terms, the interest rate is most appropriately treated as endogenous, not as a predetermined variable.

Suppose government decided to utilize monetary instead of fiscal policy to manipulate the level of aggregate demand. What would be the change in equilibrium income associated with a given change in the interest rate, i?

Expressing the model in terms of changes, and keeping in mind that Δa, ΔE, and ΔG are all equal to 0,

$$\Delta Y = \Delta C + \Delta I + \Delta X_n$$
$$\Delta C = b \, \Delta Y$$
$$\Delta I = d \, \Delta Y - h \, \Delta i$$
$$\Delta X_n = -m \, \Delta Y$$
$$\Delta i = \Delta i$$

Making the appropriate substitutions,

$$\Delta Y = b \, \Delta Y + d \, \Delta Y - h \, \Delta i - m \, \Delta Y$$
$$\Delta Y - b \, \Delta Y - d \, \Delta Y + m \, \Delta Y = -h \, \Delta i$$

Therefore, the *interest rate multiplier* will be

$$\frac{\Delta Y}{\Delta i} = \frac{-h}{1 - b - d + m}$$

Any change in the interest rate will result in a shift of the aggregate demand schedule by the amount

$$\Delta D = \Delta I = -h \, \Delta i$$

and an ultimate change in the equilibrium level of income of

$$\Delta Y = \frac{-h}{1 - b - d + m} \, \Delta i$$

The interest rate multiplier is negative, reflecting the inverse relationship between interest rates and income. If interest rates rise in this model, other things being equal, aggregate demand will fall.[2]

Tax policy is a third tool with which the central government might manipulate the level of aggregate demand. Suppose the government decides to raise revenues by means of a personal income tax. What will be the effect

---

[2] The empirical observation that income and interest rates often rise and fall together may be due to other components of demand changing simultaneously.

on the equilibrium level of income when the central government varies the amount of tax it assesses?

Since individuals must pay part of their income to the government in the form of taxes, the consumption function must be altered to take this into account. Consumption is a function of *disposable income,* or income after taxes; that is,

$$C = a + b(Y - T)$$

Assuming for simplicity that all imports are consumption goods, then import demand will also be a function of disposable income, and

$$X_n = E_0 - m(Y - T)$$

Incorporating these new relationships into the complete model,

$$Y = C + I + X_n + G$$
$$C = a + b(Y - T)$$
$$I = dY - hi$$
$$X_n = E_0 - m(Y - T)$$
$$G = G_0$$
$$i = i_0$$

Expressing the model in terms of changes, and assuming that Δa, ΔE, ΔG, and Δi will all be equal to 0,

$$\Delta Y = \Delta C + \Delta I + \Delta X_n$$
$$\Delta C = b\,\Delta Y - b\,\Delta T$$
$$\Delta I = d\,\Delta Y$$
$$\Delta X_n = -m\,\Delta Y + m\,\Delta T$$

Making the appropriate substitutions,

$$\Delta Y = b\,\Delta Y - b\,\Delta T + d\,\Delta Y - m\,\Delta Y + m\,\Delta T$$

Therefore,

$$\frac{\Delta Y}{\Delta T} = \frac{-(b - m)}{1 - b - d + m}$$

Assuming that the marginal propensity to consume is greater than the marginal propensity to import, that is,

$$0 < m < b$$

the *tax multiplier* will be negative, reflecting the inverse relationship between taxes and consumption. An increase in personal income taxes will result in a decrease in the equilibrium level of income by

$$\Delta Y = \frac{-(b - m)}{1 - b - d + m} \Delta T$$

Since the marginal propensity to consume minus the marginal propensity to import is positive and less than unity,

$$0 < b - m < 1$$

the tax multiplier is smaller in absolute value than the expenditure multiplier, since

$$\frac{1}{1 - b - d + m} > \frac{b - m}{1 - b - d + m}$$

A reduction in taxes will result in a smaller increase in aggregate demand than an equal increase in government expenditure. This is because a part of the tax reduction will be saved rather than spent. An increase in government expenditure of \$100 million will shift the aggregate demand schedule up by \$100 million:

$$\Delta D = \Delta G = \$100 \text{ million}$$

A reduction in taxes of \$100 million will shift the aggregate demand schedule up by \$100 million multiplied by the marginal propensity to consume minus the marginal propensity to import:

$$\Delta D = \Delta C + \Delta X_n = -b\, \Delta T + m\, \Delta T = -(b - m)\, \Delta T$$

Since

$$0 < b - m < 1$$

the aggregate demand schedule shifts upward by a smaller amount when taxes are reduced by \$100 million than when expenditures are increased by \$100 million.

The conclusion that the expenditure multiplier is greater than the tax multiplier leads to an interesting question. At first glance a balanced government budget appears to be fiscally neutral. That is, if the government increases expenditures and finances them through an equal increase in taxes, one would expect there to be no change in aggregate demand. But since the expenditure multiplier is greater than the tax multiplier, an increase in spending accompanied by an equal tax increase will have a net effect of *increasing* the level of aggregate demand. Since

$$\frac{\Delta Y}{\Delta G} = \frac{1}{1 - b - d + m}$$

and

$$\frac{\Delta Y}{\Delta T} = \frac{-(b - m)}{1 - b - d + m}$$

then assuming

$$\Delta G = \Delta T$$

$$\Delta Y = \frac{1}{1 - b - d + m} \Delta G - \frac{b - m}{1 - b - d + m} \Delta T$$

$$= \frac{1}{1 - b - d + m} \Delta G - \frac{b - m}{1 - b - d + m} \Delta G$$

$$= \frac{1 - b + m}{1 - b - d + m} \Delta G$$

The *"balanced budget"* multiplier is

$$\frac{\Delta Y}{\Delta G} = \frac{1 - b + m}{1 - b - d + m}$$

which is greater than 1. In the special case in which there is no induced effect on investment, so that

$$d = 0$$

the balanced budget multiplier is

$$\frac{\Delta Y}{\Delta G} = \frac{1 - b + m}{1 - b + m} = 1$$

and

$$\Delta Y = \Delta G = \Delta T$$

Aggregate demand will increase by the size of the government budget when the change in spending is completely financed by taxes.

It is sometimes believed that the government budget must be in deficit to have an expansionary impact on the economy. But it is clear that a *balanced* budget also has an impact on aggregate demand. In addition, the total size of the government budget is relevant in determining that impact. Thus, the net budget deficit or surplus alone is not indicative of the role of the public sector in the total demand picture. The absolute size of the budget is also important.

It is clear that a variety of alternative fiscal policies can be employed to produce a given change in the level of aggregate demand. The greater the increase in taxes that accompanies an increase in government expenditure, the greater is the increase in expenditure necessary to effectuate a given increase in aggregate demand. Theoretically, a budget change can show a surplus, that is, taxes can increase by more than expenditures, and still have an expansionary effect on aggregate demand.[3] In fact, for a budget to have no effect on aggregate demand, that is, for

$$\Delta Y = 0$$

the change in taxes must exceed the change in expenditure by a definable amount. Since

$$\Delta Y = \frac{1}{1 - b - d + m} \Delta G - \frac{b - m}{1 - b - d + m} \Delta T$$

when

$$\Delta Y = 0$$

then

$$\frac{1}{1 - b - d + m} \Delta G = \frac{b - m}{1 - b - d + m} \Delta T$$

and

$$\Delta G = (b - m) \Delta T$$

or

$$\Delta T = \frac{1}{b - m} \Delta G$$

Thus, the change in taxes must be $1/(b - m)$ times the change in expenditure for a budget change to be fiscally neutral. If

$$b - m = \tfrac{3}{4}$$

---

[3]To achieve a given expansionary effect on aggregate demand, government spending must increase more, the greater the proportion of it financed by taxes. Those who deplore the ever-increasing size of the public sector might note that deficit spending achieves a greater impact on income with considerably smaller increases in public spending than is necessitated if the budget is to be kept in balance.

the requisite change in taxes will be $1\frac{1}{3}$ times the change in expenditure. The smaller the marginal propensity to consume minus the marginal propensity to import, the greater is the change in taxes needed to offset the expenditures in a fiscally neutral budget.

4-2 Deflationary Gap Analysis

A policy planner may approach the multiplier analysis from a different point of view from that of the forecaster. A forecaster asks the question, "What will be the ultimate impact of a particular monetary or fiscal policy on the level of aggregate demand?" The policy maker, on the other hand, will want to know, "What monetary or fiscal programs will effectuate a particular change in the level of aggregate demand?"

In Figure 4-1, income is in equilibrium at E, while full employment is at F. The difference between actual income and full-employment income is EF. The distance HG between the aggregate demand function and the 45° line at full-employment income is called the *deflationary gap*. It represents the difference between spending and income at full employment. An autonomous shift in aggregate demand by the amount of the deflationary gap, HG, will, taking into account the multiplier effects, result in an ultimate change in equilibrium income equal to EF. The deflationary gap shows the increase in autonomous spending which is necessary to bring an economy to the level of income associated with full employment.

The relationship between the deflationary gap and the difference between equilibrium and full-employment income can be derived from the multiplier analysis. Since

$$Y_F - Y_E = \Delta Y = \frac{\Delta D}{1 - b - d + m}$$

therefore,

$$\Delta D = (1 - b - d + m)(Y_F - Y_E)$$

The deflationary gap is the difference between equilibrium and full-employment income multiplied by the reciprocal of the multiplier. Obviously, the deflationary gap is smaller than the required change in income.

Suppose the economy has a deflationary gap of $200 million. With a multiplier of 5, this implies the required change in income is $1 billion. Several alternative monetary and fiscal policies will be appropriate to bring income to its full-employment level. Assume the marginal propensity to

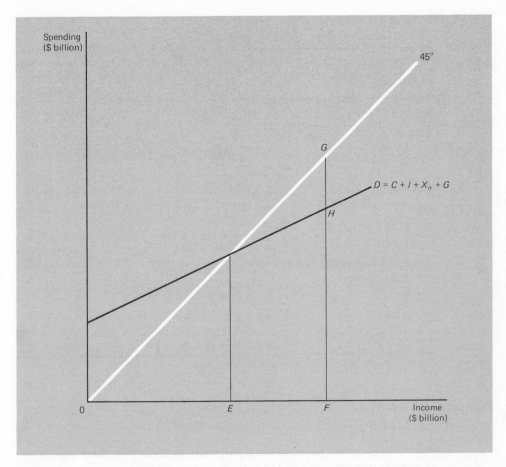

Figure 4-1   A Deflationary Gap

consume is 0.7, the marginal propensity to import is 0.1, and the investment function is

$$I = 0.2Y - 100i$$

Table 4-1 shows some alternative measures which can close the deflationary gap and bring the economy to a full-employment level of income. Actually, an infinite variety of policy combinations can be employed to close the deflationary gap. If the policy maker finds one measure not politically feasible, he will have a vast number of alternative choices.

Table 4-1 Alternative Measures to Close
a Deflationary Gap of $200 Million

Policy	Effect on D	Actual Change in Policy Parameter
Increase in G	$\Delta D = \Delta G$	$200 million
Reduction in T	$\Delta D = \Delta C + \Delta X_n = -(b - m)\, \Delta T$ $= -0.6\, \Delta T$ $\Delta T = 1.66\, \Delta D$	$332 million
Reduction in i	$\Delta D = \Delta I = -h\, \Delta i$ $= -100\, \Delta i$ $\Delta i = \frac{1}{100} \Delta D$	2 points
Equal increase in G and T (balanced budget change)	$\Delta D = \Delta G + \Delta C + \Delta X_n$ $= \Delta G - b\, \Delta T + m\, \Delta T$ $= \Delta G - (b - m)\, \Delta G$ $= 0.4\, \Delta G$ $\Delta G = 2.5\, \Delta D$	$500 million

4-3 Period Analysis of the Multiplier

When forecasting the effect of a particular monetary or fiscal policy, the planner is generally concerned with its impact on income and employment *within some definite period of time.* Our previous examples have taken a *comparative statics* approach, examining the movement from one equilibrium to another in response to changes in the underlying conditions, policy parameters, or functional relationships. The passage of time has been ignored.

For some purposes, however, the ultimate equilibrium position of the economy may be irrelevant. In the example illustrated in Table 4-2, the sum of the marginal induced spending effects is 0.8. Notice that we have ignored the foreign sector to simplify the exposition. An increase in government expenditure of $100 million will *ultimately* cause an increase in income of $500 million. Thus, given sufficient time the total multiplier will be 5. But our time horizons are generally short. We want to know what will happen this year or next.

Suppose the central authority is considering increasing public expenditure by $100 million. A forecaster is asked to estimate the impact on total GNP within one year after the expenditure is made. He must examine the time path of income as it is moving to its new equilibrium. The forecaster will need to know not only the magnitude of the marginal induced spending effects, but also the average length of time which will pass between expenditure and income receipt and income receipt and expenditure.

Suppose that the expenditure–receipt–expenditure period is estimated to be three months. Furthermore, assume the government increases its expenditure by $100 million (per three-month period) and maintains it at that new level. Referring to Table 4-2, we can see that the level of income will be increased by $295 by the end of the year (at the end of four three-month expenditure–receipt–expenditure periods), or about $\frac{3}{5}$ of the ultimate

Table 4-2   Time Path of Income for a Continuous Increase in Government Expenditure

Period	Increase in Government Expenditure (in millions of dollars)	+	Increase in Consumption Expenditure (in millions of dollars)	+	Increase in Investment Expenditure (in millions of dollars)	=	Total Increase in Expenditure and Income (in millions of dollars)
1	100		0		0		100
2	100		60		20		180
3	100		108		36		244
4	100		146		49		295
5	100		177		59		336
6	100		220		67		387
7	100		232		77		409
8	100		245		82		427
9	100		256		85		441
10	100		265		88		453
11	100		272		91		463
12	100		278		93		471
	–		–		–		–
	–		–		–		–
	–		–		–		–
	100		300		100		500

effect of $500. Using *period analysis,* we find that after one year the multiplier is 2.95 rather than 5. The total multiplier will still be 5, however, given a sufficiently long time horizon.

Table 4-2 suggests that the multiplier can be treated as a decreasing geometric series. In period 1, $100 million in new government expenditure is paid out as income in the form of wages, profits, interest, and rent. The quantity $b + d$, or 80 percent, is spent on consumption and investment in period 2. Thus, including the autonomous increase in spending by the public sector, additional spending in period 2 is

$$\text{Spending} = \$100 \text{ million} \times (1 + 0.8)$$
$$= \$100 \text{ million} + \$80 \text{ million} = \$180 \text{ million}$$

In period 3, income is $100 million $\times$ (1 + 0.8). Additional induced expenditure is

$$\text{Induced spending} = \$100 \text{ million} \times (1 + 0.8) \times 0.8$$
$$= \$100 \text{ million} \times (0.8 + 0.8^2)$$
$$= \$80 \text{ million} + \$64 \text{ million} = \$144 \text{ million}$$

Thus, including the autonomous increase in spending by the public sector, total expenditure in period 3 is

$$\text{Spending} = \$100 \text{ million} \times (1 + 0.8 + 0.8^2)$$
$$= \$100 \text{ million} + \$80 \text{ million} + \$64 \text{ million} = \$244 \text{ million}$$

Letting

$$k = b + d$$

where k represents the sum of the marginal induced effects, and assuming $0 < k < 1$, the ultimate multiplier can be represented by the decreasing geometric series,

$$\text{Multiplier} = 1 + k + k^2 + k^3 + k^4 + \cdots = \frac{1}{1 - k}$$

At the end of any period, t,

$$\text{Multiplier} = 1 + k + k^2 + \cdots + k^{t-1} + k^t$$

If the expenditure–receipt–expenditure period is known, it is easy to calculate the multiplier for any time period. In our example,

$$\text{Multiplier} = 1 + 0.8 + 0.8^2 + 0.8^3$$
$$= 1 + 0.8 + 0.64 + 0.512$$
$$= 2.95$$

The period multiplier can be traced in Figure 4-2. A shift in the aggregate demand function from D_1 to D_2 results in an initial increase in income of $CH = E_1F = AB$. This induces spending in period 2 of GI. In period 2, the increase in income is

$$CM = AB(1 + k)$$

Figure 4-2   The Period Multiplier

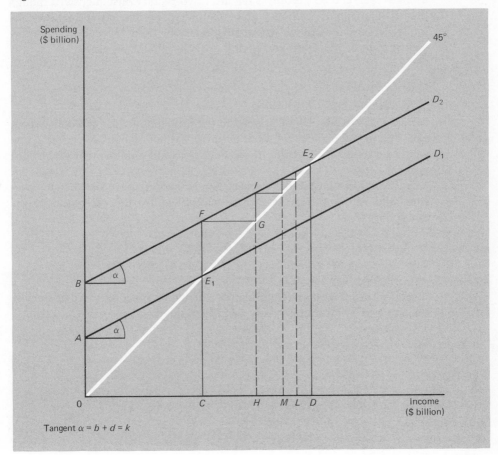

At the end of period 3, income is

$$CL = AB(1 + k + k^2)$$

The process continues until a new equilibrium is reached at E_2, with an ultimate change in income of CD, where

$$CD = \frac{AB}{1-k}$$

Because the multiplier is a decreasing geometric series, the largest impact of an autonomous change in spending is felt soon after it is made. In our example, 60 percent of the ultimate change in income is felt after a single year, and 85 percent is felt after two years. Consequently, although the time horizon of the policy maker is limited, he may often treat the total multiplier as an acceptable approximation to the short-term effect. For more precise forecasting, however, period analysis should be used.

PERIOD ANALYSIS
AND THE DEFLATIONARY GAP

Period analysis can also be applied to the problem of closing a deflationary gap. The policy maker may wish to know, "What amount of tax reduction would be necessary to bring the economy to full employment within one year?"

We know that the deflationary gap is the difference between equilibrium and full-employment income multiplied by the reciprocal of the multiplier,

$$\Delta D = (1 - b - d)(Y_F - Y_E)$$
$$= (1 - k)(Y_F - Y_E)$$

where ΔD represents the autonomous change in spending needed to close the gap and bring the economy to full employment.

Since

$$\frac{1}{1-k} = 1 + k + k^2 + k^3 + k^4 + \cdots$$

after four three-month periods

$$\Delta D = \frac{1}{1 + k + k^2 + k^3}(Y_F - Y_E)$$

In our example, $k = 0.8$, so that

$$\Delta D = \frac{1}{2.95}(Y_F - Y_E)$$

Since

$$\Delta D = \Delta C = -b\,\Delta T$$

and

$$b = 0.6$$

then

$$\Delta D = -0.6\,\Delta T = \frac{1}{2.95}(Y_F - Y_E)$$

Therefore,

$$\frac{Y_F - Y_E}{\Delta T} = -1.77$$

and

$$\Delta T = -\frac{1}{1.77}(Y_F - Y_E) = -0.56(Y_F - Y_E)$$

The tax reduction should be over half the desired change in equilibrium income.

Since the period multiplier is only a partial multiplier, the policy maker should keep in mind that the tax reduction will continue to have an expansionary influence in future years. If the deflationary gap is closed in the first year, it will have an inflationary effect in the future.[4] However, since the multiplier effect decreases over time, the bulk of the impact will be felt in the first year. Offsets such as a restrictive monetary policy or gradually increasing taxes might be used in the next year if the policy maker wishes to halt the expansion or inflationary trend.

4-4   The Employment Multiplier

We have seen that an autonomous change in spending in any sector of the economy will induce changes in spending in other sectors. The ratio of the total change in spending to the initial autonomous change in spending is the income multiplier.

In Chapter 2 we defined the aggregate supply function relating em-

---

[4]If all resources are already fully employed, a further increase in the value of output, or GNP, can only reflect price increases, or inflation, not an increase in real output.

96

ployment to expected total revenue, which in equilibrium will equal total spending. For any autonomous change in spending, there will be a corresponding change in employment. As additional changes in spending are induced, additional changes in employment will occur as firms revise their sales revenue expectations. The ratio of the total change in employment, which occurs as a result of a change in autonomous spending, to the initial change in spending is the *employment multiplier*.

In Figure 4-3, the economy is in equilibrium at E_1 when the aggregate demand function is D_1. The aggregate supply function is Z. Aggregate supply equals aggregate demand at an income of $0A$ and an employment level of $0I$. Consider a shift in the aggregate demand function to D_2. The initial increase in autonomous spending is $JK = E_1F$. The new equilibrium is at E_2. Aggregate supply equals aggregate demand at income $0B$ and an employment level of $0L$. The autonomous change in spending, JK, generates a total change in spending and income of $GH = AB$, and a total change in employment of IL. The income multiplier is

$$\frac{\Delta Y}{\Delta D} = \frac{AB}{JK} = \frac{1}{1-k}$$

Figure 4-3   The Employment Multiplier

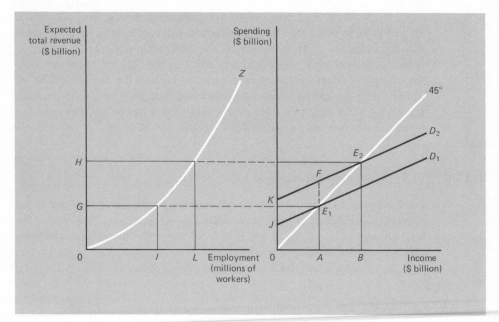

where k represents the sum of the marginal induced components.

The employment multiplier is[5]

$$\frac{\Delta N}{\Delta D} = \frac{IL}{JK}$$

Since employment and income are related through the aggregate supply function,

$$N = f(Y)$$

where N represents employment in number of workers and Y represents the level of income, which in equilibrium is equal to spending, the employment multiplier is functionally related to the income multiplier.

Suppose

$$N = Y^\alpha$$

If the aggregate supply function is convex to the employment axis then α will be between zero and unity; that is,

$$0 < \alpha < 1$$

This implies that successively greater increments to income are required to induce firms to hire additional workers as employment increases. Once the functional relationship between employment and output is specified, the employment multiplier can be calculated.

The income multiplier is

$$\frac{\Delta Y}{\Delta D} = \frac{1}{1 - k}$$

where ΔD is the autonomous change in spending and k is the sum of the marginal induced spending effects.

Let

$$Y_2 - Y_1 = \Delta Y$$

where Y_1 is the initial equilibrium level of income and Y_2 is the new equilibrium income attained as a result of the autonomous change in spend-

---

[5]Because income and employment are measured in different units, the actual value of the multiplier will depend upon the units of measurement along the axes.

ing, ΔD. From the aggregate supply function, the level of employment before and after the change in spending can be found:

$$N_1 = Y_1^\alpha$$

and

$$N_2 = Y_2^\alpha$$

Therefore,

$$\Delta N = N_2 - N_1 = Y_2^\alpha - Y_1^\alpha$$

The employment multiplier is

$$\frac{\Delta N}{\Delta D} = \frac{Y_2^\alpha - Y_1^\alpha}{\Delta D}$$

Suppose

$$k = 0.8$$

and the initial level of income is \$400 million. What would be the impact on employment of an autonomous increase in spending of \$100 million? Since

$$\Delta Y = \Delta D \frac{1}{1 - k}$$
$$= \$100 \text{ million} \times 5$$
$$= \$500 \text{ million}$$

the income multiplier is 5.

Therefore, at the new equilibrium, income, Y_2, will be \$900 million.

$$Y_2 = Y_1 + \Delta Y = \$400 \text{ million} + \$500 \text{ million} = \$900 \text{ million}$$

Suppose that the functional relationship between employment and income is

$$N = Y^{1/2}$$

Then

$$\Delta N = N_2 - N_1 = Y_2^{1/2} - Y_1^{1/2}$$
$$= (900 \text{ million})^{1/2} - (400 \text{ million})^{1/2}$$
$$= 30 \text{ million} - 20 \text{ million}$$
$$= 10 \text{ million}$$

and

$$\frac{\Delta N}{\Delta D} = \frac{10 \text{ million}}{100 \text{ million}} = \frac{1}{10}$$

The total change in employment which occurs in response to an autonomous increase in spending of $100 million is 10 million workers. The employment multiplier is $\frac{1}{10}$.

A period analysis can also be employed. Suppose the planner wishes to ascertain the impact on employment *after one year* of an autonomous increase in spending of $100 million. Expenditure is to be increased by $100 million every three months. If the expenditure–receipt–expenditure period is also three months, we know that

$$\Delta Y = \Delta D(1 + k + k^2 + k^3)$$
$$= \$100 \text{ million} \times (1 + 0.8 + 0.8^2 + 0.8^3)$$
$$= \$100 \text{ million} \times 2.95$$
$$= \$295 \text{ million}$$

The period multiplier is 2.95.

If income was $400 million initially, after one year the new income level will be

$$Y_2 = Y_1 + \Delta Y = \$400 \text{ million} + \$295 \text{ million} = \$695 \text{ million}$$

Since

$$N = Y^{1/2}$$

then

$$\Delta N = N_2 - N_1 = Y_2^{1/2} - Y_1^{1/2}$$
$$= (695 \text{ million})^{1/2} - (400 \text{ million})^{1/2}$$
$$= 26 \text{ million} - 20 \text{ million}$$
$$= 6 \text{ million}$$

and

$$\frac{\Delta N}{\Delta D} = \frac{6 \text{ million}}{100 \text{ million}} = \frac{6}{100}$$

The change in employment after one year in response to an autonomous spending increase of $100 million is 6 million workers. This is 60 percent of the ultimate effect. The period employment multiplier for one year is $\frac{6}{100}$.

4-5   Impact on the Balance of Trade

One goal of national economic policy is to avoid excessive balance-of-payments deficits. While we shall not consider the complete payments balance here, we can analyze the impact of fiscal and monetary policy on the trade balance. While some countries can support substantial trade deficits by accepting aid from abroad or by maintaining a surplus on capital account, others require perpetual trade surpluses to compensate for large capital outflows and unilateral transfers abroad. Nevertheless, for any country concerned with avoiding increased payments deficits, the impact of public economic policy on the trade balance must be considered.

Consider the national income model:

$$Y = C + I + X_n + G$$
$$C = a + b(Y - T)$$
$$I = dY - hi$$
$$X_n = E_0 - m(Y - T)$$
$$G = G_0$$
$$i = i_0$$

What will be the impact of an increase in government spending, G, on the trade balance, X_n? Expressing the model in terms of changes and assuming that Δa, ΔT, ΔE, and Δi will be zero,

$$\Delta Y = \Delta C + \Delta I + \Delta X_n + \Delta G$$
$$\Delta C = b \, \Delta Y$$
$$\Delta I = d \, \Delta Y$$
$$\Delta X_n = -m \, \Delta Y$$
$$\Delta G = \Delta G$$

By substitution,

$$\Delta Y = b \, \Delta Y + d \, \Delta Y - m \, \Delta Y + \Delta G$$
$$= \frac{1}{1 - b - d + m} \Delta G$$

and

$$\Delta X_n = -m \, \Delta Y = \frac{-m}{1 - b - d + m} \Delta G$$

The impact, therefore, of a change in G on the trade balance is

$$\frac{\Delta X_n}{\Delta G} = \frac{-m}{1 - b - d + m}$$

which is negative if the marginal propensity to import is positive. An increase in government spending will, other things being equal, cause imports to increase and, with exports fixed, reduce the net export surplus.

The process is seen graphically in Figure 4-4. In Figure 4-4(B), exports, E, are fixed, and imports, M, increase with income. Net exports, X_n, decline

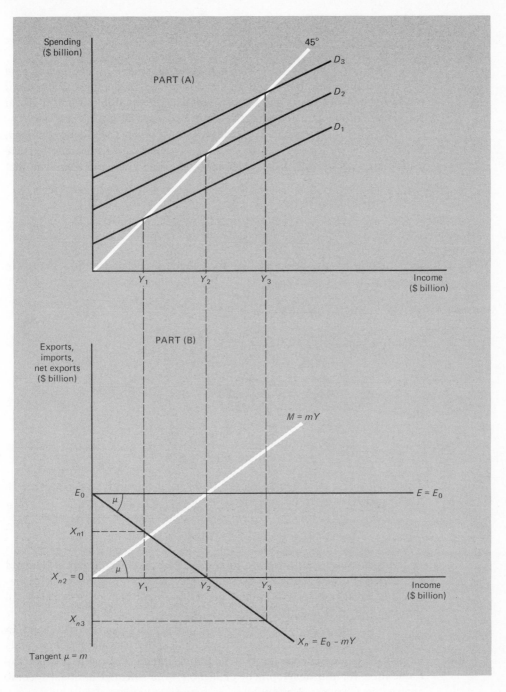

Figure 4-4 The Impact of a Change in Aggregate Demand on the Balance of Trade

with income. In Figure 4-4(A) when aggregate demand is D_1, national income is Y_1, and the trade balance is in surplus at X_{n1}. If demand is increased to D_2, income will be Y_2 and exports will exactly equal imports. If demand increases beyond D_2, however, the trade balance will go into deficit.

Suppose the government decides to use tax policy to influence demand. What will be the impact on the balance of trade? Since the trade balance multiplier associated with an autonomous change in demand is known, that is,

$$\frac{\Delta X_n}{\Delta D} = \frac{-m}{1 - b - d + m}$$

then solving for the initial change in demand associated with a change in taxes results in

$$\Delta D = \Delta C + \Delta X_n = -b\,\Delta T + m\,\Delta T = -(b - m)\,\Delta T$$

Therefore, since

$$\frac{\Delta X_n}{\Delta D} = \frac{\Delta X_n}{-(b - m)\,\Delta T} = \frac{-m}{1 - b - d + m}$$

then

$$\frac{\Delta X_n}{\Delta T} = \frac{m(b - m)}{1 - b - d + m}$$

The impact of a tax increase on the trade balance will be positive; that is, it will increase the trade surplus as long as

$$0 < m < b$$

In general, if imports tend to rise with income and if export demand is independent of domestic economic conditions, then expansionary monetary and fiscal policies will reduce net exports and restrictive policies will improve the trade balance.

Having developed the basic model of national income equilibrium, in Chapters 5 and 6 we shall take a closer look at the two major components of private demand: consumption and investment. This will provide the foundation for the development of a more sophisticated national income analysis in Chapters 8 and 9.

Questions for Study and Review

1. Consider an economy represented by the following macroeconomic model,

$$D = C + I + X_n + G$$
$$Z = N^2$$
$$C = 200 + 0.6(Y - T)$$
$$I = 0.3Y - 15i$$
$$X_n = E - 0.1(Y - T)$$
$$E = 50$$
$$G = 200$$
$$T = 100$$
$$i = 4$$

where

D = aggregate demand (in millions of dollars)
Z = aggregate supply (in millions of dollars)
Y = national income (in millions of dollars)
N = employment (in millions of workers)

and the other notation follows that of the text.

(a) Find the equilibrium level of income and employment in this economy.

(b) Calculate the government expenditure multiplier, the tax multiplier, and the interest rate multiplier. Consider both the income and employment multipliers as well as the multiplier effect on the trade balance.

(c) What will be the effect on income, employment, and the trade balance of the following policies:

(i) increasing government expenditure by $25 million,
(ii) increasing taxes by $25 million,
(iii) increasing simultaneously government expenditure and taxes by $50 million,
(iv) reducing the interest rate by two percentage points,
(v) reducing the interest rate by one percentage point and increasing taxes by $50 million?

2. In the economy represented in the above model, the income-expenditure–receipt period is three months.

(a) Calculate the multiplier effect *after one year* of a change in government spending, taxes, and the interest rate on income, employment, and the trade balance.

(b) What will be the effect *after one year* of the following policies on income, employment, and the trade balance:

(i) increasing government expenditure by $10 million every three months for one year,

(ii) reducing taxes by $15 million every three months for one year,

(iii) increasing simultaneously government expenditure and taxes by $50 million every three months for one year,

(iv) reducing the interest rate by two percentage points at the beginning of the year?

(c) For each policy in part (b), find the percentage of the total economic impact of the program experienced after one year.

3. Consider an economy whose structure is exactly like that of the economy represented by the model above except that investment is not a function of income. In this economy

$$I = 300 - 1500i$$

(a) Find the government expenditure multiplier, the tax multiplier, and the interest rate multiplier. Consider both the income and employment multipliers as well as the multiplier effect on the trade balance.

(b) Explain why the expenditure and tax multipliers are always lower in this economy than in the former economy, in which investment is a function of income.

4. Return to the economy represented by the model in Question 3. Suppose 10 million workers are unemployed.

(a) What is the deflationary gap?

(b) Design three alternative fiscal and/or monetary programs that will close the deflationary gap and bring the economy to full employment.

(c) Can monetary policy *alone* close the deflationary gap? Be sure to justify your answer.

5. For the model in Question 3, suppose the government desires to increase spending, but because of serious balance of payments problems, it cannot allow the trade balance to deteriorate. If the government is willing

to increase taxes, how much will they have to increase (as a percentage of the increased government spending) so that the increase in spending has no impact on the trade balance? (*Hint:* An example in the text showed the increase in taxes required to neutralize the impact of an increase in government spending on national income.)

6. Can you distinguish between a policy-planning model and a forecasting model? Why is accurate behavioral or structural specification so important in designing these models?

7. Explain why an analysis of economic policy planning is an important part of macroeconomic theory.

Additional Reading

Machlup, Fritz, "Period Analysis and Multiplier Theory," *The Quarterly Journal of Economics*, LIV (November, 1939), 1–27.

Musgrave, Richard A., *The Theory of Public Finance*. New York: McGraw-Hill Book Company, Inc., 1959, Chapter 18.

Suits, Daniel B., "Forecasting and Analysis with an Econometric Model," *The American Economic Review*, LII (March, 1962), 104–32.

"Tax Revision: Impact on Output and Employment," *Economic Report of the President*. Washington, D.C.: U.S. Government Printing Office, January, 1963, pp. 45–52.

5

The
Theory
of
Consumption

In the last three chapters we developed a model of national income equilibrium. Such a model, with more accurate and complete behavioral specification, is actually used for macroeconomic forecasting and policy planning at the national level.

In Chapters 6 and 7 we shall examine some hypotheses about consumption and investment behavior. An understanding of the behavior of the economic groups in the private sector (consumers and investors) is vital to the development of a forecasting model. Even though the model-building approach to economic decision making may seem "impersonal," we shall see that the economist must know a great deal about human behavior so that his quantitative relationships actually mirror real-world events.

In this chapter we are concerned with the factors which influence consumption. Chapter 6 deals with the investment decision.

5-1   The Keynesian Consumption Function

The notion that consumption is primarily a function of disposable income lies at the heart of Keynesian economics. The hypothesis is reasonable, since disposable income is the principal source by which consumption expenditures are financed. An individual cannot live beyond his means indefinitely. Keynes postulated that aggregate consumption would increase with disposable income, but that the increment to consumption would not be as great as the increment to income. In technical terms, he suggested that the *marginal propensity to consume* (MPC) would be less than 1 or algebraically,

$$\frac{\Delta C}{\Delta Y} < 1$$

Not only did he expect the *amount* of saving to increase with income, but he expected the *proportion* of income saved to increase as well. This implies that the *average propensity to consume*, C/Y, declines with income. (Note that this is not equivalent to the observation that the poor spend a higher proportion of their income than the rich. On an aggregate level, we are examining the behavior of *total* consumption as the level of national income changes.) The *a priori* reasoning behind what Keynes called "fundamental psychological laws" is somewhat tenuous. The idea seems to be that as a society becomes richer, wants become less urgent. Alternatively, it may suggest a diminishing marginal utility of consumption. While this idea may be appealing superficially, it is important to keep in mind that the alternative to consumption is saving, presumably for the purpose of future consumption.

Thus, the theory actually implies that the preference for present over future consumption is weaker when the income level is higher. This hypothesis may be valid for individuals, but it is not necessarily applicable to a whole economy, particularly after national income has surpassed the subsistence level.

Nevertheless, as a first approximation it is reasonable to assume that at least part of an increment to income will be saved (or conversely, that a decline in income will be partly offset by a decrease in saving) and that the proportion of income saved rises with the general level of national income.

A consumption function such as Keynes had in mind is shown in Figure 5-1.[1] Along the 45° line which bisects the quadrant, consumption is equal to income. Consequently, the vertical distance between the consumption function and the 45° line represents saving.

As we saw in the earlier chapters (especially, Chapter 2), Keynes' consumption function is vital to his theory of employment. Unless there is sufficient investment to offset the additional saving as income and output increase, aggregate demand will not equal aggregate supply and firms will reduce employment levels. Thus, the level of employment is determined by the level of demand. Furthermore, since he expected saving to increase as a percentage of income in the process of economic development, Keynes believed a wealthy economy would have a particularly difficult time generating adequate aggregate demand for the maintenance of full employment. Investment and government spending would have to increase indefinitely relative to consumption.

Classical, or pre-Keynesian, economists felt that saving and investment would be equated at any level of income by movements of the interest rate. Keynes pointed out that if saving is solely a function of the interest rate, then consumption is also solely a function of the interest rate and does not depend on income—a rather unlikely hypothesis.

5-2 Empirical Tests and New Hypotheses

Keynes' model of income determination is theoretical in design. The behavioral relationships, such as the consumption function, are hypothetical and are not based on actual empirical relationships. Keynes was concerned with

---

[1]Keynes may have had a curvilinear relationship in mind since he suggested that the marginal propensity to consume may decline with income. A linear relationship is easier to handle algebraically, however, and does not essentially alter the conclusions of the analysis as long as the slope is less than 1.

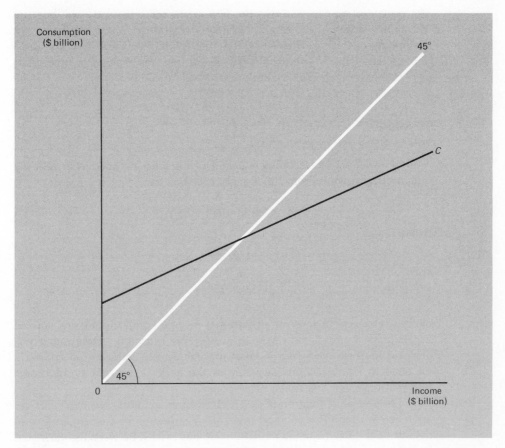

Figure 5-1   The Keynesian Consumption Function

explaining the phenomenon of generalized unemployment in a market economy. Although his policy prescriptions were an important outgrowth of the analysis, his model was not intended to be used for actual policy planning and forecasting. It lacked complete behavioral specification, and the actual values of the various parameters (e.g., the MPC), were not estimated. Furthermore, the stability of the relationships had not been established.

Precisely because it indicated a need for active government intervention in the economy, Keynesian economics demonstrated the need for a planning model. The parameters of such a model had to be estimated empirically on the basis of data reflecting past experience. Following World War II, economists of the "new" Keynesian school began to devise such models.

The consumption function was the first relationship they studied, because it is at the heart of the model and because consumption represents the largest component of GNP. Furthermore, they felt it might be the easiest and most stable relationship to specify, since consumption was believed to be primarily a function of a single variable, disposable income.

APPROACHES TO ESTIMATING
THE CONSUMPTION FUNCTION

A priori or deductive reasoning is useful as a first approximation in devising a theoretical model. From the *a priori* specification,

$$C = a + b(Y - T)$$

where

$$a > 0$$

and

$$0 < b < 1$$

many useful conclusions about national income equilibrium were derived in Chapters 3 and 4. However, to answer the question, "How much will demand increase next year if taxes are cut by $50 million this quarter?" we need to know the precise value of the *MPC*, b, as well as additional information about the speed of response.

For precise estimation of parameter values, an inductive, or *a posteriori*, approach is used. This method involves examination of past experience to determine if indeed a reliable relationship has existed between the variables. In the case of the consumption function, it is necessary to examine data which measure consumption and disposable income.[2]

Two sources of such data are available. First, the relationship between consumption and income can be measured for different periods of time. As income changed between 1950 and 1960, for example, how did consumption move? Such a study is called *time series analysis*.

An alternative approach is to examine the consumption of families at different levels of income. How does the consumption of a family earning $10,000 differ from that of a family earning $15,000? This is a *cross-section* or *budget study* approach.

While both use valid sources of data, the relationships found in the two analyses may differ considerably. Suppose, for example, that over a

[2]For the remainder of this chapter, the terms income and disposable income will be used interchangeably except when it is necessary to make the distinction.

10-year period, average disposable income rises by 50 percent. Family A earns $10,000 in the base year and $15,000 10 years later. Consider family B earning $15,000 in the base year. Would you expect the consumption of family A at the end of the 10-year period to be the same as that of family B in the base year? Probably not, for a number of reasons. Family B is likely to consume less than family A out of its $15,000 income, since in the base period family B is more affluent in relation to the general standard of living of the society than family A at the end of the period. As average income rises so does the average level of consumption, or standard of living, so that the average propensity to consume (APC) from $15,000 will rise as average income increases. Thus, while time series and cross-section studies both measure the relationship between consumption and income, they are actually examining different behavioral relationships.

The question facing a forecaster is which approach best suits his needs. He wants to know how aggregate consumption will change in response to short-run changes in disposable income. Suppose we ignore distributional problems and assume everyone is to receive a $100 transfer payment from the government. Will families adjust fully to the improved standard of living in the short run? If not, a time series analysis measuring behavior over long periods of time may not be useful in a short-run situation. A time series study using quarterly data (data collected every three months) over a fewer number of years would be preferred. However, in the short run there are often considerable lags in consumer responsiveness to income changes. These lags are often unpredictable and difficult to estimate. Budget studies can also be useful since in the short run individuals may be subject to a *distributional illusion*. That is, they may feel their relative economic status is improved by an increase in income and indeed behave like the more affluent families of the cross section. As we shall see, budget studies and short-run time series analysis often yield similar parameter estimates.

REAL VERSUS MONEY SPECIFICATIONS

In the model which we have developed, the variables were expressed in terms of their money value. We were concerned with how total money spending in the economy affects employment decisions of firms. Total money spending is comprised of consumption, investment, net exports, and government spending, all measured in money value.

Empirical studies of consumption and investment behavior typically measure the variables in *real* terms. A variable measured in real terms is deflated by a price index to abstract from price changes. This practice is based on the assumption that households and firms are not subject to a "money illusion"; that is, they take price changes into account before making decisions. Suppose money income rises by 10 percent and consumer prices rise by 10 percent simultaneously. If households are not subject to a money illusion, real consumption will be unaffected and money consumption will increase by 10 percent. If they are subject to money illusion, families will behave as if their purchasing power had increased, real consumption will rise, and money consumption will increase by more than 10 percent.

Because consumption and investment functions are generally specified in real terms for the purposes of empirical study, we shall treat them as real relationships in Chapters 5 and 6. However, to incorporate them in a model of national income equilibrium, they must be converted into money relationships by multiplying the variables measured in real terms by a price index.

If we assume for simplicity that all the variables in the relationship were originally deflated by the same price index, that is, if variations in consumer prices were about the same as for the price level in general, then the MPC will be the same, regardless of whether the variables are in real or money form. Denoting real variables with the subscript r, and money variables with the subscript m, then if

$$C_m = a + bY_m$$
$$C_r = \frac{C_m}{p}$$

and

$$Y_r = \frac{Y_m}{p}$$

where p is the common price index,

$$\frac{C_m}{p} = \frac{a}{p} + \frac{bY_m}{p}$$

or

$$C_r = \frac{a}{p} + bY_r$$

Only the constant term, reflecting the amount of consumption which would occur independently of income variation, will change when the variables are transformed from money into real terms.

We shall return to a more detailed consideration of real versus money models in Chapter 8.

EARLY EMPIRICAL INVESTIGATIONS

One of the first attempts to study consumption behavior empirically was made by Simon Kuznets in 1946.[3] He plotted a consumption function from annual time series data covering the period 1869–1938. The consumption relationship he obtained is shown in Figure 5-2. Kuznets found that over a long period, real consumption was roughly proportional to real national income. Furthermore, the *APC* remained nearly stable, varying between 0.85 and 0.89.

[3]Simon Kuznets, *National Product Since 1869* (New York: National Bureau of Economic Research, 1946), p. 119.

Figure 5-2 Consumption Function Estimated
from Long-Period Time Series

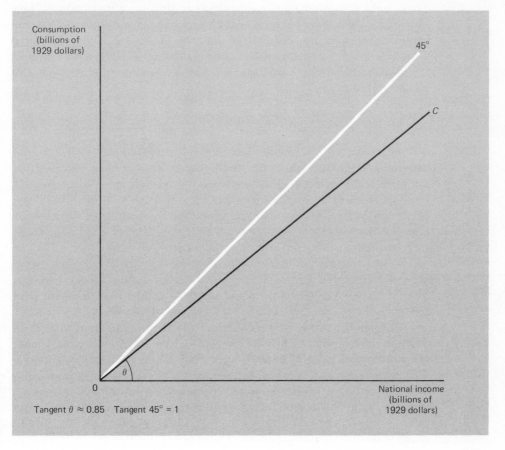

Notice that for a linear consumption function which intersects the origin, the *APC* and the *MPC* are equal. Algebraically, the relationship is expressed as

$$C = bY$$

where b is both the *APC* and *MPC*. Note that b is a constant; it does not decline with income.

Kuznets' study supported Keynes' hypothesis that consumption is a stable function of income and that the *MPC* is less than 1. The idea that the *APC* and perhaps the *MPC* decline with income did not receive empirical support.

Kuznets' study was primarily intended to be descriptive. Other economists were concerned with actually forecasting postwar consumer demand. They decided to estimate the consumption function using quarterly time series data collected over a relatively short period, 1929–1941.[4] The consumption function they obtained is shown in Figure 5-3. The function has a positive intercept of $26.5 billion and a slope of 0.75 when the variables are measured in 1954 dollars and the independent variable is disposable income. Algebraically, this is expressed as

$$C = 26.5 + 0.75Y$$

Since the *MPC* is smaller than for the Kuznets' consumption function, this implies that the short-run multiplier is smaller than the long-run multiplier. If Kuznets had used disposable income rather than national income in his relationship, the long-run *MPC* and the multiplier would have been even greater. It is reasonable to expect the short-run *MPC* to be smaller than the long-run *MPC*, considering that it takes time for a family to adjust its consumption behavior to a new, higher level of income.

The consumption relationship derived from short-run time series generally supported Keynes' *a priori* reasoning about consumption behavior. The *APC* declines with income and the *MPC* is less than 1. There is no tendency for the *MPC* to decline with income, however.

Economists using the short-period consumption function to estimate postwar consumption grossly underestimated the level of postwar demand for consumption goods. The *MPC* turned out to be considerably higher than 0.75. This is not surprising since they were using a relationship reflecting behavior during a severe depression to predict consumption following a wartime boom. As income increased after the war, consumption increased

[4]Gardner Ackley, *Macroeconomic Theory* (New York: The Macmillan Company, 1961), p. 226.

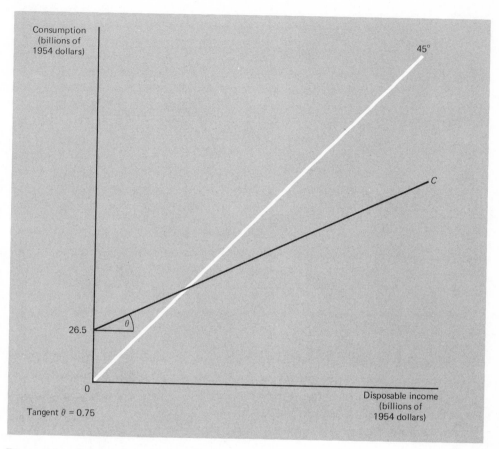

Figure 5-3   Consumption Function Estimated
from Short-Period Time Series Data

by a greater proportion than in the prewar experience due to a general feeling
of optimism as well as the availability of liquid assets accumulated during
the wartime rationing which could be used to satisfy the "pent-up" demand.

The following question then arose: "Should we use long- or short-
period data to estimate our forecasting model?" Furthermore, "Is there a
theoretical reconciliation of the two approaches?"

Arthur Smithies contended that the short-period consumption relationship is basically nonproportional, as shown in Figure 5-3, but that the
function has shifted up over time, as shown in Figure 5-4.[5] The C_s are

[5] Arthur Smithies, "Forecasting Postwar Demand," *Econometrica*, XIII (January, 1945), 1–14.

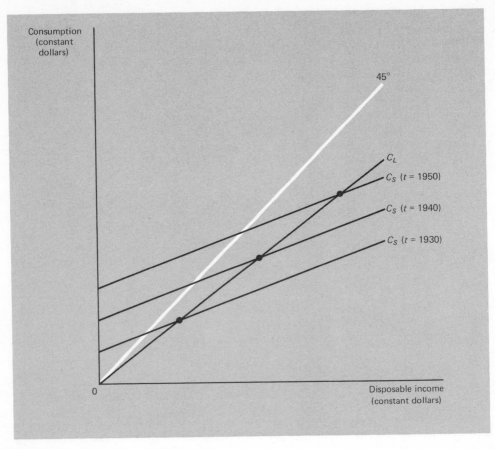

Figure 5-4   Shifts in the Short-Period
Consumption Function

short-period consumption functions, estimated at different periods of time.
The line C_L is a long-period consumption function such as Kuznets found.
It is obtained from points on different short-period consumption functions.
Thus, Smithies argued, the forecasters of postwar consumption demand
failed to recognize that the short-period consumption function was likely
to shift upward after the war, reflecting an increase in the *APC* at all levels
of income.

Smithies did not provide a complete *a priori* explanation for why the
consumption function shifts upward over time. He attributed much of the
shift to increases in the standard of living as median family incomes increased. But, if the magnitude of shifts in the function over time are random

or arbitrary, his theory does not explain why the long-run relationship is almost exactly proportional.

Smithies estimated a relationship which took the passage of time into account. Algebraically, he found

$$C = a + bY + ct$$

where t is the year in which the variables are observed. If c is positive, then as t increases, consumption will increase, even in the absence of increases in disposable income. The exact relationship Smithies found is

$$C = 76.58 + 0.76Y + 1.15(t - 1922)$$

This is a per capita relationship. It implies that in 1922, autonomous per capita consumption (in 1929 prices) was $76.58 and increased by $1.15 every year thereafter. The MPC from disposable income is 0.76.

THE RELATIVE INCOME HYPOTHESIS

Despite the weakness of Keynes' *a priori* hypotheses about consumption, empirical (or *a posteriori*) evidence has tended to substantiate his view, at least in part.

James Duesenberry, one of Smithies' students, formulated a more complete *a priori* explanation for the observed discrepancy between long- and short-period consumption behavior.[6] Furthermore, he performed cross-section budget studies of income and consumption. The consumption function derived from cross-section data (collected for a single time period from various income groups) is similar to the short-period time series relationship shown in Figure 5-3. It has a positive intercept on the consumption axis and an MPC less than 1 and less than that of the long period found by Kuznets. Duesenberry's theory was designed to explain the discrepancy between the cross-section and short-period time series consumption functions on the one hand and the long-period relationship on the other.

Unlike Smithies, Duesenberry suggested that the most basic consumption relationship was long run and proportional. That is, since saving is undertaken primarily for the purpose of future consumption, there is no reason to expect saving to increase as a percentage of income as income

---

[6]James S. Duesenberry, *Income, Saving, and the Theory of Consumer Behavior* (Cambridge, Mass: Harvard University Press, 1949). Chapter 3 is especially interesting. Also see James S. Duesenberry, "Income-Consumption Relations and their Implications," in *Income, Employment, and Public Policy: Essays in Honor of Alvin H. Hansen* (New York: W. W. Norton and Company, 1948), pp. 54–81.

rises. This is equivalent to saying that time preference is independent of the level of income.

Duesenberry's explanation of cross-section behavior is based on his idea that consumption patterns are principally social. People's tastes are so interdependent that an individual's consumption pattern may be more influenced by the income and consumption of his friends than by his own income. An individual earning $10,000 will consume more if he lives in a rich neighborhood than in a poor one. Thus, lower-income families attempting to keep up with the Joneses will spend a higher proportion of their income than high-income families. Duesenberry labeled this phenomenon the *demonstration effect*. As individuals come into contact with superior goods, the impulse to increase their own consumption will become more intense. This hypothesis has also been used to explain why the average propensity to save (*APS*) is relatively low in developing countries.

For the economy as a whole, families with below-average income will have a higher *APC* than higher-income families. This explains why the *APC* declines with income in budget studies. As *median* (or average) family income increases with economic growth, however, there is no reason to expect the average *APC* to decline. Instead, on the average all families enjoy an increased standard of living. This explains the proportionality of the long-period consumption function.

Finally, Duesenberry provides an explanation for the observed nonproportional function derived from short-period time series data. If consumption is influenced by the "demonstration effect" of the goods others enjoy, then it also must be influenced by the "own-demonstration effect" of goods previously enjoyed. That is, consumption patterns must be influenced by past living standards, particularly in the short run. Thus, if disposable income declines in the short run, families attempt to maintain their old living standards and the *APC* rises. On the other hand, when disposable income rises, families do not adjust fully to the new income level, and although consumption increases, they are still tied to their old living standard to some extent. Consequently, the *APC* falls. Duesenberry labels this tendency for families to maintain living standards in periods of temporary declines in income the *rachet effect*.

He formulates the short-period consumption function as

$$\frac{C_t}{Y_t} = b - e\frac{Y_t}{Y_{pp}}.$$

where the subscript t refers to the time period at which the variable is measured and Y_{pp} refers to previous peak income.

This relationship states that the *APC* declines as the ratio between current income, Y_t, and previous peak income, Y_{pp}, rises. The *MPC* will be somewhat less than b and depends upon how widely income is varying. Thus, the multiplier to be applied to a small change in income will be greater than that to be applied to a larger variation when a forecast of total spending is required.

For the period 1929–1940, Duesenberry found the relationship between real consumption and real disposable income to be

$$\frac{C_t}{Y_t} = 1.196 - 0.25\frac{Y_t}{Y_{pp}}$$

or

$$C_t = 1.196Y_t - 0.25\frac{Y_t^2}{Y_{pp}}$$

During that period, for instance, if current real income were equal to its previous peak, the *APC* would have been 0.946:

$$APC = 1.196 - 0.25 = 0.946$$

If current income were 5 percent above its previous peak, the *APC* would have fallen to 0.934:

$$APC = 1.196 - 0.25\tfrac{105}{100} = 0.934$$

THE PERMANENT INCOME HYPOTHESIS

Another explanation of the inconsistency of the short- and long-period data has been provided by Milton Friedman.[7] Like Duesenberry, Friedman argues that the consumption function is essentially proportional; that is, there is no tendency for the proportion of income saved to increase at higher income levels. He contends, however, that households do not adapt their consumption behavior to current income alone, but to the general level of their resources over extended periods of time. Income measured on a quarterly or even yearly basis, he argues, is not necessarily a good measure of the variable which influences consumers' behavior.

Consider the example of seven men, each earning $100 per week and each paid on a different day of the week. Suppose we collect budget data for these men on a daily basis. On each day, one man will have income

[7] Milton Friedman, *A Theory of the Consumption Function* (Princeton, N. J.: Princeton University Press, 1957).

of $100, and the others will have no income. If they distribute their consumption expenditures fairly uniformly over the week, we will find that the *APC* falls drastically with income (from infinity to something less than 1).[8] Friedman argues correctly that these results tell us nothing meaningful about consumption behavior but merely reflect the use of inappropriate measures of income and consumption. If we had measured income and consumption on a weekly basis, our results would have been more interesting.

Friedman contends that a three-month period (generally used for short-run time series data) or even a year may be inappropriate. Households make their budget plans on the basis of a more permanent measure of income. He argues that consumption, in the aggregate, will be proportional to permanent income at all income levels.[9] The difficulty in testing Friedman's hypothesis is, of course, that permanent income cannot be measured directly.

Friedman argues that individuals do not know their permanent income any more than the forecaster does. Therefore, they base their consumption behavior on their past income, as well as on current income. Friedman estimates permanent income by a weighted average of current and past measured income with exponentially decreasing weights. His consumption relationship is

$$C_t = KY_p = 0.9Y_p$$

and

$$Y_p = 0.33Y_t + 0.22Y_{t-1} + 0.15Y_{t-2} + \cdots$$

where Y_p is permanent income, Y_{t-i} is income measured i periods before t, and K is the marginal and average propensity to consume out of permanent income.

This expression for Y_p represents a weighted average of past and present values of Y with the weights declining in a geometric progression with coefficient $\frac{2}{3}$; that is,

$$Y_p = 0.33 \sum_{i=0}^{\infty} (\tfrac{2}{3})^i Y_{t-i} = 0.33(\tfrac{2}{3})^0 Y_t + 0.33(\tfrac{2}{3})^1 Y_{t-1}$$

$$+ 0.33(\tfrac{2}{3})^2 Y_{t-2} + \cdots + 0.33(\tfrac{2}{3})^\infty Y_{t-\infty}$$

[8]This example is taken from *ibid.*, Chapter 9.
[9]Friedman defines *permanent income* rather tautologically as that income to which households adapt their consumption behavior.

Notice that since

$$C_t = KY_p = 0.33K[Y_t + \tfrac{2}{3}Y_{t-1} + (\tfrac{2}{3})^2Y_{t-2} + \cdots + (\tfrac{2}{3})^\infty Y_{t-\infty}]$$

then

$$\tfrac{2}{3}C_{t-1} = 0.33K[\tfrac{2}{3}Y_{t-1} + (\tfrac{2}{3})^2Y_{t-2} + \cdots + (\tfrac{2}{3})^\infty Y_{t-\infty}]$$

Subtracting,

$$C_t - \tfrac{2}{3}C_{t-1} = 0.33KY_t$$

Therefore, since

$$K = 0.9$$

Friedman's consumption function can be written as

$$C_t = 0.297Y_t + \tfrac{2}{3}C_{t-1}$$

For purposes of statistical estimation, this formulation is preferred to the earlier one, since it involves only two explanatory variables, present income and past consumption. The earlier expression required knowledge of past income over a very long period.

The alternative formulation of Friedman's permanent income hypothesis states that if consumption is a function of past income, it is also a function of past consumption. Thus, consumption is a function of past consumption as well as current income. Mathematically, this is strikingly similar to the Duesenberry model, although the *a priori* basis for the hypothesis is somewhat different. Because past consumption influences present consumption, the *APC* will rise in response to short-run declines in income and will fall when income rises in the short run. This explains the observed nonproportionality of the short-run consumption function. In the long run, permanent and measured income are equivalent, so that the long-run *APC* from measured income is approximately constant. To the extent that current changes in disposable income are considered temporary, the *MPC* and hence the multiplier will be smaller than for income changes expected to be permanent. According to the permanent income hypothesis, for instance, an increase in personal income taxes that is expected to be temporary will have less impact on consumption spending than a permanent increase.

Friedman's hypothesis has also been used to explain cross-section behavior. He contends that families with an above-average income will, on the average, have a positive, transitory (nonpermanent) component to their income. Families with a lower-than-average income will, on the average, have a negative transitory component. Furthermore, the higher the level of income, the greater is the transitory component of income, on the average, for that income group. This accounts for the observed tendency of the APC to decline with income and for the MPC to be lower than for the long-run time series relationship.

THE LIFE-CYCLE HYPOTHESIS

A variant of the permanent income hypothesis is based on the idea that the consumer wishes to allocate his resources to enable him to maintain approximately the same level of consumption each year of his life.[10] Consumption is estimated by the formula

$$C_t = \frac{Y_t + (N - T)Y_p + A_t}{L_t}$$

where

Y_t = current income
Y_p = permanent income
L_t = number of years of life remaining
$N - T$ = earning years remaining
A_t = nonearning assets

This theory is similar to the permanent income hypothesis in that consumption is based on a long-run measure of household resources. In this model, however, the MPC out of permanent income will vary with age and family size. Other things being equal, the younger the family, the lower is the MPC out of permanent income, since the future consumption horizon is longer than for older families. This may be important if the age distribution of the population is expected to change in the short run, as has been the case in certain postwar periods.

CONCLUSION

All the theories we have studied are reasonable explanations of consumer behavior. Furthermore, the equations which specify the hypotheses are all

---

[10] Albert Ando and Franco Modigliani, "The 'Life Cycle' Hypothesis of Saving," *The American Economic Review*, LIII (March, 1963), 55–84.

more or less representative of the actual empirical evidence. In fact, all the equations boil down to the general form

$$C_t = b_1 + b_2 Y_t + b_3 C_{t-1}$$

or

$$C_t = d_1 + d_2 Y_t + d_3 C_{pp}$$

where C_{pp} is the previous peak consumption.

Graphically, the short-run relationship can be formulated in terms of a family of linear nonproportional consumption functions such as shown in Figure 5-4. While in the Smithies formulation these shift with time, in the Duesenberry model they shift with previous peak income. In the Friedman and life-cycle models they shift with the previous period's consumption. The long-run relationship is derived by connecting various points on the short-run functions as shown in Figure 5-4.

Both algebraically and graphically, the various models of consumption behavior are quite similar. This is not surprising, since they were all developed as attempts to explain the same *a posteriori* relationships. Since the theoretical basis for the various hypotheses are different, however, the policy implications may be somewhat different. In the next section we shall examine the effect of various economic policies on consumption behavior.

5-3 Consumer Behavior and Economic Policy

In our simple model of income determination, changes in spending initiated in the public sector induce further changes in consumption spending. This phenomenon, called the multiplier, occurs because consumption is a function of disposable income. Keynes assumed that the sole impact of public policy on consumption spending would be the effect induced by the change in disposable income. Post-Keynesian theories suggest, however, that public policy might have an impact on the *MPC* itself. Thus, the multiplier associated with any spending or tax program should be expected to vary with the exact nature of the program.

In this respect, Smithies' analysis is not very helpful. Since he attributes shifts in the short-run consumption function primarily to the passage of time, the influence of public policy on the *MPC* is unknown.

The relative income hypothesis suggests, however, that the *MPC* will be lower, the greater the magnitude of the change in disposable income, since consumption is influenced by the relationship of current income to the previous peak income. The *MPC* would also be reduced to the extent that the program increased the inequality of the income distribution, since consumption is influenced by other peoples' spending habits.

The permanent income and life-cycle hypotheses suggest that the *MPC* will be lower to the extent that the income change is viewed to be temporary. The life-cycle hypothesis includes the further notion that the *MPC* will be lower the younger the population.

Consider, for example, a guaranteed annual income plan. This is essentially a transfer scheme, and if financed by taxes, would not initially affect aggregate disposable income at all. The relative income hypothesis would suggest that the program might increase the *MPC* of those income groups affected, since it (1) reduces inequality in the income distribution and (2) provides a buffer to large changes in disposable income. According to the permanent income hypothesis, the same conclusion would be reached for a different reason. A guaranteed annual income should increase the *MPC* by reducing the transitory component of income. Thus, the program could have an expansionary effect on aggregate demand, even though net aggregate disposable income was left unchanged by the initial transfer.

On the other hand, a tax increase specifically designed to be temporary, such as the income tax surcharge of the Johnson administration, would have the effect of reducing the *MPC* from that income. In fact, after the Johnson tax, increased consumption spending was not reduced to the extent many observers expected on the basis of the pretax consumption function. While this may have been due in part to a reaction lag, it was probably also attributable to the fact that households viewed the decline in their take-home pay as transitory. The relative income hypothesis is not as useful in explaining this behavior as the permanent income hypothesis.

5-4 Other Variables
Affecting Consumption

Relationships which treat consumption as a function of disposable income and past consumption or income have proved to be good forecasting tools. The stability of the consumption–income relationship or "consumption function" has been demonstrated with both time series and budget study data. The introduction of other variables into the equation has provided little if any improvement in the predictions obtained, except in the case of durable consumer goods which we shall treat later in this section. However, some observers have felt it necessary to consider the significance of non-income variables, particularly financial variables. We turn to these briefly.

FINANCIAL VARIABLES

The life-cycle hypothesis suggests that the value of an individual's financial assets may affect his consumption patterns. Ando and Modigliani have found that very short-run changes in the value of assets may have considerable impact on short-run consumption.[11] They found, for instance, that movements of the stock market had some effect. Most other studies have concluded, however, that assets are not a very important determinant of consumption.

Pigou, the proponent of classical economics attacked by Keynes in *The General Theory*, argued that a general price deflation, by increasing the real value of money balances held by individuals, might stimulate consumption. This "real balances effect" suggested that deflationary monetary policy could be a remedy for unemployment. This, of course, was in direct contradiction to the Keynesian position that expansionary monetary policy is the appropriate antirecession weapon. Since empirical evidence does not support the hypothesis that the value of assets is an important determinant of consumption spending, the likelihood of a Pigou effect on consumption is generally considered to be negligible.

Classical economists believed that the interest rate would affect consumption. An increase in the interest rate was expected to stimulate saving and discourage consumption. Since interest rates and income generally move together over the cycle, it is difficult to separate their influence. Consumption rises and falls with income and interest rates, but whether rising interest rates provide some brake on consumption as income rises is uncertain. There is no indication, however, whether in theory or from the empirical evidence, that changes in interest rates have an appreciable effect on consumption, except in the case of consumer durables which are often financed by credit.

CONSUMER DURABLES

A *durable* consumer good can be defined as one which provides a flow of services over a period of time, generally in excess of a single year. These goods are much like capital goods, except that they are purchased by households for their own use rather than by firms for the purpose of producing goods and services for sale.[12] Durable consumption goods include such items as automobiles, televisions, and refrigerators.

Expenditure on durables is likely to be influenced by credit conditions,

---

[11] *Ibid.*

[12] Traditionally, residential housing is categorized as an investment, even though it is purchased by households, not firms. Residential housing will be discussed in Chapter 6.

since these items are largely financed by credit. Since they yield a stream of services which extends over a relatively long period of time, the initial cost of consumer durables may be great in relation to the immediate benefit to the household. Consequently, many families prefer to distribute the cost of the item over its useful life—a sort of pay-as-you-go arrangement at the household level. About 65 percent of new cars are financed by credit. By contrast, not more than 15 to 20 percent of business investment is financed externally.

The purchase of a durable consumer good can often be postponed, at least temporarily. Consequently, consumers are willing to wait for credit to ease. While consumption of durables is not as sensitive to credit conditions as residential housing (since the length of the debt obligation is considerably shorter in the former case), it is reasonable to expect that some measure of consumer credit cost and availability should be included in the consumption relationship. In most models, separate equations are used for consumption of durables and nondurables.

Despite the appeal of the *a priori* reasoning, however, present data on consumer expenditure for durables do not appear to support the hypothesis that this component of GNP is particularly sensitive to credit conditions. Using the Federal Reserve discount rate as roughly indicative of the state of the credit market,[13] Table 5-1 shows consumption of durables to be highest in those years when interest rates are also high. This is particularly apparent when we examine the ratio of consumption of durables to consumption of nondurables. With the exception of 1970, this ratio has risen and fallen with the Federal Reserve discount rate.

How can we account for the observed insensitivity of purchases of durables to rising interest rates? The answer most likely lies in the fact that the rate of interest generally rises and falls with disposable income. Since most durable goods are luxury items to many families, these are most often purchased when the family experiences a short-run increase in disposable income. A family feeling a new sense of affluence may choose this time to replace an old washing machine or automobile. On the other hand, when disposable income falls in a recession, purchases of durables are often postponed until better times.[14] A family makes do with old, worn-out equipment.

---

[13] Although there is some lag between changes in the Federal Reserve's discount rate and changes in consumer credit rates, it is not too important when yearly data are used.

[14] The year in which there was an exception to the positive relationship between durables purchases and the interest rate, 1970, was a recession year. The monetary authorities maintained interest rates at a high level, despite declining real income and rising unemployment, and durables purchases receded.

Table 5-1   Expenditures on Durable
                Consumption Goods

Year	Federal Reserve Discount Rate (%)	Purchases of Durable Consumer Goods (in billions of dollars, 1958 prices)	Ratio of Durable to Nondurable Consumption Expenditures
1958	2.16	37.9	0.270
1959	3.36	43.7	0.298
1960	3.53	44.9	0.300
1961	3.00	43.9	0.287
1962	3.00	49.2	0.311
1963	3.23	53.7	0.331
1964	3.55	59.0	0.346
1965	4.04	66.6	0.373
1966	4.50	71.7	0.383
1967	4.19	72.9	0.383
1968	5.17	81.4	0.414
1969	5.87	84.9	0.422
1970	5.95	82.1	0.395

Source: U.S. Department of Commerce, Office of Business Economics. *Survey of Current Business,* 1958–1970.

This is not to say that credit conditions do not influence consumer spending on durables. Without the tightening of credit in a boom, consumption of durables can rise even faster than it has in recent experience. On the other hand, rising interest rates can lead the public to believe credit will become even tighter in the future, stimulating current expenditures. Nevertheless, a reliable durable goods consumption function must include disposable income as well as the interest rate; that is,

$$C_d = \alpha + \beta(Y - T) + \gamma i$$

where α, β, and γ are constants.

The data in Table 5-1 indicate that the *MPC* from short-run changes in disposable income is higher for consumption of durables than for consumption of nondurables.

Questions for Study and Review

1. Discuss and compare the theories of consumption represented by the equations

(a) $C_t = a_1 + a_2 Y_t + a_3 C_{t-1}$

(b) $C_t = b_1 + b_2 Y_t + b_3 Y_{pp}$

(c) $C_t = c_1 + c_2 Y_t + c_3 i_t$

(d) $C_t = d_1 + d_2 Y_t + d_3 C_{t-1} + d_4 A_t$

where

C_t = aggregate consumption in period t
Y_t = aggregate disposable income in period t
Y_{pp} = previous peak income
i_t = market rate of interest in period t
A_t = financial assets held by individuals in period t

What signs should the various parameters have?

2. A theory of consumption must be consistent with the

(a) long-run stability of the APC,

(b) cyclical (short-run) variation in the APC,

(c) tendency for the APC to fall relative to income in budget study data.

How do several well-known theories of consumption reconcile these superficially incompatible observations?

3. One of the most important contributions of the Keynesian analysis was to show the effect of monetary and fiscal policy on consumption spending. Outline the effect which Keynes described. On the basis of post-Keynesian consumption theory, can you suggest any further role that public policy might play in influencing consumption behavior?

4. Consumption of durable goods is generally more volatile (varies more over the cycle) than consumption of nondurables. How do you account for this behavior?

5. The government is considering a program which would increase social security payments to the aged and provide free medical care for the aged

and needy. The program is to be financed from general tax revenue and by increasing social security contributions. What effect, if any, would such a program have on aggregate consumption?

Additional Reading

Ando, A. and F. Modigliani, "The 'Life Cycle' Hypothesis of Saving," *The American Economic Review*, LIII (March, 1963), 55–84.

Duesenberry, J. S., "Income-Consumption Relations and Their Implications," in *Income, Employment, and Public Policy: Essays in Honor of Alvin H. Hansen*. New York: W. W. Norton and Company, 1948, pp. 54–81.

Duesenberry, J. S., *Income, Saving, and the Theory of Consumer Behavior*. Cambridge, Mass: Harvard University Press, 1949, Chapter 3.

Ferber, Robert, "Research on Household Behavior," *The American Economic Review*, LII (March, 1962), 19–54.

Friedman, Milton, *A Theory of the Consumption Function*. Princeton, N. J.: Princeton University Press, 1957, Chapter 9.

Keynes, John Maynard, *The General Theory of Employment, Interest, and Money*. New York: Harcourt Brace Jovanovich, Inc., 1965, Chapters 8 and 9; originally published by Macmillan & Co., Ltd., 1936.

6

The
Theory
of
Investment

$\mathbf{W}$hile consumption represents the largest component of GNP, investment is the most difficult to forecast and analyze. In the previous chapter we saw that consumption is a fairly reliable function of disposable income. Investment expenditures, on the other hand, are influenced by a multitude of economic variables. These factors, moreover, assume varying degrees of importance in different situations, particularly in different phases of the business cycle. Investment, therefore, is not a reliable function of any one variable.

In this chapter several different theories of investment are considered. Because of the complexity of the investment decision, no one theory is applicable all the time. In addition, we shall examine the various types of economic policy that might be used to manipulate this important component of aggregate demand.

6-1 The Role of Investment in the Economy

Analytically the most troublesome, investment is the component of GNP of most concern to forecasters and policy planners. In recent years, private investment expenditures have represented about 15 percent of GNP in the United States. Despite its relatively small size in absolute terms, however, the *percentage fluctuations* in investment have been considerably greater than for any other component of GNP. These fluctuations in turn generate changes in GNP through the multiplier process. Since no other component of GNP fluctuates so widely, changes in investment account for much of the cyclical instability of the economy.

In addition to its role as a component of aggregate demand, investment is also the foundation for economic growth. Keynes predicted that in the long run the private sector would not generate sufficient investment to absorb saving at high levels of income. Whether or not Keynes' *secular stagnation thesis* is tenable, it is important to consider the long-run prospects for growth of investment opportunities as a society becomes increasingly affluent. Not only is long-run growth of investment requisite to maintaining full employment of a growing labor force, but such growth is also necessary if output and real income per worker is to increase.

Finally, investment, more than any other component of aggregate demand, is particularly sensitive to external influences such as wars and financial panics, both domestic and foreign. While the impact of such events on investment expenditures is difficult to predict, an understanding of the economic factors involved in the investment decision is helpful to the forecaster.

DEFINITION OF INVESTMENT

By *investment* the economist generally refers to the production of goods used to produce or sell other goods, that is, goods not directly consumed. Such goods are called *capital goods*. Some items, such as a blast furnace, a tractor, or a lathe, are obviously capital goods. Other items, such as automobiles and buildings, are less easily categorized.

There are three major types of expenditures which are included in Gross Private Domestic Investment as defined in the national accounts. These are expenditures on new plant and equipment, net inventory accumulation, and new residential housing construction. So-called theories of investment are primarily concerned with explaining investment in new plant and equipment. The determinants of investment in inventories and residential housing are different and will be treated at the end of this chapter.

PROBLEMS ASSOCIATED
WITH THE INVESTMENT DECISION

The analysis of the investment decision, that is, the determinants of capital goods purchases by the private sector, must incorporate the notion that capital goods are basically productive factor inputs. Because capital goods are used solely as inputs into the production or sale or other goods, they have no value of their own apart from the value of the final product. Like all productive factors, the demand for capital goods is a *derived demand*.

Let us consider for a moment the motives which determine how much of a factor of production a firm will wish to employ (i.e., the demand for that factor). If the firm is maximizing profits, it will employ a factor as long as its marginal contribution to the total product, that is, the *marginal revenue product*, exceeds its marginal cost. Algebraically, the firm will demand additional units of a factor as long as

$$MP_f \times MR_p > P_f$$

where

$$MP_f = \text{marginal product of the factor}$$
$$MR_p = \text{marginal revenue from sale of the good}$$
$$P_f = \text{price of the factor}$$

If the marginal revenue product of the factor is declining as more of the factor is utilized, as shown in Figure 6-1,[1] the firm will hire additional units

---

[1] A sufficient condition for a negatively sloped marginal revenue product schedule is diminishing returns to the factor and a negatively sloped product demand curve. Both are reasonable assumptions.

Figure 6-1   The Demand for a Factor of Production

of the factor until the marginal revenue product is equal to the factor price, or

$$MP_f \times MR_p = P_f$$

In Figure 6-1, when the price of the factor is P_{f1}, F_1 units will be employed. When the price falls to P_{f2}, employment will increase to F_2. If the marginal revenue product schedule ($MP_f \times MR_p$), is negatively sloped, changes in employment are inversely related to changes in the price of the factor; that is, as the factor price falls more will be demanded, and conversely, as the factor price rises less will be demanded.

In this model, the firm is expected to estimate the demand for the final product (to determine MR_p), the marginal productivity of the factor, and the factor price. The problem is particularly complicated when the factor of production is a capital good.

Consider the case of a corner grocer who must decide how many clerks to keep on the floor on any one day. He must take into account only those influences which will affect the volume of business on that day, including his own advertising and that of his competitors, the season of the year, the particular day of the week, and so forth. If he becomes short-handed, he presumably has a reserve of labor that he can call upon with little notice. He can even man a checkout counter himself. Furthermore, the payoff derived from having extra help on a particular day should be realized immediately (unless the grocer has overestimated the marginal revenue product), so that provision for the payment of the extra wages is internally generated through an increase in the day's receipts.

The decision to purchase a piece of capital equipment (e.g., a new building) is more complex than deciding how many clerks to have on the floor on a particular day. Generally, considerable time elapses between the purchase of the capital equipment and the realization of the proceeds derived from sale of the output. Not only does the process of producing or delivering the capital good take time, but capital equipment is generally durable, capable of producing output over an extended period of time. Consequently, the firm must estimate such things as the following:

1. The demand for the final good produced over an extended period of time. This becomes increasingly complex if the firm itself produces capital goods or is in a highly competitive market.
2. Not only the cost of capital, but the cost of labor and other inputs over the relevant period.
3. The possibility of technological change which would make the capital good obsolete before the end of its useful life.

Furthermore, the notion of a marginal product is somewhat ambiguous for a factor of production that yields a "stream" of product returns over time, particularly when the return stream is not uniform over time.

Because the proceeds derived from the use of capital goods are realized over a long period of time, the initial cost generally exceeds the immediate return. Consequently, they must be financed by some source other than their own revenue.

Thus, the durability of capital equipment provides two unique features to the investment decision. The firm must make long-term estimates of certain economic and technological market conditions. In addition, it must make some provision for financing the expenditures other than through the extra revenue generated by the new capital equipment itself.

In this chapter we shall consider three major investment theories.[2] The classical approach, emphasizing the rate of return on investment projects, was taken by Keynes in *The General Theory*.[3] One post-Keynesian school has emphasized the relationship of capital stock to output. Another has focused upon the sources of finance for firms undertaking investment in capital goods.

6-2 The Classical Approach: Marginal Efficiency of Capital

A rational investor weighs the potential or expected returns from a project against its cost. As a rule of thumb, he will purchase a capital good if he expects the return to exceed the cost. While all theories of investment recognize this general principle, there is disagreement concerning how the investor estimates his potential returns and costs.

In the classical approach, the market rate of interest is the cost of investment. If the project must be financed by borrowed funds, the investor must pay interest. If, on the other hand, the investor has his own funds available, he must consider the possibility of using his money to purchase a financial asset (e.g., a bond which yields interest). The return on the bond is the *opportunity cost* of using his own money to purchase the capital good. By so doing, he foregoes the potential interest earnings on the bond, and hence, the market rate of interest again represents the cost of investment, even if borrowed funds are not used to finance it.

It is recognized, of course, that different financial assets yield different rates of interest. If, however, this is a reflection of differences in risk, then we can simply view the difference between the actual rate of return on a bond and some "prime" interest rate on a riskless asset as the return to the purchaser of the bond for bearing the risk. Assuming that an individual prefers a promise of $100 with certainty to $100 with some chance of default, only part of the return on a risky bond represents the return to the lender for loaning his funds; the rest is a premium to induce him to purchase the risky asset instead of a safe one. Consequently, only the rate of interest on a riskless bond represents the true cost of a dollar used for investment; higher interest rates reflect risk, which involves a cost of a different type.

If the cost of a dollar used to purchase a capital good is the market rate of interest, what is the return? Suppose a company is considering the

---

[2]These theories are primarily concerned with investment in plant and equipment.

[3]This is not to be confused with the so-called "classical" macroeconomics in general, which Keynes *attacked* in *The General Theory*.

purchase of a new machine which costs $1000. If the firm expects output to increase by 100 units per year as a result of using the new equipment, and if the output sells for $1 per unit, then the rate of return on the investment will be 10 percent. That is, the annual return will be $100/$1000 = 0.10 = 10 percent. The firm will purchase the machine if the market rate of interest is less than 10 percent.

Most investment projects do not generate a constant income stream over time. It may take some time for the machine to be delivered after it is ordered. This is particularly true in the case of buildings and expensive, specialized equipment. Here a cost might be incurred with no immediate return. When a machine is new, it takes time for the labor force to learn to use it most efficiently. Finally, as the machine wears out it becomes less productive. Most capital goods do not last forever and generally become obsolete and need to be replaced. While the money used to purchase the item can earn interest indefinitely in the financial market (assuming that money can always be reinvested if a bond falls due), the earning stream of a capital good is definitely limited. Hence, the concept of a single "rate of return" *in perpetuity* is usually not applicable to a real capital investment.

Suppose a machine which costs $1000 yields a return of $200 in the first year, $500 in the second, $400 in the third, $100 in the fourth, and then wears out. How does a potential investor decide whether or not to buy the machine? He must ask the question, "How does this income stream compare with the yield on a bond costing $1000 and paying the market rate of interest in perpetuity?" Suppose the market rate of interest is 5 percent. The alternatives are shown in Table 6-1 and graphically in Figure 6-2.

The difficulty stems from the fact that if the return stream of the investment project is not uniform over time, as in the case of the bond, a yearly average rate of return is difficult to compute. Of course, if the return

Table 6-1 Return on Capital Good Versus Return on Financial Asset Each Costing $1000

Year	Revenue Gained from Use of Machine (dollars)	Interest Yield from Bond (dollars)
1	200	50
2	500	50
3	400	50
4	100	50
5	0	50

Figure 6-2   Payoff Stream on a Capital Good Versus the Return
on a Financial Asset Shown as a Function of Time

were all realized in one year, computing the return would be a relatively
simple matter.

Consider the following example: Suppose the present cost of a project
is $100 and this project is expected to return $110 next year, after which
no further returns are expected. Since

$$r = \frac{\$110 - \$100}{\$100}$$

or

$$\$100(1 + r) = \$110$$

the rate of return, r, can be computed by the formula

$$1 + r = \frac{\$110}{\$100}$$

$$\$100 = \frac{\$110}{1 + r}$$

or

$$C = \frac{R}{1 + r}$$

where C is the cost and R is the return. In this case

$$r = 0.10 = 10 \text{ percent}$$

If i is the market rate of interest, then P, derived from the formula

$$P = \frac{R}{1 + i}$$

is called the *present value* of the asset.[4] If r exceeds i, the rate of return exceeds the market rate of interest, and the present value of the project will exceed its cost. The converse is also true.[5]

Since financial assets earn compound interest, an investment project must earn a compound return to be equally attractive. This applies to projects with a return stream which exceeds one year. One hundred dollars

---

[4] The term *present value* derives from the fact that an asset yielding R dollars after one year is worth exactly as much as a financial asset costing P dollars this year if i is the market rate of interest.

[5] The proof is as follows:

$$C = \frac{R}{1 + r}$$

$$P = \frac{R}{1 + i}$$

if

$$r > i$$

Then,

$$1 + r > 1 + i$$

and since

$$R = R$$

$$P > C$$

loaned at 5 percent interest will be worth $105 in one year:

$$\$100 + (\$100 \times 0.05) = \$105$$

or

$$\$100(1 + 0.05) = \$105$$

In two years it will be worth, not $110, but $110.25, since

$$\$100 + (\$100 \times 0.05) + (\$105 \times 0.05) = \$110.25$$

or

$$\$100(1 + 0.05)^2 = \$110.25$$

The present value of $110.25 to be paid after two years is $100, or

$$\$100 = \frac{\$110.25}{(1 + 0.05)^2}$$

Algebraically,

$$P = \frac{R_2}{(1 + 0.05)^2}$$

where R_2 is the return expected after two years.

Let the symbol R_i refer to a return expected after i years. Then the formula for the present value of an asset yielding a return stream over n years is

$$P = \frac{R_1}{1 + i} + \frac{R_2}{(1 + i)^2} + \frac{R_3}{(1 + i)^3} + \cdots + \frac{R_n}{(1 + i)^n}$$

If the cost C is known, the compound rate of return, r, can be computed by the formula

$$C = \frac{R_1}{1 + r} + \frac{R_2}{(1 + r)^2} + \frac{R_3}{(1 + r)^3} + \cdots + \frac{R_n}{(1 + r)^n}$$

Keynes called the compound rate of return on an investment project the *marginal efficiency of capital* (*MEC*).[6] As in the previous example, if the present value exceeds the cost, then the compound rate of return on an asset, or the *MEC*, exceeds the market rate of interest.

---

[6]Some economists distinguish the *marginal efficiency of capital*, a rate of return on capital, from the *marginal efficiency of investment*, the rate of return on investment.

Returning to our earlier problem, the firm can compute the *MEC* for the machine whose lifetime earnings are shown in Table 6-1 by the formula

$$\$1000 = \frac{\$200}{1 + r} + \frac{\$500}{(1 + r)^2} + \frac{\$400}{(1 + r)^3} + \frac{\$100}{(1 + r)^4}$$

This equation can best be solved by trial and error. In this case

$$r \approx 8 \text{ percent}$$

Since the market rate of interest is 5 percent, the machine should be purchased because the return exceeds the cost. Equivalently, since the market rate of interest is known, the firm can compute the present value of the return stream and compare it with the known cost of the machine.

The present value formula is

$$P = \frac{\$200}{1 + 0.05} + \frac{\$500}{(1 + 0.05)^2} + \frac{\$400}{(1 + 0.05)^3} + \frac{\$100}{(1 + 0.05)^4}$$

so that

$$P = \$1081$$

Since the present value exceeds the cost of $1000, the machine is worth more than a bond costing $1000 yielding the market rate of interest in perpetuity.[7]

THE MARGINAL EFFICIENCY OF CAPITAL SCHEDULE

At any one time there is a large number of potential investment projects open to the firms in the economy. Let us assume that for each project the *MEC* is known. Starting with the project or projects yielding the highest *MEC*, we can add the dollar volume of investment projects available at successively lower rates of return. The function relating the *MEC* to the dollar volume of aggregate investment is called the *MEC schedule*.

For the economy as a whole, since each investment project will be small relative to the total, the *MEC* schedule can be represented as a smooth function, as shown in Figure 6-3. As investment increases, successively less profitable projects are undertaken. Consequently, the *MEC* schedule will be negatively sloped.

If all projects are undertaken whose *MEC* exceeds the market rate of

[7] The present value of such a bond is, of course, equal to its cost.

Figure 6-3   The MEC Schedule

interest, then the level of aggregate investment can be determined from the *MEC* schedule if the interest rate is known.[8] In Figure 6-4, when the interest rate is i_0, investment will be I_0. If the interest rate falls to i_1, investment will increase to I_1. Thus, changes in investment will be inversely related to changes in the market rate of interest.

    Shortly after the publication of *The General Theory*, a series of interviews with businessmen indicated that changes in the interest rate had a minimal effect on their decision to invest. In fact, in the depths of the depression, interest rates were quite low while investment fell to nearly zero. More recent

[8]Note that this is not a theory of interest. The interest rate must be known.

Figure 6-4 Determination of the Level of Investment

experience has shown that investment and interest rates generally move together over the cycle rather than inversely, as the theory suggests. This tends to support the skepticism with which many economists have viewed the classical approach to investment theory. The solution is apparent when time is introduced into the analysis. The MEC schedule is constructed for a single level of aggregate demand. Thus, it is static with respect to time. If, over time, aggregate demand increases, expected returns $(R_1, R_2, \ldots, R_n)$ are likely to increase too. Since the MEC is the compound rate of return on an investment project, then if expected returns increase, the MEC will rise as well. Thus, the MEC schedule generally shifts up and down with aggregate demand as well as with expected changes in aggregate demand.

If the authorities are undertaking a countercyclical monetary policy, then interest rates will also be moving with income. As shown in Figure 6-5, even though the "instantaneous" *MEC* schedules are all negatively sloped, investment can actually increase with interest rates if income is also increasing at the same time.[9]

Thus, as income increases from Y_0 to Y_2, the *MEC* schedule shifts upward and to the right. Even if the interest rate rises from i_0 to i_2, invest-

[9]In other words, the partial derivative, $\partial I/\partial i < 0$, may be negative when income is held constant while the total derivative, $dI/di > 0$, may exceed zero when income changes are taken into account.

Figure 6-5   Shifts in the MEC Schedule

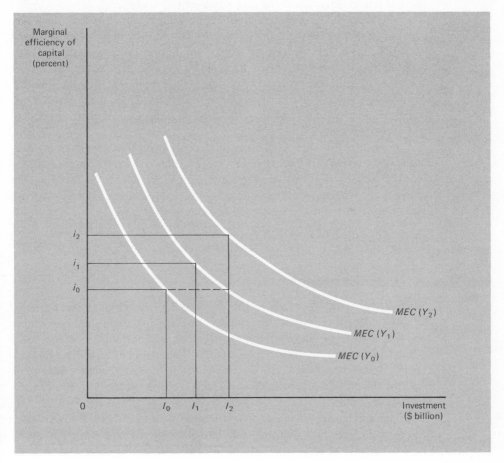

ment will increase from I_0 to I_2. These changes in investment are induced by income. Note, however, that the induced effect on investment of the rise in income would have been considerably greater had the rising interest rate not provided a brake. If the interest rate had remained at i_0 when income rose to Y_1, investment would have been I_2 rather than I_1.

This theory, taking into account the effect of aggregate demand on the MEC schedule, is the basis for the investment equation in our earlier model in which investment is treated as a function of both income and the rate of interest; that is,

$$I = f(Y, i)$$
$$I = g + dY + ei$$

where d is a positive constant and e is a negative constant.

Since the MEC depends upon expectations about future demand, investment can be influenced by a wave of optimism or pessimism about the future. The "announcement effect" of a proposed tax increase, for instance, could cause producers to expect a decline in demand, the MEC schedule to shift leftward, and the level of investment to fall, thereby reducing aggregate demand through the multiplier. Thus, the proposed tax increase could effectively reduce the level of aggregate demand even if it were never enacted.

When shifts in the MEC schedule are induced by changes in income or expected changes in income, investment may appear to be insensitive to credit conditions. The two post-Keynesian theories of investment which follow may provide additional insight into the observed insensitivity of aggregate investment to changes in the interest rate.

6-3   The Accelerator Model

While the classical approach to the demand for capital goods emphasizes the rate of return on investment projects, accelerator models are concerned with the relationship between the capital stock and output. As we shall see, accelerator models represent a substantial departure from the Keynesian theory of income determination. The concept of equilibrium yields to a dynamic theory of economic activity which lays the foundation for a theory of business cycles.

The accelerator theory of investment is based on the hypothesis that for the firm there is an optimal relationship between the level of output,

q, and the capital stock, K. This relationship may be expressed algebraically as

$$\frac{K}{q} = \widehat{\beta}$$

or

$$K = \widehat{\beta}q$$

where $\widehat{\beta}$ represents the desired capital–output ratio. Furthermore, it is assumed that if output is to be increased, the firm will desire to increase its capital stock proportionately, so as to maintain the capital–output ratio at $\widehat{\beta}$[10]; that is,

$$\Delta K = \widehat{\beta}\,\Delta q$$

where Δ refers to a change in the variable. (Notice that since the change in output can also be negative, the equation implies that a reduction in output will be followed by a proportional reduction in the capital stock.)

Remember that investment, I, is nothing more than a change in the capital stock, so that

$$\Delta K = I$$

and, therefore,

$$I = \widehat{\beta}\,\Delta q$$

That is, investment, or the demand for capital goods, will be proportional to changes in output. Assuming for simplicity that prices do not change, the accelerator model suggests that investment is a function of changes in national income or GNP. The distinction between this theory and the one described previously is that here investment is induced by a *change* in income, while in the former it was induced by the *level* of income. Algebraically, the accelerator is expressed as

$$I = \widehat{\beta}\,\Delta pq = \widehat{\beta}\,\Delta Y$$

---

[10]With constant returns to scale and a homogenous production function this implies the labor force will also be increased proportionately. This will be the case if the wage–interest rate ratio is unchanged. Even if there is some change in this ratio, it is still likely that an increase in output will require *some* increment to both the capital stock and the labor force. The assumption of proportionality is not necessary to the model and is convenient as a first approximation.

146

Excluding the public sector, we know that a constant level of GNP can be maintained only if investment stays constant. Yet the accelerator theory would conclude that positive net investment can be maintained only if GNP is growing. (If GNP were constant, then

$$\Delta Y = 0$$

and investment would also be zero.) Consequently, the accelerator theory rejects the possibility of a static national income equilibrium for a more dynamic approach to national income determination. In Chapter 13 we shall examine in some detail models in which national income moves over time, never reaching a static equilibrium in the Keynesian sense.

Apart from its dynamic implications, the accelerator theory is useful in explaining the observation that a static economy, one in which output is not growing rapidly, is generally considered to be in a state of quasi-recession. As the growth of output tapers off, investment may actually decline even though the cycle is still technically in an upswing. The decline in investment may eventually generate a downturn due to the induced effects of the multiplier.

LIMITATIONS TO THE ACCELERATOR

Undeniably, firms will adjust their capital stock as aggregate demand changes. However, the accelerator equation in its simple form is not a good description of investment behavior. In fact, if investment were as responsive to changes in national income as the model suggests, the economy would be subject to extreme fluctuations in GNP. Remember that changes in investment are multiplied due to the induced components of GNP. These changes in GNP would in turn, through the accelerator, produce further changes in investment. (We shall consider this process of multiplier–accelerator interaction further in Chapter 13.) In fact, it is unlikely that the changes in capital stock would be proportional to changes in demand for a number of reasons.

The model assumes that the firm can adjust its capital stock to achieve the optimal capital–output ratio in a very short time. However, generally some time elapses between the decision to invest and the acquisition of capital goods. Furthermore, because of the long-term nature of capital investment, the firm will not act strictly on the basis of immediate past experience (as the model implies) but will examine experience over a longer • period of time and perhaps will act on the basis of expectations about the future. Hence, the mere *announcement* of a planned government policy (e.g., an increase in armaments spending) may affect current investment demand even before the spending program is actually put into effect. Both the lag in the implementation of the investment decision and the tendency of firms to take a long-run view of past and future changes in demand before adjusting capital stock reduce fluctuations in investment demand and add stability to the model.

The model assumes that the firm will act symmetrically in response to both increases and declines in output or demand. In fact, a firm might increase its capital stock when demand increases, but be unable or unwilling to disinvest as quickly when demand declines. Disinvestment takes place as the firm fails to replace worn-out or obsolete equipment. Since the wearing-out process takes time, the speed at which a firm can disinvest is much more limited than the speed at which it can accumulate capital. Furthermore, if a firm expects the decline in demand to be short lived, it may continue to replace or maintain its equipment even though it has excess capacity. In a recovery period, the existence of excess capacity would preclude new investment by the firm, even if demand were increasing rapidly. Thus, it is likely that the accelerator model would be most applicable to an economy during a boom period in which demand had been increasing for some time, and less applicable in a recession or in the early phases of a recovery. Since the model allows for no autonomous investment (independent of changes in income), it is incapable of explaining why there is generally some positive investment even when income is not increasing.

Not only does the accelerator theory fail to explain investment in all but boom periods, it may actually understate investment even during periods of high demand, due to the fact that it attempts to explain aggregate investment based on a model of a single firm's behavior. In fact, aggregate income may remain constant, so that

$$\Delta Y = 0$$

but output in different firms may be increasing or decreasing. If there is some asymmetry to the response of investment to increases and declines in output, investment in those firms experiencing positive changes in demand will not be matched by proportional disinvestment by firms experiencing negative changes in demand. Consequently, even though there is no change in aggregate demand, aggregate investment induced by income changes should be positive (even excluding the possibility of autonomous investment). No matter what the change in aggregate demand, it is likely that growing firms invest more than declining firms disinvest in response to output changes; hence, the aggregate accelerator equation will tend to understate even that investment which is induced by output changes at the level of the firm.

Finally, the accelerator theory completely avoids consideration of the cost of capital. In fact, it assumes the firm has unlimited funds to carry out its capital expansion program. If funds are limited or if the cost of capital is very high, the firm may reduce its capital–output ratio, and consequently, capital accumulation will not be proportional to increases in output, even in the upswing.

The accelerator theory is not a realistic explanation of aggregate investment in recessions or early recovery periods. While it is most likely applicable in boom periods, the theory should be modified to take into account the lags in response as well as the effect of the rising cost of capital in boom periods. Nevertheless, since capital is a productive factor input, it is important to recognize that additions to capital stock will be made as output is increasing. There is no reason to expect capacity-expanding investment to take place as long as output remains constant. If investment is at least partly "change-induced," we would expect to see investment declining as the growth of demand tapers off in a boom. A "level-induced" theory would not be able to explain this phenomenon.

Both the classical and accelerator theories of investment assume that firms have unlimited access to funds at some constant cost or rate of interest. Although the accelerator model seems to ignore the possibility of prohibitively high capital costs in boom periods, the classical approach views changes in capital costs over the cycle as the most important stabilizer of investment. While the accelerator theory suggests that expenditure or tax policy which generates changes in aggregate demand should be used to manipulate investment and through it aggregate demand, the classical approach puts more reliance on monetary policy.

Both theories ignore the possibility that the cost of capital to a firm at any given stage of the business cycle may itself be a function of the amount of investment the firm is undertaking. A third school of thought emphasizes the role of the cost of capital in the investment decision.

6-4 The Cost of Capital

A rational businessman will undertake investment expenditure if the rate of return or *MEC* exceeds its cost. Until now we have assumed that the market rate of interest represents the cost of capital to the firm and that this cost is invariant to the amount of investment in which the firm is engaged.

The *cost-of-capital schedule* relates the cost of capital to the level of investment. We have assumed that this schedule is infinitely elastic (horizontal) with respect to investment at the market rate of interest. Experience tells us, however, that for the typical firm the cost of capital rises as more and more funds are required for investment spending. To see why this is so, let us consider the sources of finance capital, that is, money available to the firm for capital expenditures.

The cheapest source of funds is *retained earnings*, that is, depreciation allowances and undistributed profits after taxes. Most firms consider the cost of using these funds negligible, at least in the short run. True, there is an opportunity cost to consider; the firm could use the funds to buy bonds or purchase equity in some other business. However, apart from the possibility of running afoul of antitrust laws (a very real problem in some cases), most managers prefer not to turn their enterprise into a financial management concern. "If I wanted to manage a financial portfolio," says one top executive of a manufacturing corporation, "I would have gone into the banking business. Here our major concern is products." A second possibility is the distribution of unused earnings to stockholders. This is unappealing, however, in view of the lack of identity between ownership and management in most large enterprises. As a rule of thumb, most managers prefer to keep a fairly stable dividend payout ratio, which averages roughly one-third of total corporate profits. Thus, the cost to the corporation of finance capital coming from retained earnings is near zero.

Empirically, over 85 percent of private, nonfarm, nonfinancial investment is financed from retained earnings. As shown in Table 6-2, investment in plant and equipment (column 2) is generally within 10 percent of retained earnings for the economy as a whole. Notice that, even in the quasi-recession periods 1958–1959 and 1961–1962, investment does not fall drastically below the level of retained earnings. This suggests that the latter provides a floor or cushion to the accelerator, or demand forces acting to inhibit the level of investment.

It may be profitable, particularly in boom periods, to seek external financing for investment projects when internal sources are exhausted. A firm may issue *bonds* or debt instruments. While a limited amount of debt may be marketable at or near the market rate of interest, the bond price will fall, or alternatively, the effective interest rate will rise as the firm's debt–equity ratio or *leverage* rises. As the firm borrows additional funds for investment projects, its fixed obligations to pay interest on its debt rises as a percentage of its equity. Not only will increasing leverage affect bond prices, but it also will drive down the price of the firm's common and preferred stock.[11] These effects must be considered part of the cost of the bond issue. In general, the marginal cost of funds raised by a bond issue rises as more funds are required.

[11] In the limiting case, in which the bond yield is exactly equal to the *MEC*, all the return from an investment project will go to the bondholders and none to the holders of preferred or common stock. Since investment always requires some risk, the total risk is borne by the stockholders with no expectation of gain. This will make the stock less desirable than before the project was undertaken.

Table 6-2   Relation of Internal Funds to Purchases of Physical Assets
by Nonfarm, Nonfinancial Corporate Business, 1957–1968
(in billions of dollars)

Year	(1) Internal Funds*	(2) Nonresidential Fixed Investment	(3) Purchases of Physical Assets†	(4) (1)/(2)	(5) (1)/(3)
1957	30.6	33.4	34.7	0.916	0.882
1958	29.5	28.4	27.3	1.039	1.081
1959	35.0	31.1	36.9	1.125	0.949
1960	34.4	34.9	39.2	0.986	0.878
1961	35.6	33.2	37.0	1.072	0.962
1962	41.8	37.0	44.7	1.130	0.935
1963	43.0	38.6	53.5	1.137	0.940
1964	50.5	44.0	53.5	1.148	0.944
1965	56.6	53.2	64.9	1.064	0.872
1966	61.1	63.0	79.8	0.970	0.766
1967	61.5	64.9	74.1	0.948	0.830
1968	63.8	70.1	81.3	0.910	0.785

*Internal funds include undistributed profits, corporate inventory valuation adjustment, and capital consumption allowances.
†Purchases of physical assets includes nonresidential fixed investment, residential investment, and inventory change.
Source: Board of Governors of the Federal Reserve System, *Federal Reserve Bulletin*, 1957–1968.

A third source of funds is from sale of *equity*, that is, the issue of additional common or preferred stock. This may be undesirable for a number of reasons and is generally considered to be the most costly. Duesenberry contends that "if current earnings can be regarded as bearing any relation to the earnings expected in the future by the management, the yield cost of equity finance is usually of the order of 7 to 10 percent for large firms. To this must be added flotation costs plus any reduction in the value of existing shares resulting from the issue. The differential is further increased by the differential tax treatment of bond and equity finance."[12]

The cost of capital to the firm will vary according to its source, and how much is required. Figure 6-6 shows a cost-of-capital schedule which takes into account the various sources of finance capital. When investment

[12] J. S. Duesenberry, *Business Cycles and Economic Growth* (New York: McGraw-Hill Book Company, Inc., 1958), p. 95.

Figure 6-6 . A Cost-of-Capital Schedule

is financed from retained earnings, the cost of capital is negligible. When external financing is required, the cost of debt issue rises rapidly with leverage. Once the cost of debt reaches the cost of issuing equity, the cost-of-capital schedule becomes flatter.

6-5 A General Theory of Investment

The classical and accelerator approaches emphasize the role of demand for capital goods. In the classical model, the level of income influences investment demand through its impact on expected profits. The accelerator theory views investment as changes in productive capacity which will vary with changes in income. The corporate finance school is concerned with the role of retained earnings in determining the level of investment. A study of investment behavior by John Meyer and Edwin Kuh has shown neither theory to be applicable all the time.[13] Their results indicate that the need for capacity expansion and other demand-generating forces are most important in explaining business investment during boom periods of economic activity. In recessions and the early stages of recovery, however, investment spending rarely falls far below the level of retained earnings.[14]

Consider a typical MEC schedule. This tells us the amount of investment desired or, alternatively, the demand for investment funds at any given rate of return. In Figure 6-7 we have superimposed a set of MEC schedules on a cost-of-capital schedule. The intersection of these curves represents equilibrium in the market for investment funds.

As aggregate demand increases, the MEC schedule shifts upward from $MEC (Y_1)$ to $MEC (Y_3)$. Because of the rising cost of capital, investment does not increase as rapidly as a pure demand-oriented theory would suggest. Suppose, however, demand becomes so slack that the MEC schedule shifts to the left of $MEC (Y_1)$. In the short-run view, investment should decline proportionately. However, Meyer and Kuh found that firms take a longer view than this short-run model would suggest. In fact, firms will generally spend most of their retained earnings in recessions on technological improvements to reduce costs and advertising campaigns to increase their market share. While the distribution of spending among firms producing capital equipment may be different from that of a boom period when firms are primarily investing in capacity expansion, the overall level of investment will not fall as much as might be indicated by a simple short-run model.

Another reason why the accelerator model fails to provide an adequate explanation of investment behavior in a recession is the asymmetry of investment and disinvestment. When demand falls, firms simply permit facilities to lie idle; there is generally no mechanism for rapid disinvestment. As explained earlier, the accelerator theory is a poor description of behavior in recessions, even in the absence of financial considerations.

POLICY IMPLICATIONS

Traditionally, monetary policy (i.e., changes in the market rate of interest) was viewed as the appropriate instrument for manipulating the level of

[13] J. Meyer and E. Kuh, *The Investment Decision* (Cambridge, Mass: Harvard University Press, 1956).

[14] Of course, profits and hence retained earnings tend to be lowest in periods of slack activity, so that investment spending falls concomitantly.

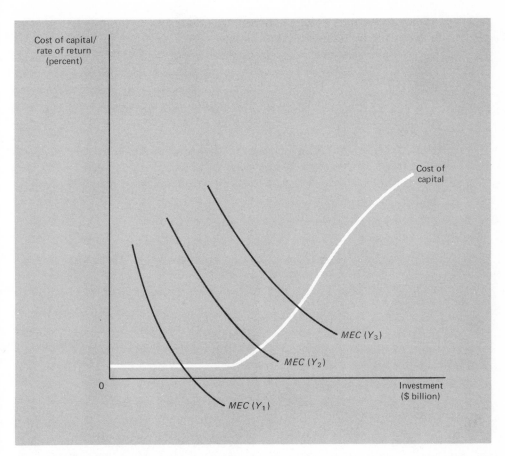

Figure 6-7   The Market for Investment Funds
                 (Short Run)

investment. This practice was supported by the classical theory of investment. But recent developments in the theory of investment indicate that
monetary policy might be the least effective of all the macroeconomic policy
instruments. In the analysis represented by Figure 6-7, the market rate of
interest plays only a small role in determining the cost of capital to a firm.
The principal effect of rising interest rates would probably be to reduce the
elasticity (increase the steepness) of the second phase of the schedule. This
would serve to brake investment, once internal sources had been exhausted.
Conversely, an easing of credit would increase the elasticity (flatten) the
second phase of the curve. This would have no effect in a recession if firms
were financing all investment strictly from internal sources. Thus, monetary

154

policy would most likely be more useful in dampening a boom than in stimulating investment in a recession.

A more effective policy instrument would control the internal sources of funds. The impact of a change in internal sources of funds on investment is shown in Figure 6-8. A reduction in corporate taxes in a recession, for instance, could stimulate investment if firms are taking a long-run view and investing all of their retained earnings in research and development and cost-reducing improvements. This policy may have the additional advantage of preventing rapid price increases as the level of economic activity recovers. In a boom, an increase in corporate taxes would shift the cost of capital curve to the left, as shown in Figure 6-8, discouraging marginal projects.

Figure 6-8   The Impact of a Change in Internal Funds
on Investment

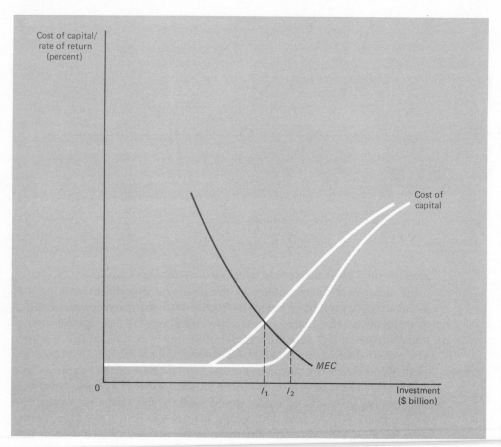

In our example, investment falls from I_2 to I_1 as the cost-of-capital schedule shifts to the left. Our present system of corporate taxation, based on income, does have this stabilizing feature built in. Since the tax is based on income, receipts rise in booms and decline in recessions. Discretionary changes in corporate tax rates and depreciation allowances, however, would be an even more powerful tool for manipulating investment and, through it, aggregate demand.

Investment expenditures are also induced by the level of and changes in the level of aggregate demand. Consequently, tax and expenditure policy, through their effect on aggregate demand and the *MEC* schedule, will strongly influence the level of investment. Whenever the government is using these measures to influence aggregate demand, the indirect, induced effects on investment must be taken into account. Again, the importance of complete specification of the forecasting and policy-planning model is apparent.

6-6   Inventory Investment

While the accelerator model is too simplistic to provide an adequate explanation of plant and equipment investment, it is useful as a theory of inventory investment. Generally, a firm will wish to hold fixed a certain ratio between its inventory and its sales. This ratio will vary among firms depending upon such factors as how fast the stock turns over, distance from suppliers, and so forth, but in the aggregate and in the short run, the desired inventory–sales ratio can be treated as approximately constant.

Then,

$$\hat{\pi} = \frac{H}{R}$$

where

H = inventories
R = sales
$\hat{\pi}$ = desired inventory–sales ratio

Inventory investment, I_i, or the net change in inventories will then be proportional to the *change* in sales, or

$$I_i = \Delta H = \hat{\pi} \, \Delta R$$

Since the change in sales, ΔR, is equal to the change in aggregate demand, ΔY, then inventory investment will be induced by changes in aggregate demand; that is,

$$I_i = \widehat{\pi}\, \Delta Y$$

The limitations in applying the accelerator approach to investment in plant and equipment which we discussed earlier are largely inapplicable to inventory investment. Unlike plant and equipment, inventories can be accumulated and sold (disinvested) rapidly. Initial outlays which are large in relation to current revenue are not required to finance them, and they can be liquidated quickly if necessary.

The empirical evidence bears out the theoretical approach. Although net inventory investment is a small component of total investment (generally less than 10 percent), it is by far the most volatile. In fact, some recent observers have attributed much of the cyclical activity in the U.S. economy since the Korean conflict to the multiplier–accelerator interaction associated with inventory investment.[15]

6-7 Investment in Residential Housing

Of the three major components of investment, residential housing is the most likely to be sensitive to conditions in the credit market. Because the commodity in question is very durable and expensive and because it is generally purchased by households without sufficient "internal" resources to incur the entire cost at one time, residential housing is generally financed by mortgages.[16] Except in the case of very large building corporations, even the building contractor finances his expenses in the mortgage market.

Not only are most homes financed by credit, but potential home buyers are quite sensitive to credit market conditions. Because the purchase of a home involves a long-term commitment (a 20- or 30-year mortgage is standard) and because the purchase of a home, unlike other consumption goods, can be postponed for months and even years if necessary, the home buyer will generally wait to purchase his dwelling until credit conditions

---

[15]In a model simulating the U.S. economy in the recession of 1957–1959, Duesenberry, Eckstein, and Fromm found the change in inventory investment accounted for as much as 62 percent of the change in GNP. See James Duesenberry, Otto Eckstein, and Gary Fromm, "A Simulation of the United States Economy in Recession," *Econometrica*, XXVIII (October, 1960), 749–809.

[16]A mortgage is a promissory note secured by real property.

are favorable. This is particularly true if there is uncertainty about the future or if interest rates are expected to fall. The decision to purchase a home is less likely to be affected by short-run changes in disposable income. Because of the long-term commitment, the decision is probably more closely related to the buyer's dollar view of his *permanent income* (see Chapter 5).

In a study of residential housing during the 1950's, Guttentag found housing starts to be quite sensitive to credit conditions, moving inversely with disposable income.[17] (This is because interest rates and disposable income move together over the cycle.) Thus, he contends, residential housing is the one component of investment which adds stability to the economy since it moves inversely with the general business cycle. In 1966, there was a sharp drop in private nonfarm housing starts, from 1.473 million in 1965 to 1.165 million. At the same time, FHA mortgage yields rose from 5.46 percent to 6.29 percent. Mortgage yields continued to climb throughout the decade. While residential housing starts began to recover slowly, they had not reached their 1965 level by 1968.

Unfortunately, residential housing is such a small part of total aggregate demand (normally about 5 percent) that it is not a powerful automatic stabilizer. It is, however, one of the first industries to feel the pinch of a credit squeeze. Localized structural unemployment may result, and pressure for an easier money policy is often strong from the powerful interests in this sector.

Questions for Study and Review

1. Suppose you are evaluating some projects which require certain investments (I) this year and which are expected to earn returns (R) next year. There are no returns in later years. The projects are the following:

Project	I	R
A	$ 400	$ 420
B	500	530
C	600	780
D	800	1200
E	1000	1400

[17] J. M. Guttentag, "The Short Cycle in Residential Construction," *The American Economic Review*, LI (June, 1961), 275–298.

The market rate of interest is 10 percent.

(a) Which projects ought to be undertaken?

(b) Compare projects D and E by computing the *MEC*. If they are mutually exclusive, which ought to be undertaken?

(c) There are also some interactions among the projects. If A is undertaken, the return on C becomes $750; if B is undertaken, the return on E becomes $1500; and if both A and B are undertaken, the return on D becomes $1300. There are no other interactions and there is no change in any of the costs. If C, D, and E are mutually exclusive, which projects ought to be undertaken?

2. Investment has always been the most difficult component of GNP to forecast and analyze, since investment is such a small proportion of GNP.

(a) How do you account for the difficulty?

(b) Why do economists attach such importance to this part of the macro-economic model?

3. The corporate finance theory of investment can be combined with the accelerator theory to provide a complete explanation of business investment.

(a) How do the considerations introduced by the corporate finance school alter the conclusions of the pure accelerator theory?

(b) How would you design an empirical test to determine which of the theories provides the *best* explanation of business investment on the basis of time series data *alone?*

4. The classical theory of investment suggests that monetary policy is the appropriate policy instrument for influencing the general level of investment. Discuss the analysis from which this conclusion is derived. Then, on the basis of what you know about post-Keynesian investment theory and empirical findings, argue *against* this position.

5. It has been suggested that inventory cycles have accounted for most of the instability in the U.S. economy in recent years. Why should investment in inventories be any less stable than investment in plant and equipment and residential housing?

6. Can you explain the observed tendency for investment in residential housing to move inversely with the other components of gross private domestic investment over the cycle?

Additional Reading

Clark, J. M., "Business Acceleration and the Law of Demand," *The Journal of Political Economy*, XXV (March, 1917), 217–235.

Duesenberry, J. S., *Business Cycles and Economic Growth*. New York: McGraw Hill Book Company, Inc., 1958, Chapters 3–7.

Duesenberry, J. S., O. Eckstein, and G. Fromm, "A Simulation of the United States Economy in Recession," *Econometrica*, XXVIII (October, 1960), 749–809.

Guttentag, J. M., "The Short Cycle in Residential Construction," *The American Economic Review*, LI (June, 1961), 275–298.

Keynes, J. M., *The General Theory of Employment, Interest, and Money*. New York: Harcourt Brace Jovanovich, Inc., 1965, Chapters 11 and 12; originally published by Macmillan & Co., Ltd., 1936.

Meyer, J., and E. Kuh, *The Investment Decision*. Cambridge, Mass: Harvard University Press, 1956, Chapters 2 and 12.

7

The Theory
of Interest
and Monetary
Policy

Since both consumption and investment are influenced by credit conditions, a model of income determination would not be complete without a theory of interest. In particular, we shall be concerned with how actions of the monetary authorities who control the money supply affect the interest rate.

Ever since Keynes described the relationship between the rate of interest and the level of income, economists have questioned the efficacy of monetary policy both as an antirecession weapon as well as a means for combating inflation. Although Keynes himself was pessimistic about the usefulness of monetary policy in recession, in recent years political considerations and institutional factors have made monetary policy the most flexible of our economic policy instruments, and in the United States it has been central to anti-inflation programs. A careful study of the factors determining the rate of interest must precede a more general analysis of the use of monetary policy to achieve the various macroeconomic goals.

7-1   Theories of Interest Rate Determination: Keynes and the Classics Compared

A salient feature of Keynesian economics is its usefulness as a policy model. As we shall see, a theory of interest can be approached from many angles. The advantage of the Keynesian treatment is that it clearly demonstrates the link between monetary policy (changes in the money supply) and the rate of interest.

Traditionally, interest has been viewed as the price a borrower pays for the use of money. If the borrower provides the lender with a promissory note, or bond, the interest rate is the difference between the face value of the bond and the amount actually borrowed (expressed as a percentage of the face value). Thus, interest may be viewed either as the cost of issuing the bond or, alternatively, the price paid for the use of money.

Classical economists viewed interest as the price which clears the bond market. Since the supply of bonds should decline as the interest rate (or cost) increases, while the demand for bonds should increase with the interest rate (or return), an equilibrium rate of interest would be achieved where the supply of bonds, B_S, is equal to the demand for bonds, B_D, as shown in Figure 7-1.

If the rate of interest were to exceed i_e, the demand for bonds would exceed the supply (i.e., lenders would wish to lend more than borrowers wished to borrow), and the rate of interest would be bid down. If the interest rate were below i_e, borrowers would not find sufficient funds available at

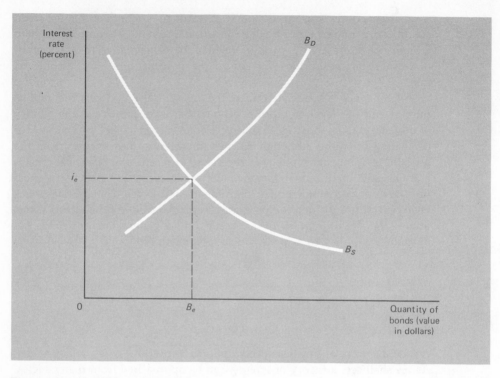

Figure 7-1   Equilibrium Rate of Interest Determined
in the Bond Market

that rate and would be forced to pay a higher rate. An equilibrium in which borrowers could obtain exactly the amount they wished to borrow would be achieved at i_e. At this rate of interest, all bonds offered would be sold, and the bond market would be cleared.

While this approach to the determination of the interest rate is theoretically valid, it is not particularly useful from a policy point of view, since the link between monetary policy and the interest rate is not clearly established. Moreover, it was the bond market approach to interest theory which led the classical economists to the erroneous conclusion that the rate of interest equilibrates saving and investment. If, indeed, all investment not financed directly from saving is financed from bond sales,[1] and if all saving not directly invested is used to purchase bonds, then equilibrium in the

[1]Corporate profit, of course, is a type of saving, and hence, internally financed investment is financed directly from saving.

bond market would ensure the equality of saving and investment. That is, if

$$I \equiv B_S$$

and

$$S \equiv B_D$$

then

$$B_S = B_D$$

implies that

$$I = S$$

Since the interest rate is the mechanism by which the bond market is cleared, then implicitly, the interest rate also equates saving and investment, regardless of the level of income. Fluctuations in the rate of interest produce the saving–investment equality required for national income and employment equilibrium at full employment, as long as the bond market is cleared. Such reasoning was the basis of Say's Law, the idea that a full-employment level of income could always be achieved by the automatic operation of market forces.

Keynes recognized the validity of the bond market, or *loanable funds*, approach to interest theory, but pointed out that the extension of the analysis to the so-called saving–investment market involved a fundamental fallacy. It is not necessarily true that all saving will be either directly invested or placed in the bond market, and hence, the equality

$$B_D = B_S$$

does not ensure that

$$S = I$$

Keynes pointed out that in the absence of an interest rate, a man would hold his savings in the most liquid form. To induce him to part with liquidity, a premium or rate of interest must be paid. The less liquid the bond, other things being equal, the greater is the rate of interest which the borrower must pay. This *portfolio* approach to interest theory is useful in explaining the structure of interest rates on bonds of different periods of maturity. For the Keynesian model, it is important in explaining the pure rate of interest on a riskless bond, traded in a market. Such a bond has the greatest liquidity of any asset except cash. The interest rate on such a bond will be determined in the market where people choose between holding their assets (savings) in the form of money or in interest-bearing securities. Hence, it is determined by the demand for money and the money supply. If the demand for money increases as the interest rate (or price of money) falls, then conversely, the interest rate must fall to induce people to hold more money. Increases in the money supply must be accompanied by a decline in the rate of interest if the money market is to be cleared.

In Figure 7-2, the money demand function, M_D, is downward sloping, reflecting the inverse relationship between the demand for money and the interest rate. As the money supply increases from M_{S1} to M_{S2}, the interest rate must fall from i_1 to i_2 to induce individuals to hold the increment to the money supply in money balances and hence to maintain equilibrium in the money market.

With his *liquidity preference* theory of interest, Keynes pinpointed the relationship between changes in the money supply and the interest rate.

Figure 7-2   Equilibrium Rate of Interest Determined
in the Money Market

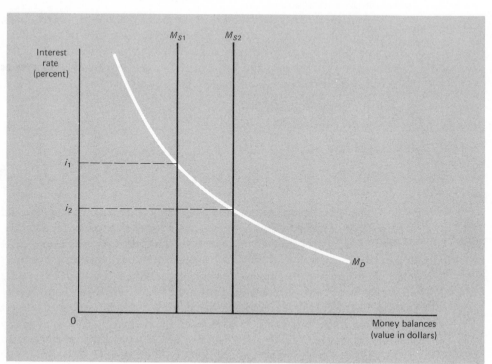

Furthermore, he isolated the fallacy which resulted in adherence to Say's Law in classical macroeconomics.

The portfolio approach demonstrates that the demand for bonds is not identical to saving. In fact, the demand for bonds consists of saving minus the net change in money holdings. Algebraically,

$$B_D = S - (\Delta H - \Delta M) = S - \Delta H + \Delta M$$

where

B_D = demand for bonds
S = saving
H = cash balances held
M = money supply

The supply of bonds is equal to investment (not financed directly out of saving); that is,

$$B_S = I$$

Now consider the implications for equilibrium in the various markets. Suppose the interest rate adjusts so as to clear the bond market; that is,

$$B_S = B_D$$

This implies that

$$I = S - \Delta H + \Delta M$$

or

$$I - S = \Delta M - \Delta H$$

Only if the money market is cleared, that is, if

$$\Delta M = \Delta H$$

will a national income equilibrium be achieved; that is,

$$I = S$$

Equilibrium in the bond market does not ensure a national income equilibrium as the classical economists believed. While fluctuations in the interest rate may serve to clear the bond market, they do not necessarily ensure that saving will be equal to investment. As Keynes pointed out, the saving–investment equality will only be achieved by fluctuations in the level of income.

The portfolio approach underscores another interesting relationship between the various markets. Consider the basic relationships,

$$I = B_S$$
$$S = B_D + \Delta H - \Delta M$$

Suppose the economy is in macroeconomic equilibrium, so that

$$S = I$$

Then,

$$B_D + \Delta H - \Delta M = B_S$$

or

$$\Delta H - \Delta M = B_S - B_D$$

If the interest rate has adjusted so that the bond market is in equilibrium, that is, if

$$B_S = B_D$$

then the money market must also be in equilibrium:

$$\Delta H = \Delta M$$

The reverse is also the case. If a national income equilibrium is attained, then the interest rate that clears the money market will also clear the bond market. In equilibrium, the *liquidity preference* (money market) and *loanable funds* (bond market) approaches produce equivalent results. The choice between the two is hence one of methodological preference rather than theoretical validity.

The liquidity preference approach which incorporates the relationship between money supply and the interest rate has more to recommend it methodologically. Incorporation of the money supply, a policy parameter, into the theoretical discussion will facilitate the adaptation of the model into a policy-planning framework. In addition, a theory which views the interest rate as the price paid for the use of money avoids the possibility of the fallacious misunderstanding that the interest rate equilibrates saving and investment.

The liquidity preference theory of interest is not without imperfections. However, before examining its faults, it will be useful to consider the liquidity preference theory in some detail. After an examination of the determinants of the demand for money and money supply, we shall consider the question of the efficacy of monetary policy in achieving the macro-economic goals.

7-2   The Demand for Money

Keynes observed that people are willing to forego interest income when they hold their assets in the form of money rather than as interest-bearing securities. Consequently, there must be some utility attached to money which would explain an individual's preference for liquidity. Keynes suggested three distinct motives for holding money balances: Individuals require money for transactions, and to meet unexpected contingencies. In addition, money may be temporarily preferred as an asset when the price of interest-bearing assets is expected to fall.

THE TRANSACTIONS DEMAND

Individuals require money balances in the form of cash and demand deposits to make day-to-day transactions. If a person expects to make $500 in transactions in a month, spread about evenly over the month, and if he is paid at the beginning of the month, his average cash balance would be $250.

Several factors influence the amount of cash balances held for transactions purposes. The transactions demand for cash increases with total expenditures. Suppose expenditures increase by $100. Again, assuming they are distributed uniformly over the period, then average money balances will increase by $50. Therefore,

$$\Delta M = \frac{\Delta E}{2}$$

where ΔM is change in money balances and ΔE is change in expenditures.

Not only do individuals hold cash balances for transactions purposes, but so do firms and government. Therefore, the demand for transactions balances can be expressed as a function not only of household expenditures, but of total aggregate demand or income; that is,

$$M_1 = l_{11}C + l_{12}I + l_{13}G = l_1(C + I + G) = l_1 Y$$

where M_1 is the *transactions demand for money,* l_{11}, l_{12}, and l_{13} are the proportions of C, I, and G respectively which are held by individuals, firms, and government in the form of money balances, and l_1 is the proportion of national income held by these groups in the form of money balances.

Institutional factors also influence the demand for money. If individuals are paid more frequently, the demand for transactions balances is reduced. In the previous example, a man who spends $500 uniformly over the month and who is paid biweekly will hold an average cash balance of $125 as compared with $250 if paid every month. Even though his expenditures remain the same, the demand for money is reduced by one-half because the pay period is shortened.

The use of credit cards reduces the transactions demand for money. If individuals pay most of their bills at the beginning of the month and the individuals are also paid then, there will be no reason to hold large transactions balances during the month. The practice of tax withholding precludes the need for accumulating balances for tax payments. Institutional influences in the United States have served to reduce the fraction of aggregate expenditure held by individuals in the form of cash balances.

Industrial organization plays a role in determining the demand for transactions balances by firms. In particular, vertical integration will reduce the requirement for cash in transactions between firms. An integrated company will simply record a transaction as a bookkeeping entry with no actual transfer of cash.

The rate of interest may also affect the demand for transactions balances. The higher the rate of interest, the more profitable it becomes to enter the bond market for short periods of time. However, the typical individual is paid at intervals not exceeding one month. At the same time, it is unlikely that he is sophisticated enough in financial practice to deal in that market in which he can realize interest income for periods shorter than a month.[2] Even at high rates of interest, the average individual will probably not enter the bond market with his transaction balances.[3] This may not be true of a large corporation, however, which may invest balances it is holding to meet an order which it expects six weeks in the future. In this case, transactions demand for money may decline as interest rates rise.[4]

[2]Conventional sources generally require that the asset be held for at least a month before the holder is eligible to receive interest.

[3]In this connection, it is important not to confuse transactions balances with savings which are not destined to be spent within the pay period.

[4]For a further discussion of this point see J. Tobin, "The Interest Elasticity of the Transactions Demand for Cash," *Review of Economics and Statistics,* XXXVIII (August, 1956), 241–247 and W. J. Baumol, "The Transactions Demand for Cash: An Inventory Theoretic Approach," *Quarterly Journal of Economics,* LXVI (November, 1952), 545–556.

THE PRECAUTIONARY DEMAND

Individuals and firms hold money balances in excess of their transactions needs to meet unexpected contingencies. Suppose, because of a clerical error, a paycheck is delayed. The man's family still must eat and make other necessary expenditures. It would not be prudent for him to allow his checking account balance to fall to zero on the day before payday. Instead, it would be advisable to keep some buffer cash in reserve as a precaution.

The amount of such precautionary balances held depends largely upon the level of transactions or income. Indeed, as a rule of thumb, an individual or firm may hold adequate precautionary balances to meet expenditures for a certain period of time, say, one week. Therefore, both precautionary and transactions balances can be viewed as a function of income, or algebraically,

$$M_1 + M_2 = l_1 Y + l_2 Y = (l_1 + l_2)Y = lY$$

where M_2 is precautionary balances and l_2 is the fraction of income held in precautionary balances.

The proportion of income held in the form of precautionary balances will vary with the amount of uncertainty associated with receipts and expenditures. This suggests that the percentage of income held in precautionary balances may rise in times of recession. Also, the availability of so-called "near-moneys" may encourage individuals to convert precautionary balances into interest-bearing securities, particularly if interest rates are high.

Both the transactions and the precautionary demand for money are directly related to income and, to a lesser extent, inversely related to the rate of interest. Figure 7-3 shows a family of money demand functions each for a different level of income. As income increases, M_D shifts rightward, from M_{D1} to M_{D3}. For any rate of interest, the demand for money will be greater the higher the level of income. For any level of income, the demand for money will increase slightly as the interest rate falls.

THE SPECULATIVE DEMAND

An individual who wishes to maximize the return on his portfolio investment will not purchase bonds if he expects their price to fall. Thus, he may find it most profitable temporarily to hold money rather than bonds as an asset, even though the former bears no interest, if the expected capital loss associated with a decline in the bond price exceeds the interest income he will forego by holding his assets in the form of money.

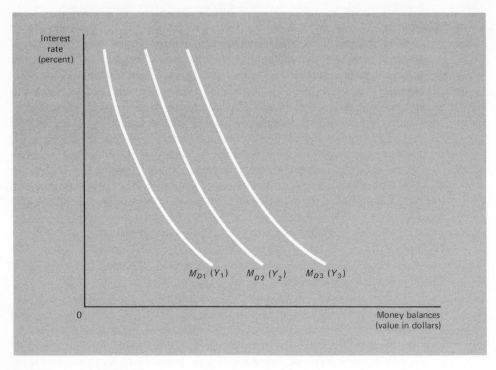

Figure 7-3 The Transactions and Precautionary Demand
for Money

For example, suppose an individual purchases a bond for $100 with a 5 percent coupon interest rate. If, after a year, the bond is worth only $90 and he receives $5 in interest, the net gain from holding the bond is −$5. Since there is no loss associated with holding cash, the latter is a preferable asset.

The market value of a bond with a fixed-coupon rate varies inversely with the market rate of interest. If the market rate of interest is 5 percent, a bond with a fixed-coupon rate of $5 is worth $100 in the bond market. Suppose the market rate of interest increases to 10 percent. Unless the bond yields the market rate of interest, there will be no buyers for it in the bond market. For the relationship between the bond price and the coupon premium of $5 to reflect the market rate of interest, 10 percent, the price of the bond must fall to $50. Thus, an individual will prefer to hold money rather than bonds, if he expects the market rate of interest to rise, thereby producing a decline in the market value of the bond which is greater than the original yield. In this case, the expected gain associated with buying a bond is $-\$45$ (the decline in the bond price, $-\$50$, plus the $\$5$ coupon), if interest rates are expected to rise from 5 percent to 10 percent.

The demand for money balances as a hedge against capital losses in the face of rising interest rates is what Keynes called the *speculative demand for money*. Keynes reasoned that, at very high interest rates, most people expect interest rates to fall (bond prices to rise), and consequently, the speculative demand for money is very low. Most people will prefer to hold bonds, since there is little risk of capital loss. At successively lower rates of interest, however, fewer people anticipate interest rates to fall still further and some expect them to rise. Those expecting rising interest rates (falling bond prices) liquidate their bond holdings in the expectation of capital losses and increase their money balances. At very low rates of interest, no one expects the rate of interest to fall, and everyone expects it to rise; consequently, any new additions to asset holdings are in the form of money balances.

Keynes labeled the phenomenon of a virtually infinite demand for money at very low interest rates the *liquidity trap*.[5] In this range, all increments to the money supply are "trapped" in speculative balances. Since these funds are not used to purchase bonds, the interest rate will be unaffected by increases in the money supply. A schedule of the speculative demand for money as suggested by Keynes is shown in Figure 7-4. The schedule becomes flatter as the interest rate falls and more people hold money as a hedge against the anticipated decline in bond prices.

Algebraically, the speculative demand, M_3, can be expressed as

$$M_3 = \frac{K}{i} \qquad \text{for } i_2 > i > i_1$$
$$M_3 = 0 \qquad \text{for } i \geq i_2$$
$$M_3 = \infty \qquad \text{for } i = i_1$$

where K is a constant.

The liquidity preference theory of interest is based on expectations. The rate at which the demand for money may become infinitely elastic depends upon what individuals expect "normal" rates to be. In periods in which interest rates range between 2 percent and 4 percent for as long as 10 years, a 1.5 percent rate of interest may represent the lower limit. If rates are uniformly higher, the money demand schedule may flatten at higher rates. In periods of greatly fluctuating rates, there may be no rate considered

---

[5]By similar reasoning, it can be argued that at high interest rates the demand for bonds is infinite. We shall consider the implications of this possibility in the discussion of monetary policy.

Figure 7-4   The Speculative Demand
for Money

"normal," and consequently, there may be no liquidity trap. In fact, Keynes himself doubted that the liquidity preference function would actually flatten out in practice except in "very abnormal circumstances."[6]

In some cases, falling interest rates may be associated with a decline in the demand for money if rates are expected to fall still farther. The reverse may also be true in the case of rising interest rates. Such behavior would result in highly unstable bond markets. Since the monetary authorities, through open market operations, are responsible for controlling bond prices (interest rates), the situation is unlikely to develop unless the authorities are expected to allow interest rates to move outside of their "normal" range.

THE DEMAND FOR MONEY

The demand for money varies directly with income and inversely with the market rate of interest. Demand for transactions and precautionary purposes increases with income. The demand for speculative balances increases as

[6]J. M. Keynes, *The General Theory of Employment, Interest, and Money,* (New York: Harcourt Brace Jovanovich, Inc., 1964), p. 207. Originally published by Macmillan & Co., Ltd., 1936.

interest rates fall. Algebraically, the demand for money is the sum of the transactions, precautionary, and speculative demands,

$$M_D = M_1 + M_2 + M_3 = lY + \frac{K}{i} \qquad \text{for } i_2 > i > i_1$$

$$= M_1 + M_2 + M_3 = lY \qquad \text{for } i \geq i_2$$

$$= M_1 + M_2 + M_3 = \infty \qquad \text{for } i = i_1$$

The money demand schedule for a given level of income can be represented as a function of the rate of interest as shown in Figure 7-5. The distance $0M_Y$ represents the transactions and precautionary demands at the specified income level. If the demand for transactions and precautionary balances were inversely related to the interest rate, the total money demand schedule would be flatter than the speculative demand schedule over the nonhorizontal portion.

As shown in Figure 7-6, the demand for money as a function of the interest rate can also be represented as a family of liquidity preference schedules, one for each level of income. At successively higher income levels,

Figure 7-5   The Demand for Money for a Specified
Level of Income

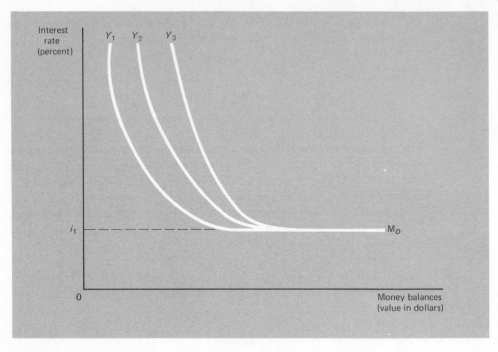

Figure 7-6   A Family of Liquidity Preference Schedules
Associated with Different Income Levels

the transactions and precautionary demands increase so the liquidity preference schedule shifts to the right. For interest rates above i_1, the demand
for money increases as the level of income increases. Notice, however, that
at the interest rate i_1, the demand for money balances becomes infinite,
regardless of the level of income. This corresponds with the algebraic
statement presented above.

CHANGES IN THE PRICE LEVEL

The demand for money balances will increase and decrease in proportion
to changes in the price level. If prices increase by 5 percent, the amount
of money required to purchase the same goods and services also increases
by 5 percent, and the demand for transactions and precautionary balances
increases proportionately.[7] Thus, interest rates will increase if the money
supply remains fixed. If the variables in the model are measured in money

[7] In a chronic inflation, the percentage of expenditures held in money balances may fall
since individuals will be anxious to exchange money which is decreasing in value for goods
as rapidly as possible. This phenomenon is not likely to occur when price changes are slight.

terms, price changes are reflected in the money income variable. In such a model, M_1 and M_2 can be treated as a function of money income which reflects the effect of price changes as well as changes in real expenditures. Since bonds have a fixed-money value, price changes will not affect the relative desirability of bonds and money, but they may cause individuals to convert speculative money holdings into real property, such as gold, jewelry, and real estate, as well as paper equity such as common stock. Since bonds have a fixed value in terms of money, however, they will not be any more attractive than money in inflationary times, and bond prices will most likely fall simultaneously with the shift from money and bond holdings into real assets. Thus, even though the speculative demand for money is likely to decline in periods of chronic inflation, interest rates will also rise. A rise in the money rate of interest during an inflation does not necessarily reflect an increase in the real rate. Suppose a bond yields 10 percent. If prices are expected to increase by 4 percent before the premium is due, the real yield on the bond is only 6 percent.

If inflation persists and the money supply remains fixed, money rates of interest will rise, causing speculators to revise their expectations concerning the floor below which bond yields will not fall. This will shift the liquidity preference function (in money terms) upward, with the liquidity trap located at a higher money rate of interest. If, however, speculators are subject to a "money illusion," they may not revise their expectations about the normal range of interest rates, and the liquidity preference function will not shift with changes in the price level.

7-3 Monetary Policy and the Money Supply

Given the demand for money for transactions, precautionary, and speculative purposes, the monetary authorities can manipulate the interest rate by changing the money supply. The Federal Reserve can increase the money supply by buying bonds on the open market, lowering the discount rate at which commercial banks can borrow from the Federal Reserve banks, and reducing reserve requirements for member banks.

An increase in the money supply will have the effect of reducing the interest rate, except in the liquidity trap, as shown in Figure 7-7. As the money supply increases from M_{SA} to M_{SB} to M_{SC}, the interest rate falls from i_A to i_B to i_1 as individuals and firms convert some of the additional balances into bonds, driving bond prices up. At an interest rate of i_1, however, increases in the money supply will not cause interest rates to fall farther. In the liquidity trap, bond prices are so high that everyone prefers to hold the additional money in speculative balances rather than enter the

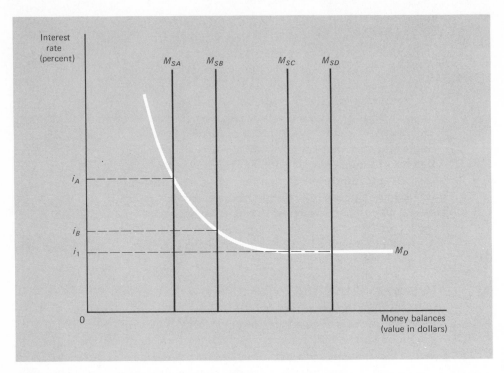

Figure 7-7 Determination of the Interest Rate
for a Specified Level of Income

bond market, since they expect bond prices to fall. If the money supply
is increased from M_{SC} to M_{SD}, the interest rate will remain fixed at i_1.

Notice that the higher the rate of interest, the greater is the change
in the interest rate associated with a given change in the money supply.
Thus, monetary policy is likely to be most effective at higher interest rates.
At very low rates of interest, changes in the money supply are less effective
in controlling the interest rate, and in the liquidity trap, monetary policy
cannot influence the interest rate at all.

CHANGES IN THE DEMAND FOR MONEY

The monetary authorities must consider certain factors which might affect
the demand for money. These include price level changes, increased use
of credit cards (reducing transactions demand), and increased national health
and retirement insurance coverage. Suppose an increase in the price level
results in an increased demand for money.[8] Figure 7-8 shows the effect

---

[8] In cases of runaway inflation, the demand for money might actually weaken.

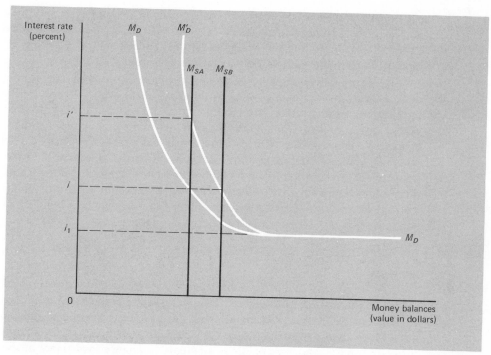

Figure 7-8   An Increase in the Demand for Money

on the market rate of interest. As the money demand schedule shifts rightward from M_D to M'_D, the market rate of interest rises from i to i', when
the money supply is M_{SA}. If the monetary authorities were interested in
maintaining a stable interest rate in the face of inflationary pressure, they
would have to increase the money supply from M_{SA} to M_{SB}, which intersects
M'_D at i.[9]

7-4 Limitations
to the Effectiveness
of Monetary Policy

Two major factors limit the effectiveness of monetary policy as an instrument
for manipulating aggregate demand. If the demand for money is extremely

---

[9]The increased money supply may stimulate aggregate demand, causing national income
and the demand for transactions balances to rise. This will cause the money demand schedule
to shift again. Thus, to maintain the interest rate at i, the monetary authorities would be forced
to increase the money supply again, feeding continuous inflation. Undoubtedly, in such a
situation the policy of maintaining the interest rate at i would be called into question.

elastic with respect to the interest rate, changes in the money supply may not result in significant changes in the interest rate. A second and quite distinct factor inhibiting the effectiveness of monetary policy is the inelasticity of investment with respect to the interest rate.

The speculative demand for money in Keynesian analysis might produce a liquidity trap at low rates of interest. There are important policy implications to this rather esoteric theoretical innovation. It suggests that expansionary monetary policy, that is, increases in the money supply, might be ineffective in stimulating investment demand in a recession since it could not push interest rates below the marginal efficiency of capital.[10] Direct government intervention in the spending stream through reduced taxes and, more effectively, through increased public spending would be the only policy instrument capable of moving the economy to full employment. On the other hand, the rate of interest is likely to be much more responsive to monetary management in boom periods when interest rates are higher, since the liquidity preference function becomes much steeper at higher rates of interest.

As suggested in the previous chapter, investment demand may be inelastic with respect to changes in the interest rate, particularly in periods of inadequate aggregate demand. Not only is the investment demand schedule relatively steep in times of slack demand and uncertainty, but many firms find internal sources of funds adequate to finance investment at this time. Furthermore, in a slump they are often actually faced with excess capacity, so there is no incentive to undertake new investment.

In boom periods, as well, accelerator effects which stimulate investment may outweigh considerations of capital cost, again weakening the impact of a tight money policy on investment. In boom periods, however, restrictive monetary policy may be particularly effective in limiting demand in those sectors in which external financing is the rule and accelerator influences are weaker. In particular, the housing industry and certain consumer durables industries might face a cutback in demand, as sources of finance dry up or become prohibitively expensive.

Milton Friedman, a noted monetary economist, has suggested an additional factor which not only limits the effectiveness of monetary policy but also implies that it may actually make things worse. Friedman argues that the lag between discretionary changes in the money supply by the Federal Reserve and its influence on spending is so great that the overall effect may be destabilizing. For instance, the Fed may decide to increase

---

[10]Theoretically, the idea of the liquidity trap was not a real innovation, since the classical economists had implicitly recognized an interest rate floor of zero. At zero or negative rates of interest, everyone would prefer money to bonds, and hence, the demand for money balances would be infinitely great.

the money supply when the unemployment rate rises, but by the time interest rates have time to adjust downward and have the desired (if any) effect on aggregate demand, the economy might well be on its way to an inflationary boom (due presumably to a faster-acting fiscal policy package). Thus the increased money supply may serve to add fuel to the inflation. Friedman proposes a system whereby the money supply is automatically changed as the level of GNP changes. This would at least eliminate the lag in the recognition and decision-making process.

7-5 Evaluation of the Liquidity Preference Theory of Interest

Perhaps the most important contribution of the liquidity preference theory of interest is that it provides a framework for an analysis of monetary management. Classical economists, by focusing on the bond market, had viewed money as something of a "veil" which determined the absolute level of prices, but which had no influence on real variables in the economy. By showing the link between the money supply and the interest rate, Keynes demonstrated that money is more than a veil. By determining the interest rate, in the Keynesian model, the money supply determines the level of investment and, through the multiplier, national income.

By introducing the notion of the liquidity trap, Keynes made a strong theoretical point for increased reliance on fiscal policy as an antirecession weapon. However, there is little historical evidence to support the premise that the demand for money becomes infinite at low rates of interest. It is ironic that Keynes did not place more emphasis on the interest elasticity of investment demand. Empirical findings indicate that interest inelasticity of investment demand is a far more serious limitation to monetary policy in a recession than the speculative demand for money. Nevertheless, Keynes' misgivings about the effectiveness of monetary policy represented an important milestone in the history of economic thought and policy.

Questions for Study and Review

1. Assume the following functional relationships:

$$C = 10 + \frac{3}{4}(Y - T)$$

$$I = \frac{1}{4}Y - 100i$$

$$M_1 + M_2 = \frac{1}{4}Y$$

$$M_3 = \frac{10}{i} \qquad \text{for } i > 2$$

$$= \infty \qquad \text{for } i \leq 2$$

$$T = \frac{1}{3}Y$$

$$G = 300$$

$$M = 115$$

The notation follows that in the text.

(a) What is the equilibrium level of income?

(b) If full-employment income is 500, can it be reached by monetary policy alone?

(c) Show how fiscal policy might be used to bring the economy to full employment.

2. How might a decline in the transactions demand for money affect national income and employment? How would it affect the general level of prices? What policy measures would serve to neutralize these effects?

3. The argument that Keynes' theory of interest was not significantly different from the bond market theory has been defended and denied. State your position in this controversy, with some argument on *both* sides of the question.

4. Keynes made a strong case for the use of fiscal policy as a weapon to stimulate a sluggish economy. Outline the arguments on which this case was made.

5. Show how Keynes' theory of interest and money provides a planning model for monetary management. What behavioral parameters need specification?

Additional Reading

Bronfenbrenner, Martin, and Thomas Mayer, "Liquidity Functions in the American Economy," *Econometrica*, XXVIII (October, 1960), 810–834.

Friedman, Milton, "A Monetary and Fiscal Framework for Economic Stability," *The American Economic Review*, XXXVIII (June, 1948), 245–264.

Hansen, Alvin, *A Guide to Keynes*. Book Four. New York: McGraw-Hill Book Company, Inc., 1953, Chapter 6.

Keynes, J. M., *The General Theory of Employment, Interest, and Money*. New York: Harcourt Brace Jovanovich, Inc., 1965, Chapters 13, 14, and 15; originally published by Macmillan & Co., Ltd., 1936.

Pigou, A. C., "The Value of Money," *The Quarterly Journal of Economics*, XXXII (November, 1917), 38–65.

8

The
Complete
Model

Having examined the forces which influence the consumption and investment components of aggregate demand, we are now ready to develop a complete model of income determination. While the basic framework of the policy-planning and forecasting models of the early chapters will be left intact, the complete model will incorporate the analysis of consumption, investment, and interest rate determination of Chapters 5, 6, and 7.

Aggregate demand and conditions in the money market are closely interrelated, and as a consequence, fiscal and monetary policy may interact in important ways. A study of the complete macroeconomic model will serve to emphasize the importance of coordination of the various monetary and fiscal measures undertaken to attain the goals of full employment, price stability, payments equilibrium, and growth.

8-1 The Variables of the Model

If the model is to be used for policy planning, it is necessary to establish links between the policy variables—government spending, taxes, and money supply—and the target variables—employment, price level, and GNP. As the model explains how these target variables are determined, however, other important indicators of economic conditions can be derived. These include the rate of interest, the level of real wages, and the distribution of the net private product between consumption and investment.

Treating the so-called "policy parameters" as exogenous, or predetermined, does not imply that the public authorities have complete discretionary control over all policy instruments. In fact, it is likely that public expenditures, taxes, and money supply are themselves dependent in part on economic conditions in the private sector. The scope of this particular model, however, is to show how public policy decisions affect the various target variables and, implicitly, how public policy can be used to effectuate desired changes or to attain certain goals. Consequently, policy instruments are treated as exogenous; the model is designed to show how changes in these instruments produce changes in the endogenous variables of the system.

REAL VERSUS MONEY MODELS

The variables in an economic model can be expressed in *real* or in *money* terms. If a variable is expressed in real terms, it is deflated by a price index so as to abstract from price level changes. For example, if GNP were to rise from $500 billion to $600 billion while prices increased by 10 percent, then the *money* increase in GNP would be $100 billion while the *real* increase would be $45 billion. The real increase is calculated as follows: For a 10 percent increase in prices from the base year, the price deflator is 110 (100 for the base year plus 10 percent of 100), so that when GNP rises to $600 billion, *real* GNP is

$$\frac{\$600 \text{ billion}}{110} \times 100 = \$545 \text{ billion}$$

Thus, the *real* change in GNP is $45 billion. The money change in GNP measures the change in the value of goods and services produced. The real change measures the change in output when valued at the prices of the base period.

In *The General Theory*, Keynes converts money variables into real variables by using a *wage unit deflator*, an index of average wages, rather than a price deflator. This practice has two major advantages. First, when a money variable is expressed in constant wage units (rather than constant money units), the variable is directly tied to the level of employment. If the proportion of national income earned in the form of wages is constant, then national income in wage units, Y, is proportional to the level of employment, N, since if

$$\lambda Y = wN$$

where λ represents the percent of national income earned as wages, and w is the wage unit deflator, then

$$\frac{Y}{w} = \frac{1}{\lambda} N$$

Income in wage units will only increase if employment increases or if the relative share of national income earned in nonwage form decreases. A second advantage of using wage units is that changes in average wages will tend to be uniform with respect to capital goods and consumer goods industries if labor is mobile between them. On the other hand, price level changes may vary considerably between capital and consumer goods industries, often necessitating the use of separate price deflators for the investment and consumption sectors. A difficulty with the wage unit approach is that changes in the distribution of income between wage and nonwage sources must be taken into account explicitly.

If money variables are deflated by a price index, a measure of output (real income) is obtained. If money variables are deflated by a wage index, a measure of employment is obtained. Wages and prices are related to each other through the marginal productivity of labor, since

$$w = p \times MP$$

With the wage unit fixed, an increase in aggregate demand and employment implies an increase in prices, since the marginal productivity of labor will generally fall as more workers are employed with a fixed capital stock. Thus, output measured in constant dollars will not increase as rapidly as output measured in wage units. This is equivalent to saying that output will not increase as fast as employment, or alternatively, that there are diminishing returns to labor with a fixed capital stock.

Economists have traditionally developed macroeconomic models in real terms. The practice may be attributable to the classical belief that money is a veil which has no impact on real variables. In a Keynesian system, however, in which the quantity of money in circulation has an important relationship to the value of the real variables, this justification for abstracting from money no longer applies.

Some economists continue to construct models in real terms, even though their models are essentially Keynesian in the sense that they recognize the impact of the money supply on the real variables. This is generally done because of the assumption that spending units make their decisions in terms of the real values of income, interest rates, and the like. In most cases it is assumed that spending units are not subject to "money illusion"; that is, they take price changes into account before making their spending decisions. Thus, real consumption is essentially a function of real income. If prices and income were to increase by 10 percent, then after a lag, consumption expenditures would also increase by 10 percent.

Although the behavioral relationships of the model may be correctly specified in terms of real variables, it is a mistake to examine the complete Keynesian system in real terms. Changes in the real variables of the system will always have an impact on the price level through the aggregate supply function. These price level changes in turn affect the real value of the money supply and hence the rate of interest, investment, and real income. For instance, consider an increase in government spending which generates an increase in employment through the multiplier. As shown in Figure 8-1, with a fixed money wage, prices will increase as the economy moves along the aggregate supply function from E_1 to E_2, and the marginal productivity of labor declines. The price increase has the impact of increasing the transactions demand for money proportionally and raising the real rate of interest. Unless the monetary authorities increase the money supply in proportion to the price increase, the employment multiplier will be smaller than that predicted by an analysis of the real system alone. Thus, abstraction from the price changes generally associated with changes in employment ignores the impact of these changes on the value of transactions balances and hence on the rest of the system. There are important feedbacks which are ignored when variables are measured in real terms. In this case the increase in government spending must be combined with expansionary monetary policy (increased money supply) if the full impact of the multiplier is to be felt.

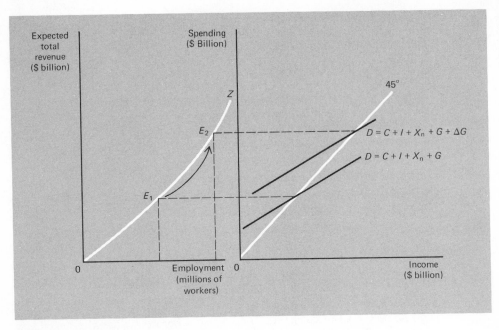

Figure 8-1 Impact of an Increase
on Government Spending

Converting consumption, investment, and money demand functions from real into money terms implies no loss of generality, even though the relationships which we examined in Chapters 5, 6, and 7 were essentially real in the sense that they implied no "money illusion." Empirical studies of consumption and investment behavior generally work with variables deflated by a price or wage index. However, these can easily be converted into money terms by multiplying the deflated variables by the deflator. Thus, if real consumption, C_r, is obtained by dividing the money value of consumption, C_m, by a price index,

$$C_r = \frac{C_m}{p}$$

then money consumption can be found by multiplying real consumption by the price index; that is,

$$C_m = C_r p$$

If all variables in the relationship have been deflated by the same index, then the relationship, except for constant terms, will be the same regardless of whether the variables are in real or money form.

Converting behavioral relationships into money form has the additional advantage that money illusion can be taken into account whenever it occurs. Money illusion implies that individuals react to money changes in economic variables, such as income and wages, independent of price level changes. An example of money illusion in the Keynesian system is the liquidity trap. The demand for money becomes infinite at some low rate of interest. But this floor below which the interest rate is not expected to fall and hence will not fall is presumably (according to the standard analysis) independent of the rate of change of the price level. Speculators have a money illusion if they believe that the interest rate will not fall below 2 percent even if the general price level is falling. Money interest rates will be lower in periods of falling prices than when prices are rising if the real rate remains unchanged.

In conclusion, the complete Keynesian model can be developed in either real or money terms. By abstracting from price level changes, however, we fail to account for the effect of changing levels of employment on the price level and, hence, on the real value of the money supply. The simple model developed in Chapters 2, 3, and 4 was presented in money terms. The analysis that follows will be based upon that framework.

It should be noted that while a model which involves money relationships may be most useful for policy planning and forecasting, we are often interested in separating price changes from real changes in national income aggregates. While real increases in GNP may be desirable, since they represent increases in real goods and services, price level increases are not, since they represent changes in the value of money. In fact, whether or not the government should stimulate GNP will often depend upon how much of the increase will be pure price inflation. In Chapters 10 and 11 we shall consider the process of inflation and analyze the problem of how to maintain high levels of employment without encountering inflation. It is clear, however, that the problem of inflation cannot be solved by abstracting from price level changes in the analysis.

8-2   The General Equilibrium

A SIMPLE KEYNESIAN MODEL

In its simplest form, the Keynesian system of income determination can be built from the consumption or saving function, the *MEC* schedule, the liquidity preference or money demand function, and the aggregate supply function. The model is analyzed graphically in Figure 8-2. Given the money demand function and the money supply, the rate of interest is determined

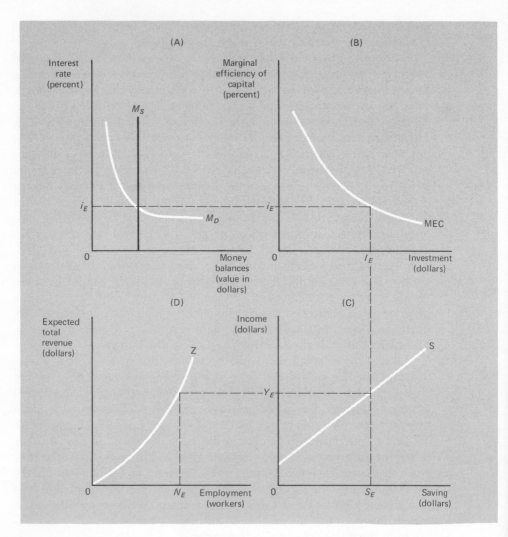

Figure 8-2   A Simple Keynesian System

by the equality of money supply and demand in part A. In part B, investment is determined from the *MEC* schedule once the interest rate is known. Given the level of investment and the saving function in part C, the equilibrium level of income is found at the point on the ordinate where saving equals investment. The equilibrium level of employment is determined from the aggregate supply function in part D.

Algebraically, the model can be represented as follows:

Part A

Money demand $\qquad M_D = \dfrac{K}{i}$

Money supply $\qquad M_S = M_0$

Equilibrium interest
  rate $\qquad M_D = M_S \longrightarrow \dfrac{K}{i} = M_0$

$$i = \dfrac{K}{M_0}$$

Part B

Interest rate
  determined from part A $\qquad i = i_0 = \dfrac{K}{M_0}$

MEC schedule $\qquad I = ei = \dfrac{eK}{M_0}$

Part C

Investment determined
  in part B $\qquad I = \dfrac{eK}{M_0}$

Saving function $\qquad S = -a + sY$

Equilibrium income $\qquad I = S \longrightarrow \dfrac{eK}{M_0} = -a + sY$

$$Y = \dfrac{a}{s} + \dfrac{eK}{SM_0}$$

Part D

Income determined
  in part C $\qquad Y = \dfrac{a}{s} + \dfrac{eK}{SM_0}$

Aggregate supply
  function $\qquad N = Y^{\alpha}$

Equilibrium
  employment $\qquad N = \left[\dfrac{a}{s} + \dfrac{eK}{SM_0} \right]^{\alpha}$

190

Notice that in this model, equilibrium values for the variables are determined *recursively*, or in succession. First, the rate of interest is determined in the money market. Once the rate of interest is known, investment is determined from the *MEC* schedule. Given the level of investment, equilibrium income is found from the saving function. Given the level of income, equilibrium employment is derived from the aggregate supply function.

While this approach is useful as a first approximation, it disguises some important interrelationships and feedbacks. If the transactions demand for money is taken into account, money demand is a function of the income level as well as of the rate of interest. Thus, the interest rate will depend upon the level of income as well as money supply. It is ironic that Keynes criticized the classical economists for ignoring the impact of the interest rate on the income level, because the simple Keynesian model ignored the effect of the income level on the interest rate. Furthermore, investment may depend upon the level of income and saving on the rate of interest. It is obvious that a complete macroeconomic model must account for the *interdependence* of income and the rate of interest in determining the various macroeconomic relationships.

THE EXTENDED KEYNESIAN MODEL

Suppose that the demand for money is composed of both transactions and speculative demand and, hence, is a function of the level of income as well as the rate of interest. Graphically, such a money demand function is represented as a family of liquidity preference schedules shown in Figure 8-3. The higher the level of income, the greater is the demand for transactions balances and the further to the right the money demand function will lie. The equilibrium rate of interest is determined by the intersection of the money supply schedule with the money demand schedule for each level of money income. Notice that for a fixed money supply, the rate of interest required to achieve money market equilibrium is higher for higher levels of income. As income rises from Y_1 to Y_3, for instance, the interest rate will rise from i_1 to i_3 with the money supply fixed at M_S. At very low levels of income, for instance, Y_0, the transactions demand for money is very small, and the rate of interest may lie in the liquidity trap. This may be true for several different levels of income.

Consider the relationship between the level of income and the rate of interest required to clear the money market given a fixed money supply. This relationship, called the *LM* curve, is shown in Figure 8-4. The total

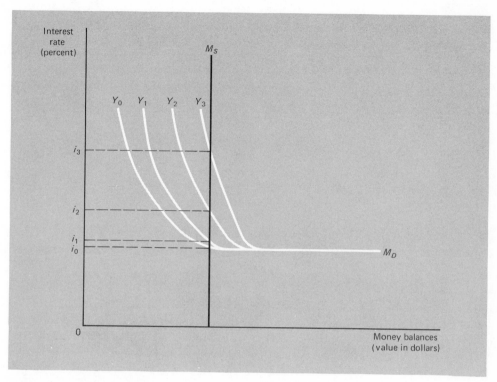

Figure 8-3   Money Market Equilibrium at Different
Levels of Income

demand for money is the sum of the transactions, precautionary, and speculative demands. At low income levels, the transactions and precautionary
demand is weak; at low interest rates the speculative demand is infinite.
Since the rate of interest is determined by the equilibrium between money
demand and money supply, and assuming a fixed-money supply, the *LM*
curve will be positively sloped with a horizontal portion to the far left,
reflecting the infinite speculative demand for money in the liquidity trap.
Because of the transactions demand for money, the equilibrium rate of
interest rises with the level of money income, since bond prices must fall
if speculative balances are to be released for transactions purposes; but due
to the speculative demand for money, the interest rate will not fall below
a certain level even when income is very low.

Algebraically, the *LM* function is derived as follows: The demand for

Figure 8-4 The LM Curve

transactions and speculative money balances is a function of both income and the interest rate:

$$M_D = lY - ji \qquad \text{for } i > i_0$$
$$M_D = \infty \qquad \text{for } i = i_0$$

Setting

$$M_D = M_S$$

the LM equation becomes[1]

$$lY - ji = M_S \qquad \text{for } i > i_0$$

$$Y = \frac{M_S}{l} + \frac{ji}{l} \qquad \text{for } i > i_0$$

[1] If $i = i_0$, the level of income is inconsequential, since the speculative demand for money is infinite and hence consistent with money market equilibrium regardless of the level of income.

The *LM* curve relates money income and the rate of interest and assumes a constant money supply.

The *LM* curve shows the rate of interest consistent with financial equilibrium at different income levels. Will these same rates of interest be consistent with national income equilibrium? National income equilibrium occurs when saving is equal to investment. This equilibrium can occur at any income level, depending on the level of investment and saving. If saving and/or investment are functions of the rate of interest, then different rates of interest should be consistent with different levels of investment and saving and, hence, of income. The relationship between the rate of interest and the equilibrium level of national income is called the *IS* curve. The *IS* curve is shown in Figure 8-5. The lower the rate of interest, the greater is the level of investment, and hence, the higher is the level of national income equilibrium consistent with that rate of interest. Consequently, the *IS* curve

Figure 8-5   The IS Curve

will be negatively sloped, reflecting the inverse relationship between the rate of interest and national income equilibrium.[2]

Algebraically, the IS curve is derived as follows. In the most general formulation, saving can be a function of both income and the rate of interest:

$$S = -a + sY + wi$$

Investment is also a function of income and the rate of interest:

$$I = dY + ti$$

In equilibrium, saving is equal to investment,

$$S = I$$

or

$$-a + sY + wi = dY + ti$$

Rearranging terms, the IS curve becomes

$$(s - d)Y = a + (t - w)i$$

$$Y = \frac{a}{s - d} + \frac{t - w}{s - d}i$$

Since saving should increase with the rate of interest,

$$w > 0$$

and investment declines with the interest rate,

$$t < 0$$

Assuming

$$0 < s - d < 1$$

that is, the marginal propensity to save exceeds the marginal propensity to invest, then

$$\frac{t - w}{s - d} < 0$$

---

[2]See Appendix A, pp. 377–80 for a more detailed discussion of the shape of the IS curve.

and the *IS* curve,

$$Y = \frac{a}{s-d} + \frac{t-w}{s-d} i$$

has a negative slope.

The rate of interest and the level of income cannot be in total equilibrium, unless both financial equilibrium (i.e., the clearing of the money market) and national income equilibrium are achieved simultaneously. If the demand for money exceeds the supply, for instance, the rate of interest will rise and national income will fall. If investment exceeds saving, the level of money income will rise and with it, the transactions demand for money and the interest rate. Only when

$$M_D = M_S$$

and

$$I = S$$

will both income and the interest rate be in equilibrium, with no tendency for either to change.

The rate of interest, i_E, and the money income level, Y_E, consistent with both financial and national income equilibrium can be found at the point of intersection of the *IS* and *LM* curves. This general equilibrium, shown in Figure 8-6, involves the simultaneous determination of the interest rate and the level of money income. In general equilibrium, the money market will be cleared, saving will equal investment, and there will be no tendency for income or the interest rate to change unless the equilibrium is disturbed, or *displaced,* by a shift in *IS* or *LM.*

8-3 Displacement of General Equilibrium

The equilibrium level of income and interest rate will be displaced (changed) by a shift of the *IS* or *LM* curve, or both. Policies designed to manipulate the level of income and employment involve a shift in one of the curves.

SHIFTS IN THE *LM* CURVE

Measures which affect money supply or demand will cause the *LM* curve to shift to the right. With more money available, a lower rate of interest will clear the money market for each income level. For a given *IS* curve,

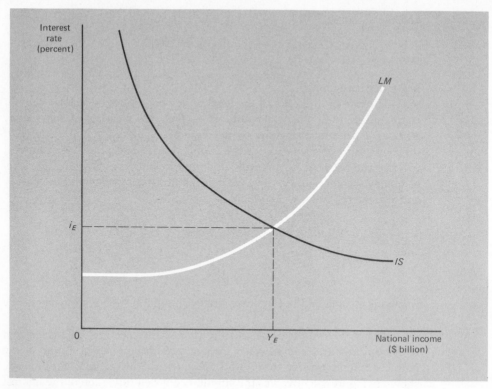

Figure 8-6   General Equilibrium of National Income

increases in the money supply will result in a lower interest rate and a higher level of money income, as shown in Figure 8-7. Suppose an increase in the money supply causes the LM curve to shift from LM_1 to LM_3. The interest rate will fall from i_1 to i_3, and the level of money income will rise from Y_1 to Y_3.

An increase in the demand for money which is due to factors other than changes in income and the interest rate will also cause the LM curve to shift.[3] Suppose the widespread introduction of a credit card system reduced the transactions demand for money. At each income level, the demand for money balances would fall and a lower rate of interest would be consistent with equilibrium. This would cause the LM curve to shift to the right, and for a given IS curve, the interest rate would fall and money

[3] Changes in money demand resulting from changes in income and interest rates are represented by *movements along* the LM curve.

income would rise as seen in Figure 8-7. Notice that the effect is the same
as if the money supply had increased.

Suppose a prolonged period of tight money caused speculators to alter
their expectations about future interest rates. If the structure of interest rates
were expected to be generally higher than before, the *LM* curve would shift
upward as shown in Figure 8-8. At any interest rate, the speculative demand
for money would increase, raising the interest rate and causing a decline
in the level of income. In Figure 8-8, the upward shift in the *LM* curve causes
the interest rate to rise from i_1 to i_2 and the level of income to fall from
Y_1 to Y_2. Notice that this same effect will occur during a price inflation if
speculators are not subject to money illusion concerning the interest rate.
Money interest rates may rise with no change in the speculative demand
for money provided that the real rate does not increase. If prices are rising,
for any given money rate of interest, the real rate will be lower and the
speculative demand for money will be greater.

Figure 8-7   Impact of Shifts in the LM Curve
                  on General Equilibrium

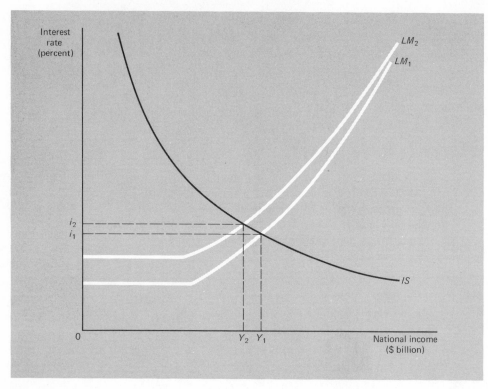

Figure 8-8   Impact of Changing Expectations About the Structure
of Interest Rates

SHIFTS IN THE *IS* CURVE

Events which affect national income equilibrium will cause shifts in the *IS* curve. Expansionary fiscal policy, by reducing the level of investment required to offset a specified level of saving, causes any national income equilibrium to be consistent with a lower rate of interest than before. This is represented by a rightward shift in the *IS* curve as shown in Figure 8-9. For a fixed *LM* curve, national income will rise and so will the rate of interest. Suppose an increase in government spending causes the *IS* curve to shift rightward from IS_1 to IS_2, as shown in Figure 8-9. Money income will rise from Y_1 to Y_2, and the interest rate will increase from i_1 to i_2.

The *IS* curve may also shift as aggregate demand changes, even if no policy changes are undertaken. Suppose, for instance, that business confidence is undermined by rumors of a cutback in government spending. Pessimistic expectations about future demand may cause the *MEC* to decline

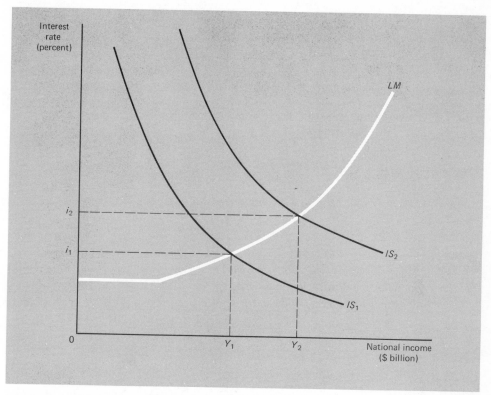

Figure 8-9   Impact of a Shift in the IS Curve
on General Equilibrium

for all levels of investment. The impact will be to reduce the level of investment associated with a given rate of interest, and the IS schedule will shift leftward. For a fixed LM curve, national income and the rate of interest will fall.

A GENERAL EQUILIBRIUM
MULTIPLIER ANALYSIS

Let us consider the algebra of equilibrium displacement. In Chapter 3, we saw that when equilibrium is displaced by an autonomous change in public spending, the ultimate impact on income and spending was greater than the initial change. This *multiplier effect* was derived from the national income equilibrium condition that saving equal investment.

Suppose saving and investment are both functions of income and the rate of interest. Algebraically,

$$S = -a + sY + wi$$
$$I = dY + ti$$

Government spending is set at some level, G_0.

In equilibrium,[4]

$$S = I + G$$

or

$$-a + sY + wi = dY + ti + G_0$$

$$Y = \frac{1}{s-d}[a + (t-w)i + G_0]$$

Since the interest rate is assumed to be determined independently by the monetary authorities, then when government spending increases, Δi is assumed to be zero, and

$$\frac{\Delta Y}{\Delta G} = \frac{1}{s-d}$$

Since

$$s = 1 - b$$

where s is the marginal propensity to save and b is the marginal propensity to consume,

$$\frac{\Delta Y}{\Delta G} = \frac{1}{1-b-d}$$

which is the same multiplier which we derived in Chapter 3.

The above analysis measures the impact of a displacement of equilibrium through a shift in the IS schedule with a given interest rate. The change in income from Y_1 to Y_2 is shown in Figure 8-10. Essentially, we have ignored the impact of the increase in income on the demand for money and, hence,

[4]Note that since

$$S = Y - C$$

this is equivalent to

$$Y = C + I + G$$

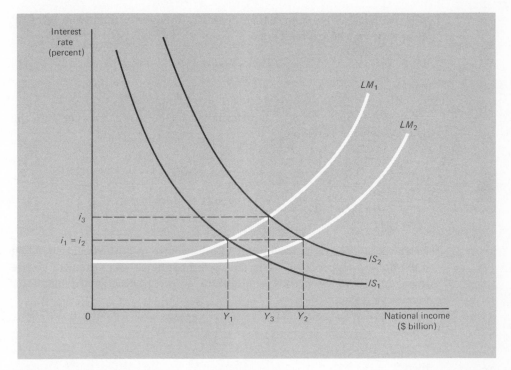

Figure 8-10 Shift in IS with Interest Rate Constant

on the interest rate. If the complete model were taken into account, that is, if the money market had been examined, our analysis would have predicted a smaller change in income, from Y_1 to Y_3, as the interest rate rises with income along the function LM_1 to i_3.

Suppose we drop the assumption that the interest rate is independent of the fiscal action (increase in government spending) and is determined in the money market. Assuming the demand for money is a function of income and the interest rate[5] and that the money supply is fixed,

$$M_D = lY - ji$$
$$M_S = M_0$$

then equilibrium in the money market occurs, where

$$M_D = M_S$$

or

$$lY - ji = M_0$$

---

[5] We have ignored the liquidity trap in this example.

Now we have an equation which expresses the rate of interest in terms of income. It can be expressed as

$$i = \frac{l}{j}Y - \frac{M_0}{j}$$

Substituting the value of i, as determined in the money market, into the national income equation,

$$Y = \left(\frac{1}{1 - b - d}\right)[(t - w)i + G_0]$$
$$= \left(\frac{1}{1 - b - d}\right)\left[\frac{(t - w)lY}{j} + \frac{(w - t)M_0}{j} + G_0\right]$$

we can now determine the impact of an increase in government spending if the money supply is held constant and the interest rate is allowed to rise to maintain money market equilibrium as the transactions demand for money increases.

Expressing the model in terms of changes and recalling that

$$\Delta M = 0$$

then

$$\Delta Y = \left(\frac{1}{1 - b - d}\right)\left[\frac{(t - w)l}{j}\Delta Y + \Delta G\right]$$

Letting

$$\mu = \frac{(t - w)l}{j}$$

then

$$\frac{\Delta Y}{\Delta G} = \frac{1}{1 - b - d - \mu}$$

Since the signs of w, l, and j are positive, while the sign of t is negative, then the sign of μ is clearly negative. Thus, when the impact of the change in income on the transactions demand for money and the interest rate is taken into account, the size of the multiplier is reduced. The parameter μ can be called the *monetary effect* of the change in demand.

If the government undertakes an expansionary fiscal policy without increasing the money supply, interest rates will rise, discouraging investment and reducing the expansionary impact of the fiscal operation. Since we have assumed no increase in taxes, the expenditure increase must have been financed by the issue of debt, which would of course have the effect of reducing bond prices and raising interest rates. Suppose, however, the fiscal operation were accompanied by an increase in the money supply just large enough to prevent the interest rate from rising. Such a program is shown graphically in Figure 8-10. If a shift in *IS* from IS_1 to IS_2 is accompanied by a shift in *LM* from LM_1 to LM_2, then income will rise from Y_1 to Y_2 as predicted by the simple multipler analysis in which the interest rate was assumed to be determined independently of the level of national income.

The simple multiplier analysis may be relevant to current policy planning if the monetary authorities view the rate of interest rather than the money supply as the primary policy instrument. Suppose, for example, it is determined to undertake expansionary fiscal policy and neutral monetary policy. If monetary authorities view the interest rate as the relevant policy instrument, they will increase the money supply as the expansion takes place to keep the interest rate at its previous level. If, on the other hand, the money supply is viewed as the appropriate policy instrument, the monetary authorities will not increase the money supply and will allow the rate of interest to rise. Although both types of behavior can be called neutral, the impact of the fiscal operation on national income will be greater if it is financed totally or in part by money creation rather than bond issue. Consequently, policy planners must be careful to specify what they mean by monetary neutrality before they can forecast the multiplier effect of a fiscal operation when monetary policy is neutral.

The question of whether the money supply or the interest rate should be the primary planning instrument for monetary policy has been a major source of controversy between Milton Friedman, a monetary theorist, and such neo-Keynesian economists as Walter Heller. Friedman, adhering to the quantity theory of money, argues that not only is the level of national income determined by the money supply, but also that the money supply should be the principal policy instrument for economic stabilization. Heller, on the other hand, views national income as essentially determined by aggregate demand and feels that monetary policy should essentially be effectuated by interest rate changes.[6] We shall consider Friedman's macroeconomic theory in more detail in Chapter 9.

8-4   The Impact
of Alternative
Economic Policies

MONETARY VERSUS FISCAL POLICY

As we have seen, any change in fiscal policy will have a monetary impact since changes in income produce changes in the demand for money. In

---

[6]Heller, like most neo-Keynesians, often questions the efficacy of monetary policy of any sort and would urge more reliance on tax and expenditure policy for controlling aggregate demand.

addition, changes in the money supply will affect income as changes in the rate of interest influence aggregate demand. In the preceding chapters we have suggested that the impact of monetary policy on demand is less reliable than the impact of fiscal policy. In particular, demand may be insensitive to changes in the money supply, especially in periods of recession.

Let us assume, for the moment, however, that monetary policy can be used effectively as a substitute for fiscal policy for purposes of economic stabilization. Suppose the policy maker desires to increase the level of income and employment as shown in Figure 8-11. Note that we have reversed the axes of the IS–LM diagram to make it comparable with the aggregate supply function. When the IS schedule is IS_1 and the LM schedule is LM_1, equilibrium is at Y_E with employment N_E and the rate of interest is i_E. Full employment is N_F, so the desired change in income is $Y_F - Y_E$.

The target level of income can be attained by either fiscal or monetary policy. However, while the impact on income will be the same, the effect on other variables in the system will be different. An increase in government

Figure 8-11 Use of Monetary and Fiscal Policy
to Close a Deflationary Gap

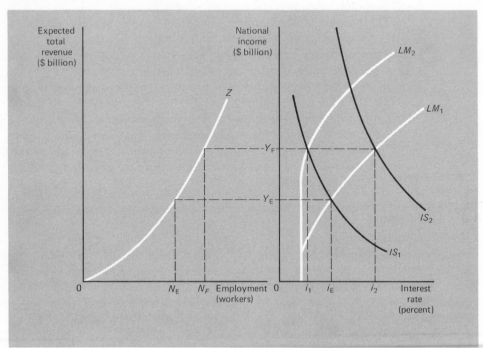

spending sufficient to shift IS to IS_2 will achieve the target income level. If there is no increase in the money supply, the interest rate will rise to i_2. If monetary policy is used, a shift in LM to LM_2 will also produce the desired change with no change in IS. In the absence of any change in fiscal policy, the interest rate will fall to i_1.

If fiscal policy alone is used to engineer an expansion, demand in the public sector will increase. Demand in those sectors sensitive to changes in the interest rate (investment and consumption) may also rise but not as much as if the interest rate had not increased. Any increase in consumption and investment will be due to the effect induced by the change in income, but the effect will be impeded by the rising interest rate.

Because the impact of an increase in public spending is smaller when the greater proportion is financed from taxes, the change in government spending required to close any deflationary gap will be greater if financed from taxes than if financed by a bond issue or money creation. Consider the ways in which a public spending increase can be financed as shown in Table 8-1.

Closing the deflationary gap by a "balanced budget" increase in spending increases public spending at the expense of both consumption and investment, depending on the incidence of the tax. A bond issue will only restrict consumption if the latter is affected by the rise in interest rates and will have the greatest impact on investment. If financed by money creation, the smallest increase in public spending will be required to close the gap since there will be no increase in interest rates, and consequently, consumption and investment will rise by the greatest amount.

Monetary policy used alone can also close a deflationary gap if aggregate demand is sufficiently elastic to changes in the money supply. As shown

Table 8-1 Methods of Financing an Increase in Government Spending to Close a Deflationary Gap

	Required Increase in Public Spending	Increase in Consumption	Increase in Investment	Increase in Interest Rate
Tax finance				
Personal income tax	largest	smallest	largest	intermediate
Corporate income tax	largest	intermediate*	smallest	intermediate
Bond issue	intermediate	intermediate	smallest	largest
Money creation	smallest	largest	largest	smallest

*If the tax causes a reduction in dividends and hence personal income.

in Figure 8-11, as LM shifts from LM_1 to LM_2, the rate of interest falls from i_E to i_1. Thus, the expansion in income is attributable to increases in investment and consumption with no increase in public spending.

If monetary and fiscal policy were combined so that the deflationary gap could be closed with no increase in interest rates, then the traditional multiplier analysis would apply. The change in income is due to an autonomous change in government spending with no initial (noninduced) changes in the other sectors. In Figure 8-12 the deflationary gap $Y_F - Y_E$ can be closed with no impact on the interest rate by an increase in IS from IS_1 to IS_2 coupled with an increase in the money supply which will shift the LM curve from LM_1 to LM_2.

We have seen that under the assumption that monetary policy can be used as effectively as fiscal policy to control aggregate demand, the policies will have different impacts on the distribution of spending among consumption, investment, and the public sector. Furthermore, the means by which a public expenditure change is financed will also affect the distribution of spending. Consequently, when deciding whether to use monetary

Figure 8-12 Closing a Deflationary Gap with no Change
in Interest Rate

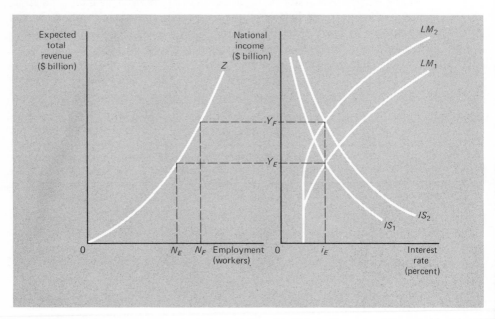

or fiscal policy for stabilization purposes, the planner must consider not only the efficiency or reliability of his policy instruments for controlling demand, but also their distributional impact on spending in the various sectors of the economy. In general, monetary policy relies more heavily for stabilization on changes in investment than does fiscal policy. Thus, a tight money policy is more likely to cause a cutback in investment spending than a personal income tax increase or a reduction in public spending. Of course, an increase in corporate income taxes can also precipitate a decline in investment expenditure.

EVALUATING MACROECONOMIC POLICY

Consider a simple macroeconomic model which takes into account conditions in the money market. Such a model can be used to design alternative programs for closing a deflationary gap. Assume the following relationships:

$$Y = C + I + G$$
$$C = 100 + 0.6Y$$
$$I = 0.2Y - 50i$$
$$M_D = 0.25Y - 30i$$
$$M_S = 65$$
$$G = 100$$

Substituting the consumption and investment functions into the national income identity, the *IS* curve is derived:

$$Y = C + I + G$$
$$Y = 200 + 0.8Y - 50i$$
$$0.2Y = 200 - 50i$$
$$Y = 1000 - 250i$$

The *LM* curve is found by setting money demand (M_D) equal to the money supply (M_S):

$$M_D = M_S$$
$$0.25Y - 30i = 65$$
$$Y = 260 + 120i$$

Solving the equations for the *IS* and LM curves simultaneously,

$$Y = 1000 - 250i$$
$$Y = 260 + 120i$$

the equilibrium level of income is found to be 500, and the interest rate is 2.

Suppose that the full-employment level of income is 600, so that the desired change in income is 100. If the money supply is held constant, what change in government spending will be required to close the deflationary gap?

Letting

$$Y = 600$$

allowing for a change in G, and substituting into our model, the IS curve becomes

$$600 = 200 + 0.8(600) - 50i + \Delta G$$
$$50i - 80 = \Delta G$$

and the LM curve is

$$600 = 260 + 120i$$
$$120i = 340$$
$$i = 2.83$$

Since the equilibrium rate of interest can be found from the LM curve when the equilibrium level of income is known, we can now determine the required change in G from IS:

$$\Delta G = 50(2.83) - 80$$
$$= 141.5 - 80$$
$$= 61.5$$

The required change in G could also have been found from the multiplier analysis of the preceding section. Recall that when M_s is assumed constant,

$$\frac{\Delta Y}{\Delta G} = \frac{1}{1 - b - d - \mu}$$

where μ is the "monetary effect" reflecting the impact of the increase in demand on the interest rate.

In our model

$$b = 0.6$$
$$d = 0.2$$

and

$$\mu = \frac{(t - w)l}{j}$$

$$t = -50$$
$$w = 0$$
$$l = 0.25$$
$$j = 30$$

so that

$$\mu = \frac{-50}{30}(0.25) = -0.415$$

Therefore,

$$\frac{\Delta Y}{\Delta G} = \frac{1}{1 - 0.6 - 0.2 + 0.415} = \frac{1}{0.615}$$

To induce a change in Y of 100,

$$\Delta G = 61.5$$

Suppose the monetary authorities decide to neutralize the impact of the fiscal operation on credit conditions and increase the money supply to hold the interest rate constant at 2 while income rises to 600. Letting M_s vary and substituting in the LM equation,

$$0.25(600) - 30(2) = 65 + \Delta M_s$$

or

$$\Delta M_s = 25$$

To find the required change in G, substitute in the IS equation:

$$600 = 200 + 0.8(600) - 50(2) + \Delta G$$

or

$$\Delta G = 20$$

Notice that

$$\frac{\Delta Y}{\Delta G} = 5$$

This result is the same as we would have obtained from the simple national income model which ignores the monetary effect. That multiplier gives

$$\frac{\Delta Y}{\Delta G} = \frac{1}{1 - b - d} = \frac{1}{1 - 0.6 - 0.2} = 5$$

Notice that in this case the change in the money supply required to neutralize the impact of the spending increase on the interest rate was greater than the spending increase itself. Thus, even if policy planners had financed the entire increase in government spending by money creation, the rate of interest would still have risen slightly, and the change in G required to close the deflationary gap would have been slightly larger.

Finally, suppose policy planners desired to achieve the target level of income using monetary policy only. From the IS curve, the required rate of interest can be found:

$$Y = 200 + 0.8Y - 50i$$
$$600 = 200 + 0.8(600) - 50i$$
$$50i = 80$$
$$i = 1.6$$

The change in M_S required to achieve this rate of interest when income is 600 can be found from the LM equation,

$$0.25Y - 30i = 65 + \Delta M_S$$
$$0.25(600) - 30(1.6) = 65 + \Delta M_S$$
$$\Delta M_S = 37$$

Notice that, in this particular model, the highest level of income which can be achieved using monetary policy alone is 750. Because the demand for money becomes infinite at an interest rate of 1, the interest rate cannot fall below this level no matter how great the increase in money supply. Consequently, from the IS curve,

$$0.2Y = 200 - 50$$
$$Y = 750$$

Now we are ready to evaluate the impact of the three policies used to effectuate an increase in income of 100 as shown in Table 8-2. Notice that the greater the change in the money supply, the smaller is the proportion of the total change in income attributable to government spending and the larger is the increase in investment. Since the change in consumption is always 60 and the change in income 100, then the change in investment plus government spending must be 40. Thus, the greater the change in government spending, the smaller is the change in investment.

In this section we assumed that monetary and fiscal policy are equally effective and reliable stabilizing instruments. However, much of the contro-versy about the use and design of macroeconomic policy centers around

Table 8-2 Impact of Alternative Policies
for Increasing Income by 100

Policy	Impact					
	ΔY	ΔG	Δi	ΔM_g	ΔI	ΔC
Government expenditure increase (money supply unchanged)	100	61.5	+0.83	0	−21.5	60
Government expenditure increase (interest rate unchanged)	100	20	0	25	+20	60
Money supply increase (government spending unchanged)	100	0	−0.4	37	+40	60

the effectiveness of the various policy instruments. The discussion involves different assumptions about behavior as well as the hypothetical elasticities or slopes of the IS and LM curves with respect to interest rates and changes in GNP.

To gain further insight into the appropriate monetary–fiscal policy mix, in Chapter 9 we shall examine some alternative models of national income equilibrium.

Questions for Study and Review

1. Refer to the model on p. 207 of the text:

(a) Construct a diagram to show the equilibrium level of income.

(b) What would be the effect of increasing M_g to 125?

(c) If the full-employment level of income is 800, can it be reached in this model by increasing the money supply alone? Explain.

(d) What would be the impact of a shift in the investment demand function so that

$$I = 0.2Y - 20i$$

2. How would the following events affect the equilibrium level of national income and the rate of interest:

(a) increasing the velocity of circulation,

(b) increasing corporate income taxes,

(c) increasing government spending financed by debt issue,

(d) open market purchasing by the Federal Reserve,

(e) increasing unemployment compensation financed from general tax revenues,

(f) increasing unemployment compensation financed by money creation?

3. Keynes criticized the classical economists for failing to recognize that the rate of interest is an important determinant of the level of income. Can a similar criticism be made of his model? Explain.

4. Show how the introduction of monetary considerations affect the multiplier analysis developed in Chapter 3.

5. Both the *IS* curve and the *LM* curve are derived from macroeconomic equilibrium relationships, yet neither presents a complete picture of macroeconomic equilibrium. Explain.

6. Assume that monetary policy can be used effectively as a substitute for fiscal policy for purposes of economic stabilization. Compare the effects of the two policies on consumption, saving, investment, and rate of growth.

Additional Reading

Hansen, Alvin H., *A Guide to Keynes*. Book 4. New York: McGraw-Hill Book Company, Inc., 1953, Chapters 7 and 9.

9

Some Models
of National Income
Determination

Having developed the complete Keynesian model of income determination, it is interesting to view it in the perspective of some alternative models. *The General Theory* was conceived by Keynes as a refutation of what he called classical economics. This was essentially the analysis described by A. C. Pigou in his *Theory of Unemployment*. Following the publication of *The General Theory*, the Keynesian model was the subject of a lively and critical debate among the economists of the so-called classical tradition. In this chapter we shall examine the classical model and its similarities to and differences from the Keynesian model.

A more recent attack on Keynesian economics has come from a group of economists who believe that the quantity of money, rather than aggregate demand, is the essential determinant of national income. The spokesman for this group, Milton Friedman, has had a particularly important influence on economic policy during the Nixon Administration. In examining the Friedman model and its relation to the Keynesian analysis, particular emphasis will be placed on the implications for economic policy.

9-1 Keynes and the Classics

Following the publication of *The General Theory* and after a reasonable time had been allowed for it to be absorbed and understood by the scholars of economics, it became fashionable to remark that Keynes had not said anything new, that all the Keynesian results could have been derived from the classical analysis of Pigou. No one felt this more strongly than Pigou himself, who argued that Keynes had introduced a new twist in his "liquidity trap," but that essentially the analysis was the same as his own.

In analyzing the relationship between the classical and Keynesian models, it is important to bear in mind that not only the equilibrium, but also the means by which the equilibrium is reached is important. The classical analysis begins with the assumption of full employment, based on Say's Law. It then proceeds to examine the relationship between the macroeconomic variables in this full-employment equilibrium. The Keynesian approach, on the other hand, presumes that the level of employment is determined by aggregate demand. If it can be shown that full employment will be achieved automatically (i.e., without government intervention) within the framework of a Keynesian system, one might conclude that this system is equivalent to the classical model. It is true that, in this case, the equilibrium is the same for the two models, but the sequence in which the variables adjust to equilibrium is different. Because of the differences in the adjustment process, the policy implications for a disequilibrium situation are different for the two models.

THE CLASSICAL MODEL

In the classical model, attention is focused on the labor market for determining the "real" variables in the system.[1] Assuming that the real wage will always adjust to clear the labor market, real wages and employment are simultaneously determined there.

To maximize profits, firms will hire workers until the contribution of the last worker to total revenue, his marginal value product, is just equal to the money wage, or

$$p \times MP = w$$

Equivalently, firms will hire workers until the marginal productivity of labor is equal to the real wage (the money wage divided by the product price), or

$$\frac{w}{p} = MP$$

If labor supply is also a function of the real wage, then both the demand for and supply of labor depends on the real wage. In such a market both the level of employment and real wages are simultaneously determined. Algebraically,

$$\frac{w}{p} = MP = f'(N_D) \qquad \text{demand for labor}$$

$$\frac{w}{p} = g(N_S) \qquad\qquad \text{supply of labor}$$

$$N_D = N_S \qquad\qquad\quad \text{equilibrium condition}$$

In this three-equation model, the three variables w/p, N_S, and N_D can be determined.

The determination of employment and output in a classical model is shown graphically in Figure 9-1. In Figure 9-1(A), the level of employment and the real wage is determined in the labor market by the equilibrium between labor supply and demand. Once the level of employment is de-

---

[1] Since the classical model was always elaborated in real terms, we shall compare it with a Keynesian model developed in real terms. Alternatively, the classical model can also be developed in money terms and compared with a Keynesian model with the variables in money units. The comparison produces the same similarities and differences, regardless of how the variables are expressed. Since the analysis presented here is for comparative purposes only and not for forecasting, it is legitimate to work with the real relationships of the models.

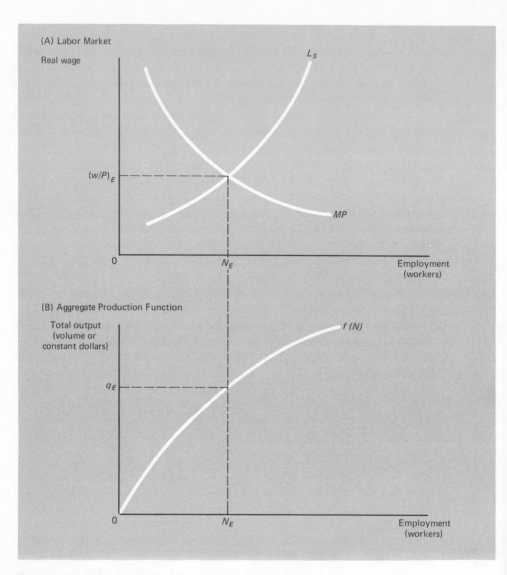

Figure 9-1   Determination of Aggregate Output
in a Classical Model

termined in the labor market, aggregate output (or real income) can be found from the production function in Figure 9-1(B).

In the classical analysis, this simple model completely describes the determination of real GNP. The level of prices and interest rates can be found by looking at monetary and financial relationships, but these do not enter into the determination of real income and employment.

The quantity theory of money is used to explain price level changes. Given the money supply, the level of money GNP or national income can be found. The quantity theory states that the money value of all transactions must exactly equal the total quantity of money in circulation multiplied by the number of times the money changes hands, or the *velocity of circulation*. Algebraically,

$$MV = pT$$

where

$$M = \text{money supply}$$
$$V = \text{velocity of circulation}$$
$$P = \text{price level}$$
$$T = \text{total transactions}$$

Assuming that transactions are proportional to real income, y,

$$T = \lambda y$$

then

$$MV = p\lambda y$$

or

$$M = KY$$

where

$$K = \frac{\lambda}{V}$$

and

$$Y = py$$

where Y is money income.

Quantity theorists assume K to be independent of changes in any of the macroeconomic variables. Since real income, y, is determined by the level of employment, then changes in the money supply, M, must result in proportional changes in the price level. While monetary policy may be useful in controlling prices, it has no impact on real GNP. Note that real GNP is also unaffected by price level changes, since it is determined by conditions in the labor market.

The rate of interest, as well as the distribution of real GNP between consumption and investment, is determined in the bond market. Investment, or the supply of bonds, is a function of the interest rate. Recalling that interest rates move inversely with bond prices, the supply of bonds increases as interest rates fall (bond prices rise) as shown in Figure 9-2. Saving, or

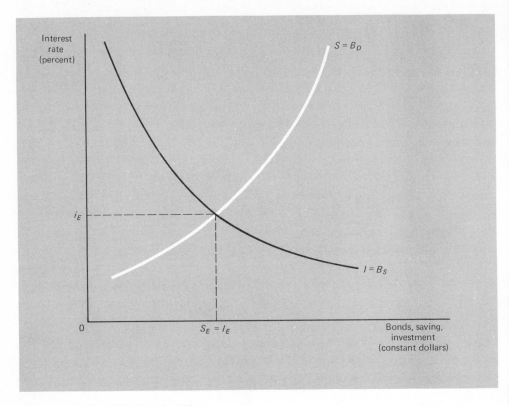

Figure 9-2   Bond Market Equilibrium
in a Classical Model

the demand for bonds, rises with the interest rate (falls with the bond price). Equilibrium in the bond market determines not only the rate of interest, but also the levels of saving and investment, which are always brought into equality in this market.[2] Algebraically,

$$S = S(i) \qquad \text{saving function}$$
$$I = e(i) \qquad \text{investment demand function}$$
$$S = I \qquad \text{equilibrium condition}$$

These three equations are sufficient to find the three unknowns, S, I, and i. Notice that since

$$Y = C + S$$

[2]This theory of interest is analyzed critically and in more detail in Chapter 7.

the equilibrium level of consumption is also determined in this market, given the level of national income.

Since the level of employment and real income are determined in the labor market, the rate of interest, saving, investment, and consumption do not have any impact at all on these variables. While the bond market may be of interest to students of finance, it has nothing to do with the analysis of income determination in the short run. Since it does determine the level of investment, however, the interest rate will affect the rate of growth and hence labor productivity, real wages, and output in the long run.

To summarize, the classical model may be represented algebraically in seven equations:

$$\left.\begin{array}{l} \dfrac{w}{p} = MP = f'(N) \\[2mm] \dfrac{w}{p} = g(N) \end{array}\right\} \quad \begin{array}{l}\text{labor market}\\ \text{equilibrium}\end{array}$$

$$\left.\begin{array}{l} y = q(N) \\ Y = KM \end{array}\right\} \quad \begin{array}{l}\text{real income}\\ \text{money income}\end{array}$$

$$\left.\begin{array}{l} S = S(i) \\ I = e(i) \\ S = I \end{array}\right\} \quad \begin{array}{l}\text{bond market}\\ \text{equilibrium}\end{array}$$

Seven variables can be determined: real wages, employment, real income, money income, saving, investment, and the rate of interest. Given the identities,

$$py \equiv Y$$

and

$$Y - S \equiv C$$

the price level and consumption can also be found.

THE KEYNESIAN
AND CLASSICAL MODELS COMPARED

The Keynesian model has been described in detail in Chapter 8. Table 9-1 provides a brief summary and comparison of the way in which the various macroeconomic variables and relationships are explained in the two models.

In the classical model, full employment was assured by the adjustment of wages which would clear the labor market. Since both the demand for and supply of labor are determined by the real wage, the condition for

Table 9-1 The Classical and Keynesian Models Compared

Macroeconomic Variable or Relationship	Determination in a Classical Model	Determination in a Keynesian Model
Employment	labor market	aggregate demand
Real income or output	employment	employment
Money income	employment/money supply	aggregate demand
Prices	money supply	aggregate demand/money wage
Interest rate	bond market	money market
Saving/consumption	interest rate	income
Investment	interest rate	interest rate
$S = I$ (equilibrium)	bond market/interest rate	national income
Real wages	labor market	level of output
Best way to stimulate employment	reduce wages	increase aggregate demand

achievement of full employment (labor market equilibrium) is that real wages must be flexible in the downward direction when labor is in excess supply. Thus, in this model, attention is focused on the labor market and, in particular, wages. Policies designed to maintain full employment were essentially aimed at promoting competitive conditions in the labor market and at convincing labor that the only way full employment could be attained in a recession was for labor to accept lower wages.

The level of output was simply a function of employment. Changes in the money supply would not affect employment or real output but only the level of prices. Investment, consumption, and the real rate of interest were determined independently in the bond market. While the level of investment affected the rate of growth and, hence, the future relationship between output and employment, conditions in the bond market had no effect on employment and output in the short run.

Keynes argued that full employment was not assured by the wage-adjustment process, and that, on the contrary, employment was determined by aggregate demand rather than the reverse. He argued that negotiations between labor and management are not generally based on *real* wages, but on money wages. Real wages are determined by the marginal productivity of labor which in turn depends upon the level of employment.

Consider a period in which demand is falling, due, let us presume, to a reduction in public spending. Firms begin to lay off workers and labor in turn agrees to work for lower wages. The reaction to this by firms may be to reduce product prices, to increase sales, and conceivably, the real wage may rise. Keynes observed that

> . . . I think, that the change in real wages associated with a change in money-wages, so far from being usually in the same direction [as the classical economists assumed], is almost always in the opposite direction when money-wages are rising, that is to say, it will be found that real wages are falling; and when money wages are falling, real wages will be rising. This is because, in the short period, falling money-wages and rising real wages are each, for independent reasons, likely to accompany decreasing employment; labor being readier to accept wage-cuts when employment is falling off, yet real wages inevitably rising in the same circumstances on account of the increasing marginal return to a given capital equipment when output is diminished.[3]

Since wage bargains affect money wages rather than real wages, there is no assurance that labor–management negotiations can assure labor market equilibrium (full employment). Consider the underemployment equilibrium shown in Figure 9-3. Suppose real wages are $(w/p)'$, employment is at A, and AB workers are unemployed. Since the real wage is determined by marginal productivity, the impact of a money wage cut will simply be a corresponding reduction in prices, with no change in the real wage and no change in the level of employment.

The only way real wages can be reduced is for the level of employment to increase, thereby reducing marginal labor productivity. Note that the sequence in which events occur is crucial. In the classical model, real wage cuts must precede increases in the level of employment, while Keynes argued that employment must increase before real wages can fall. The only way in which the level of employment can be expected to increase, in the Keynesian view, is for aggregate demand to increase. Only then will firms find it profitable to hire more workers, and only then will marginal labor productivity and real wages fall.

Since real wages, not money wages, must fall to assure labor market equilibrium, money wage cuts are neither necessary nor sufficient for full

[3]J. M. Keynes, *The General Theory of Employment, Interest, and Money* (New York: Harcourt Brace Jovanovich, Inc., 1965), p. 10. Published originally by Macmillan & Co., Ltd., 1936.

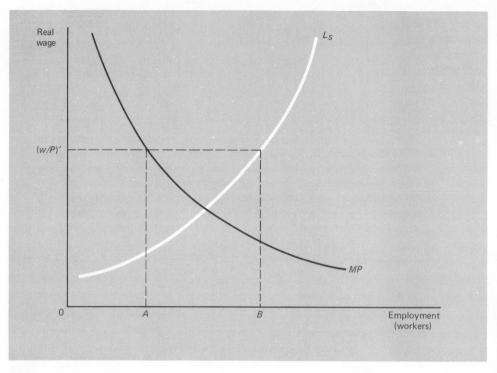

Figure 9-3 An Underemployment Equilibrium

employment. The only way full employment can be attained is for aggregate demand to increase to the level required to induce firms to employ all those who wish to work. In the process, real wages will fall, whether money wages have declined or not.

EQUILIBRIUM ANALYSIS
OF THE KEYNESIAN AND CLASSICAL MODELS

Classical rebuttal to *The General Theory* was essentially based on two arguments:

1. Money wage reductions will eventually cause real wages to fall and produce full employment, although the adjustment process may be different from that originally hypothesized in classical theory.
2. Downward rigidity of money wages is a principal cause of labor market disequilibrium.

A graphical presentation of the relationship between the Keynesian national income equilibrium and the classical labor market is shown in Figure 9-4. Here the Keynesian model is described in real terms. The *IS* curve shows the level of real income for which real saving and real investment are equated at different real rates of interest. The *LM* curve shows

Figure 9-4   Equilibrium Analysis of the Keynesian and the Classical Model

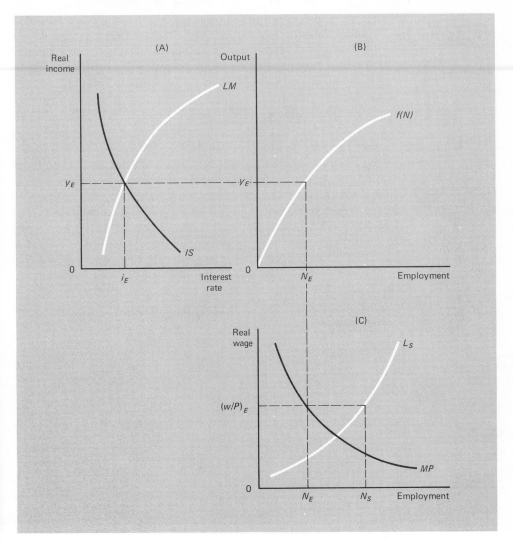

the real rates of interest for which the demand for real money balances is equal to the real value of the money supply for different levels of real income.[4]

Aggregate demand is in equilibrium in Figure 9-4(A) where the IS and LM curves intersect.[5] The demand for labor, N_E, is then found from the production function in Figure 9-4(B). The marginal productivity schedule, derived from the production function,[6] together with the labor supply function determine labor market conditions in Figure 9-4(C).

The equilibrium level of employment, N_E, represents an underemployment situation. When employment is N_E, the real wage is $(w/p)_E$. At that wage the labor supply is N_S and $(N_S - N_E)$ workers are unemployed. Suppose workers agree to accept cuts in money wages. Can full employment be achieved in this manner without any autonomous increases in aggregate demand? If so, the classical position would presumably be vindicated.

If the real wage, w/p, is determined by the level of employment, N_E, then the initial impact of a decline in money wages, w, will be a reduction in prices. If the money supply is fixed, a fall in prices will cause the LM curve to shift upward,[7] as shown in Figure 9-5. The price reduction causes an increase in the real value of the money supply and a decline in the interest rate.[8] Aggregate demand increases, inducing an increase in the level of employment and a reduction in the real wage. The process continues as the money wage is bid down until full employment is attained.

Viewed in a Keynesian framework, the impact of money wage cuts is exactly as described by the classical model. Money wage reductions cause real wages to decline and the level of employment to increase. Notice that if workers resist money wage cuts in the underemployment situation depicted in Figure 9-4, full employment will only be attainable by fiscal policy, which causes IS to shift rightward, or increases in the money supply, causing LM to shift upward.

[4]Notice that by abstracting from price level changes for the LM relationship we implicitly assume that speculators are not subject to money illusion with respect to the interest rate and, therefore, that the real interest rate at which the liquidity trap occurs is independent of price level changes. In the analysis using money-valued variables, we assumed that speculators are subject to money illusion with respect to the interest rate, and therefore that the money interest rate at which the liquidity trap occurs is independent of price level changes.

These assumptions can be relaxed in either case by allowing the LM curve to shift perpendicular to the interest rate axis in response to price level changes.

[5]Note that the axes measuring income and the interest rate are inverted from the traditional position.

[6]Marginal productivity for any level of employment is the slope of the production function (total productivity function) there.

[7]Note that the upward shift is equivalent to a rightward shift if the income and interest rate axes had not been inverted.

[8]The effect is the same as if the money demand for money declined in a money value model. This will occur as money wages and money income fall.

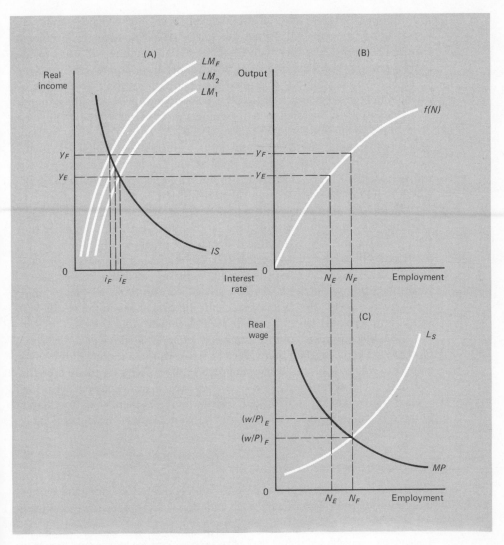

Figure 9-5   Impact of Money Wage Cuts on
National Income Equilibrium

The mechanism by which money wage cuts can stimulate employment
is by the impact of falling prices on money market equilibrium. As prices
fall, the real value of the money supply increases, causing the interest rate
to fall. Thus, money wage cuts can be no more effective than expansionary
monetary policy as a mechanism for stimulating employment.

Suppose interest rates fall to the level at which speculators uniformly expect bond prices to fall. When this happens, all increases in the money supply will be held as speculative balances (since no one will want to buy bonds) and the economy will be in a "liquidity trap." Increases in the real value of the money supply associated with falling prices will have no impact on the rate of interest and, hence, will have no impact on aggregate demand.[9]

In Figure 9-6, national income equilibrium is shown by the intersection of IS and LM in the vertical portion of the LM curve. As prices fall and LM shifts upward, the equilibrium level of income is unaffected. In this case, wage cuts will not affect the level of employment. The only route to full employment in this situation is to undertake expansionary fiscal policy which will shift the IS curve upward to the right.

Pigou, in rebutting the Keynesian position that wage cuts will not necessarily produce full employment, argued that, even in a liquidity trap, falling wages and the concomitant decline in prices would stimulate employment. He argued that as prices fell, the real value of assets with fixed-money value held by creditors would increase, causing creditors to feel wealthier and to increase their level of consumption.[10] Thus, falling prices would cause the IS curve to shift rightward (as autonomous consumption increases), and income and employment would rise.

Many economists doubt that a price deflation would ever result in this *Pigou effect*. Keynes argued that workers are subject to a money illusion with respect to wages. If money wages and prices fall, workers are likely to reduce consumption, because a decline in money wages makes them feel poorer even if real wages are unchanged. Furthermore, as mentioned in Chapter 5, there is no empirical evidence that the value of asset holdings is a significant determinant of consumption spending.[11]

EVALUATION OF THE CONTROVERSY

We have seen that if wages and prices are completely flexible and if there is no liquidity trap, then money wage deflation will theoretically be sufficient

[9] If speculators are subject to a money illusion concerning the interest rate, a price deflation should result in a rightward shift of the LM curve (away from the income axis), causing the liquidity trap to occur at a higher real rate of interest. This is because, as prices fall, the real rate of interest corresponding to a given money rate rises. In this case a price deflation will cause speculators to sell bonds and hold more money balances at each real rate of interest, and consequently, the impact of the deflation may be to raise real interest rates and actually reduce the level of aggregate demand.

[10] Note that by this reasoning, debtors should feel poorer and their consumption should decline. Pigou argued, however, that since government is a net debtor, the private sector is a net creditor, so that the net effect of falling prices on private wealth and consumption is positive.

[11] See, for instance, Thomas Mayer, "The Empirical Significance of the Real Balance Effect," *Quarterly Journal of Economics*, LXXIII (May, 1959), 275–291.

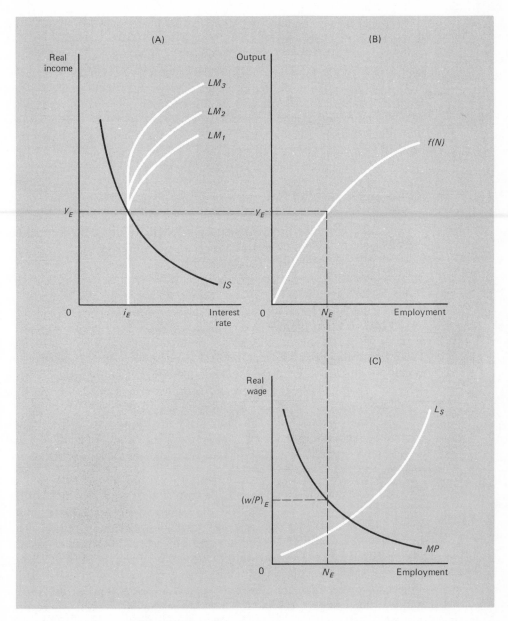

Figure 9-6 Impact of Money Wage Cuts
in the Liquidity Trap

to produce full employment. Money wages and real wages will move together to clear the labor market. A Keynesian underemployment equilibrium will result only if (1) workers refuse to accept money wage cuts, or (2) the economy is in the liquidity trap and the Pigou effect is inoperative.

The Keynesian position in the controversy is that the Pigovian rebuttal ignores the institutional realities of the situation. In general, there is a significant amount of money illusion in all sectors of the economy, so that individuals' actions depend more upon the money value of variables than on their real values.

Keynes believed that workers would resist money wage cuts, even in the face of high rates of unemployment. Moreover, he argued that even if they would accept wage cuts, the mechanism by which employment would be stimulated in a classical system is through the monetary effect on the interest rate.[12] Presumably the same purpose could be served by maintaining the old level of money wages and increasing the money supply. Keynes noted that classical analysis associated increases in the money supply with inflation, but that, in an underemployment situation, inflation from this source is unlikely. If it did occur, however, it would be a tolerable price to pay for the increase in the level of employment. Furthermore, if speculators are subject to a money illusion with respect to the interest rate, price inflation will cause the liquidity trap to occur at a lower real rate of interest. Thus, if the price inflation is accompanied by appropriate increases in the money supply, real interest rates will fall, thereby stimulating real aggregate demand and employment even when the economy had previously been in a liquidity trap.

In view of the conclusion that, from the viewpoint of the macroeconomy, wage deflation serves exactly the same function as an increase in the money supply, Keynes criticized wage deflation as an antirecession weapon on three counts:

1. Increasing the money supply is preferred to wage deflation. In the absence of money illusion, both have the same initial impact on conditions in the money market. Wage and price deflation, however, must have a depressing effect on both consumption and investment demand which will tend to shift the IS curve downward to the left, reducing the level of income and employment. Falling wages inhibit consumption when households are subject to money illusion. Furthermore, falling prices tend to reduce the marginal efficiency of capital for investment. Since investment requires incurring costs now for the prospect of future returns, in a deflationary economy firms invest when costs are relatively high and sell after prices have fallen.

Since an increase in the money supply will have the same impact on

---

[12]This effect is often called the *Keynes effect*.

the interest rate without the depressing effects of a deflation, it is a better antirecession weapon than money wage cuts.

2. Ignoring the depressing impact on the IS curve, wage–price deflation can be no more effective than an increase in the money supply for stimulating employment. In a recession, Keynes doubted that monetary policy would effectively stimulate demand. If interest rates are already low, speculators may hold all increments to the money supply in the form of idle balances in the expectation that bond prices will fall. If they do not enter the bond market, bond prices cannot rise and interest rates will not fall. This is the liquidity trap situation depicted in Figure 9-6. Furthermore, even if the interest rate can be reduced by increasing the money supply, it may have little effect on aggregate demand. As we saw in Chapter 6, investment tends to be interest-inelastic in periods of recession.

3. It is likely that speculators will be subject to some money illusion with respect to the interest rate; that is, their expectations concerning the future course of interest rates may depend upon the prevailing money rate of interest rather than the real rate. This being the case, during a deflation money rates are below real rates of interest, and the liquidity preference function is likely to flatten out at a higher real rate of interest than when prices are stable. If prices are rising, the liquidity preference function will flatten out at lower real rates of interest. Thus, other things being equal, if speculators are subject to a money illusion, it will be easier for the monetary authorities to effectuate a reduction in the real rate of interest during a period of stable or rising prices than during a price deflation.

IMPLICATIONS
FOR ECONOMIC POLICY

While the Keynesian model, given certain assumptions, can be made to produce so-called "classical results" (i.e., full-employment equilibrium in the absence of government intervention), the policy implications of the two approaches are quite different. Both are concerned with the question of how to remedy a situation of massive and persistent unemployment.

The classical analysis suggests that the appropriate remedy is wage deflation. Keynes argued that such a policy would reduce unemployment only in the very long run. Since an increase in the money supply will produce the same effect more quickly and less painfully, it is a preferable remedy for unemployment.

But the Keynesian model actually represented a radical new approach to macroeconomic policy in shifting attention from the labor market and wage rates to the level of aggregate demand. Since employment is determined by aggregate demand, Keynes argued, then the most effective remedy for unemployment is that which most effectively raises the level of aggregate demand. He ranked deficit spending, tax cuts, and expansionary monetary policy in that order. Deficit spending was by far, Keynes believed, the most effective way of stimulating demand and employment in a hurry. While other measures were theoretically effective, given adequate time for the appropriate adjustments to occur, the impact on employment must eventually come from demand, and consequently, the choice between them should depend on speed and efficiency and not on the necessity to vindicate traditional theories and ideologies.

9-2 Monetary Versus Fiscal Policy: A Post-Keynesian Debate

Keynes' economics represented an attack on the classical model of income determination and the macroeconomic policies which it espoused. In recent years, a fresh attack on Keynesian macroeconomic theory and policy has come from the monetarist school, led by Milton Friedman. While Friedman recognizes the essential Keynesian link between employment and aggregate demand, he argues that aggregate demand is itself determined by the quantity of money in circulation. Thus, an increase in government spending matched by an equal increase in taxes will have no impact on aggregate demand.[13] As a result of this analysis, Friedman concludes that the best policy measure for stimulating employment is increasing the money supply.

The economic policy implied by Friedman's model has been the subject of considerable debate in recent years. The Nixon administration, relying heavily on monetary policy for economic stabilization, was greatly influenced by Friedman's ideas.

THE FRIEDMAN MODEL

Friedman's model of income determination is based on the quantity theory of money. In the classical model the quantity of money determined the absolute level of prices through the relationship

$$MV = pT$$

where

$$M = \text{money supply}$$
$$V = \text{velocity of circulation}$$
$$p = \text{prices}$$
$$T = \text{transactions}$$

[13] In the Keynesian view, of course, the effect of a "balanced budget" increase in spending is expansionary. See Chapter 4.

Assuming that transactions are proportional to real income, that is,

$$T = \lambda y$$

the relationship becomes

$$MV' = py$$

where $V' = V/\lambda$ is called the income velocity of circulation.

The relationship

$$MV' = py$$

is an identity, because the money value of all transactions in the economy must exactly equal the amount of money that changes hands. A quantity theory of money, however, for it to be more than a tautology, must be based on an assumption that some of the variables in the relationship remain stable while others are varied.

In the classical model, it was assumed that both velocity, V', and real income, y, remain fixed when the quantity of money varies. Velocity is determined by institutional factors such as the availability of alternative means of exchange (credit cards, barter relationships, etc.) and length of the pay period. Real income is determined by the level of employment. Thus, the sole effect of a change in the money supply is a proportional change in the level of prices:

$$\Delta M = \left(\frac{1}{V'}y\right)\Delta p$$

The modern quantity theory recognizes that the level of income is also a variable. In Friedman's view, however, the income velocity of circulation is a stable relationship, essentially unaffected by changes in the money supply. Thus, changes in the money supply must produce proportional changes in money income, or

$$\Delta M = \frac{1}{V'}\Delta Y$$

where $Y = py = $ total money income. If V' is stable with respect to changes in all macroeconomic policy instruments—government spending, taxes, interest rates, and money supply—then the only way in which aggregate demand can be increased is for the money supply to increase also.

Notice that the quantity theory relationship

$$M = \left(\frac{1}{V'}\right)Y = KY$$

where

$$K = \frac{1}{V'}$$

is a theory of the demand for money. If V' is presumed to be independent of all macroeconomic policy instruments, this is true of K as well. The demand for money balances, therefore, is independent of the interest rate and depends only on the level of income.

A graphical view of the neoquantity theory model is shown in Figure 9-7. Suppose the economy is in an underemployment equilibrium at N_E. Full employment, N_F, can be attained by increasing the money supply to M_F. Note that in this model, full employment can also be achieved by a policy of wage and price deflation with no change in the money supply, since presumably the velocity of circulation will increase (the demand for money would decrease) as the price level falls. However, since the impact of the wage deflation is the same as an increase in the money supply, the latter policy is presumably a quicker and less painful way out of a recession.

Because the validity of his theory is based on the assumption that velocity is stable, Friedman has undertaken extensive empirical studies of the validity of his position.[14] He has found, for instance, that in the period 1929–1933, U.S. monetary authorities actually reduced the money supply by one-third. "The Great Contraction," Friedman has observed, "is tragic testimony to the power of money—not as Keynes and so many of his contemporaries believed, evidence of its unimportance."[15]

Furthermore, Friedman's studies have shown that the velocity of circulation for the United States has been considerably more stable than the multiplier relationship on which the Keynesian model is based. He even goes so far as to suggest that "most of the evidence was consistent with the view that the multiplier is useless for predictive purposes except as a disguised reflection of monetary change."[16]

Although Friedman's empirical work has been strongly criticized by some economists on methodological grounds, it has convinced others that

[14]See, for example, Milton Friedman and David Meiselman, "The Relative Stability of Monetary Velocity and the Investment Multiplier in the United States, 1897–1958," in *Stabilization Policies*, Committee on Money and Credit (Englewood Cliffs, N.J.: Prentice-Hall, Inc., 1963).
[15]Milton Friedman, *Dollars and Deficits* (Englewood Cliffs, N.J.: Prentice-Hall, Inc., 1968), p. 14.
[16]*Ibid.*

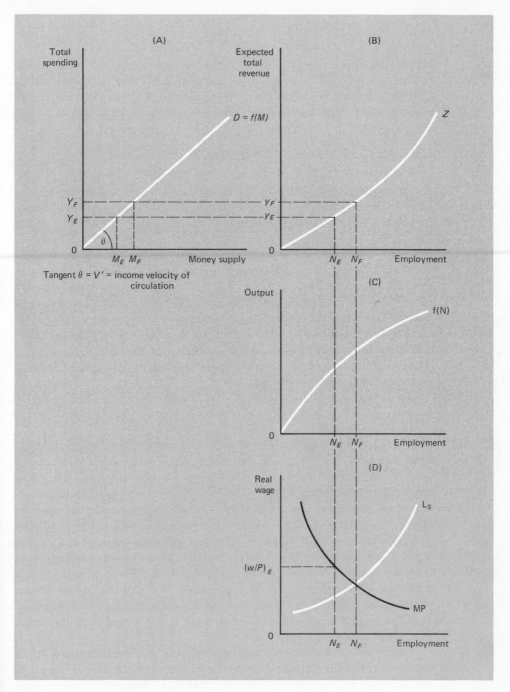

Figure 9-7 A Monetary Model
of National Income Equilibrium

his position concerning the importance of money indeed has merit. While Friedman may at times be guilty of overstating his case, most economists agree that monetary policy cannot be ignored. Even a modern Keynesian recognizes the importance of the monetary effects of fiscal operations.

KEYNESIAN AND FRIEDMAN'S MODEL COMPARED

"In one sense," Milton Friedman once remarked, "we are all Keynesians now; in another, no one is a Keynesian any longer. We all use the Keynesian language and apparatus; none of us any longer accepts the initial Keynesian conclusions."[17]

The Friedman model incorporates the Keynesian notion that the sequence of adjustment is from aggregate demand to employment rather than the other way around, as the classical model presumed. Both models concentrate on the factors which influence demand rather than on wages and the labor market for the design of policies to stimulate employment.

For both Keynes and Friedman, the relation between aggregate demand and its essential determinants can be expressed as an identity. For Keynes, demand is the sum of its components—consumption, investment, government spending, and net exports:

$$D \equiv C + I + G + X$$

If the relationship between demand in the private sector and income is stable with respect to changes in demand in the public sector, then a link can be established between the policy instruments (fiscal policy) and the policy target (aggregate demand). The relationship between demand in the private sector and income is represented by the marginal propensity to consume and the marginal propensity to invest. If these are stable, then the multiplier (the link between fiscal policy instruments and aggregate demand) is also stable. Friedman argues that if the multiplier does not remain constant when taxes are reduced or public spending is increased, then fiscal policy is not a reliable macroeconomic policy instrument. Not only might the desired effect not be achieved, but if the multiplier is subject to unknown lags (e.g., as in the case of consumer reaction to a tax cut), the impact of the policy may occur at some inopportune time.

Suppose, for instance, taxes are reduced to stimulate demand. If consumers view the increase in their take-home pay as transitory rather than permanent (a possibility consistent with Friedman's *permanent income hypothesis*

---

[17]*Ibid.*, p. 15.

concerning consumption), consumption spending may not rise as much as a Keynesian model would predict. In the absence of an increase in consumption, public authorities may decide to increase government spending to close the deflationary gap. If the policy is successful, full employment may be achieved. Now suppose consumers begin to react to the tax cut and consumption spending rises. The effect will be inflationary and will involve taking measures to reduce demand. Friedman argues that the marginal propensities to consume and invest are subject to such unreliable lags that fiscal policy is apt to be destabilizing and necessitate repeated on-again-off-again measures which constantly overshoot the mark.

The Friedman model views aggregate demand as identically related to the money supply and the velocity of circulation:

$$Y \equiv MV'$$

This can also be expressed as a money demand identity,

$$M \equiv KY$$

where

$$K = \frac{1}{V'}$$

If the demand for money is stable with respect to changes in the money supply, then changes in the money supply must necessarily produce changes in aggregate demand.

Keynes argued that the demand for money is a function of the rate of interest which, in turn, depends upon the money supply. Furthermore, in a recession, the money demand schedule tends to be most elastic with respect to the interest rate. In the liquidity trap, for instance, increases in the money supply are all held as idle balances so that changes in money supply have no impact whatsoever on aggregate demand.

The dispute between the followers of Keynes and Friedman boils down to the question of which is the more reliable: the relation between private demand and income or the demand for money. Keynes' position was based on *a priori*, or deductive, reasoning. Friedman, on the other hand, has provided empirical studies which, he claims, support his view. Unfortunately, Friedman's critics base their rebuttal more on logic and rhetoric than on cold data.

Figure 9-8 shows the impact of a change in demand on GNP under alternative assumptions about the relationship between the interest rate and the demand for money. Notice that the more elastic the demand for money with respect to the interest rate, the greater is the increase in GNP associated

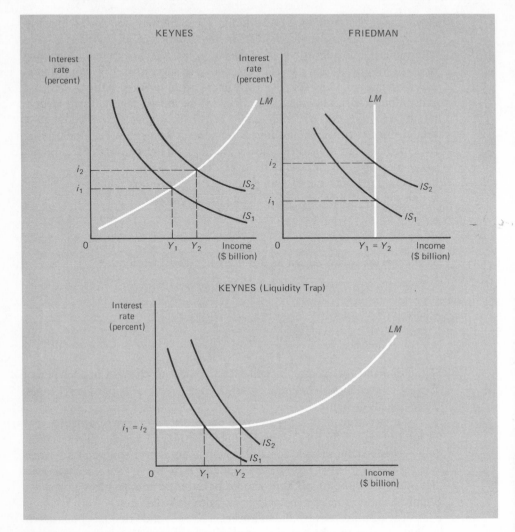

Figure 9-8 Impact of a Change in Demand
on GNP

with a given shift in the *IS* curve. For Friedman, the demand for money
is independent of the interest rate, so that the *LM* curve is completely
inelastic. In this case, changes in demand represented by shifts in *IS* have
no impact on GNP, despite the fact that they cause the interest rate to rise.
Note that this is true even where *IS* is interest elastic.

Figure 9-9 shows the impact of a change in the money supply on GNP
under alternative assumptions about the relationship between the interest

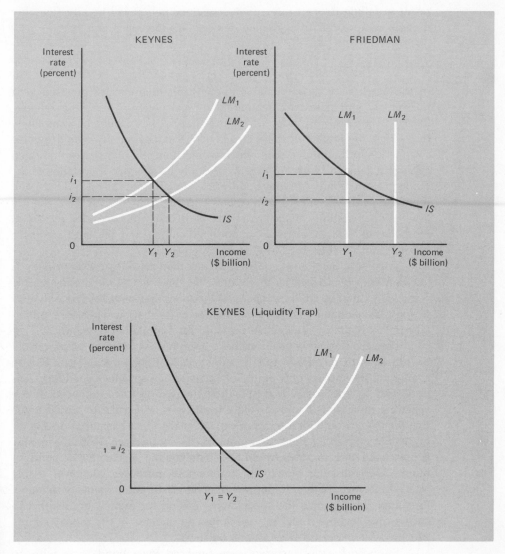

Figure 9-9   Impact of a Change in the Money Supply
on GNP

rate and the demand for money. A given increase in the money supply will
affect GNP only if the *LM* curve rises with the interest rate, and the impact
is greater the flatter the *IS* curve, that is, the more responsive total spending
is to changes in the interest rate. In the Keynesian liquidity trap, increases
in the money supply have no effect on GNP. If increases in the money supply

result in falling interest rates, then monetary policy will be effective only if some components of aggregate demand are interest elastic.

POLICY IMPLICATIONS

In the Keynesian view, monetary policy can theoretically be used as a measure to stimulate employment, but fiscal policy is far more reliable. Except in the liquidity trap, where monetary policy would be completely ineffective, the impact of the increase in the money supply would involve a reduction in the interest rate which would then stimulate investment and aggregate demand. Such a policy would only be effective if speculators are willing to buy bonds (driving bond prices up and interest rates down) and if investors increase spending in response to the fall in interest rates. Keynes doubted the reliability of such reactions, particularly in a period of recession. He believed that an increase in public spending and tax cuts are more efficient and reliable ways to stimulate demand.

Friedman, on the other hand, argues that the demand for money is not significantly affected by the interest rate and that, if the money supply is increased, money will be exchanged for goods and services. The only way to stimulate demand is to put more money in circulation. Therefore, monetary policy is the most effective measure for stimulating demand.

Between these two positions lies a compromise which involves careful coordination of monetary and fiscal policy. In Chapter 8 we saw that in evaluating the impact of a policy of increased government spending, it is important to know how that spending increase is to be financed. If the spending increase is financed solely from taxes, a Keynesian would argue that the effect would be somewhat expansionary, since consumption spending would not fall by the full amount of the tax increase. With the money supply fixed, interest rates would rise, reducing the speculative demand for money and releasing money for transactions purposes. However, rising interest rates would tend to depress interest-elastic components of demand. Friedman, who ignores the speculative demand for money, argues that in such a case, income could not rise unless an increase in the money supply provided for increased transactions balances.

Suppose the tax increase were financed by a bond issue with no increase in the supply of money. In the Keynesian view demand would increase more than by tax financing since presumably consumption spending would not fall. As bond prices fall due to the bond issue, funds are released from speculative balances to satisfy transactions demand. Again, Friedman would argue that such a measure would have no impact on GNP, if the money supply were not increased.

Only if the increase in spending were financed by money creation would both Keynes and Friedman predict an expansionary effect. For Keynes, the impact on GNP would be greater than by using tax finance or debt creation since new transactions balances are available without having to release funds from speculative balances. Consequently, interest rates would not necessarily rise.

Generally, fiscal and monetary policy is coordinated so that an increase in public spending is accompanied by some increase in the money supply. If expansionary measures are called for, it is unlikely that the monetary authorities will permit interest rates to rise very much. Because of this coordination, it is difficult to determine whether the expansion is due to the increased spending or the increased money supply. Indeed, this phenomenon has provided fuel for the fires of both camps.

In fact, under these circumstances, the expansion should be attributed to the interaction of fiscal and monetary policy working together. Walter Heller, taking the Keynesian position in a debate with Milton Friedman over economic policy, aptly stated:

> The monetarists have taught us much. We are far richer for their analyses and painstaking research. But we would be far poorer, I believe, for following their policy prescription. It is high time that they stop trying to establish a single variable—money supply—as all-powerful, or nearly so, and stop striving to disestablish another variable—fiscal policy—as impotent, or nearly so. The path to progress in economic policy lies, instead, in a mutual undertaking to work out the best possible combination of fiscal, monetary, and wage–price policies—coupled with measures to speed the rise in productivity—for reconciling sustained high unemployment with reasonable price stability.[18]

Questions for Study and Review

1. A policy planner wishes to achieve full employment. These programs are available to him:

(a) wage deflation,

(b) fiscal policy,

(c) monetary policy.

Which of these would you recommend to him and why? In justifying your answer, be sure to explain why you rejected the alternatives.

[18] Walter Heller, in *Monetary vs. Fiscal Policy: A Dialogue*, ed. by Milton Friedman and Walter Heller (New York: W. W. Norton and Company, 1969), p. 41.

2. One of the major conclusions to be drawn from Keynesian economics is that an underemployment equilibrium can be maintained indefinitely in the private sector of an economy. Another school of thought argues that the economy cannot be in equilibrium if a major market (in this case, the labor market) is left uncleared. How can the controversy be reconciled?

3. "Deficit spending by the federal government during a recession is not an effective means of eliminating a deflationary gap if the deficit is financed solely by the issuance of bonds." Outline the theoretical framework on which that statement is based and discuss it critically.

4. Trace, in detail, the impact on real wages of a general increase in the level of money wages.

5. Recently it has been argued that "Keynesian economics is dead," and that the Friedmanian (monetarist) position essentially represents a return to the classical tradition. Do you agree?

Additional Reading

Friedman, Milton, *Dollars and Deficits*. Englewood Cliffs, N.J.: Prentice-Hall, Inc., 1968, Introduction.

——, and Walter Heller, *Monetary vs. Fiscal Policy: A Dialogue*. New York: W. W. Norton and Company, 1969.

——, "The Quantity Theory of Money—A Restatement," in *Studies in the Quantity Theory of Money*, ed. by Milton Friedman. Chicago: University of Chicago Press, 1956.

Hansen, Alvin H., *A Guide to Keynes*. New York: McGraw-Hill Book Company, Inc., 1953, Chapters 1 and 10.

Hicks, J. R., "Mr. Keynes and the 'Classics'; A Suggested Interpretation," *Econometrica*, V (April, 1937), 147–159.

Keynes, John Maynard, *The General Theory of Employment, Interest, and Money*. New York: Harcourt Brace Jovanovich, Inc., 1965, Chapters 2 and 19. Published originally by Macmillan & Co., Ltd., 1936.

Modigliani, Franco, "Liquidity Preference and the Theory of Interest and Money," *Econometrica*, XII (January, 1944), 45–88.

Patinkin, Don, "Price Flexibility and Full Employment," *The American Economic Review*, XXXVIII (September, 1948), 543–564.

Smith, Warren, "A Graphical Exposition of the Complete Keynesian System," *The Southern Economic Journal*, XXIII (October, 1965), 115–125.

10

The
Theory
of
Inflation

The previous analysis has examined the relationship between money values of national income aggregates and economic policy instruments. The model was developed in money terms to take account of the impact of price level changes as the economy moves from one national income equilibrium to another.

While the models presented in money terms are appropriate for establishing the links between policy instruments and national income aggregates, planners may be interested in separating price level changes from real changes in output in view of the goals of national economic policy. One of the goals is full employment. We have assumed that the level of employment necessarily increases with the level of aggregate demand and that monetary and fiscal policy which increases demand or GNP will also increase the level of employment. This is not always the case. In 1969 and the first quarter of 1970, money GNP rose steadily from $908 billion to $960 billion as shown in Table 10-1. Beginning in the third quarter of 1969, however, the unemployment rate rose from 3.4 percent to 3.8 percent, dipped to 3.5 percent, and rose again to 4.2 percent. Both real GNP and industrial production declined steadily from the third quarter of 1969 through the beginning of 1970. Thus, the rise in money GNP was attributable to price increases rather than to increases in the output of goods and services. The recession was characterized by the phenomenon of inflation and rising unemployment occurring simultaneously.

To frame policies designed to maintain full employment and economic growth without inflation, planners must view changes in real GNP separately

Table 10-1   Indicators of Economic Activity
in the Recession of 1969-1970

Quarter	GNP (current prices, in billions of dollars)	GNP (1958 prices, in billions of dollars)	Industrial Production Index (1957-1959)	Unemploy- ment Rate	Consumer Price Index (1957-1959)	Wholesale Price Index (1957-1959)
1969 (I)	908.7	723.1	170.1	3.4	124.6	111.1
1969 (II)	924.8	726.7	172.5	3.4	126.8	111.9
1969 (III)	942.8	730.6	174.3	3.8	128.7	113.4
1969 (IV)	952.2	729.8	171.4	3.5	130.5	114.7
1970 (I)	960.4	726.9	169.8	4.2	132.5	116.4

Source: Council of Economic Advisors, *Economic Indicators,* United States Government Printing Office, Washington, D.C., monthly. Jan., 1969-June, 1970.

from money changes. Stimulating money GNP is not sufficient to increase the level of employment. In this chapter we shall be concerned with de-terminants of price level changes and their impact on the variables such as GNP and employment. The analysis will be useful in developing policies to stabilize prices.

10-1   A Digression on Price Indices

To separate price changes from real changes in GNP, an index of price changes must be compiled. If GNP rises from $500 billion to $690 billion and prices increase by 20 percent, then real GNP is said to have increased to $575 billion or 15 percent. Real GNP is the value of output that would have resulted had prices not risen. Thus,

$$\text{Real GNP} = \frac{\text{GNP}}{\text{price index}} \times 100$$

or

$$\$575 \text{ billion} = \frac{\$690 \text{ billion}}{120} \times 100$$

The price index measures the percentage increase in prices over the base year price level, conventionally set equal to 100.

What is meant by a price increase of 20 percent? Of course, all prices do not increase by 20 percent. Some may increase more and others may fall. A price index is a weighted average of price changes for many goods; the weights are determined by the relative importance of the goods in the GNP.

Price indices, constructed in this manner, provide an imperfect measure of pure price change. This is particularly true when the distribution of demand among various products and services changes over time. This means that the weights to be associated with price level changes may vary consid-erably over the period studied. An index using weights appropriate to the beginning of the period may indicate prices have increased while an index using weights from the end of the period may show a price decline. Statisti-cians can make price indices act in strange and contradictory ways by ingenious selection of commodities and services to be included in the index (obviously, all commodities and services can never be included in a practical index) and by assigning different weights to them. Since the choice of commodities and weights to be used is arbitrary, it is difficult to determine which index is the most reliable. In addition, policy makers, and certainly the general public, rarely evaluate an index in terms of its composition. Yet many policy decisions are based on the movement of such commonly watched price indices as the Consumer Price Index and the Wholesale Price Index. Indeed, it is unfortunate that an indicator which contains so much that is arbitrary is given so much credence as an index of inflation.

Not only are price indices subject to easy manipulation, but they tend to be biased upward. Because of the fact that commodities are treated generically (i.e., a Chevrolet is a Chevrolet), quality improvements are not taken into account. This is particularly true for the service sector in which prices are generally equivalent to wage remuneration. Wages may rise in a nonservice industry such as steel with no concomitant price increase if marginal productivity rises proportionally. However, the only way a dentist can obtain a wage increase is to increase the price of his services. Presumably, this increase reflects, at least in part, an improvement in the quality of those services.

Paradoxically, policies undertaken by the government to control inflation also contribute to the upward bias in the price indices, generating the appearance of the very inflation those policies are designed to prevent. Since the Consumer Price Index is expected to reflect changes in the "cost of living," indirect taxes and interest rates are included in the index. When increases in indirect taxes and increases in interest rates are used as anti-inflationary measures, governments will promote an appearance of the very price increases they are trying to halt. Actually, increases in the index may not be due to increased prices of goods and services at all.

The built-in upward bias of price indices has often caused governments to undertake anti-inflationary actions which drive the economy into recession. As demonstrated in the 1969–1970 recession, both the Consumer Price Index and the Wholesale Price Index rose throughout the period as industrial production declined and the unemployment rate rose.

Traditional price indices should be discounted as measures of inflation, particularly in periods during which governments are undertaking anti-inflationary policy. This is not to say that measures should not be taken to stabilize an obvious inflationary trend, particularly if these measures can be designed so as not to interfere with the goals of full employment and a high rate of growth. In the analysis which follows we shall show how such anti-inflationary policy can be designed.

GRAPHICAL METHOD
OF SHOWING PRICE LEVEL CHANGES

An analysis of price level changes can be incorporated into the complete model using the aggregate supply function and the aggregate production function. The aggregate supply function relates the level of employment with the expected total revenue of all firms in the economy. Expected total revenue is equal to the expected money value of output, or

$$ETR = py = g(N)$$

where p is a price index and y is the real value of output or income.

The aggregate production function relates real output to employment. If the capital stock is fixed in the short run, output will increase with employment, but at a decreasing rate, as shown in Figure 10-1. Thus,

$$y = f(N)$$

A price index can be derived by deflating (dividing) the aggregate supply function by the aggregate production function, since

$$p = \frac{py}{y} = \frac{g(N)}{f(N)}$$

Such an index shows the price level as a function of the level of employment, as shown in Figure 10-1.

Suppose for instance that

$$ETR = g(N) = N^\alpha$$

and

$$y = f(N) = N^\beta$$

then

$$p = \frac{g(N)}{f(N)} = N^{(\alpha - \beta)}$$

In Chapter 2 the general equation for the aggregate supply function was shown to be

$$py = \frac{wAP}{MP} N$$

where w is the money wage, AP is the average product of labor, and MP is the marginal product of labor.

Note that total output is equal to output per worker, AP, multiplied by the number of workers employed:

$$y = AP \times N$$

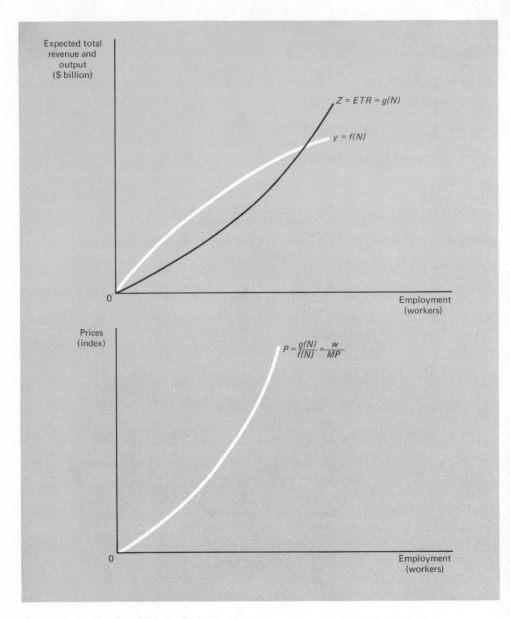

Figure 10-1 Graphical Method of Showing
Price Level Changes

Therefore, a general form for the relation between prices and employment is

$$p = \frac{py}{y} = \frac{(wAP \times N)/MP}{AP \times N} = \frac{w}{MP}$$

The price level varies directly with the level of money wages and inversely with marginal labor productivity.[1] Notice that if money wages are fixed, prices will rise with employment if the marginal productivity of labor declines with employment.[2]

The price-employment relationship may be steeper or flatter than the aggregate supply function. Although the relationship between the slopes of the two functions is complicated to derive, it essentially depends upon how fast the average productivity of labor declines as employment increases. In general, the faster the rate of decrease of AP, the flatter will be the aggregate supply function with respect to the price-employment relationship.

10-2 Aggregate Demand and the Price Level

A cursory study of Keynesian economics suggests that the level of prices is determined by the level of aggregate demand. This notion has influenced public policy to such a large degree that measures such as tax increases, spending cuts, and tight money are sometimes viewed as the only effective and indeed the only legitimate anti-inflationary policy instruments.

It is important to bear in mind, however, that Keynesian economics is basically depression economics. Keynes pointed out that the way to increase employment is to increase aggregate demand and that decreases in demand reduce the level of employment. His analysis did not extend in any depth to an analysis of the relation between price level changes and demand. Perhaps this orientation was due to the fact that in recovering from a depression, inflation is generally not a serious problem. Furthermore, Keynes believed that a moderate amount of inflation is a healthy thing for a stagnating economy.

Price determination in a Keynesian model is shown in Figure 10-2. The level of money income is determined simultaneously with the interest rate by the general equilibrium relationship between IS and LM as shown

[1]This same condition can be derived by assuming that firms are perfect competitors, maximizing profits. It implies that price will be equal to the cost of the last unit produced.
[2]Diminishing marginal productivity of labor is implied by a production function in which total output increases with employment but at a decreasing rate.

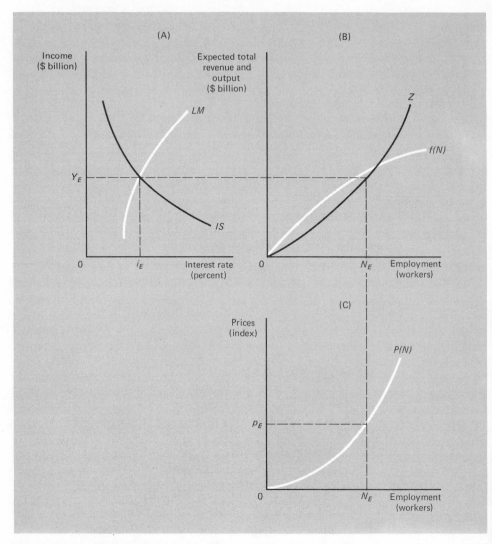

Figure 10-2 Price Determination in a Keynesian Model

in Figure 10-2(A). The equilibrium level of employment associated with this level of money income is found from the aggregate supply function in Figure 10-2(B). Employment equilibrium occurs when producers' expectations concerning sales are fulfilled. Once the level of employment is known, the price level can be found from the price–employment relationship in Figure 10-2(C).

EFFECT OF CHANGES IN DEMAND
ON THE PRICE LEVEL

The impact of a change in demand on the price level is determined by the shape of the aggregate supply function and the price–employment relationship. Assume, as a first approximation, that the aggregate supply function and the price–employment relationship are independent of changes in aggregate demand. In this case the impact of a shift in the IS curve from IS_1 to IS_2 is shown in Figure 10-3. Such a shift could have been initiated by an increase in government spending or a reduction in taxes. As income rises from Y_1 to Y_2, firms increase employment from N_1 to N_2 and prices rise from p_1 to p_2. Notice that the impact of a change in demand on the price level will be greater, the steeper the aggregate supply function and the price–employment relationship in the relevant region. The steeper these curves, the greater is the change in prices and the smaller is the change in employment associated with a given change in aggregate demand.

Since the price–employment relationship and the aggregate supply function incorporate the assumption that money costs of labor and other inputs are fixed, then the slope depends upon the rate at which the marginal productivity of labor changes as the level of output increases. Once full employment is attained, there can be no further increases in real output, and any increase in money GNP will have to be attributed to pure price rise.

Keynes assumed for simplicity that marginal labor productivity would remain constant until full employment was reached. Thus, increases in demand would not produce inflation until full employment was attained, after which, all expansionary measures would be inflationary. An aggregate supply function incorporating this assumption is shown in Figure 10-4. As long as the labor force is not fully employed, increases in demand will generate increases in output and employment, with no price increases. Constant returns to labor implies constancy of both marginal and average labor productivity. Hence, for a shift in demand from IS_1 to IS_2, along the aggregate supply curve,

$$Y = \frac{wAP}{MP} N$$

output will increase in proportion to employment. Prices, determined by the relationship

$$p = \frac{w}{MP}$$

will remain constant. Once full employment is attained, however, further shifts in demand will result in price increases with no further increase in

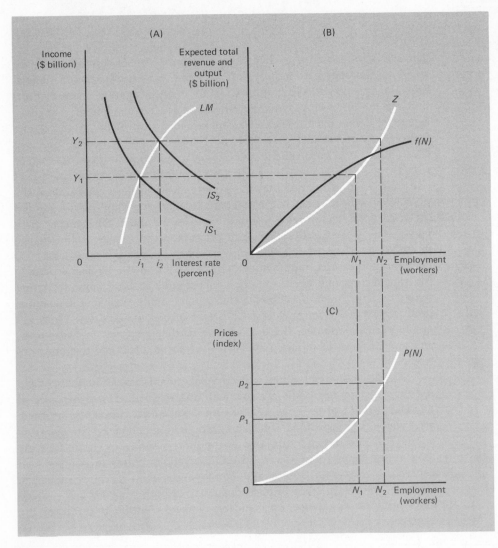

Figure 10-3   Impact of a Shift in the *IS* Curve
on the Price Level

employment. The simple Keynesian model suggests, therefore, that if the labor force were not fully employed, full employment could be attained without inflation merely by increasing aggregate demand. On the other hand, it follows that the best way to stop an inflation is to reduce demand. Furthermore, demand can be reduced in such a way that full employment can be maintained once the inflation is halted.

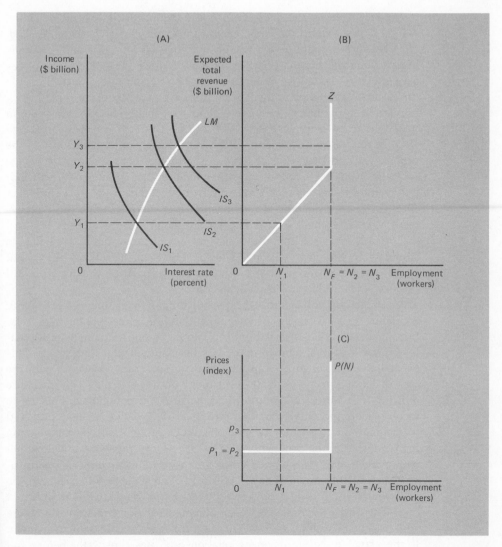

Figure 10-4   Price Level Changes in a Simple
                   Keynesian Model

The simple Keynesian assumption of a constant marginal labor product may have been an adequate approximation for describing a situation in which both the labor force and capital stock are chronically underemployed. However, as full-capacity production is achieved, marginal labor productivity begins to fall rapidly. This occurs as the capital stock becomes fully utilized and as less efficient workers are drawn into the labor force. Thus, as employment increases, the price level should begin to rise with the declining marginal productivity of labor even before full employment is reached.

Because the rate of decrease in marginal labor productivity depends in part upon the amount of excess capital capacity, the shape of the price–employment relationship depends upon the size and rate of growth of the capital stock in relation to the labor force. Given the size of the capital stock in relation to the labor force in the short run, there will be some range in which the price–employment relationship becomes very steep, as in Figure 10-5. In this range, increments to the labor force can be made only at the expense of rather large price increases, and as a consequence, this range is often considered to reflect full employment of the labor force even though it may more accurately reflect full employment of the capital stock. In Figure 10-5, the price–employment relationship rises sharply before full employment, N_F, is reached. If IS is IS_1, income is Y_E, employment is N_E, and the price level is p_E. Suppose policy makers increase public spending to stimulate employment, shifting IS to IS_2. Employment will rise to N_G, but in the process, prices will rise to p_G. Substantial inflation has occurred, but full employment has not been achieved.[3]

To design policies to achieve full employment and price stability simultaneously, it would be desirable that the price–employment relationship remain relatively flat until full employment is attained, or alternatively, that marginal labor productivity be maintained at high levels. This necessitates ample capital capacity, growing at a rate consistent with the rate of labor force growth. If investment declines, it may become more difficult to achieve full employment without price inflation. Policies to increase labor mobility, to train or retrain labor, as well as policies designed to maintain an adequate rate of capital stock growth will, by maintaining high rates of labor productivity at all levels of employment below full employment, prevent the price–employment relationship from rising drastically before full employment is reached. Such policies will facilitate the achievement of the dual objective of full employment without inflation.

The simple Keynesian price–employment relationship, shown in Figure 10-4, can be viewed as an ideal situation for macroeconomic management. If the actual price–employment relationship rises drastically before full employment is attained, it will be impossible to design policies for achieving full employment and price stability simultaneously. One goal must be sacrificed if the other is to be achieved.

[3] The shape of the *aggregate supply function* depends upon the *ratio* between average and marginal labor productivity. Assuming average labor productivity falls more slowly than marginal labor productivity as the capital stock becomes more heavily utilized, the slope of the aggregate supply function will increase, but not as rapidly as that of the price–employment relationship.

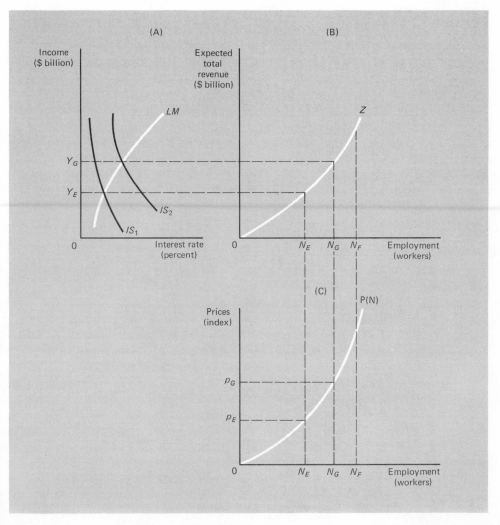

Figure 10-5   Price Level Changes with Declining
                 Marginal Labor Productivity

MONETARY VERSUS FISCAL POLICY

It is sometimes presumed that monetary policy is a more appropriate anti-
inflationary weapon than fiscal policy. Perhaps because of the association
of fiscal policy with Keynesian (or depression) economics, fiscal policy is
considered to be more useful for effectuating changes in employment.
Although monetary policy is generally more effective in slowing a boom

than in stimulating demand in a recession, it does not follow that monetary policy is necessarily more effective than fiscal policy as an anti-inflationary weapon. Confining ourselves to the demand model, the impact of monetary policy on the price level works through its impact on aggregate demand. Suppose the initial national income equilibrium is at Y_1, corresponding to IS_1 and LM_1 in Figure 10-6. Employment is at N_1 and the price level at

Figure 10-6   The Impact of Monetary and Fiscal Policy
on the Price Level (Demand Model)

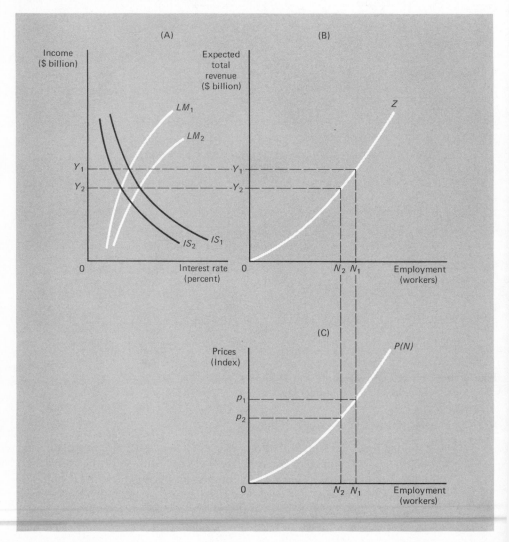

p_1. If policy makers decide that the price level should be deflated to p_2, this can be engineered by a reduction in the money supply sufficient to shift LM to LM_2. Notice, however, that the same impact on prices will result from a reduction in government spending or a tax increase which will shift IS to IS_2 when LM is at LM_1. In each case, monetary and fiscal policy have the same impact on aggregate demand, and in this model, changes in the price level are determined solely by aggregate demand.

In this model, prices can be deflated only at the expense of increasing unemployment of labor. Indeed, unless the aggregate supply function and the price–employment relationship are completely inelastic (vertical) with respect to changes in employment, a reduction in prices will always result in an increase in unemployment. Conversely, however, inflation is always accompanied by increases in the level of employment. Consequently, this model cannot be used to explain the phenomenon of rising prices and increasing unemployment which the United States experienced in the recessions of 1957–1958 and 1969–1971.

In the previous example we examined the impact of a policy designed to deflate the price level. In actual practice, however, price deflation is rarely attempted. In most cases the goal is merely to stop prices from rising. Such a policy implies a more dynamic analysis of inflation than we have presented thus far. In fact, a complete model must take into account certain interactions between all the variables in the system which affect the price level. Nevertheless, within the framework of the demand model we can analyze the following problem.

Suppose policy makers are aware that the level of aggregate demand is in the inelastic range of the aggregate supply function, as shown in Figure 10-7, where income is Y_1. Producers are optimistic about future demand, and there is an accelerator effect to investment. Policy makers expect the projected increase in investment to push the IS curve to IS_2, which would cause income to rise to Y_2 and prices to increase to p_2. In the process, the level of employment would rise from N_1 to N_2.

Since the price–employment relationship is steep in this range, the increase in demand will produce an increase in the price level with little impact on the level of employment. Consequently, the public authorities may decide to take anti-inflationary measures. Monetary or fiscal policy can be used to halt the threatened price inflation. If the policy goal is to maintain prices at p_1, a reduction in public expenditure or a tax increase could counteract the effect of the increased investment on IS, thereby maintaining equilibrium at Y_1 with employment at N_1 and prices at p_1. The same effect could be achieved by a reduction in the money supply sufficient to shift the LM curve to LM_2. Equilibrium would be maintained at Y_1 with employment N_1 and prices p_1.

Notice that, by using an excess demand approach to anti-inflationary

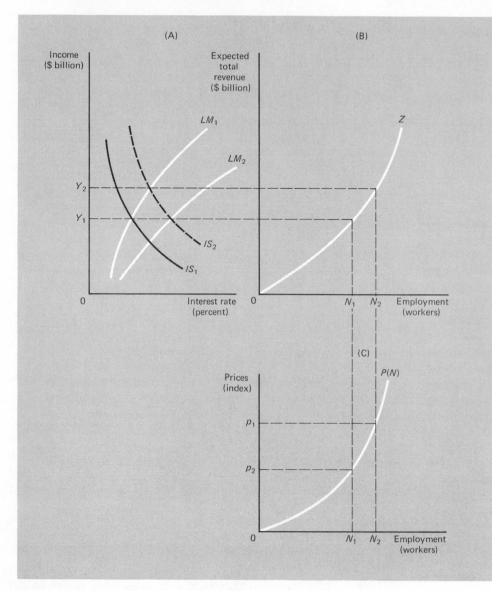

Figure 10-7 Anti-Inflationary Policy When
Aggregate Demand Is Increasing

policy, price stability can be achieved only if the level of employment is not permitted to rise in the short run. The inflationary aspects of a boom cannot be dampened without also dampening the effects of the boom on output and the level of employment. The only way to stop prices from rising is to stop all the other variables in the system from increasing.

Thus, the problem of halting demand-induced inflation is that of effectuating a transfer of resources from one sector to another. If investment demand increases and prices are to be kept stable, the level of employment and hence of output must also be held constant. Increased investment can occur only if resources are released from consumption or the public sector. A tight money policy may dampen some types of investment so that resources are reallocated within the capital goods sector.

10-3 Aggregate Supply and the Price Level

In the previous section we examined a modified Keynesian model of inflation, which emphasized the role of aggregate demand in determining the level of prices. In such a model, inflation is viewed as the price to be paid for increasing levels of employment. Despite the fact that this model has dominated anti-inflationary policy planning since the Keynesian revolution, it is not applicable to recent experience with inflation in the United States in which the price level rises continually regardless of whether the level of employment and economic activity is rising or falling.

The major difficulty with any model which emphasizes the role of aggregate demand in determining the price level is that it fails to take account of the influence of aggregate supply. If, in fact, price increases are caused by upward shifts in the aggregate supply function, then a policy designed to stop inflation by reducing aggregate demand may fail to reduce prices without a sizeable reduction in employment below previous levels.

Remember that the aggregate supply function and the price–employment relationship were constructed with the assumption that money wages are fixed. In fact, however, money wages are likely to rise both in boom periods and in periods of less than full employment. If any inflation is occurring at all, labor unions argue that money wages must be increased so that members recoup the losses in real income associated with price increases.

Suppose money wages increase. Both the aggregate supply function,

$$Y = \frac{wAP}{MP} N$$

and the price–employment relationship,

$$p = \frac{w}{MP}$$

will shift upward and to the left as shown in Figure 10-8. Initially, equilibrium is at Y_1 with employment at N_1 and prices p_1. The wage increase causes the expected total revenue required to maintain employment at N_1 to rise by the amount of the wage increase to ETR_3.

Notice, however, that if firms increased wages without cutting back employment, income would rise to Y_3. This would cause an increase in the transactions demand for money, and given a fixed money supply, the interest rate would rise to i_3. Notice, however, that the interest rate consistent with product market equilibrium at Y_3 is i_0. Since equilibrium in both the product and financial markets cannot be achieved at Y_3 with the original money supply, money income must remain at Y_1. Given the new aggregate supply function, Z_2, employment would fall to N_2.

Whether or not the price level would rise or fall as a result of the decline in employment depends upon the relative rates of increase of the Z functions and the $P(N)$ functions. In Figure 10-8, the $P(N)$ are steeper than the Z functions in the relevant range, and there is a slight decline in prices (to p_2) associated with the decline in employment. It is important, however, to note that, in any case, the price level associated with the old level of employment, N_1, is p'_1, which is substantially higher than p_1.

As the unemployment rate rises, the monetary or fiscal authorities may undertake expansionary measures. A return to the previous level of employment can be achieved only if total demand rises to Y_3. This could be accomplished by fiscal measures, which would shift the IS curve to IS_2, or by an increase in the money supply which would shift the LM curve to LM_2, as shown in Figure 10-9. In either case, prices would rise to p'_1, assuming no further shifts in aggregate supply.

In the demand model, an increase in prices was always associated with an increase in employment (unless full employment was attained). But if inflation is caused by a shift in the aggregate supply function, then the old price level can be achieved only at the cost of substantial unemployment.

Suppose the monetary authorities increased the money supply and caused the LM curve to shift to LM_2, as shown in Figure 10-9. The fiscal authorities may attempt to head off the inflationary rise in prices by demand-reducing measures which cause the IS curve to fall to IS_0. Income falls to Y_0, the level of employment falls to N_0 and prices to p_0, still well above the original level, p_1, with a substantially reduced level of employment. Inflation and a rising unemployment rate appear simultaneously.

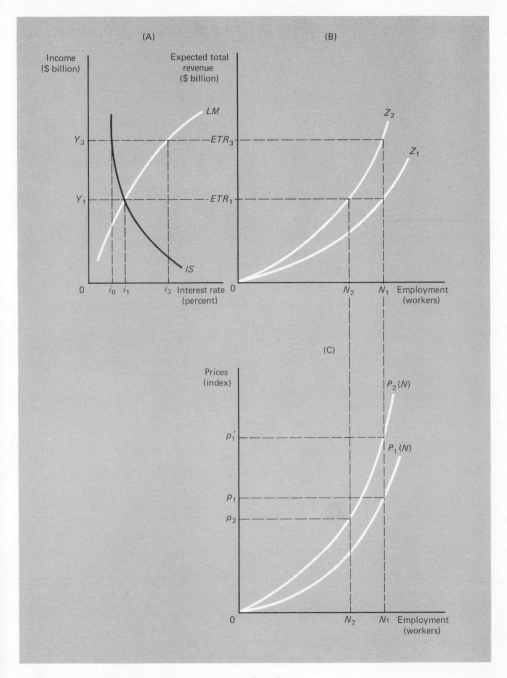

Figure 10-8 Impact of a Shift in Aggregate Supply on the Price Level

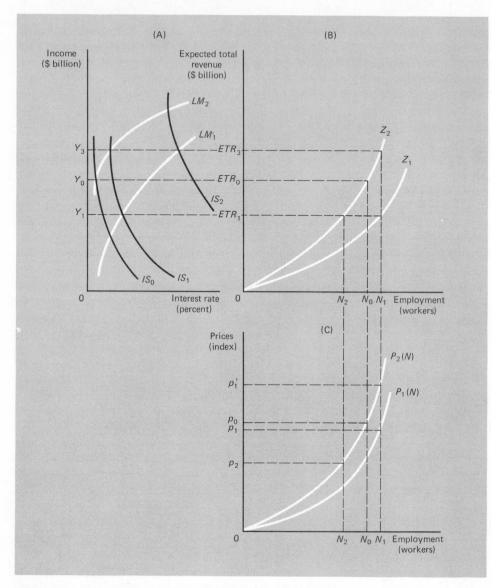

Figure 10-9 Attempts to Maintain the Level of Employment
After a Shift in Aggregate Supply

THE WAGE–PRICE SPIRAL

A rise in money wages may initially be triggered by an increase in aggregate demand. This could be due to several factors. If increasing demand initiates a price increase, workers request higher money wages to recoup losses in real income. In addition, as the level of employment increases with demand, labor markets tighten and the bargaining position of labor improves. Suppose, for instance, that the threat of war induces government to increase spending. The increase in demand will trigger a price increase, the magnitude of which will be determined by the steepness of the price–employment relationship. If there is little excess capacity in the economy, prices will rise sharply since resources will have to be transferred to the public sector from consumption and investment or other public uses. As shown in Figure 10-10, prices will rise from p_0 to p_1 as IS shifts from IS_0 to IS_1.

If the initial price increase triggers demands for higher wages, the aggregate supply curve and the price–employment relationship will shift from Z_0 to Z_1, and $P_0(N)$ to $P_1(N)$. Unless the monetary authorities increase the money supply, the level of employment may actually fall below the initial level, N_0, to N_1 as shown in Figure 10-10,[4] with prices slightly above the initial level at p_1'.

The inflation will stop here if there is no further impact on demand. However, the fiscal and monetary authorities may take expansionary action as the unemployment rate increases. Also, the Fed may increase the money supply to avoid the large increase in the interest rate associated with the inflationary spiral. In Figure 10-10, the interest rate rises from i_0 to i_1. Normally, monetary authorities will take action to prevent interest rates from skyrocketing, even if a tight money policy is being followed.

As the Fed buys bonds to support bond prices and prevent interest rates from rising, the LM curve will shift leftward, increasing demand and prices and perhaps triggering money wage increases and concomitant shifts in the aggregate supply function.

Other factors may tend to keep the wage–price spiral moving. If inflation and high levels of money demand remain unchecked, both consumption and investment demand may rise in expectation of further price increases. In extreme cases, a runaway inflation might ensue. However, unless expectations result in "panic spending," further increases in demand can normally be checked by restrictive monetary and fiscal policy.

A wage–price spiral cannot be held in check by restricting demand if it is reinforced by continued shifts in the aggregate supply function and price–employment relationship. If inflation produces recurrent increases in

---

[4]Employment will not necessarily fall below the initial level in a demand-pull–cost-push spiral, although it does in this example.

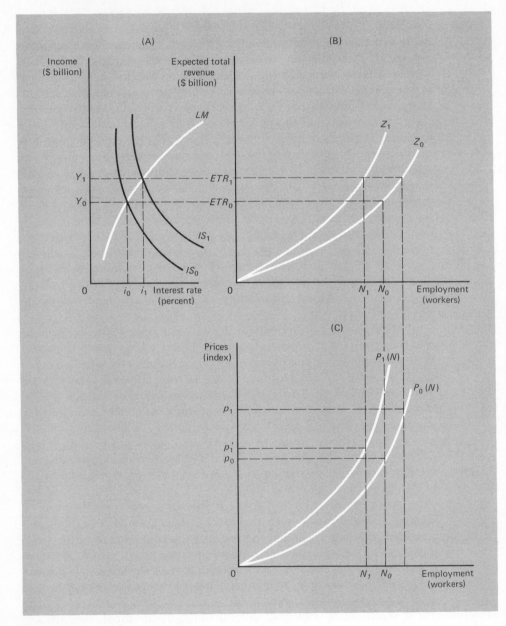

Figure 10-10 A Wage-Price Spiral

money wages, for instance, with no autonomous increases in demand, prices can be stabilized only at the expense of increases in the level of unemployment.

RIGID MONEY WAGES
AND THE PRICE LEVEL

The fact that money wages tend to rise in boom periods but remain rigid in recessions builds in an inflationary bias for an economy. Suppose expected demand rises from ETR_1 to ETR_2 as shown in Figure 10-11. As the demand for labor increases (moving along Z_1) money wages increase, shifting the aggregate supply function to Z_2 and the price–employment relationship to $P_2(N)$. Expected total revenue rises to ETR_3 as wages increase, and prices rise from p_1 to p_3. Note that prices would have moved only to p_1' if money wages had remained stable.

Suppose the shift in expected demand was only temporary, due perhaps to an expected tax cut which never materializes. Expected demand returns to ETR_1 but money wages remain rigid. Firms adjust employment along Z_2 and prices along $P_2(N)$. To maintain employment at the previous level (N_1), prices will be p_2', higher than before.

If demand were to increase again, a money wage increase would shift aggregate supply to Z_3, and so on, with a still higher price level associated with the old level of employment. Thus, wage rigidity means that to maintain a stable price level (i.e., to keep prices from rising with respect to a base year) the level of employment must continually fall.

From this analysis it is clear that the mere *announcement* of a tax cut or an increase in spending may set off an inflationary spiral even if the actual program is not carried out. This may be the case for a tax cut being debated for so long that it produces inflation. Obviously, a tax cut would not be desirable in the presence of a rising price level, so the plan is abandoned. Expected demand falls, firms cut back production, but prices do not return to their old level and the unemployment rate rises.

DEMAND SHIFT INFLATION

The observation that money wages are flexible only in the upward direction has led some economists to conclude that a shift in the sectoral composition of demand will produce inflation even if there is no overall increase in aggregate demand.[5] Suppose demand increases by $100 million in the steel

[5] This theory has been developed by C. L. Schultze, "Recent Inflation in the United States," in *Employment, Growth, and Price Levels*. Joint Economic Committee Study Paper No. 1 (Washington, D.C.: U.S. Government Printing Office, 1959).

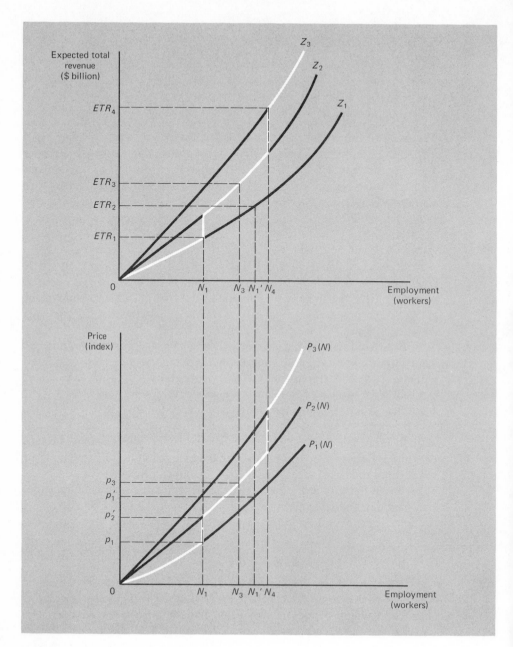

Figure 10-11 Rigid Money Wages and the Price Level

industry and declines by $100 million in the textile industry. As expected total revenue rises, the demand for labor in the steel industry rises, and money wage rates increase for that industry. Since money wages are rigid downward, there is no offsetting fall in wages in the textile industry. In fact, textile workers may press for wage increases to match increases in sectors for which demand is rising. Thus, even though the initial wage increase and concomitant price rise is in a single sector of the economy, there is a "spillover" into other sectors if all sectors compete for labor by increasing wages.

In this example, the impact of the price increase for steel is intensified by the fact that steel is a basic input in many other industries. Rising steel prices increase the cost of production for these industries, shifting the aggregate supply function leftward. It has been estimated that 40 percent of the total increase in wholesale prices over the period 1947–1958 was attributable to the increase in steel prices.[6] It is a small wonder then that steel prices have been a major target of anti-inflationary policy. One of the most dramatic tests of presidential strength in recent years was the ability of President Kennedy to force the steel industry to rescind a price increase when inflation threatened in 1962.

OTHER INFLUENCES
ON AGGREGATE SUPPLY

The aggregate supply function relates expected receipts with the demand for labor. Consequently, any factors which influence either costs of production or desired profits will cause a shift in the aggregate supply function as well as in the price–employment relationship which is derived directly from it.

Suppose, for example, an economy relies very heavily on imports for industrial raw materials. A currency devaluation would effectively raise import prices and hence production costs. Such a situation is shown in Figure 10-12. The aggregate supply curve will shift from Z_1 to Z_2 and the price–employment relationship from $P_1(N)$ to $P_2(N)$. Unless there is an offsetting increase in demand, employment will fall from N_1 to N_2 and prices will rise from p_1 to p_2.[7]

[6]See Otto Eckstein and Gary Fromm, "Steel and the Postwar Inflation," in *Employment, Growth, and Price Levels*, Joint Economic Committee Study Paper No. 2 (Washington, D.C.: Government Printing Office, 1959).

[7]The direction of change in prices when demand is unchanged will depend upon the shape of the price–employment relationship relative to that of the aggregate demand curve. In all cases, however, the price level associated with any given level of employment will always increase when the price–employment relationship shifts upward.

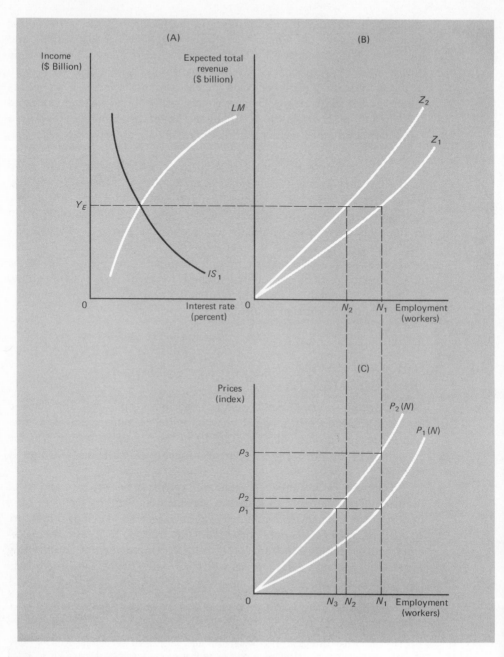

Figure 10-12 Impact of Increasing Production Costs
on National Income Equilibrium

Within a Keynesian framework, the appropriate remedy is unclear. Unemployment has risen, so an increase in demand is called for. But a return to N_1 would cause the price level to increase still further to p_3, even assuming no further leftward shifts in aggregate supply due to wage increases.[8] On the other hand, a policy designed to promote price stability would call for a reduction in demand. Such a policy, however, would serve to intensify the unemployment situation, since employment at p_1 would be N_3.

Any influences which increase production costs will tend to produce this dilemma for policy planning. This is also the case if firms decide to increase their profit margins. In all cases an increase in prices is accompanied by a reduction in the level of employment (assuming no change in the level of money demand). Should public policy be expansionary, or should the level of spending be reduced? The Keynesian approach provides no clear answer because it does not deal with the phenomenon of rising prices occurring simultaneously with rising unemployment rates.

Some economists would argue that such a situation is not truly inflationary. They contend that an increase in prices due to an autonomous increase in production costs, caused perhaps by a currency devaluation, is a once-and-for-all occurrence which will not produce a price spiral if other factors are held constant.

This argument is vacuous in two respects. First, given the institutional structure of labor markets in most economies, price increases are generally accompanied by increases in money wages as workers argue they are experiencing a decline in real income. These wage increases will trigger further shifts in the aggregate supply function and trigger more inflation and demands for even higher wages.

In addition, inflation is generally measured by changes in the various price indices mentioned at the beginning of this chapter. As these price indices rise, inflation is indicated, regardless of the source of the increase and whether it is expected to be the once-and-for-all or the spiraling variety. This is particularly true when the policy makers in power are inflation conscious and watch the price indicators with a wary regard for upward movements. For practical purposes, inflation means an increase in the price indices and, for the policy planner, anti-inflationary measures are indicated.

In the next chapter we shall analyze the problem of designing policies to combat inflation, particularly in periods of slack economic activity. With these in mind, we will be better equipped to tackle the job of policy planning for full employment without inflation.

---

[8]If such a policy is adopted, that is, if demand is increased so that employment returns to N_1, the authorities are said to have "validated" the increase in costs.

Questions for Study and Review

1. On the basis of the model on p. 207 of the text (referred to in Question 1 in Chapter 8) answer the questions below:

(a) If the aggregate supply function is

$$Z = N^2$$

and the aggregate production function is

$$y = \sqrt{N}$$

where

Z = aggregate supply
y = output
N = employment

find the relationship between employment and the price level.

(b) What is the equilibrium level of employment and prices?

(c) What would be the effect of increasing G to 150?

(d) Suppose the authorities desire to increase G without increasing prices. Show how price stability can be achieved by the use of monetary policy.

(e) What would be the impact of the measures taken in parts (c) and (d) on
(i) employment,
(ii) the distribution of GNP between consumption, investment, and the public sector?

(f) Can you design a policy by which the increase in G would increase the level of employment without causing a price rise?

2. President Johnson based his argument for an increase in personal income tax rates on the grounds that it would combat inflation. Discuss the theory on which the president's argument was based. Then, from your knowledge of inflation theory, argue *against* this justification for a tax increase.

3. Under what circumstances would Keynesian policy remedies be unable to ensure overall price stability in an economy? What policies might be more

effective? In discussing these policies, be sure to weigh their economic, social, and political implications against the social inequities and economic problems associated with inflation.

Additional Reading

Eckstein, Otto, "The Theory of the Wage-Price Process in Modern Industry," *The Review of Economic Studies,* XXXI (October, 1964), 267–286.

Hansen, Alvin H., *A Guide to Keynes.* New York: McGraw Hill Book Company, Inc., 1953, Chapter 11.

Keynes, John Maynard, *The General Theory of Employment, Interest, and Money.* New York: Harcourt Brace Jovanovich, Inc., 1965, Chapter 21. Published originally by Macmillan & Co., Limited, 1936.

Samuelson, Paul, and Robert Solow, "Analytical Aspects of Anti-Inflation Policy," *The American Economic Review,* L (May, 1960), 177–194.

Schultze, C. L., "Recent Inflation in the United States," in *Employment, Growth and Price Levels,* Joint Economic Committee Study Paper No. 1. Washington, D.C.: U.S. Government Office, 1959.

11

Inflation
and
Economic
Policy

The Keynesian model implied that the price level, like the level of employment, can be manipulated solely by policies which affect the level of aggregate demand. The idea that there is a one-to-one correspondence between the price level and the level of employment implies that the price–employment relationship and the aggregate supply function are stable with respect to changes in aggregate demand. In this view, the only source of inflation is a rising level of aggregate demand. This means that if aggregate demand is prevented from increasing, a stable price level can be maintained at any level of employment which is less than full employment. For example, it suggests that a 3 percent rate of unemployment can be maintained with no price level increases, once the appropriate level of aggregate demand is attained, by allowing demand to grow at the same rate as the labor force.

Empirical evidence suggests that this is not the case. After examining some of this evidence, we shall evaluate Keynesian remedies for inflation. This will be followed by a discussion of other measures for promoting price stability.

11-1 The Stability of the Aggregate Supply Function and the Price–Employment Relationship

The notion that inflation is caused primarily by too much demand is based on the assumption that prices rise only when the level of employment increases. The relationship between prices and employment,

$$p = \frac{w}{MP}$$

where p is the price level, w is the money wage, and MP is the marginal productivity of labor, implies that firms will hire workers as long as the price of the product exceeds the cost of production. According to this relationship, prices will rise and fall with the level of employment if marginal labor productivity moves inversely with employment. If money wages are fixed or if they rise only when employment increases, the price–employment relationship will be positively sloped as shown in Figure 11-1.

In this case, increases in demand will cause the level of employment to increase and prices to rise. If demand falls, so will the level of employment and prices. An increase in unemployment will always be accompanied by a reduction in prices, if money wages do not rise and marginal productivity increases.

Figure 11-1   The Price-Employment Relationship

Studies have shown, however, that money wages in the United States have increased continuously since World War II, despite the fact that the unemployment rate climbed as high as 6.8 percent in 1958. Samuelson and Solow have estimated that money wages would not stop increasing unless the unemployment rate rose to 8 percent. Wages would rise at a rate of 2 to 3 percent per year even with 5 to 6 percent of the labor force unemployed.[1]

Notice that rising money wages will produce upward shifts in the price–employment relationship only if they are not offset by increases in marginal productivity. If productivity is increasing by 2 to 3 percent per year, the economy could maintain price stability with a 2 to 3 percent increase in wages each year.

If, however, the unemployment rate must be maintained at a 5 to 6

[1]Paul A. Samuelson and Robert M. Solow, "Analytical Aspects of Anti-Inflation Policy," *The American Economic Review*, L (May, 1960), 177–94.

percent level to achieve this stability, the economy would have to be kept in a state of semirecession (by the standards of the 1950's and 1960's). In such an atmosphere, it is doubtful that productivity would increase at the 2 to 3 percent rate. Indeed, reducing the level of demand may discourage the investment that is responsible for gains in labor productivity. If continual money wage increases are an institutional fact of life in the United States, then measures which encourage investment and increase productivity may be better anti-inflation remedies than those which aim to stop wages from rising by increasing the rate of unemployment.

This is particularly true when an inflation is already in full swing and the unemployment rate is not declining. In such a situation, the source of inflation may not be entirely an excess of demand. Suppose there is an initial increase in demand which causes the IS curve to shift from IS_1 to IS_2 as shown in Figure 11-2. With the aggregate supply function at Z_1, the initial impact is to increase employment from N_1 to N_2. Prices rise along $P_1(N)$ from p_1 to p_2. As prices rise, labor unions demand higher wages to recoup losses in real income, and since employment is rising, their bargaining position is improved. Sometimes wage increases are automatically built into union contracts in "escalator clauses." The rise in wages will cause the price–employment relationship and the aggregate supply function to shift upward to $P_2(N)$ and Z_2 as shown in Figure 11-2. The level of employment will fall to N_0 (below the initial level, N_1), while the price level rises still further to p_0.

Although prices are rising due to an initial demand–pull situation, measures which restrict demand and discourage investment will do more harm than good. Productivity will not increase, but wages will rise anyway. In this case an easing of monetary policy or a tax stimulus to investment might have the effect of increasing investment and labor productivity—a measure which would be conducive to price stability in an economy with a persistent money wage rachet. Furthermore, such measures would increase the demand for labor in a situation in which the unemployment rate is rising simultaneously with increases in the price level.

Note that the best anti-inflationary policy in this case may look "expansionary" from a Keynesian point of view. Expansion and inflation are not always synonymous (although they sometimes are). A Keynesian might suggest that instead of increasing total demand, the current level of demand should be shifted from consumption to investment spending by means of increasing personal income taxes and easing money or subsidizing investment. This policy might be appropriate if total demand were the only factor involved. Consider the impact of this policy on prices, however. Increased personal taxes would strengthen labor's argument for money wage increases as take-home pay is reduced. Often personal taxes are included in the

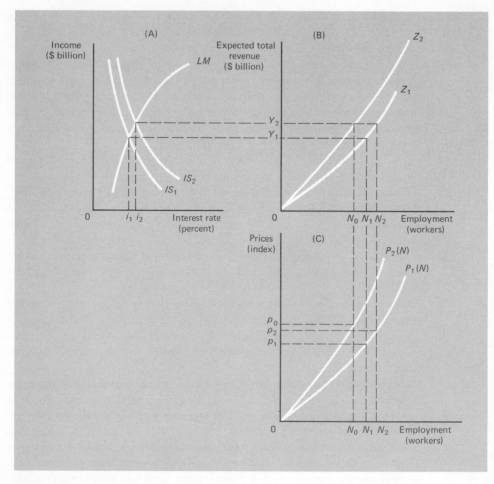

Figure 11-2 Impact of Rising Money Wages
on the Price Level

cost-of-living indices which automatically escalate wages through clauses
in union contracts. Tax hikes are not a useful anti-inflationary measure in
periods when labor is using the "loss-in-real-income" argument to justify
wage increases.

OTHER FACTORS AFFECTING
THE PRICE–EMPLOYMENT RELATIONSHIP

The price–employment relationship shows the number of workers firms will
employ for a given price level. Any factors which influence production costs
or desired profit margins will have an impact on this relationship. We saw

in the preceding chapter how a currency devaluation might produce an upward shift in the price–employment relationship for an economy which imports raw materials.

Other factors which may produce these results are the following:

1. *Increases in desired profit margins*—When demand falls, firms may try to recoup their losses in volume by increasing profit rates on units actually sold. This is particularly true if the firm follows monopolistic pricing practices. In that case the firm will hire workers until the marginal revenue equals cost per worker, or

$$MR = \frac{w}{MP}$$

Recall that

$$MR = p\left(1 - \frac{1}{E_D}\right)$$

where E_D is elasticity of demand.[2] Therefore,

$$p = \frac{w}{MP[1 - (1/E_D)]}$$

Firms will attempt to increase their total profits by raising profit margins (and hence prices) if they expect demand elasticity to be falling.

2. *Increases in interest rates*—Rising interest rates increase capital costs to firms and living costs to households. They may be passed on to consumers by firms in the form of higher prices and from households to firms in the form of wage increases. Although tight money has traditionally been viewed by the followers of Keynes and Friedman alike as an anti-inflationary measure, since it presumably reduces both aggregate demand and the quantity of money, it will generally cause the aggregate supply and price–employment relationships to shift upward and thus may generate the very inflation it is intended to prevent.

3. *Increases in taxes*—Tax increases raise living costs for households which may provide a justification for wage increases. In addition, many firms

[2] The derivation of this result is as follows:

$$E_D = -\frac{p}{q}\frac{\Delta q}{\Delta p}$$

$$MR = p + q\frac{\Delta p}{\Delta q} = p\left(1 - \frac{1}{E_D}\right)$$

view increased corporate taxes as increased unit costs of production, which they pass on to consumers in the form of higher prices. Although taxes are viewed as demand inhibitors from the Keynesian viewpoint, they are also an element of production cost and, hence, play a role in the determination of prices.

4. *Increases in price of primary products*—Rising food prices almost always provide justification for money wage increases. Primary products such as steel are inputs in many other industries, and increases in these prices represent increased production costs in secondary industry. Consequently, price increases in a limited sector of the economy, particularly in food and basic industries, will often shift the price–employment relationship upward for the economy as a whole.

11-2 Inflation and Keynesian Economic Policy

Keynesian models emphasize the role of demand in determining prices. In the preceding discussion we have suggested that, given the institutional structure of the U.S. economy as it has evolved since World War II, costs of production also play an important role. Price determination is undoubtedly a two-edged sword, and any theory of inflation must take demand as well as cost factors into account.

Suppose the unemployment rate is 3 percent and a national emergency requires an increase in defense expenditure. No one would argue that such an increase would not be inflationary unless demand were reduced in other sectors. As marginal workers enter the labor force, marginal productivity will fall and money wages will be bid up. If the capital stock is fully utilized, bottlenecks will develop, again raising unit labor costs. Keynesian remedies such as tax increases and a reduction in government spending in other areas would be appropriate measures for shifting resources into the military sector with a minimum of inflation. Tight money would be less desirable since it presumably would slow down the rate of investment. Though the short-run impact of a decline in investment might be equivalent to a reduction in consumption or other spending, in the long run this impedes the growth of labor productivity which is required for price stability in an economy in which money wages are expected to rise continually.

In the situation described above, it is clear that a reduction in demand is called for. However, the amount of inflation which occurs will depend in large measure upon the way in which demand is depressed. Increased taxes and interest rates will tend to be more inflationary than direct cuts in public spending. Furthermore, as we have suggested, tight money may have long-run consequences not immediately apparent. Nevertheless, monetary policy is often the most flexible policy instrument, and a tax increase to pay for a war is likely to be more palatable to the congress than spending cuts. In an overheated economy in which the problem is essentially too much demand, any measure which inhibits spending is better than no measures at all, and tax increases and tight money would be appropriate, although they are not the best policy instruments for controlling inflation.[3]

Suppose, on the other hand, prices are increasing at a rate of 5 percent while industrial production is declining and the unemployment rate is rising. This was the case in the United States in 1969–1970 as indicated in Chapter 10. In that period, the business community was so pessimistic about future prospects that the Dow-Jones Index of industrial stock prices suffered its most severe downturn since the crash of the late 1920's. In this case the problem was obviously not excess demand since resources were not being fully utilized. It was clearly a case of wages, profit rates, and other production costs rising faster than productivity. Policies designed to restrict demand not only intensified the unemployment problem, but they were designed in such a way that production costs were increased and investment discouraged.

President Nixon had inherited an inflationary situation from the Johnson Vietnam War era. Yet from early 1969, the unemployment rate was rising with the consumer price index, and by the third quarter, industrial production had declined with no indication that the inflation was slowing down.

Under these conditions, the anti-inflationary program of the Nixon administration was essentially Keynesian with lip service paid to the Friedman viewpoint. A temporary tax increase effected during the Johnson administration was extended. Money was tightened, credit was rationed, and the budget was balanced. With soaring interest rates, no tax relief, and a rising consumer price index, money wage increases of 10 percent and more were sought by labor unions. As prices continued to rise, Nixon's economic advisors promised to stop the inflation without increasing the rate of unemployment by using Keynesian remedies alone. They argued that any other method, such as wage guidelines, would interfere with competitive market forces and hence would be unacceptable.[4]

11-3   Non-Keynesian Remedies

From the preceding analysis, it is clear that while Keynesian remedies are appropriate for handling an inflation caused by excessive demand, they may produce disastrous results when inflation is occurring during a recession

[3]Note that if the distributive consequences of the measures are considered, tax hikes and tight money, which restrict demand in the private sector, might be preferred to cutbacks in public spending. The point made here is that tax increases and tight money are likely to be more inflationary than spending cuts.

[4]See comments by A. F. Burns, economic advisor to President Nixon, in "Wages and Prices by Formula?" *Harvard Business Review* (March–April, 1965), 59.

or when the growth of demand is slower than the growth of resources—labor force and capital stock. Not only do Keynesian remedies reduce an already slack level of demand and increase unemployment still farther, but generally (with the exception of direct cuts in government spending) they tend to increase production costs, the real culprits in this particular scenario.

An alternative to Keynesian policy is the concept of *wage–price guidelines*. The guidelines consist of holding money wage increases in all industries to average annual productivity increases for the economy as a whole. If firms maximize profits and set

$$p = \frac{w}{MP}$$

and assuming that changes in marginal and average productivity are proportional, then existing price levels can be maintained in firms with average productivity increases, raised in firms with smaller productivity increases, and lowered in firms with greater than average increases.

Such a system would result in price stability if it is assumed that the principal factor causing the inflation is cost push rather than excessive demand and that the primary source of the cost push is attributable to wage increases. Each of these assumptions will be examined in turn.

COST PUSH VERSUS DEMAND PULL

In practice it is often difficult to distinguish between cost–push and demand–pull inflation because in many inflationary situations demand and output are rising and so are wages and other costs of production. In such cases, wage–price guidelines may serve to limit the inflation associated with a boom, provided that the growth of demand is adequately controlled. If aggregate demand is allowed to grow at the same rate as average productivity and if wage–price guidelines are effective, then aggregate supply and demand can grow at the same rate, with no price increases. In such an inflation, however, Keynesian demand-oriented remedies must be combined with the guidelines for price stability. It should be noted that it is important for price stability to be attained quickly and maintained effectively so that workers do not suffer losses in real wages as a result of the guidelines.

In some inflationary situations, however, it is obvious that cost push and not demand pull is the culprit. In the recessions of the late 1950's and late 1960's, industrial production, employment, and real aggregate demand actually declined in the face of price increases. In this case, wage–price guidelines would have been an effective way of stabilizing prices without inhibiting an already slack level of demand.

COST PUSH
AND THE LEVEL OF MONEY WAGES

A wage–price policy aims at money wage increases as the principal target of anti-inflationary pressure. As we have seen, any increase in production costs will be pyramided into higher price levels, particularly if the authorities adjust demand to maintain at least a constant rate of unemployment, that is, if they "validate" the cost push. Normally, however, such factors are once-and-for-all occurrences which cause initial price increases but do not continue. Wages, on the other hand, will nearly always rise *pari passu* with these costs because the latter inflate the cost-of-living indices in which wage contracts are negotiated. Rising interest rates, taxes, and import prices all have this effect. Furthermore, escalator clauses cause wages to rise in response to all price increases so that a wage increase may, through the price rise it generates, initiate demand for further wage increases. The drive to maintain a rising real wage in the face of inflationary pressures causes a wage–push inflation to have a serious potential for an ever-increasing price spiral.

While it is important to control rising costs from any source, it is clear that, if wage-push inflation is brought under control, a good bit of the battle would be won. Since wages represent the largest element of total variable cost for most industries and since wages have the greatest tendency to rise consistently throughout periods of inflation, then it is clear that they should be the principal target in a policy of cost control at the national level. However, policy makers should also view with concern the inflationary consequences of tight money, tax increases, and currency devaluations.

CRITICISMS OF WAGE–PRICE GUIDELINES

Despite the neat theoretical justification for the guidelines, such a policy was avoided by Presidents Eisenhower and Nixon, both of whom confronted inflationary recessions in which the guidelines would have been useful. Some of the arguments put forward by critics of the guidelines are vacuous, but others have merit and should be considered in any decision to use such a policy in an anti-inflationary program.

Interference with the Market System. A major objection to the wage–price guidelines has been the contention that such a policy would interfere with the allocation of resources by the market system. Such reasoning ignores the fact that resource allocation depends upon *relative* prices and is essentially independent of the overall price level. The guidelines would not interfere at all with relative prices. Supply price would fall in fast-growing industries and presumably output and demand would increase in these firms. The reverse would hold for slower-growing industries. Since the guidelines affect only the general price level and not relative prices, they do not interfere with the market system any more than Keynesian remedies do.

Impact on Income Distribution. It is sometimes held that, if wages are allowed to increase by as much as productivity, all the gains will be to labor and none will be to profits. This is a specious argument. Suppose total output is 100, with labor receiving 80 percent and 20 percent going to profits. If, with the same labor force, productivity and wages both increase by 5 percent, output will rise to 105 and labor will receive an increase of $80 \times 0.05 = 4$. There will be a residual of 1, which will represent an increase in profits equal to 5 percent of 20 ($20 \times 0.05 = 1$). Thus if productivity increases by 5 percent, *both* wages and profits can be increased by 5 percent.

A more serious argument is that the wage–price guidelines do perpetuate the existing *relative* distribution of income between wages and profits. Robert Solow has provided two answers to this argument.[5] First, relative factor shares have changed very little in the United States during the experience of industrial development. Therefore, the guidelines would not weaken any inherent tendency for these to change. Furthermore, we must presume that the guidelines would not be adhered to precisely. In some years average productivity may be overestimated, in which case labor's share would increase. If productivity gains were understated, labor's relative share would decline.

Inflation Due to Increasing Profit Margins. It is sometimes argued that even if unions agreed to hold wage increases to the level of productivity gains, there is no assurance that firms would not jack up profits and raise prices.

Assuming that firms desire to maximize profits, they will set prices so that the value of the marginal product of the last worker is equal to the money wage they must pay that worker. This reasoning results in the formula

$$p \times MP = w$$

or

$$p = \frac{w}{MP}$$

on which the guidelines are based. Rational firms will raise or lower prices according to whether they have experienced lower or higher productivity

[5] In J. P. Schultz and R. Z. Aliber, eds., *Guidelines, Informal Controls, and the Market Place* (Chicago: Chicago University Press, 1966), pp. 48–49.

increases than the national average, and the net impact on the general price level will be stabilizing. According to this theory, there can be no profits inflation.

Suppose, however, that a firm monopolizes a product market or shares the market in such a way that its selling price is affected by the amount it sells. In this case the value of the marginal product is not $p \times MP$ but $MR \times MP$, where MR is the marginal revenue, or increment of total revenue associated with the last unit sold. Marginal revenue is the change in total revenue with respect to output, or

$$MR = \frac{\Delta TR}{\Delta q} = p + q\frac{\Delta p}{\Delta q}$$

Marginal revenue is price, minus the reduction in price required to make the last sale, multiplied by all units for which the price was reduced.[6]

Recalling the definition of demand elasticity,

$$E_D = -\frac{p}{q}\frac{\Delta q}{\Delta p}$$

and rearranging terms,

$$MR = p\left(1 - \frac{1}{E_D}\right)$$

Marginal revenue and price are related through the elasticity of demand. The greater the elasticity of demand, the smaller is the difference between marginal revenue and price.

Thus, for a monopolist or imperfect competitor, labor is hired until

$$MR \times MP = w$$

and prices are set so that

$$p = \frac{w}{MP[1 - (1/E_D)]}$$

[6]Note that if a firm is a perfect competitor and can sell its entire output at a fixed price, then

$$\frac{\Delta p}{\Delta q} = 0$$

and

$$p = MR$$

Suppose labor unions follow the guidelines and hold wage increases to productivity increases. There will still be no tendency for prices to rise in response, since the price equation should be unaffected by equal increases in w and MP. Even though the *level* of monopoly prices may be higher than would have been the case under competitive conditions, there is no indication that price *changes* would tend to be greater. It is true that these firms will increase prices (and profit margins) in response to an expected decline in demand elasticity. Conversely, they will reduce prices if they expect demand elasticity to fall. There is no evidence, however, that the guidelines per se will affect expectations concerning demand elasticity, and consequently, inflationary price increases in response to a perceived reduction in elasticity would have occurred in the absence of guidelines.

Many firms, particularly in oligopolistic industries such as steel, do not follow the principle of profit maximization described so far, but in fact follow an *administered pricing* scheme, at least in the short run. In practice, prices are determined by the "cost-plus" rule:

$$Price = Unit\ cost + Profit$$

where profit is generally set as a percentage of the cost base. Thus, wage increases are matched by proportional increases in profits. Such a policy can be highly inflationary in periods of substantial wage push but would produce price stability if a guidelines' policy were adopted. Under the guidelines, if productivity were increased by 5 percent, wages would rise by 5 percent, and if a policy of administered prices were followed, profits would increase by 5 percent. Such a practice would be consistent with price stability under the guidelines. Hence, it is not true that the guidelines would not work if administered pricing were practiced.

Difficulty in Measuring Productivity Gains. Critics have argued that wage–price guidelines are impossible to administer because it is not feasible to obtain an accurate estimate of average productivity gains. Provided, however, that estimates are approximately accurate, the guidelines are an effective means of controlling inflation. If, however, productivity gains are overstated, the general price level will probably rise even if unions adhere to the guidelines. On the other hand, if gains are understated, the price level will fall. In most cases guidelines based on slightly inaccurate estimates of productivity increases are better than no guidelines at all. Presumably they would prevent a wage–price spiral, since wages would increase only with the estimated rise in productivity and not in response to any increase in the price level which may result.

Impact on Real Wages. In practice, it is difficult to justify the use of wage–price guidelines once an inflation is in full swing. Suppose prices are increasing by 5 percent per year, while real productivity gains are estimated to be 3 percent. If labor holds wage increases to 3 percent, this represents a *decline* in the real wage of 2 percent. How can such a decrease in real wages be justified in the face of increased productivity? Someone must be reaping the return and, labor unions argue, that someone is management.

Underlying the argument, of course, is the assumption that inflation will continue at the same rate in the future as it has in the past. Real wages will decline only if inflation *continues* at a rate greater than 3 percent. Presumably, the implementation of the guidelines will eliminate the inflation so that real wages will rise by 3 percent—the same rate as the increase in money wages and the productivity increase.

However, the argument that real wages should increase by the amount of the productivity increase is a convincing one, particularly the popular version in which the price index used to compute real wage gains is taken from the past inflationary experience. Consequently, it is important to implement guidelines early in a boom period, before labor becomes accustomed to seeing wage gains frittered away by rising prices. In an inflationary situation it is difficult to convince labor that price stability will be achieved as a result of labor's own restraint.

Moral Suasion as a Policy Instrument. Some observers question the feasibility of using moral suasion or "jawboning" as a policy instrument. It is sometimes contended that those unions and management who conscientiously follow the guidelines are penalized relative to those who ignore them. J. T. Romans has observed that moral suasion works best when aimed at small groups of individuals.[7] In this way the noncompliers can be singled out and the responsibility for failure of the policy can be laid at their door. Thus, in the experience with guidelines in the Kennedy administration, only a few major, basic industries were singled out for special observation. The steel industry was of particular concern, because of the impact of steel prices on the general price level as well as the fact that the steel industry is a highly concentrated one.

It is necessary that the policy measures being imposed by moral suasion be generally popular with the public at large so that noncompliance be met with disapprobation. At the same time, the target population must be small enough that noncompliers be recognized.

[7]In J. T. Romans, "Moral Suasion as an Instrument of Economic Policy," *The American Economic Review*, LVI (December, 1966), 1220–1225.

The Role of the Quantity of Money. Some economists such as Milton Friedman argue that prices cannot rise unless the quantity of money in circulation increases. If the level of GNP is determined by money supply multiplied by the velocity of circulation

$$MV = GNP$$

then increases in M will necessarily increase GNP and, hence, prices. We have examined this model in Chapter 9. Despite its limitations, it is essentially a model which explains the determination of aggregate demand, or total GNP. It does not allow for the fact that the same level of GNP might be associated with different price levels, depending upon the level of employment and output. While it may help to explain an excess demand inflation when resources are fully employed, it is not useful in explaining why prices may rise in the face of a falling level of GNP (presumably associated with a decreasing supply of money).

In fact, the quantity theory of money is not only inapplicable to an analysis of inflation in a recession, but it is also dangerous to apply. The quantity theorists argue that tight money, with its higher interest rates, is the only way to stop an inflation of any sort. In an inflationary recession, however, tight money raises capital costs, causing an upward shift in the price–employment relationship. In addition, it will tend to discourage investment, the source of the productivity gains required to achieve price stability in the face of the upward creep of money wages.

EXPERIENCE WITH THE GUIDELINES

Recent experience with wage–price guidelines as an anti-inflationary measure has been encouraging. Gary Fromm has estimated that for the period 1962–1966, when the guidelines were more or less in effect, they

1. reduced the annual rate of increase of average hourly earnings by about 1.25 percent,
2. reduced the rate of increase of unit labor costs by about 2 percent,
3. reduced the rate of increase of the wholesale price index by about 1.4 percent.

He also concluded that the benefit of the guidelines accrued to business more than labor.[8] These findings have been supported by other observers.[9]

[8]Gary Fromm, "The Wage-Price Issue: The Need for Guideposts," in Joint Economic Committee Hearings (Washington, D.C.: Government Printing Office, 1968), 3–7.
[9]See George W. Perry, "The Wage-Price Issue: The Need for Guideposts," in Joint Economic Committee Hearings (Washington, D.C.: U.S. Government Printing Office, 1968), 12–19.

Both the Eisenhower and Nixon administrations have shied away from the use of guidelines for the various reasons listed above. However, the experience with the guidelines in the 1962–1966 period was promising. During this time, economic expansion took place with considerably less inflation than had occurred during the less buoyant conditions of the late 1950's and late 1960's.

Questions for Study and Review

1. Referring to the model in Question 1 of Chapter 10, answer the following questions:

(a) Suppose the government imposed a 5 percent tax on each unit of output. What would be the impact on the price–employment relationship as well as on the equilibrium level of employment and prices?

(b) If the government wishes to impose this tax without affecting employment, what compensatory measures would be necessary? What would be the impact on the price level?

2. Consider an economy in which wage–price guidelines are in effect. How will changes in business taxes affect the distribution of total value added between wages and profits?

3. What is a Phillips curve? What are its implications for the theory of inflation?

4. As an anti-inflationary measure, wage–price guidelines have had strong advocates as well as harsh critics. What is the essential basis of the disagreement?

5. Critically evaluate the current economic policy of the federal government with respect to the goal of achieving price stability.

Additional Reading

Lekachman, Robert, "Inflation: Classic and Modern," in *The Age of Keynes*, by the same author (Lekachman), Chapter 10. New York: Random House, 1966.

Perry, George L., "Wages and the Guideposts," *The American Economic Review*, LVII (September, 1967), 897–904.

Phillips, A. W., "The Relation Between Unemployment and the Rate of Change of Money Wage Rates in the United Kingdom, 1861–1957," *Economica*, n.s., XXV (November, 1958), 283–299.

Samuelson, Paul, "Wage-Price Guideposts and the Need for Informal Controls in a Mixed Economy," in *Full Employment, Guideposts, and Economic Stability: Rational Debate Seminars*. Washington, D.C.: U.S. Government Printing Office, 1967.

12

Economic
Dynamics
and the Theory
of Economic Growth

287

Until now, our study of the theory of macroeconomic policy has consisted of an analysis of the determinants of national income equilibrium. We have been interested in the impact of changes in the various policy parameters on equilibrium income and employment or conversely, what changes in the policy parameters would be required to move to a desired equilibrium position.

Equilibrium analysis ignores the passage of time required for the system to move from one equilibrium to another. Yet the policy planner is often concerned with the immediate or short-run effects of economic policy rather than their projected ultimate impact. In Chapters 12 and 13 we shall explicitly take into account the time pattern of the target variables as they adjust to changes in economic conditions.

12-1   Time in Economic Analysis

Equilibrium analysis is concerned with such questions as, "What will be the impact of an increase in government spending on income and employment?" Our previous examples have taken a *comparative statics* approach, examining the equilibrium income and employment before the change and comparing it with the equilibrium which would occur after the change. The process of adjustment from one equilibrium to another has been ignored.

Suppose an increase in government spending causes the IS curve to shift rightward from IS_1 to IS_2 as shown in Figure 12-1. Comparative statics would project an increase in income from Y_1 to Y_2 and an increase in the interest rate from i_1 to i_2, assuming the money supply and the LM curve remain fixed.

Because the process of adjustment has been ignored, comparative statics does not tell us *when* the new equilibrium will be reached. Yet, generally, the policy planner is interested in predicting the impact of his policy within a specified period of time. A *dynamic* model explicitly takes into account the time pattern of adjustment to equilibrium.

Associated with every problem in comparative statics is a dynamic adjustment process. This association is known as the *correspondence principle*. If the dynamic adjustment process is known, then the policy planner can be told of the impact of his policy for any time period he specifies. The values of the target variables in disequilibrium may or may not be near the equilibrium values of the comparative statics model, depending upon the dynamic adjustment process.

If the values of the target values in disequilibrium approach the equilibrium values of comparative statics as the time period allowed for adjustment lengthens, then the new equilibrium is said to be *stable*. In some

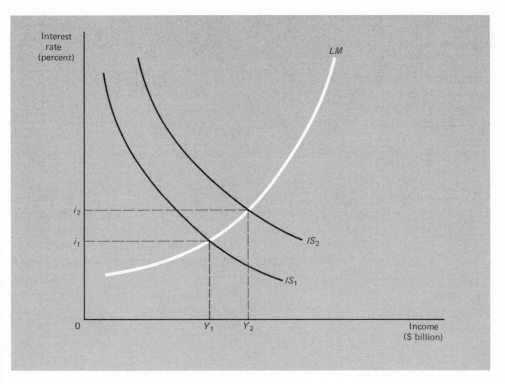

Figure 12-1   Comparative Statics Analysis of a Shift
in the IS Curve

cases, however, the target values never reach the comparative statics equilibrium, even if a very long time period is allowed for adjustment. Then
the new equilibrium is said to be *unstable*. The stability or instability of
equilibrium depends upon (1) the dynamic adjustment process specified for
the model and (2) the nature of the original functional relationships of the
model.

EQUILIBRIUM ADJUSTMENT
IN THE *IS–LM* MODEL

Consider the Keynesian model of national income determination represented
by the *IS* and *LM* curves. The *IS* curve shows the interest rate that will
equate saving and investment at different levels of national income. The
LM curve shows the interest rate that will clear the money market at different
levels of national income. Both the interest rate and national income will

be in equilibrium (i.e., there will be no tendency for either to change) when saving equals investment and the money market is cleared simultaneously. Thus, overall equilibrium occurs where IS and LM intersect, as shown in Figure 12-1. If one curve is displaced (shifts) due to a change in one of the variables or functions which define it, then the new equilibrium can be found at the new point of intersection of the curves.

Let us consider the process of adjustment to a shift in IS from IS_1 to IS_2, as shown in Figure 12-2. Suppose the banking system is slow to adjust to the initial increase in demand. In case I in Figure 12-2, the initial response to the increased demand is an increase in income from Y_1 to Y_2, with no change in the interest rate, resulting in product market equilibrium with a disequilibrium in the money market. When income is Y_2 and the interest rate i_1, the demand for money will exceed the supply, and eventually the banking system will have to raise the interest rate to i_2 (assuming the money supply and the LM curve are fixed) which will clear the money market when income is Y_2. Now the product market must adjust to restore equilibrium in saving and investment. As the interest rate rises, investment falls and the level of income must fall until saving is reduced and equilibrium restored. In case I the process continues until eventually the new equilibrium is reached at Y_e and i_e. Notice that, in the process of adjustment, both income and the rate of interest rise and fall in a cyclical pattern with the cycles becoming of successively smaller magnitude as more time passes. Such cycles are said to be *damped*. Equilibrium in case I is *stable* because the system will eventually reach it, given adequate time for adjustment.

In case II the same dynamic adjustment process is implied, yet the new equilibrium Y_e is *unstable*. Adjustments in the product and money markets produce *explosive* cycles in income and the interest rate which increase in magnitude with the passage of time. Notice that in case II the LM curve is steeper than the IS curves, while in case I the LM curve is flatter than the IS curves.

In general, a money market lag will result in explosive cycles and dynamic instability the less responsive the demand for money is to the interest rate and the more responsive investment demand is to the interest rate.

Suppose the policy maker asks the question, "What will be the impact of an increase in public spending?" Using a comparative statics analysis, the economist would project an increase in national income, employment, and the interest rate. A dynamic analysis must consider the adjustment process. If the banking system were slow in adjusting the interest rate to changes in economic conditions, the economist would predict that the change in spending will produce a cyclical pattern of income and employment. Whether the cycles will be damped or explosive will depend upon how

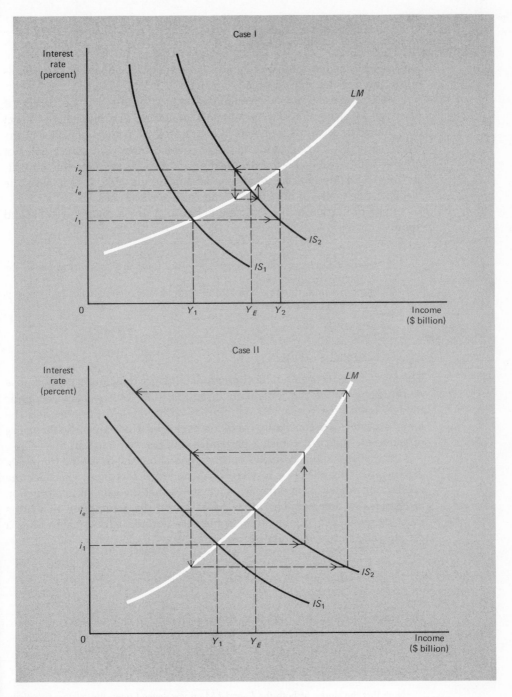

Figure 12-2 Dynamic Adjustment in the IS-LM Model
with a Money Market Lag

sensitive the demand for money and investment spending are to changes in the interest rate and income.[1]

It is apparent that a comparative statics approach is not useful if reactions to disequilibrium are not instantaneous. The immediate impact of a change in economic policy is likely to produce cyclical behavior in the target variables. Furthermore, in some cases comparative statics will not provide useful results even if the planner is not concerned with the immediate impact of his policies. If an equilibrium is unstable, it will never be reached, regardless of how much time is allowed to pass.

The projection of the dynamic behavior of the economy will depend upon

1. the dynamic adjustment process, whether there are lags and where in the economy these lags occur,
2. the functional relationships in the static model, whether the *LM* curve is steeper than the *IS* curve.

NONEQUILIBRIUM MODELS

The *IS–LM* model is an equilibrium model. It has a dynamic aspect because of the behavior of the system in disequilibrium. Other macroeconomic models ignore the concept of equilibrium altogether. In these models the target variables are constantly changing over time. Consequently, the *timing* of economic policy becomes a particular concern.

Suppose the policy maker is concerned about the best time to initiate expansionary fiscal policy to ward off a potential recession. Consider the accelerator model of investment which states that investment is a function of changes in demand. The model is based on the assumption that firms must increase their capital stock to increase output. If firms try to keep a certain ratio between capital stock and sales,

$$\frac{K}{Y} = \beta$$

and since investment is equal to the net change in capital stock,

$$I = \Delta K$$

---

[1]Note that the slopes of both the *IS* and *LM* curves depend upon the relative sensitivity of each to income and the rate of interest.

then changes in the capital stock, or investment, will be proportional to changes in demand; that is,

$$\frac{\Delta K}{\Delta Y} = \beta$$

$$I = \beta \, \Delta Y$$

The accelerator theory of investment can be incorporated into a simple Keynesian model:

$$Y = C + I$$
$$C = a + bY$$
$$I = \beta \, \Delta Y$$

Solving for income,

$$Y = a + bY + \beta \, \Delta Y$$

$$= \frac{a}{1 - b} + \frac{\beta}{1 - b} \, \Delta Y$$

This model is a nonequilibrium model. Applying the equilibrium concept would result in the nonsensical conclusion that in equilibrium net investment would be zero (since ΔY would be zero), and all GNP would be consumed or used for replacement investment. Note, however, that the model is useful for planning the appropriate timing of economic policy.

If this model is applicable, the best time to initiate expansionary public policy is not when GNP has turned down, as an equilibrium model would suggest, but when the rate of increase in GNP declines.

In Figure 12-3 the time path of GNP is shown for an economy entering a recession. Using a Keynesian equilibrium model and ignoring the lag between policy initiation and effectiveness, the best time to undertake expansionary measures is at B, where GNP declines. The accelerator model would advise the policy maker to begin his program of expansion at A, where the rate of increase in GNP declines. When ΔY declines, even if Y is still increasing, this produces a decline in investment which will trigger the downturn in GNP through the multiplier.

In Chapter 13 we shall analyze the factors which cause nonequilibrium behavior in some detail. This behavior, often called the *business cycle*, is due primarily to factors associated with aggregate demand. We shall also consider the problem of the timing of economic policy.

Figure 12-3   Optimal Timing of Anti-Recession Policy

THE CONCEPT
OF A DYNAMIC EQUILIBRIUM

Consider an economy for which aggregate supply and aggregate demand are both increasing at the same rate over time. The increase in aggregate supply may be due to increased labor productivity due to technological change, while the increase in aggregate demand may be due to increases in investment over time. As seen in Figure 12-4, equilibrium will take place at a constant level of employment. Since aggregate demand is increasing with a constant level of employment, so must income per worker. If the economy can sustain this growth rate, it will be in a dynamic equilibrium with a fixed labor force and increasing productivity and output per head.

The policy maker may ask the question, "How fast must aggregate demand grow so that full employment can be maintained in the face of a growing labor force and rising labor productivity?"

Suppose average labor productivity is rising by 3 percent and the labor force is growing by 2 percent. Then aggregate demand must grow by 5 percent in real terms to absorb the increase in productive capacity (i.e., the

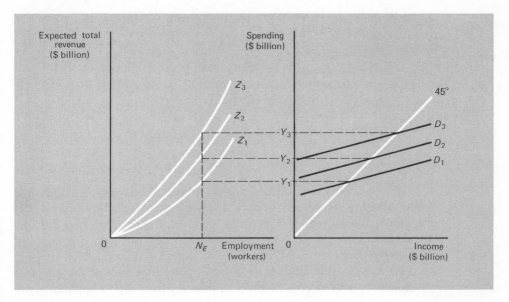

Figure 12-4   Dynamic Equilibrium with Economic Growth

increased output per worker as well as an increased number of workers) for the full-employment economy.

Can the economy sustain a dynamic equilibrium in which GNP grows by 5 percent each year? This will depend upon the rate of investment. Consider a simple Keynesian model which incorporates an accelerator theory of investment:

$$Y = C + I$$
$$C = aY$$
$$I = \beta \, \Delta Y$$

Since

$$Y = C + I$$

is an equilibrium condition, an equilibrium can be found for this model, but it will not be a static equilibrium in the Keynesian sense. Instead, because investment is a function of the change in demand over time, a dynamic equilibrium can be found. This dynamic equilibrium will represent a time path of income which can be maintained indefinitely and from which there is no tendency to move, given the underlying conditions, or parameters. Rearranging terms,

$$Y = aY + \beta \, \Delta Y$$

$$= \frac{\beta}{1-a} \Delta Y$$

or

$$\frac{\Delta Y}{Y} = \frac{1-a}{\beta}$$

This economy can maintain a rate of growth of aggregate demand equal to the marginal propensity to save divided by the capital–output ratio. If the capital–output ratio is 3, then the marginal propensity to save must be 15 percent if the economy is to sustain adequate demand in the private sector to keep the economy at full employment when labor productivity is rising by 3 percent and the labor force is growing by 2 percent. If the marginal propensity to save is only 10 percent, then if this model is applicable, the government will have to undertake expansionary measures to increase demand and absorb the growing productive capacity of the economy.

12-2 The Theory of Economic Growth

In the static Keynesian model, full employment could be achieved by attaining the appropriate level of aggregate demand and maintaining it indefinitely. Once time is incorporated into the analysis, however, it is clear that to maintain full employment over time, aggregate demand must grow to keep pace with the expanding productive capacity of the economy.

Productive capacity increases as the capital stock and the labor force grow over time. In the static, short-run analysis, investment is viewed as a component of aggregate demand. If the economy is at less than full employment, increases in investment are desirable, since these increases generate the demand necessary to induce firms to hire more workers. But more investment today means greater productive capacity tomorrow, since investment is synonymous with increases in the capital stock. Because of the dual character of investment, generating both aggregate demand and increased productive capacity, policies designed to reach full employment in the short run may result in serious unemployment problems in the long run.

Models of economic growth are concerned with three questions. First, how fast must an economy grow to maintain full employment of its resources as productive capacity increases? Second, will the private sector of the economy be able to sustain this growth rate in a dynamic equilibrium without government interference? And third, what public policies can aid an economy to maintain a stable growth rate over time?

HARROD–DOMAR MODELS

Roy Harrod and Evsey Domar independently developed models to describe the growth process.[2] Their analysis is essentially Keynesian in the sense that saving is assumed to be a function of income and national income equilibrium occurs when saving equals investment.

To maintain full employment of labor in the face of increasing productive capacity, the rate of growth of real aggregate demand must equal the rate of growth of the labor force plus the rate of growth of labor productivity. This growth rate is called the *natural rate of growth,*

$$G_N = n + p$$

where n is the rate of growth of labor force and p is the rate of growth of labor productivity.

Will the private sector be able to maintain such a growth rate? Suppose the productive capacity of the economy, P, is proportional to the capital stock:

$$P = \sigma K$$

Since

$$\Delta K = I$$

investment will produce proportional increases in productive capacity, or

$$I = \frac{1}{\sigma} \Delta P$$

If aggregate demand is sufficient to absorb productive capacity, firms will be in equilibrium (since in the absence of excess capacity, their sales expectations are being fulfilled), and investment will continue at the current rate. Therefore, in equilibrium,

$$\Delta P = \Delta Y$$

---

[2]See Roy Harrod, *Towards a Dynamic Economics* (London: Macmillan & Co., Ltd., 1948) and Evsey Domar, *Essays in the Theory of Economic Growth* (New York: Oxford University Press, 1957), Chapters 3–5.

Assuming a simple Keynesian model of income determination,

$$Y = C + I$$
$$C = aY$$

or

$$Y = \frac{I}{1 - a}$$

and

$$\Delta Y = \Delta I \frac{1}{1 - a}$$

This represents the relationship between changes in aggregate demand and changes in investment. Recalling the relationship between investment and changes in productive capacity,

$$I = \frac{1}{\sigma} \Delta P$$

and the equilibrium condition,

$$\Delta P = \Delta Y$$

then in equilibrium,

$$\sigma I = \Delta I \frac{1}{1 - a}$$

or

$$\frac{\Delta I}{I} = \sigma(1 - a)$$

In equilibrium, for aggregate demand to keep pace with productive capacity, investment must be growing at a rate equal to the output-capital ratio, σ, multiplied by the marginal propensity to save.[3]

Since

$$I = (1 - a)Y$$

[3]Note that this result is equivalent to the analysis in the previous section in which an accelerator model of investment is incorporated into a Keynesian theory of income determination. The formulation described above follows the Domar analysis, while that of the previous section is attributable to Harrod.

and

$$\Delta I = (1 - a)\,\Delta Y$$

then

$$\frac{\Delta I}{I} = \frac{\Delta Y}{Y} = \sigma(1 - a)$$

and income must also be growing at the same rate as investment. This growth rate is called the *warranted rate of growth*.

If the warranted rate of growth is exactly equal to the natural rate, that is, if

$$\sigma(1 - a) = n + p$$

then the economy can maintain a steady rate of growth at that rate indefinitely. Producers' expectations will be fulfilled, and the demand for labor will always equal the supply. The labor force will grow at a rate n and per capita income will rise by p.

Both Harrod and Domar argued that it is unlikely that the warranted rate and natural rates will be equal since they are determined by independent factors. Consider the natural rate of growth. The rate of labor force growth is determined by demographic conditions such as net birth rate, age structure of the population, and immigration patterns. These are presumably independent of economic conditions and the actual growth rate. The model presumes that the ratio between output and capital stock remains constant which, assuming constant returns to scale, implies that the ratio between the capital stock and labor force remains constant during the process of growth. Therefore, labor productivity will not increase unless a technological change occurs. The rate of growth of labor productivity will be equal to the rate of technological change. Although technological change may be embodied in investment and consequently may depend upon economic conditions and the actual growth rate, it is also governed by the rate of innovation which is presumed autonomous.

The warranted rate of growth depends upon the propensity to save which reflects households' preferences for present over future consumption. It also depends upon the relationship between capital stock and productivity which is essentially technological.

Because the natural rate and warranted rate of growth are determined by independent factors which are themselves not significantly influenced by the rate at which the economy is actually growing, then there is no reason to presume that they will be equal. Yet equality of the two rates is necessary to ensure a steady state of growth at an equilibrium rate.

THE INSTABILITY
OF HARROD–DOMAR MODELS

For the economy to grow at a steady equilibrium rate, the warranted rate of growth must equal the natural rate,

$$G_W = G_N$$

or

$$\sigma(1 - a) = n + p$$

Only then will aggregate demand be growing at the same rate as productive capacity.

We have seen that there is no inherent tendency for these two rates to be equal, and hence, steady state growth in the private sector without government intervention is unlikely. Suppose the two rates are not equal. The time path of income is shown in Figure 12-5.

If the natural rate is greater than the warranted rate, the economy will actually grow at the warranted rate. However, the growth rate will be inadequate to absorb the natural increases in the labor force, and hence, unemployment will be an ever-increasing problem. In this case the rate of capital accumulation is lower than the rate of labor force growth, and the capital stock will be inadequate to employ the national labor force.

Suppose, on the other hand, the warranted rate exceeds the natural rate. In this case, to maintain full employment, aggregate demand must grow faster than the economy is actually able to grow. Increases in labor force and productivity are inadequate to produce the required growth of output, and consequently, the economy cannot grow at the warranted rate.

The warranted rate of growth is the rate at which aggregate demand and output must grow if productive capacity is to be fully utilized. If the growth rate, G, is less than G_W, excess capacity will result. Firms will not undertake new investment, and through the multiplier, income will fall. A downturn in income will continue, as shown in case III in Figure 12-5, until sooner or later firms will need to replace their capital stock if any positive output is to be forthcoming, investment will turn up, and the economy can grow at the warranted rate until the full-capacity ceiling is reached. This will be followed by another downturn, and fluctuations will continue indefinitely with cycles becoming increasingly more severe as the productive capacity of the economy increases.

POLICY IMPLICATIONS

Unless the warranted rate and natural rate of growth happen to be equal, the private sector cannot sustain a full-employment level of income over

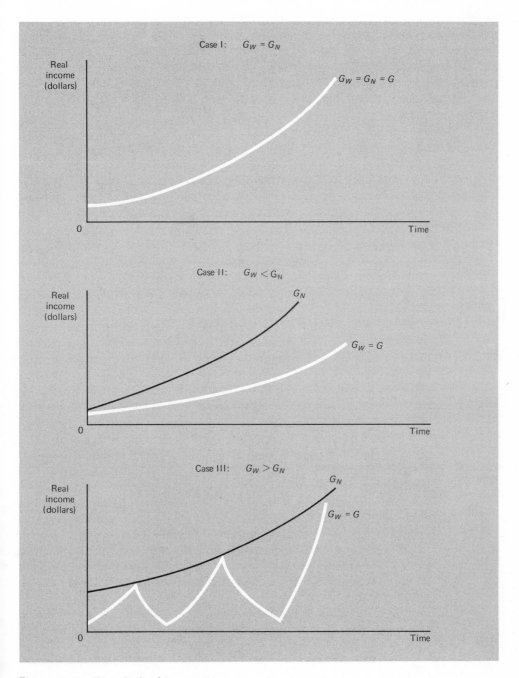

Figure 12-5 Time Path of Income in a
Harrod–Domar Model

time. In the case where

$$G_N > G_W$$

a steady rate of growth can be maintained, but it will be insufficient to absorb the growing labor force. This situation is characteristic of less-developed nations. In these countries the rate of growth of the industrial labor force is apt to be very great, since labor is flowing rapidly from the traditional agriculture and handicraft sectors into the modern sector. On the other hand, the warranted rate of growth is apt to be very low due to a low marginal propensity to save and a low output–capital ratio.[4]

For these economies, the growing labor force can be absorbed only by increasing the propensity to save and raising the output–capital ratio. While, theoretically, the propensity to save can be increased by tax policy, this approach may not be feasible in an economy in which the general population is living at the subsistence level. Tax policy must be aimed at upper income groups, and since these groups are generally powerful politically, such legislation may be impossible to obtain.

An alternative is to undertake measures which would raise the output-capital ratio. The average productivity of capital will depend, among other things, upon how much labor is being combined with capital in the production technology. In general, the more labor intensive the production process, the higher is the output-capital ratio, and the more labor can be absorbed for a given amount of investment. Underdeveloped countries, in recent years, have been plagued with well-meaning advisors from advanced nations who introduce them to the latest technological innovations of the advanced nations. These technologies are generally highly capital intensive. Given limited sources of investment funds, these projects cannot absorb as much of the labor force as projects using less capital and more labor.

The argument is often raised that if technology is labor intensive, labor productivity, and hence real wages, will be low relative to that of capital intensive processes. Supporters of this view ignore the fact, however, that if the capital stock is limited, fewer workers will be employed if production is capital intensive. If a major concern of economic development is to absorb labor into the modern economy, then labor intensive technologies, involving lower real wages but employing more workers, will be preferred to capital intensive processes for which labor productivity is higher but fewer workers are employed.

In advanced countries, the problem is generally that the warranted rate of growth outstrips the capacity of the economy to produce, so that

$$G_W > G_N$$

[4]Notice that the output-capital ratio is equivalent to the average productivity of capital.

Unless the rate of technological change can be increased, then the warranted rate must be reduced if the economy is to avoid the instability inherent in this situation. Either the rate of saving must be reduced or the output-capital ratio must fall.

Although the saving rate may be reduced by tax policy, most countries are reluctant to slow down the rate of saving and investment. Investment is presumably the source of increasing real wages which are generally a major economic goal. In addition, rising labor productivity will help to combat the inflationary trend associated with the built-in tendency for money wages to creep upward.

Increased investment will only increase labor productivity if it embodies technological change and/or if technology becomes more capital intensive. Both of these factors will also tend to bring the natural and warranted rates of growth closer together. Thus, public policy, in this situation, should be aimed at encouraging capital intensive production processes by keeping interest rates (capital costs) low. In addition, policy makers should keep in mind that very high levels of saving and investment may generate increases in productive capacity which are incompatible with full employment. Paradoxically, for mature economies a high rate of investment may not be compatible with a high growth rate if it generates recurring cycles in the level of economic activity. Instead, it will merely serve to complicate the management of macroeconomic stability for the policy maker.

NEOCLASSICAL CRITIQUE
OF THE HARROD–DOMAR ANALYSIS

The Harrod–Domar analysis concludes that if a steady state growth rate can be achieved in an economy, it will be equal to the rate of increase of the labor force plus the rate of technological change. Steady state growth can only be achieved, however, in the unlikely event that this growth rate is exactly equal to the product of the marginal propensity to save and the output-capital ratio (average product of capital). The warranted rate of growth governs the actual rate which, in the typical case, will not result in a dynamic equilibrium at full employment.

Neoclassical critics of the Harrod–Domar model argue that inherent in the market mechanism there are stabilizing forces which will automatically move the economy to a steady state growth path, compatible with a dynamic full-employment equilibrium, with a growth rate equal to the natural rate of the Harrod–Domar analysis.[5]

[5]See, for example, Robert Solow, "A Contribution to the Theory of Economic Growth," *The Quarterly Journal of Economics*, LXX (February, 1956), 65–94 and J. Meade, *A Neoclassical Theory of Economic Growth* (London: Unwin University Books, 1961).

Suppose, for instance, that

$$G_N > G_W$$

or

$$n + p > \sigma(1 - a)$$

As growth occurs at the warranted rate, labor force unemployment becomes increasingly more serious. Workers will bid down money wages, thereby causing firms to substitute labor for capital in the production process. This will increase the output-capital ratio, raising the warranted rate of growth. The process will continue as long as there is excess supply in the labor market, until the warranted rate of growth rises to equal the natural rate. At this point, steady state growth will take place at the Harrod–Domar natural rate with all resources fully employed.

Other factors may operate to speed the adjustment process. As wages fall, if the share of national income going to profits, interest, and rent rises, the aggregate propensity to save will also increase, since the propensity to save from these sources is generally much greater than the propensity to save from wages.[6] Falling wages do not necessarily imply a decreasing share of national income going to labor, however.[7] Furthermore, increased saving will only increase the warranted rate of growth if that saving is channeled into domestic investment. In many of the less-developed countries, saving from nonwage sources is consumed or invested outside the home country.

Other factors may operate to reduce the natural rate of growth. If there is serious unemployment in the modern sector of the economy or if wages there are low, workers will tend to move more slowly out of traditional agriculture and cottage industry. If neighboring countries are experiencing more rapid rates of growth, there may be some emigration to these areas, reducing the rate of growth of the labor force and, hence, the natural rate of growth.

These same influences work in reverse in the case in which

$$G_W > G_N$$

or

$$\sigma(1 - a) > n + p$$

[6]This point is made by Nicholas Kaldor, "A Model of Economic Growth," *Economic Journal* (December, 1957), pp. 591–624.

[7]This depends upon the elasticity of substitution in the production function. For many countries, relative factor shares remain remarkably constant over time, even when there is considerable variation in relative factor prices.

In such a situation, the level of investment is so great that aggregate demand must grow faster than the natural rate to keep productive capacity fully employed. As growth occurs at the warranted rate, the labor force rapidly becomes fully employed. As labor markets tighten, workers bid money wages up. If the monetary authorities do not increase interest rates proportionally, firms will substitute capital for labor in the production process, causing the output-capital ratio to fall. This process will continue until the warranted rate falls to the natural rate, at which point the economy can sustain steady state growth at the Harrod–Domar natural rate.

If investment is substantial, it is likely that the rate of technological change is also very high. This factor has been particularly important in the development of the advanced Western nations. Rapid increases in man-hour productivity have permitted high levels of investment consistent with reasonably stable growth at rates often exceeding 5 percent per year. For some countries, such as the United States, immigration has played an important role. Tight labor markets and high wages not only attract immigrants, but are generally conducive to a liberal immigration policy. Both immigration and technological change raise the natural rate of growth and reduce the disparity between the natural and warranted rates.

12-3 Economic Policy for Stable Growth

The neoclassical analysis of the process of growth concludes that a free-market system, with wage flexibility and labor mobility, will automatically settle into a stable pattern of steady state growth. The argument, like classical remedies for unemployment, does not consider the speed of adjustment. In particular, for a developing country wage deflation may be a slow and politically untenable solution to the problem of absorbing large segments of the population into the modern sector. In this section we shall consider how public policy can be used to speed and effectuate the process of stable, full-employment growth.

THE UNDERDEVELOPED MODEL

Developing countries are typically faced with rapid rates of labor force growth as workers move from traditional sectors of the economy. Labor productivity and technological change are also growing rapidly. On the other hand, saving is apt to be low, and any saving which does occur is often expatriated. That capital which is available is generally of foreign origin and often inefficiently utilized, so that the output-capital ratio tends to be low. These factors result in

$$G_N > G_W$$

producing a redundancy of labor and a scarcity of capital.

Neoclassical analysis would contend that wage deflation should encourage the substitution of labor for capital in production, raising the output-capital ratio. In a developing country, however, opportunities for factor substitution are often extremely limited. Working with imported capital and imported technologies, management may be tied to particular production techniques with little information about or interest in alternative methods. Furthermore, wage deflation will only encourage labor substitution if interest rates are not permitted to fall proportionally. In a developing economy, it is generally desirable to keep interest rates low, to encourage investment. In addition, wage deflation is not a politically or socially desirable measure, particularly when aspirations are high for improved living conditions.

As a consequence of all these factors, it is doubtful that wage deflation will effectively produce an increase in average capital productivity. This being the case, a conscious effort should be made to introduce labor intensive technologies and to discourage firms from using capital intensive techniques imported from abroad. Because, for these countries, technological change is also imported, care should be taken that the improvements are not merely "cost saving," but are aimed at increasing capital productivity in accordance with the relative scarcity of capital in the economy. Increasing the rate of growth of labor productivity will increase the natural rate of growth and serve only to intensify the problem of labor redundancy.

The second key to increasing the warranted rate of growth is to increase the propensity to save and to ensure that saving is channeled into domestic investment. If the privileged classes do not happen to be of an entrepreneurial bent, it is important to develop reliable channels of credit so that the saving of the wealthy *rentiers* can flow into the hands of those willing to invest. In the absence of native entrepreneurs, investment may become a function of the central government.

Finally, planners must recognize that the capacity for the modern sector to absorb labor from the traditional sector is limited by the warranted rate of growth. Consequently, it is important not to break down and disrupt traditional institutions too quickly, if problems of massive unemployment of an urban proletariat and concomitant social unrest are to be avoided.

GROWTH POLICY
FOR MATURE ECONOMIES

The automatic mechanisms of the neoclassical analysis are much more likely to operate speedily and effectively in a mature economy. With high levels of investment and a high propensity to save, the desired rate of capital stock growth will be greater than the rate of labor force growth. Wages will follow their inherent tendency to rise as labor markets tighten, and if the monetary authorities do not allow interest rates to rise proportionally, firms will substitute capital for labor in production. In a mature economy, opportunities for factor substitution are much greater than in a developing one, because more technologies are available and managers are more sophisticated in their use. Furthermore, technological change will be domestically developed rather than imported, and it will tend to be of the variety which increases labor productivity, since labor is the limiting factor.

Consequently, the neoclassical automatic adjustment process will tend to reduce the output-capital ratio (by increasing capital intensivity) and, hence, the warranted rate of growth, provided that the monetary authorities do not attempt to stabilize the economy by a policy of tight money. There is a danger of this, of course, because given the condition,

$$G_W > G_N$$

there will be periods of rapid growth and threatened inflation which will call for restrictive measures. Tax policy would be preferred in this case, since increased taxes would presumably reduce private saving and, hence, the warranted rate of growth.

If tight labor markets tend to produce technological change of the labor-saving type (increasing labor productivity), then the natural rate of growth will increase. Consequently, labor scarcity will tend to produce convergence of the natural and warranted growth rates and lessen the intensity of the Harrod–Domar downturn which occurs when the actual rate of growth cannot keep pace with the warranted rate.

Many mature economies are so concerned with maintaining a competitive growth rate in the world growth race that they fail to recognize their own limitations. Although, in the very short run, when there is excess productive capacity available, the actual rate of growth may be governed by the warranted rate, the growth rate of the economy is essentially limited by the natural rate. Unless technological change and the labor force are growing rapidly, high levels of saving and investment will only produce instability, and policy makers will be plagued with the necessity of managing booms and recessions of ever-increasing magnitude. An economy with an annual labor force growth rate of 2 percent and a rate of increase in labor productivity of 3 percent cannot possibly grow as fast as a country whose labor force is growing by 5 percent per year and whose labor productivity is growing by 4 percent.

Another factor tempts planners to take an overly short-sighted view of the growth process. In recovering from a recession, there is a great temptation to achieve a high rate of growth to compensate for the losses experienced in the downturn. Such a policy naturally has desirable political implications as a show of economic muscle. But while the high rates of growth can be engineered in conditions of labor market surplus, the growth rate will eventually have to slow down to the natural rate. A decline in the growth rate will cause firms to reduce their rate of investment which will, in turn, cause a further reduction in demand through the multiplier process. Such a situation may well trigger a recession.

During recovery, the economy must grow faster than the natural rate to reduce the level of unemployment. But the recovery should be carefully and cautiously engineered so that the actual rate of growth can gradually level off to the natural rate without a catastrophic reduction in the level of investment.

Mature economies have many sources of instability other than the incompatibility of the natural and warranted rates of growth. We shall consider some of these in the following chapter. However, if the potential instability inherent in the process of growth is recognized and appropriate measures are taken, the job of macroeconomic management will be much easier for the policy planner.

Questions for Study and Review

1. "The concept of equilibrium is basic to economic analysis, yet it is useless except in the context of a dynamic theory." Explain and discuss critically.

2. Suppose the monetary authorities increase the money supply, causing the *LM* curve to shift rightward.

(a) Using a *comparative statics* approach, what will be the impact of this policy on national income, employment, and the interest rate?

(b) Suppose there is a lag in the product market so that income does not respond immediately to changes in economic conditions. What will be the impact of the policy on national income, employment, and the interest rate?

(c) If the money supply changes, what are the conditions for macro-economic stability?

3. "If policy planners wait for a downturn to initiate expansionary measures, a recession cannot be avoided." Explain.

4. The Harrod–Domar model is often criticized on the grounds that its inherent instability is incompatible with the experience of growing countries. What do economists mean when they say the model is unstable? What assumptions of the model produce this instability? If the model is unrealistic, is it useless for the purposes of policy planning? Discuss critically.

5. You are an economic advisor to a country which desires to maintain a high rate of growth and full employment with a minimum of instability. The annual rate of labor force growth is 4 percent and labor productivity is growing by 3 percent. National income is $100 billion, consumption is $90 billion, and the capital stock is valued at $300 billion. What advice would you give this country?

6. It is likely that a mature economy can adjust to a steady state, full-employment growth path with a minimum of government intervention in the private sector. This is not the case for a less-developed country. The latter may experience a prolonged period of labor force surplus unless a conscious effort is made to facilitate its absorption. Explain why this statement is true.

Additional Reading

Baumol, William J., *Economic Dynamics*. London: Macmillan & Co., Ltd., 1970, Chapters 4 and 7.

Dennison, Edward, "How to Raise the High-Employment Growth Rate by One Percentage Point," *The American Economic Review*, LII (May, 1962), 67–75.

Domar, Evsey, *Essays in the Theory of Economic Growth*. New York: Oxford University Press, 1957, Chapters 3–5.

Harrod, Roy, *Toward a Dynamic Economics*. London: Macmillan & Co., Ltd., 1948.

Meade, J., *A Neoclassical Theory of Economic Growth*. London: Unwin University Books, 1961.

Solow, Robert, "A Contribution to the Theory of Economic Growth," *The Quarterly Journal of Economics*, LXX (February, 1956), 65–94.

13

Achieving and Maintaining Economic Stability

The business cycle, or periodic fluctuations in the level of economic activity, has been a phenomenon common to all industrialized economies. Although these cycles vary in their intensity, they appear with remarkable regularity despite great changes in economic structure and social upheaval. In the United States, for example, the typical duration of the cycle has been about 40 months except for certain periods of severe economic and social maladjustment. In the period 1867–1966, for example, only six cycles lasted longer than four years. Two of these were associated with wars (World War II and the Korean conflict) and two with the severe depressions of the 1870's and 1930's.

Stabilization of business fluctuations is generally considered to be a major macroeconomic goal. Figure 13-1 shows the time pattern of the various phases of a cycle. Except during late recovery and at the peak, production will be below full capacity and unemployed resources represent an undesirable waste. In the later stages of the recovery, inflation may pose a threat, while the downturn is sometimes associated with financial panic and disruption of credit channels. Cyclical instability also reduces the average rate of investment, which lowers the growth rate and the rate of technological change.

Figure 13-1   Phases of a Business Cycle

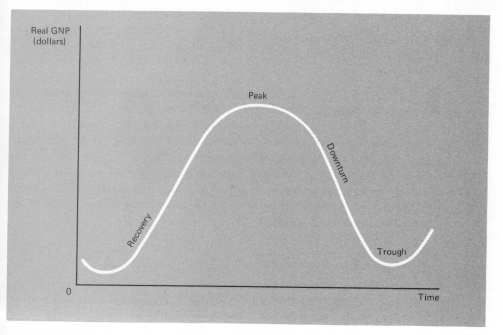

To design appropriate measures to stabilize cycles, the planner must know something about their causes. Many theories have been proposed to explain economic fluctuations—from sunspots and wars to innovation and imperialism. While some of these theories are useful for explaining recovery or downturn in particular cases, most are inadequate to explain the regularity of cycles. A theory which attributes business fluctuations to the economic consequences of war, for instance, cannot explain why cycles appear at 40-month intervals. Indeed, experience with prolonged war economies indicates that under these circumstances the recovery phase is generally longer than average.

13-1 Economic Dynamics and the Business Cycle

Because business cycles tend to be regular and recurrent, it is likely that this behavior is inherent in the macrodynamics of an economic system. In Chapter 12 we saw several possible sources of cyclical behavior for national income and employment. If the economy cannot sustain the warranted growth rate, investment demand will be highly unstable. Fluctuations in investment, through the multiplier, will generate even greater changes in GNP which in turn will affect employment, prices, interest rates, and wages.

Cyclical behavior may also result if reactions in some sectors are delayed or lagged. Given a lagged pattern of adjustment to equilibrium, income, employment, interest rates, and the price level will all follow a cyclical time path. As these vary, so do money and real wages, labor productivity, investment, consumption, and the growth rate.

Because reaction lags tend to produce instability, many economists argue that public policy tends to be destabilizing because of the lags involved in its execution. If this is the case, any policy designed to stabilize cycles must somehow be built into the system if it is not to do more harm than good. Proponents of this view contend that much of the instability in the U.S. economy is due to discretionary fiscal and monetary policy and argue that a comprehensive system of automatic stabilizers is required to achieve the goal of economic stability. In this section we shall examine each of these sources of instability in turn.

INVESTMENT AND THE CYCLE

Ignoring the public sector for the moment, it is clear that much of the instability of aggregate demand must come from the investment component. Consumption tends to be a rather stable function of income. Furthermore, since the average propensity to consume falls in booms and rises in recessions, consumption is a stabilizing influence over the cycle.

If export demand is highly volatile, then this component of private spending can produce cycles in domestic demand. This is generally a problem for developing countries, highly dependent on a single commodity and a small group of nations for its export market. For the United States, however, in which only about 5 percent of aggregate demand comes from abroad and for which both exports and export markets are well diversified, this is not a major source of instability.[1]

Since consumption and export demand in the United States are not destabilizing influences, any study of business fluctuations must concentrate on investment. If a portion of investment is undertaken for the sole purpose of capacity expansion, then that component of investment is likely to be highly unstable. If investment increases in proportion to changes in the level of demand, then as soon as the rate of increase in output declines, investment will actually decline and, through the multiplier, the economy will be plummeted into a downturn. Notice that if investment is increasing in proportion to *changes* in output, consumption must be increasing at an *increasing* rate. If the rate of growth of consumption levels off, investment must decline.[2]

If all investment is undertaken for the purpose of capacity expansion, then net investment will fall to zero as aggregate demand declines in response to the initial decline in investment. If the interaction of the multiplier and the accelerator is the source of the cycle, then the downturn should be very swift, that is, considerably faster than the recovery. Since this is the case for most cycles, this theory has a particular appeal.

The duration of the trough and early recovery phase will depend in large measure upon the durability of the capital stock. According to the multiplier–accelerator interaction model, net investment will fall to zero in the downturn. However, assuming that the economy must maintain some positive level of consumption, eventually capital equipment will have to be replaced. The more durable the equipment, the longer the trough will last. Eventually, however, some firms begin to undertake replacement investment. This stimulates aggregate demand through the multiplier. Recovery will be slow, since many firms will have excess capacity which can be used to produce the increased output. The speed of recovery will depend upon the

---

[1]Countries experiencing severe economic fluctuations may "export" their business cycles through the impact on demand abroad, particularly when they follow restrictive trade policies in an effort to increase the level of domestic employment. Such "beggar-my-neighbor" policies were followed by the developed countries in the 1930's with the impact of spreading the depression worldwide.

[2]See Chapter 12 for an algebraic formulation of this model.

durability of their capital (which will determine the effective amount of excess capacity) and the initial increase in investment. In general, the longer the recession and the less durable the capital stock, the speedier is the recovery. The more homogeneous the firms with respect to capital durability, the faster will be the recovery, since once replacement investment is initiated by some firms, most other firms will find themselves with little or no effective excess capacity and all will undertake new investment in response to the initial change in demand.

Figure 13-2 shows the time path of aggregate demand in a multiplier-accelerator interaction model. The function G_N represents the natural rate of growth which is the ceiling to real income growth that causes the downturn. The function C_S is the subsistence level of consumption which must be maintained and which initiates the replacement investment that is responsible for the recovery. If the durability of equipment does not undergo a radical change and if the values of the multiplier and accelerator (the

Figure 13-2   Time Path of Aggregate Demand in a
Multiplier–Accelerator Interaction Model

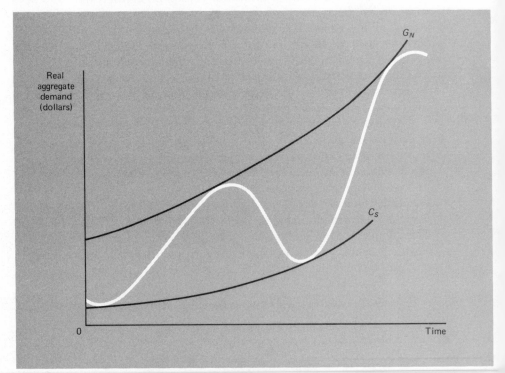

capital–output ratio) stay constant, then periodic fluctuations in economic activity should occur recurrently and with a fairly regular duration.

While the multiplier–accelerator model is useful in explaining the regularity of business cycles, it tends to explain them too well. Aggregate demand is not as unstable as this model suggests. Figure 13-3 shows the actual movement of real national income from 1957–1970. During this period real national income actually turned down only four times, and in only two cases, the recessions of 1960 and 1969–1970, did the downturn last for more

Figure 13-3   Time Pattern of Real National Income in the United States 1957–1970 (billions of 1958 dollars)

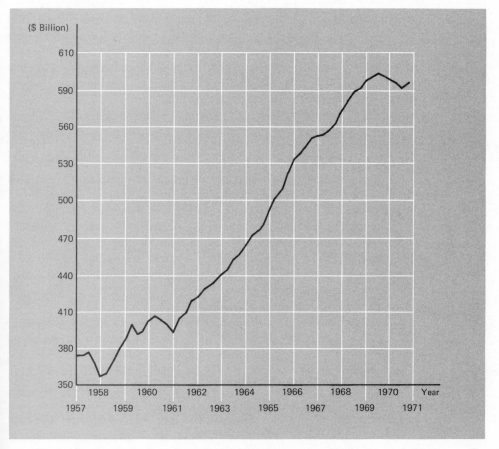

Source: U.S. Department of Commerce, Office of Business Economics. *Survey of Current Business* (Washington, D.C.: U.S. Government Printing Office, 1958–1971).

than two quarters. Recovery to the previous peak in all cases (except 1969–1970) occurred within three quarters. Between 1961 and the second quarter of 1969, the rise in real national income was constant, with a slight leveling off of the *rate* of increase in late 1966 and early 1967.

National income is not as unstable as the multiplier–accelerator model suggests for two reasons. First, investment is not governed solely by the accelerator principle. In addition, certain factors tend to cushion the impact of changes in investment on national income, effectively reducing the size of the multiplier.

In Chapter 6 we examined the determinants of investment in some detail. Investment in plant and equipment, which in 1965 comprised 67.0 percent of total investment and 10.7 percent of GNP, is affected by such factors as the availability of finance capital and credit conditions. If firms are limited in booms by the availability of funds and if retained earnings provide a floor to investment, then investment will be considerably less volatile than the accelerator model would suggest. There is an additional factor which contributes to the instability of plant and equipment investment, however. The marginal efficiency of capital is based upon producers' expectations about future demand. If previous experience has conditioned businessmen to expect a 40-month cycle, then they may begin to anticipate turning points. For instance, they may become pessimistic after a boom has lasted for more than two years. This "anticipation effect" will actually build in the very instability they fear.

Figure 13-4 shows the time pattern of plant and equipment investment over the period 1957–1970. Performance of this component of investment has been remarkably stable with no significant downturns or booms. Plant and equipment investment turned down slightly in 1958, and the downturn in late 1960 was barely perceptible. Note that the 1960 downturn *followed* rather than led the downturn in national income. In the late 1960's, plant and equipment investment began to show more instability than in the earlier period, with a decided downturn occurring in 1970. Again, the downturn followed the decline in national income.

Investment in residential housing in 1965 comprised 24.0 percent of total investment and 3.85 percent of GNP. Since investment in residential housing tends, in the short run, to be highly sensitive to credit conditions, its time pattern as seen in Figure 13-4 is actually slightly countercyclical, since interest rates tend to move in phase with the cycle. This is a stabilizing factor which reduces the volatility of total investment.

Inventory investment, which in 1965 accounted for 9.07 percent of total investment and 1.45 percent of GNP, is the most volatile component of investment. As described in Chapter 6, inventory investment is best explained by a pure accelerator model. Despite its small magnitude, some

Figure 13-4   Time Pattern of Investment in the United States 1957–1970
(billions of 1958 dollars)

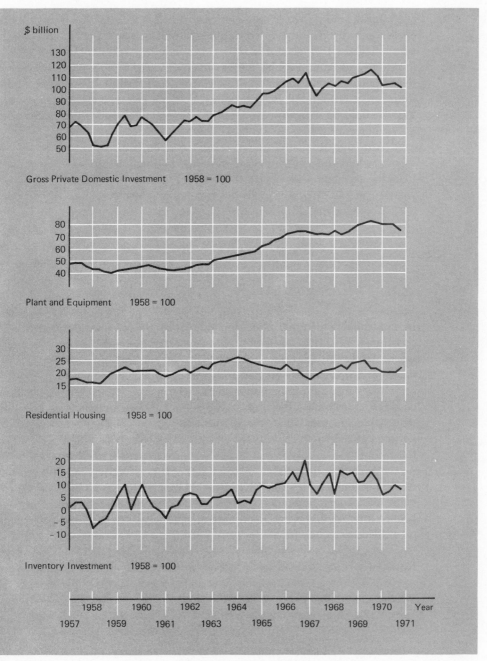

Source: U.S. Department of Commerce, Office of Business Economics. *Survey of Current Business* (Washington, D.C.: U.S. Government Printing Office, 1958–1971).

economists believe that inventory investment has accounted for most of the cyclical activity of the U.S. economy since the Korean conflict. In a model simulating the U.S. economy in the recession of 1957–1959, Duesenberry, Eckstein, and Fromm found the decline in inventory investment accounted for 62 percent of the decline in GNP.[3] Klein and Popkin, in a similar study, found that virtually all cyclical behavior in the U.S. economy since World War II could have been eliminated if inventory fluctuations were reduced by 75 percent.[4]

Although total investment is less volatile than a simple accelerator theory would suggest, it is more variable than national income, as is clear from the accompanying charts. If the multiplier analysis is correct, however, changes in investment should generate even greater changes in income.

Consider the simple multiplier of the Keynesian model,

$$Y = C + I$$
$$C = a + bY$$
$$I = f(i, \Delta Y, Y, \text{retained earnings, etc.})$$

$$Y = \frac{1}{1 - a} I$$

In this model, the multiplier depends upon the marginal propensity to consume (*MPC*). However, note that consumption depends upon *disposable income*, while the multiplier is applied to the relationship between *national income* and investment. To find the true multiplier, we need to know not only how consumption responds to changes in disposable income, but how changes in income affect the relationship between national income and disposable income. Thus, the distribution of the various components of national income as it changes, as well as its speed of adjustment, will affect the multiplier.

Appendix B discusses in some detail the accounting differences between national and disposable income. National income measures the total value of incomes earned in the process of production, including wages, profits, interest, and rent. Disposable income measures the after-tax income of individuals. Therefore,

National income − disposable income = Corporate profits − dividends
− transfer payments to individuals + personal taxes

[3] J. S. Duesenberry, Otto Eckstein, and Gary Fromm, "A Simulation of the United States Economy in Recession," *Econometrica*, XXVIII (October, 1960), 749–809.

[4] Lawrence R. Klein and Joel Popkin, "An Econometric Analysis of the Postwar Relationship Between Inventory Fluctuations and Changes in Aggregate Economic Activity," in *Inventory Fluctuations and Economic Stabilization*, paper prepared for the Joint Economic Committee (Washington, D.C.: U.S. Government Printing Office, 1961), p. 75.

The components of the difference between national income and disposable income operate to reduce the impact of an initial change in national income on disposable income. Corporate profits, which vary widely with the cycle, are the most important stabilizer of all. Fluctuations in this volatile component of national income are considerably greater than in national income itself, and consequently, disposable income varies far less than national income. Because firms are reluctant to vary dividend rates in response to short-run changes in profits, dividends are generally more stable than national income. Consequently, corporate profits less dividends display even more variation than corporate profits alone.

Personal taxes and transfer payments both vary with income. Both income and excise taxes rise and fall with changes in income and consumption. Transfer payments such as welfare payments and unemployment insurance rise when income falls. Both have the effect of reducing the impact of changes in national income on disposable income.

Thus, the complete national income multiplier,

$$\frac{\Delta Y}{\Delta D} = \frac{1}{1 - (b - m)(1 - t - p - z) - d - \mu}$$

where

b = marginal propensity to consume

m = marginal propensity to import

d = marginal propensity to invest (from national income)

μ = monetary effect

$t = \dfrac{\Delta T}{\Delta Y}$

T = personal taxes

$p = \dfrac{-\Delta W}{\Delta Y}$

W = transfer payments to individuals

$z = \dfrac{\Delta Z}{\Delta Y}$

Z = corporate profits less dividends (business saving)

is considerably smaller than the multiplier which ignores the difference between disposable income and national income.

The importance of "offsets" to changes in disposable income is indicated by the experience of the recession of 1961. During this period, personal income tax offset 17.9 percent of the decline in national income and corporate income tax offset 14.3 percent. This means that for every $100 decline in national income, individuals paid $17.90 less in personal income taxes and corporations paid $14.30 less in corporate income taxes. Unemployment insurance and welfare payments offset 6.1 percent, while excise taxes on consumer durables offset 16.1 percent.[5] These factors alone offset 54.4 percent of the decline in national income, so that disposable income declined by less than half as much as national income. Substituting into the multiplier for

$$t = 0.179 + 0.161$$
$$z = 0.143$$
$$p = 0.061$$

then

$$1 - t - p - z = 1 - 0.544 = 0.456$$

so that

$$\frac{\Delta Y}{\Delta D} = \frac{1}{1 - 0.456(b - m) - d - \mu}$$

and the impact of the marginal propensity to consume on the multiplier was reduced by over one-half.

In Chapter 5 we saw that the short-run MPC from disposable income is smaller than in the long run. In addition, it is likely that the speed with which income changes occur affects the MPC too. If income changes are rapid, they are generally viewed as transitory by households and changes in transitory income have minimal impact on consumption. Furthermore, households will attempt to maintain past living standards in the very short run. Thus, if a downturn is rapid, the MPC is likely to be much lower than it was in the recovery and boom phase, cushioning the impact of the downturn. In general, the national income multiplier tends to be considerably smaller in recessions than in booms. In recessions, offsets to changes in national income are greater than in booms. Furthermore, since downturns tend to be more rapid than recovery, the MPC tends to be lower.

THE IMPACT OF REACTION LAGS

In Chapter 12 we saw that a reaction lag in the monetary sector will cause national income, employment, prices, interest rates, and the other economic variables which depend upon them to move in a cyclical pattern over time.

---

[5] The excise tax offset in this period was unusually large due to a big decline in automobile sales in the recession.

The accelerator model of investment is also a special case of a reaction lag.

A relationship contains a reaction lag if the value of the dependent variable in period t, depends upon the values of the independent variables in time $(t - n)$, where n measures the length of the lag. Denoting the time period in which the variable is measured by a subscript, the accelerator model of investment,

$$I_t = \beta \, \Delta Y_t$$

can be expressed

$$I_t = \beta(Y_t - Y_{t-1})$$

Clearly, investment today depends upon income today as well as yesterday's income.

Suppose investment depends not only upon the change in demand, but also upon the amount of capital already available. Because desired changes in the capital stock cannot take place instantaneously but require time to implement, the actual capital stock at any time may be different from the optimal level. The *flexible accelerator* model takes into account the possibility that the increased output will be produced with excess capacity capital. Denoting actual capital stock as K_t and desired capital stock as K_t^*, the model can be expressed as

$$I_t = \beta(Y_t - Y_{t-1}) - \gamma(K_t - K_t^*)$$
$$K_t^* = \beta Y_t$$

If actual capital stock is greater than the firm desires or finds necessary to produce Y_t, then investment will be lower by some proportion of the difference.[6]

Actual capital stock, however, is equal to the accumulated investment over the life of the equipment, so

$$K_t = I_{t-1} + I_{t-2} + \cdots + I_{t-n}$$

where n is the life of the equipment. Therefore,

$$I_t = f(Y_t, Y_{t-1}, I_{t-1}, I_{t-2}, \cdots, I_{t-n})$$

Investment today depends not only upon yesterday's income but also yesterday's investment.

---

[6]The flexible accelerator can also work in the opposite direction. If the capital stock is below the optimal level in period t, then investment will be greater than that projected by a simple accelerator model.

Reaction lags are the basic source of instability in an economic system. Without these lags, the system would generally reach equilibrium instantaneously.[7] It is likely, however, that various sorts of reaction lags will exist in any economic system.

Initially, there may be a *recognition lag*. It may take some time for households, for instance, to recognize that real income has fallen. This may be followed by a *decision lag*, as households decide to readjust consumption in response to the change in income. This lag may spread over several time periods as households adjust to new standards of consumption and as they determine whether or not the decline in income is transitory or permanent. Finally, there is an *implementation lag* as households implement the decision to readjust consumption. The implementation lag may be particularly long for investment spending. Shirley Almon has estimated that the implementation lag between the decision to undertake a capital expenditure and the completion of the expenditure is about two years for most industries, with the bulk of the expenditure occurring between three and six quarters after the decision was made.[8]

DESTABILIZING LAGS
IN PUBLIC POLICY

Since cyclical behavior of macroeconomic targets can be attributed to reaction lags in the various sectors of the economy, public policy may also be destabilizing if it is subject to lags. Some economists, such as Milton Friedman, argue that lags in discretionary stabilization policy are so long that they tend to reinforce cyclical behavior rather than stabilize it. When lags in policy initiation are combined with lags in the private sector, the problem of appropriate timing of public policy can be serious. If the composite lag is as long as two years, this requires forecasting economic behavior more than two years in advance. Not only must forecasts be made, but policy makers must be convinced that the forecasts are correct and that policy measures must be taken now to reverse these future trends.

13-2 Stabilization Policy:
Rules Versus Discretion

One of the most controversial aspects of macroeconomic policy is whether or not stabilization policy should rely on automatic stabilizers or whether

---

[7]The system will not reach equilibrium, even in the absence of lags if the equilibrium is unstable. See Appendix A for an example of such a possibility for macroeconomic equilibrium.

[8]Shirley Almon, "The Distributed Lag between Capital Appropriations and Expenditures," *Econometrica*, XXXIII (January, 1965), 178–196.

automatic stabilizers should be supplemented by discretionary measures. Those who argue for "rules" support an overall strengthening of automatic stabilizers and reject discretionary measures as destabilizing because of lags. An extreme position is taken by Milton Friedman, who has proposed a completely automatic monetary mechanism for achieving stability. On the other side of the controversy, those who argue for "authority" contend that automatic stabilizers can never completely eliminate instability. As our understanding of macroeconomic relationships and our ability to forecast trends improves, it is foolish not to rely more heavily on discretionary policy where it is indicated. Because automatic mechanisms have traditionally been slow and unreliable, it would be unwise and unpolitic to allow a recession or serious inflation to run its course with no attempt to reverse the trend by discretionary measures.

Clearly, while some discretionary control is indicated in the face of catastrophic events such as war, financial panic, or a severe depression such as occurred in the 1930's, the rules versus authority controversy has taken place within the context of economic conditions that are reasonably stable. Walter Heller once viewed the role of stabilization policy in the 1960's as that of "fine tuning." In this section we shall examine some aspects of stabilization policy in such a context.

AUTOMATIC STABILIZERS

Automatic stabilizers, such as personal and corporate income taxes, excise taxes, and unemployment insurance, reduce the fluctuations in disposable income associated with changes in national income and thereby reduce the size of the multiplier. They also operate to stabilize investment, the most volatile component of GNP. These stabilizers are automatic because they are triggered by changes in the level of economic activity, usually national income. Since they are "built into" the system, no one has to decide to initiate a policy action. Because a cyclical trend must occur to activate them, the stabilizers can never be completely effective in eliminating economic fluctuations. Stabilizers can, however, significantly reduce their amplitude and duration.

In the 1960 recession we saw that automatic stabilizers offset over half the decline in national income. Furthermore, the decline in corporate taxes in this period may have provided some stimulus to investment. As indicated by the data in Figure 13-4, plant and equipment investment, which is most likely to be influenced by the availability of internal funds, remained stable despite the decline in real national income. The overall decline in investment in this recession was due to the sharp drop in inventory accumulation. Unfortunately, automatic stabilizers have little or no impact on inventory investment, which has been the major source of instability in the post-World War II economy.

In a simulation of the U.S. economy, Eilbott estimated that the stabilizers will generally offset from 35 percent to 50 percent of a decline in *GNP* and from 25 percent to 40 percent of the recovery.[9] In addition, he shows that the effectiveness of the stabilizers could be increased significantly by extending the coverage of unemployment compensation. Furthermore, he suggests that, in the absence of the stabilizers, fluctuations might be even greater than predicted by his model since psychological factors tend to reinforce swings in economic activity. On the basis of his study, Eilbott concludes that

> In general . . . the stabilizers do appear to provide, under all but unusual circumstances, a reasonably satisfactory defense against downward pressures on the economy. They do not suffer, as do discretionary policies, from problems of timing and errors of judgment, and they seem to be powerful enough (especially if the unemployment compensation system is strengthened considerably) to prevent a substantial percentage of an income decline.[10]

Other economists have argued that automatic stabilizers should be strengthened by such measures as extending the system of unemployment insurance and making income taxes more progressive. The automatic stabilizers in the U.S. fiscal package were originally designed for other purposes, however, and the distributional implications of making them more responsive to income changes are not always desirable. Consequently, some observers have suggested the development of automatic fiscal and monetary policies, designed specifically as stabilization measures, and with as neutral a distributional impact as possible. This concept is known as *formula flexibility*.

One suggestion which has received serious consideration is the possibility of automatically altering tax rates in response to changes in the level of economic activity. Tax rates would rise in booms and fall in recessions in such a way that the average tax rate for the entire period would be in line with the prevailing tax schedule. One difficulty with such a program, which presents itself whenever formula flexibility is discussed, is that no one can agree on the appropriate index of economic activity to which to tie tax rate changes. Although many economists seem to favor the unemployment rate (i.e., reduce the tax rate when the unemployment rate rises above some stipulated amount and raise the tax rate when the unemployment rate falls below some different value), this would be a poor choice for stabilization purposes. The level of employment is one of the lagging

---

[9]Peter Eilbott, "The Effectiveness of Automatic Stabilizers," *The American Economic Review,* LVI (June, 1966), 450–465.
[10]*Ibid.,* p. 464.

variables during cyclical fluctuations, since it takes time for firms to hire and fire workers in response to changes in demand. By the time the unemployment rate rises, the economy is likely to be well into the downturn. The best time to undertake expansionary action is before the peak is actually reached, when the rate of increase in demand has begun to level off, but before the unemployment rate has increased. This is because the downturn in investment generally precedes the downturn in income. Furthermore, there is likely to be some lag in the reactions of households to the tax cut. A better, but more controversial, measure would be to tie changes in tax rates to *changes* in income, to the level of total investment or, better still, to inventory investment. Duesenberry, Eckstein, and Fromm, in their simulation of the U.S. economy in a recession, found that tying tax rate changes to changes in GNP was more effective than tying them to the unemployment rate.[11] In one case, they simulated an antirecession policy which reduced the amount of personal income tax collected by a percentage which depended upon the deviation of GNP from its previous peak value. They found that this reduced the decline in GNP from $34 billion to $20.2 billion with consumption increasing throughout the recession.

A drawback to such a plan is that it may prematurely induce a recession psychology which may precipitate the downturn. Using the unemployment rate as an indicator of economic activity will not have this effect since the turning point will have already occurred. However, the lags involved might be so great as to be destabilizing.

DISCRETIONARY STABILIZATION POLICY

Automatic stabilizers have proved to be an effective means of shielding the U.S. economy from wide swings in economic activity. By extending their coverage and increasing their sensitivity to changes in national income as well as by designing measures with *formula flexibility*, they could presumably be made even more effective. However, because they must be triggered by income fluctuations, automatic stabilizers can never completely eliminate cyclical instability.

Discretionary measures, such as money supply changes, variations in the level of public spending, and changes in tax rates or structure, are all subject to lags of various sorts. First, there is the *recognition lag*. Cyclical indicators require interpretation, and many times different observers will disagree concerning the need for remedial action. Once the need for stabilizing action is recognized, there is the *policy initiation lag*. Planners must first decide on the appropriate remedy, and then they must convince policy

---

[11] J. S. Duesenberry et al., *op. cit.* pp. 749–809.

makers that it should be undertaken. All discretionary policy requires political approval, and the problem is the most acute in boom periods when such measures as tax increases, spending cuts, and tight money are politically unpopular. If lags in the private sector are expected to be long, remedial action may be called for well in advance of overt indications of a change in the phase of a cycle. Thus, restrictive policies may be called for even before full employment is reached. President Johnson, for instance, requested a tax increase from the congress nearly two years before it was finally approved. By the time the measure was approved and became effective, the economy was well into the downturn and the effect was, on balance, destabilizing.

The duration of the policy initiation lag will depend upon the type of policy under consideration as well as the phase of the cycle. The most flexible instrument in all phases of the cycle tends to be monetary policy, since discretionary changes in the money supply do not require congressional approval. The least flexible instrument tends to be tax policy, since the congress must approve all tax changes. The president has more authority on the expenditure side, particularly in the short run, so that generally there is a bias toward increasing expenditures when recession is threatened.

While tax changes have the longest policy initiation lag, they generally have a shorter *effectiveness lag* than the other discretionary measures.[12] The effectiveness lag is considerably shortened by the comprehensive tax withholding system. Recent experience, however, has shown that the effectiveness lag of a tax increase is not insignificant. The 10 percent surtax on the personal income tax imposed by the Johnson administration in 1968 had little immediate impact on consumption. One reason may have been that the tax was widely publicized as being a temporary measure, so that households considered it a transitory reduction in their income. This being the case, the MPC would have been negligible and the increased taxes would have been paid from savings.

The impact of a decision to reduce public spending may have a substantial effectiveness lag because it is not feasible to terminate spending programs at will. Not only would it be wasteful to halt construction of a highway or some other public works program in midstream, but it is also not politically feasible to do so.

The effectiveness lag in monetary policy is perhaps the most unreliable and difficult to estimate, particularly as an expansionary measure. This is because the link between increases in the money supply, a decline in the interest rate, and the stimulus to investment are all tenuous and unreliable.

---

[12] Automatic stabilizers, of course, are subject to the same effectiveness lags as discretionary measures and may, as a consequence, be destabilizing.

In boom periods, discretionary policy is generally biased toward tight money since it has the shortest policy initiation lag. Since the effectiveness lag is unreliable and generally of long duration, it is difficult for planners to determine the appropriate timing. When a downturn is threatened, fiscal measures may be easier to engineer since spending increases and tax cuts are politically more desirable than their counterparts in a boom. Since the effectiveness lag is shorter for these measures, antirecession policy is easier to time and less likely to be destabilizing than restrictive policies. The timing of the Kennedy–Johnson tax cut of 1964 was considerably better than was the Johnson surtax of 1968. For the tax cut, the total recognition plus policy initiation plus effectiveness lag was less than one year. For the 1968 surtax, the recognition plus policy initiation lag alone was about two years, and by 1970 (when the surtax was removed) many economists doubted that it had even had a significant effect on consumption. In fact, the major impact of the surtax may have been to feed a cost–push inflation rather than to restrict consumption as it was originally intended.

THE FRIEDMAN FRAMEWORK
FOR ECONOMIC STABILITY

The timing difficulties of discretionary policies and the inadequacy of automatic stabilizers have led to various proposals for formula flexibility. An extreme position is taken by Milton Friedman, who has proposed a framework for economic stability which relies completely on an automatic monetary mechanism.[13] Friedman's proposal is in line with his belief that monetary policy is the only effective and reliable means of controlling demand. His system, he argues, being completely automatic will avoid the destabilizing lags associated with discretionary policy.

The basis of Friedman's proposal is to maintain a constant and steady rate of increase of the money supply equal to the natural rate of growth of the economy. In the absence of economic fluctuations, this would allow the rate of growth of money supply to exactly equal the growth rate of output and the transactions demand for money with full employment and stable prices.

The tax system would be progressive with income, while the level of public spending would be determined by the society's requirement for public goods. Public spending would not be used for the purpose of manipulating aggregate demand. Tax rates should be set so that at full employment there would be a slight budget deficit. This deficit would be financed by money

[13]Friedman's proposal is described fully in Milton Friedman, "A Monetary and Fiscal Framework for Economic Stability," *The American Economic Review,* XXXVIII (June, 1948), 245–264.

creation and would be set so as to permit the secular increase in the money supply necessitated by the growth requirements of the economy.

The banking system would be required to hold 100 percent of its deposits as reserves. Since the sole function of the banking system would be to provide deposit facilities and check clearance, it could not make loans and, consequently, could not create money. The Fed would buy bonds from the U.S. Treasury when the government budget was in deficit and retire them when the budget was in surplus. Consequently, money would be created to meet government deficits and retired when the budget was in surplus.

Since the income tax system is designed to allow only the secular increase in the money supply at full employment, non-secular deficits and surpluses with consequent changes in the money supply will be the automatic consequences of changes in income. If income falls below the full-employment level, tax receipts will fall, the budget will go into deficit, and the money supply will be automatically increased. The reverse will occur if demand increases after full employment is achieved, since price inflation will cause money income to rise above the full-employment level, generating a budget surplus and consequent contraction of the money supply. Thus, the quantity of money is automatically determined by the needs of economic stability.

In this system, discretionary action is limited to determining the tax rates required to maintain the desired budget deficit at full employment. Since all government spending is financed either by taxes or money creation, there will be no government bonds held by the public and no open market operations. Friedman points out that debt finance is not as efficient as money creation for stimulating demand nor will debt retirement restrict demand as much as a reduction in the quantity of money.

While this proposal is internally consistent, it relies on the belief that changes in the money supply alone are adequate for controlling demand. A Keynesian would argue that the mechanism on which the program depends is the interest rate and that the interest rate may be an ineffective stabilizing instrument. Furthermore, while this proposal eliminates the recognition and initiation lags, there still may be a substantial effectiveness lag. Friedman argues that if his program is adopted the effectiveness lag may be eliminated or at least shortened, if the business community can count on automatic changes in the money supply. If they do not have to wait to see if discretionary actions will be undertaken, they will anticipate changes in monetary conditions.

An inherent weakness of the Friedman proposal is the assumption that prices will be flexible in both directions. If there is downward price rigidity, then there will not be a one-to-one correspondence between the level of money income and employment. If prices and the unemployment rate are rising simultaneously because of cost–push factors (perhaps associated with rising interest rates), the level of money income will not fall with employment, the deficit will not increase, and the automatic increase in the money supply required to stimulate the economy will not be forthcoming. Conceivably, the level of income may rise as unemployment rises, increasing the budget surplus and causing a contraction in the money supply. Not only will this reduce the level of employment still farther, but it will cause interest rates to rise, feeding the cost–push inflation. Friedman, like Keynes, views aggregate demand as the essential measure of the level of economic activity. Consequently, his remedies are more applicable to a recession than in managing a modern cost–push inflation.

As with all automatic mechanisms, it is likely that the adjustment process implicit in the Friedman proposal would be slow and painful. If unemployment became sufficiently severe, it is conceivable that money wage rates would finally fall and with them the price level and the level of money income, setting the automatic stabilizer in motion. It is doubtful, however, that, with the principles of Keynesian economics and the appropriate fiscal remedies at their disposal, policy makers would find it politically expedient to allow a recession or prolonged inflation to drag on simply for the sake of automaticity. While discretionary measures suffer from lags and while they may overshoot the mark and hence require abrupt reversal, discretionary fine tuning by a series of successive approximations may be preferred to dependence on automatic monetary stimuli.

Questions for Study and Review

1. Consider the model

$$Y_t = C_t + I_t$$
$$C_t = aY_{t-1}$$
$$I_t = b(Y_{t-1} - Y_{t-2})$$

(a) If $a = 0.5$ and $b = 2$, trace the time path of income starting at $t = 0$ where

$$Y_0 = 100$$

and

$$Y_1 = 110$$

(b) Design a time path for government spending which would stabilize this economy at $Y = 150$.

(c) If $a = 0.8$ and $b = 3$, answer the question in part (a). Does an increase in the parameter values a and b increase or reduce the stability of the system?

(d) Suppose the investment equation is altered so that

$$I_t = b(Y_{t-1} - Y_{t-2}) - \gamma(K_t - K_t^*)$$

Find the time path of part (a), assuming

$$K_t^* = bY_t$$
$$K_0 = 250$$

and

$$\gamma = 0.5$$

How does the introduction of the capital stock variable into the investment equation affect the stability of the system?

2. Consider an economy in which the personal income tax rate is a uniform 10 percent and the corporate income tax rate is 15 percent. The MPC from disposable income is 0.8 and the marginal propensity to invest from corporate income is 0.5.

(a) Find the impact on national income of an increase in government spending of 100.

(b) Suppose the personal income tax is raised to 15 percent. Will the increase in tax revenue be sufficient to finance the expenditure increase? (*Hint:* Notice that the increased tax rate changes the value of the multiplier.)

3. Discuss and analyze the cyclical behavior of the following:

(a) consumption,

(b) corporate profits,

(c) inventory investment,

(d) plant and equipment investment,

(e) residential construction.

4. Discuss the relative merits of automatic stabilizers, formula flexibility, and discretionary fiscal and monetary policy for stabilizing business cycles. You should include in your discussion some hypothetical or historical examples.

5. Discuss and critically evaluate Milton Friedman's framework for economic stability.

6. "If federal expenditure should be held constant at the current level with no increase in tax rates, a depression is inevitable." Defend or attack the quoted proposition.

Additional Reading

Bronfenbrenner, Martin, ed., *Is the Business Cycle Obsolete?* New York: John Wiley & Sons, Inc., 1969.

Clement, M. O., "The Quantitative Impact of Automatic Stabilizers," *The Review of Economics and Statistics*, XLII (February, 1960), 56–61.

Duesenberry, J. S., O. Eckstein, and G. Fromm, "A Simulation of the United States Economy in Recession," *Econometrica*, XXVIII (October, 1960), 749–809.

Eilbott, Peter, "The Effectiveness of Automatic Stabilizers," *The American Economic Review*, LVI (June, 1966), 450–465.

Friedman, Milton, "A Monetary and Fiscal Framework for Economic Stability," *The American Economic Review*, XXXVIII (June, 1948), 245–264.

Matthews, R. C. O., *The Business Cycle*. Chicago: The University of Chicago Press, 1959.

Samuelson, Paul, "Interactions Between the Multiplier Analysis and the Principle of Acceleration," *The Review of Economic Statistics*, XXI (May, 1939), 75–78.

14

The
Impact
of Macroeconomic
Policy

Now that we have completed the formal analysis of models of income determination, it will be useful to review the various macroeconomic policy instruments in terms of their impact on the objectives set forth in Chapter 1. If public policy is to achieve full employment and economic growth while maintaining price stability and avoiding excessive balance of payments deficits, that policy must be carefully designed.

As we have seen, macroeconomic policy must consist of more than simply manipulating aggregate demand, as the Keynesian model suggests. To the extent that policy targets conflict, policy must be designed to reduce the range in which the conflict occurs. Thus, if policy makers recognize an incompatibility between the goals of full employment and price stability, measures which increase labor mobility and which prevent money wages from rising as labor markets tighten may keep prices from increasing as aggregate demand and the level of employment are increased. In addition, we have seen that instruments designed to control aggregate demand may have a secondary impact on the policy objectives which may counteract the effect of the change in demand. For instance, tight money and tax increases may be used to restrict demand during an inflation, but both these policies tend to increase production costs, which may cause firms to increase prices.

When government undertakes spending programs, it must have a means of commandeering resources. How these resources are obtained—through taxes, borrowing, or money creation—will influence the policy objectives. Thus, a final analysis of the effect of economic policy must contain a discussion of the impact of federal budget operations.

In this chapter we shall consider the impact of macroeconomic policy, with particular attention paid to its secondary effects when it is designed essentially for the purpose of controlling aggregate demand.

14-1 The Problem of Conflicting Objectives

In a simple Keynesian model, the way to reach full employment is to increase aggregate demand. Inflation is brought into check by reducing demand. Since the model assumes prices will remain stable until full employment is attained, there is no conflict between the goals of full employment and price stability, and both objectives can be achieved simultaneously simply by manipulating demand. In the real world, however, prices begin to rise well before full employment is reached, so that full employment is incompatible with price stability.

Two choices are open. We can remain pure Keynesians and adhere to the view that controlling aggregate demand is the only legitimate sort of macroeconomic policy. In this case the policy objectives must be viewed as a trade-off; that is, we can only increase the level of employment at the cost of inflation. On the other hand, we can take the position that economic policy should be designed to make Keynesian policy (demand manipulation) more effective. Thus, if public policy can reduce the rate of inflation associated with each level of employment, then increases in demand may help to achieve the full-employment goal with a minimum of inflation. In this section we shall examine several potential conflicts of objectives and consider how economic policy can be designed to reduce the range of conflict.

FULL EMPLOYMENT AND PRICE STABILITY

Prices rise with the level of employment when increases in employment are associated with rising marginal costs of production. The greatest element in these costs is marginal labor cost per unit of output. Labor costs rise as money wages increase and as marginal productivity declines. Other factors which may contribute to rising costs of production are increases in the price of materials and capital goods.

Policies which could keep production costs from rising as employment increases include the following:

1. *Wage–price guidelines*—If wage increases do not exceed productivity increases, unit labor costs will not rise with employment and prices will not increase unless other production costs rise.

2. *Measures to increase labor productivity*—Given the institutional realities of an upward drift in money wages, wage–price guidelines will be difficult to enforce if labor productivity is not growing rapidly. It is particularly important to keep labor productivity from declining as the level of employment is increased. Programs to increase labor mobility, both regionally and occupationally, may reduce unemployment which was originally viewed as "structural" without decreasing productivity. These programs should include retraining experience as well as aids to relocation. To keep labor productivity high, it is also important not to interfere with the rate of investment and technological change. Technological change that raises labor productivity should be encouraged. Measures to increase labor productivity will also increase the potential for economic growth.

3. *Special attention to basic industries*—Wage–price guidelines and measures to improve labor productivity should be applied with particular vigor in basic industries such as steel, since prices in basic industries represent production costs for secondary industry. Food prices are also important since they are a significant component of the cost-of-living index. Higher food prices are often pyramided into higher wages. If an aid-to-agriculture pro-

gram is undertaken, therefore, direct subsidies to farmers will be preferred
to agricultural price supports.

ECONOMIC GROWTH, FULL EMPLOYMENT, AND PRICE STABILITY

For a mature economy, the rate of economic growth consistent with full
employment and price stability is limited by the rate of labor force growth
and the rate of growth of labor productivity. Attempts to grow more rapidly
than the productive capacity of the labor force allows will result in recurrent
periods of recession (unemployment) and inflation. Increasing the rate of
investment will not be consistent with noninflationary, full-employment
growth unless it is accompanied by labor-saving technological change (which
increases labor productivity).

Policy makers should recognize the limitations imposed by the natural
rate of growth, particularly in managing an economic expansion. If recovery
is too rapid, bottlenecks will appear, thereby increasing inflationary pressures. Attempts to slow down the boom may produce a contraction of the
level of investment and result in a downturn.

Policies to reduce the range of conflict between the growth objective
and full employment and price stability include the following:

1. *Use of monetary policy to control the warranted rate of growth*—If the
warranted rate of growth is greater than the natural rate, inflation and a
subsequent recession may ensue. Although public authorities may be
tempted to employ a tight money policy to control the expansion, such a
policy will discourage firms from substituting capital for labor as money
wage rates rise. If, however, firms are encouraged to look for more capital
intensive processes, the warranted rate of growth will decline and productivity per worker and the natural rate of growth will increase.

2. *Encouraging labor-saving innovations*—The natural rate of growth, which
limits the growth rate consistent with full employment and price stability,
can be increased by increasing the rate of growth of labor productivity. Labor
productivity can be increased by the adoption of labor-saving innovations.
Such innovations are often met with opposition by labor unions on the
grounds that they produce unemployment. For the economy as a whole,
this is not likely to be a problem if the demand for labor is growing faster
than the supply (which is equivalent to the condition that the warranted
rate exceeds the natural rate of growth). However, it can be a problem in
individual industries for which productivity increases are not matched by
increases in demand. In this case labor must be reallocated to industries
in which demand is growing more rapidly. Such reallocation may entail both

retraining and geographical relocation and should be facilitated by public policy if inflation and structural unemployment are to be avoided.

FULL EMPLOYMENT
AND THE BALANCE OF PAYMENTS

Expansionary monetary and fiscal policy may increase the level of employment at the expense of widening the balance-of-payments deficit. Imports will rise with the level of money demand, and if exports do not increase concomitantly, the trade deficit will increase. Furthermore, if interest rates are reduced to stimulate demand, capital will go abroad where interest rates are higher.

For the United States, where the foreign sector represents a small component of demand, the conflict of objectives is not serious. However, for countries such as Britain, it is often deemed necessary to maintain a state of semirecession in the domestic economy to avoid serious payments deficits.

The conflict of domestic policy objectives with that of avoiding excessive payments deficits could be eliminated by the adoption of a system of *flexible exchange rates* under which a payments deficit could not occur. If the price of each country's currency could fluctuate in response to the requirements for trade, then there would never be an excess supply of any currency, and every country would automatically experience payments equilibrium. During an expansion, as import demand increases, the supply of a country's currency would increase and its price would fall. Such an experience may be inflationary for the domestic economy, however, since it would effectively raise the price of imports in terms of the domestic currency.[1]

A policy of flexible exchange rates would have to be universally adopted by many countries. Strong vested interests in the international financial community currently support the maintenance of fixed exchange rates and an international gold standard. Since flexible exchange rates are not likely to be adopted due to the opposition of these vested interests, governments must look to second-best solutions to overcome the incompatibility of their domestic economic goals and balance of payments requirements.

Such policies include

1. *Monetary policy and interest equalization tax*—The domestic government could rely on expansionary fiscal policy to stimulate investment, employ-

---

[1]For a more complete discussion of flexible exchange rates, see Milton Friedman, "The Case for Flexible Exchange Rates," in *Essays in Positive Economics* (Chicago: The University of Chicago Press, 1953).

ment, and growth while following a tight money policy to attract foreign capital and improve the balance of payments. In some cases, however, governments prefer or are required by political pressure to keep interest rates low to stimulate investment at home. When this is the case, funds may be expatriated to foreign capital markets to take advantage of higher interest rates there. Such an outflow of domestic currency will widen the balance-of-payments deficit. An *interest equalization tax* on earnings from foreign securities will reduce the actual return to holding these bonds and eliminate the gain to expatriating finance capital.

2. *Currency devaluation*—A currency devaluation by raising the domestic price of imports and reducing the foreign price of exports should discourage imports and stimulate exports, thereby reducing the trade deficit. A currency devaluation which raises import prices may be inflationary, however, particularly for a country such as Great Britain where imports are largely composed of food and primary products.[2]

A currency devaluation operates on the same principle as flexible exchange rates except that it is a one-time discretionary action in which the currency is revalued, rather than a constant and automatic realignment of exchange rates as trade conditions change. Ideally, a currency would be valued so that payments are in equilibrium at full employment. However, this ideal value depends upon the value of other currencies and upon economic conditions abroad, all of which are constantly in flux. Changes in the structure of trade also affect the optimum currency value.

3. *Trade restrictions and export subsidies*—Most economists tend to regard trade restrictions as undesirable, at least for advanced countries. By raising import prices they prevent consumers from obtaining goods from the cheapest possible source. Furthermore, most countries will follow reciprocal practices and establish comparable restrictions on imports, so that the measures are likely to be self-defeating. Their ultimate impact is merely to reduce total world trade, with goods and services being produced by high-cost domestic firms rather than by the most efficient producer. Import restrictions, by raising import prices, also are inflationary.

Export subsidies also interfere with efficient resource allocation. They permit foreigners to buy goods more cheaply than domestic purchasers. Foreigners view such practices as an unfair incursion into the domestic market and may impose import barriers which would, of course, defeat the objective of the export subsidy. If exports are primary goods, foreign manufacturers will face lower production costs than domestic producers with the

---

[2]If the demand for imports is inelastic with respect to price, a devaluation may actually increase a payments deficit since the percentage increase in price will exceed the percentage reduction in quantity imported, and the value of imports will rise. If exports fall very little, the payments deficit might actually widen.

result that foreigners will be able to undersell domestic manufacturers in their own markets.

14-2 Choice of Policy Instruments

Keynesian analysis, by suggesting that policy targets can be attained solely by manipulating aggregate demand, implies that the policy variables move symmetrically with respect to negative and positive changes in policy instruments which affect aggregate demand. This is not the case for a number of reasons. First, the trade-offs between various targets do not operate in both directions. For instance, while an increase in the level of employment will produce an increase in prices, it is not likely that a reduction in employment will cause a decline in prices due to the downward rigidity of money wages. Furthermore, changes in policy instruments designed to influence demand have secondary effects which do not always act symmetrically when moving in opposite directions. Thus, a tax increase may be inflationary, while a reduction in taxes is not likely to cause a reduction in prices. Finally, there is an asymmetry in the response of various components of demand to changes in policy instruments. An increase in interest rates may discourage investment in a boom, but a reduction in interest rates may not stimulate it in a recession.

Because of this asymmetry, anti-inflation policy cannot be viewed as antirecession policy in reverse. Consequently, the appropriate choice of policy instruments will depend largely upon the state of the economy at the time the policy is designed.

ANTIRECESSION POLICY

The Keynesian model is most applicable to the design of antirecession policy. During a recession the primary objective is to increase the level of employment and the growth rate. Until the expansion begins, there is little danger of serious inflation or balance-of-payments difficulties. The particular problems of managing an inflationary recession will be treated later in this section. Policy instruments for antirecession action include increases in public spending, tax cuts, and increases in the money supply. Each shall be considered in turn.

1. *Increased public spending*—Increases in public spending are the most direct and effective way to stimulate demand and the level of employment. It must be kept in mind, however, that spending increases are often irreversible. The government may involve itself in a long-term program of

highway construction, for instance. If the purpose of the spending were primarily to increase the level of economic activity, presumably it would be desirable for spending to level off once full employment is reached. If there is excessive aggregate demand, the spending program should be scrapped. However, it may be difficult to justify abandoning a highway program in midstream, and consequently, the cutback in spending may have to come from consumption or investment. If government spending programs are not reversible then there will be a secular increase in the size of the public sector over the cycle if this instrument is used as an antirecession measure.

Keynes observed that it would be better

> . . . if the Treasury were to fill old bottles with banknotes, bury them at suitable depths in disused coal mines which are then filled up to the surface with town rubbish, and then leave it to private enterprise on well-tried principles of *laissez-faire* to dig the notes up again, . . . there would be no more unemployment and, with the help of the repercussions, the real income of the community, and its capital wealth also, would probably become a good deal greater than it actually is.[3]

Keynes also suggested that the ancient practice of building pyramids and cathedrals was also useful in generating full employment, since these endeavors have little use-value, and as a consequence, the populace will never complain of having too many of them. Thus he argues, "Two pyramids, two masses for the dead, are twice as good as one; but not so two railways from London to York."[4]

This philosophy appears capricious in view of the chronic need for public services in today's society. Indeed, the idea that spending for the sake of spending is a good thing presents serious questions for resource allocation in a full-employment economy. What happens when the Office of Pyramid Construction develops such economic and political power that it wins increasingly large budgetary appropriations from the congress at the expense of education, medical care, and other socially more useful endeavors?

Even when the programs have merit, however, the use of government expenditure as a means of stimulating the economy builds in a bias toward an ever-growing public sector. This is because it is easier to increase spending in a recession than it is to reduce spending in boom periods.

2. *Tax reductions*—Tax reductions stimulate both consumption and investment spending. A cut in personal income taxes generally stimulates consumption with a very short lag. In fact, the short-run marginal propensity

---

[3]J. M. Keynes, *The General Theory, op. cit.,* p. 129.
[4]*Ibid.,* p. 131.

to consume when taxes are reduced is generally greater than the immediate marginal cutback in consumption when taxes are increased.

A reduction in corporate income taxes will stimulate investment and consumption (if profits are distributed to shareholders).[5] This policy is particularly useful in the recovery phase of the cycle, since it will relieve the inflationary pressure posed by capital stock bottlenecks, if the recovery is rapid. Furthermore, if technological change occurs, the natural rate of growth may be increased by this measure. Increases in labor productivity will also offset the inflationary impact of rising money wages as labor markets tighten.

If corporations view the cost of investing retained earnings as negligible, then they will generally invest most of their internal funds in a recession. In this case tax reductions will be more effective in stimulating investment in a recession than monetary policy. Furthermore, as mentioned in Chapter 6, the type of investment undertaken in recessions is likely to be of the variety that improves labor productivity rather than mere capacity expansion.

Despite its favorable impact on investment, tax policy is not as reliable as expenditure policy for stimulating demand, particularly in periods of chronic depression. If the private sector is pessimistic about the future, increases in disposable personal and corporate income due to tax reductions are likely to be held as saving. Ideally, a policy of increased public expenditure will be combined with tax cuts in a severe recession. The implications of such deficit spending for the federal budget will be considered later in this chapter. Conceivably, however, in a minor recession, tax policy alone could perform the job of stimulating demand.

3. *Monetary policy*—Increases in the money supply, by causing interest rates to fall, may provide a stimulus to investment and consumption spending. Monetary policy is most likely to be effective immediately following a boom period in which credit has been very tight. In this case there may be a pent-up demand for housing and consumer durables as well as for certain types of capital equipment, and an easing of credit will facilitate purchases of these items.

In general, however, economists question the efficacy of monetary policy for stimulating the economy in the absence of expansionary fiscal policy.[6] Increases in the money supply may be ineffective in reducing interest rates to the level required to induce enough demand to trigger an expansion. This may be particularly true if money rates of interest have been relatively

---

[5] A reduction in corporate taxes can take the form of liberalized depreciation allowances and investment tax credit as well as a reduction in tax rates.

[6] The position of Milton Friedman is a notable exception to this viewpoint.

high in the immediate past and if speculators are subject to a money illusion with respect to the interest rate as prices stabilize in the recession. In this case it may be difficult to convince speculators that bond prices will indeed rise further, and increases in the money supply may be held in the form of speculative balances.

If there are no signs that demand will increase, investment and consumption spending may be quite inelastic to reductions in the interest rate. Any expansionary impact is likely to be restricted to particular industries in which purchases have been postponed due to tight credit conditions in the previous boom.

Clearly, however, if an expansionary fiscal policy is accompanied by an easy money policy, investment is likely to proceed more rapidly than if money is scarce. This is important during the recovery phase, particularly if money wages are rising. If capital costs are kept low, firms will substitute capital for labor, raising labor productivity. This will have the dual effect of bringing the warranted rate of growth closer to the natural rate while at the same time offsetting the inflationary pressure of rising money wages as labor markets tighten.

POLICIES FOR MANAGING AN EXPANSION

If an expansion is carefully managed, an economy can proceed along a full-employment growth path with a minimum of inflation. If the growth rate is too rapid, however, inflation will develop and measures to halt the inflation may precipitate a downturn. Furthermore, in the downturn, the inflation may persist, leaving the economy in a situation in which Keynesian economic policy is not at all helpful for achieving price stability.

While Keynesian measures (i.e., controlling the rate of growth of aggregate demand) are necessary for managing a boom, the secondary effects of these measures on the level of prices must also be considered. The use of wage–price guidelines in an expansion will help keep cost–push inflation in check as excess demand is controlled by the orthodox Keynesian policy instruments.

A second difficulty in designing policies for managing an expansion is that restrictive actions such as spending cuts, tax increases, tight money, and wage–price guidelines are bound to be unpopular and, therefore, politically difficult to implement. Because of congressional and presidential opposition, the policy initiation lag is likely to be much longer for restrictive actions than for expansionary ones, and as a consequence, the choice of policy instruments may hinge largely on the speed with which they can be adjusted.

In view of these limitations, we shall examine the available policy instruments in turn:

1. *Reductions in government spending*—Reductions in government spending are the most effective means of reducing aggregate demand. Furthermore, spending cuts do not feed a cost–push inflation as the other Keynesian policy instruments do. Government spending, however, may be difficult to curtail, particularly if on-going programs have merit from a social point of view, or if there are vested interests in their continuation. Even the Office of Pyramid Construction might argue that it would be wasteful to leave half-finished pyramids sitting around as monuments to our indecisiveness and failure to manage the economy properly.

2. *Increases in taxes*—Tax increases are less reliable than spending cuts for restricting demand. In addition, they are likely to be inflationary.

Tax increases are intended to restrict consumption and investment demand. Experience has shown them to be unreliable since the impact is subject to lags of indeterminant length. If consumers have been accustomed to a long period of expansion in which real income has been steadily rising, they may view a tax increase as a temporary measure and make no immediate adjustment in their consumption. This will be particularly true if households have accumulated substantial savings during the boom. On the other hand, investment is likely to be harder hit than consumption when corporate taxes are increased, particularly if credit markets are tight.

Tax hikes will cause firms to raise prices if taxes are viewed as an element of production cost. Furthermore, tax increases are likely to stimulate demands for higher money wages by labor, again escalating costs and prices. The unfavorable impact on investment will affect the rate of growth of labor productivity which will worsen the inflationary impact of rising money wages.

Tax increases are often used as an anti-inflationary measure because they are easier to obtain from congress than spending cuts. In this case they represent a second-best solution for stabilizing demand during an expansion. Clearly, however, tax hikes should only be viewed as anti-inflationary when an inflation is being caused by excessive demand. Otherwise, they will merely feed a cost–push inflation with an undesirable effect on the level of employment.

3. *Monetary policy*—Monetary policy can be used to limit the availability of credit and raise the cost of borrowing, thus restricting investment and consumption demand.

Monetary policy is generally considered to be the most flexible policy instrument because, not requiring congressional approval, it has the shortest initiation lag. The effectiveness lag, however, is of indeterminant length, since there are so many factors which determine how firms will react to increased capital costs in a boom period.

Tight money will be most effective when investment is being externally financed or when combined with increases in corporate taxes which deplete internal funds. Credit rationing is likely to hit certain industries harder than others with well-established lines of credit or with ample internal funds, and consequently, the overall impact on investment is difficult to determine for any particular period.

A restrictive monetary policy is likely to be inflationary for two reasons. First, rising interest rates represent increased costs of production for firms. In addition, policies which restrict investment reduce the rate of growth of labor productivity which can provide an offset to the inflationary pressure of rising money wages. Tight money also nullifies the impact of rising money wages on capital substitution, so that the warranted rate of growth cannot be brought into line with the natural rate. Restated, unless productive capacity is expanding, bottlenecks will be reached early in the recovery resulting in declining labor productivity and inflation.

Since monetary policy is the easiest measure to implement when restraint is required, it is frequently employed as a means of stabilizing demand in booms. Like tax policy, it should be viewed as a second-best solution, however. Furthermore, tight money will be useful as an anti-inflationary measure only when price increases are due to excessive demand, since it tends to reinforce cost–push inflation.

4. *Wage–price guidelines*—Wage–price guidelines attempt to stabilize unit labor costs as money wages rise. If wage increases are proportional to increases in labor productivity, then unit labor costs will not rise and firms will not raise prices unless other costs of production increase. Since labor cost represents the bulk of total unit cost in most industries, this policy could have a significant stabilizing influence on prices.

Wage–price guidelines represent a way to alleviate some of the inflationary pressures produced by tight money, tax increases, and a leveling off of investment. Presumably, using the guidelines, more reliance could be placed on tax policy and monetary policy for managing an expansion without the constant inflationary threat posed by these policy instruments. As a consequence, there would not be such pressure on congress and the president to cut back on-going public spending programs.

HANDLING AN INFLATIONARY RECESSION

In a recession, inflation is not caused by excessive demand, and consequently, Keynesian anti-inflationary measures are inapplicable. Policies which affect aggregate demand should be mildly expansionary, since the recession will be characterized by a decline in real output and an increase in the unemployment rate, reflecting inadequate aggregate demand. The inflation will undoubtedly be of the cost–push variety, so measures should be taken to reduce production costs.

Tax cuts and reductions in interest rates will have the dual impact of stimulating demand and reducing production costs. In a serious recession, increases in public spending may be needed, although these will not have the deflationary impact of tax and monetary policy. Furthermore, it is doubtful that a recession in which prices are rising will be severe enough to necessitate strong expansionary action, since the wage–push effect would eventually recede as the unemployment rate rises.

Policies to increase demand should be accompanied by wage–price guidelines. Furthermore, tax policy should be designed to encourage investment. If increases in labor productivity are forthcoming, then guidelines will be easier to implement.

When employment and the price level are moving in opposite directions, then Keynesian remedies which affect aggregate demand should be used to attain the full-employment goal. Non-Keynesian remedies, such as wage–price guidelines can be applied to the goal of maintaining price stability.

THE APPROPRIATE NUMBER
OF POLICY INSTRUMENTS

As demonstrated in Chapter 1, an effective policy package generally must contain as many policy instruments as policy targets. In a simple Keynesian model, two policy objectives—full employment and price stability—can be achieved by judicious use of a single policy instrument for controlling aggregate demand. This unfortunate oversimplification has caused many people to view generalized monetary and fiscal policy as a panacea for all the economic ills of a country.

Consider the typical case of an economy experiencing creeping inflation with less than full employment, a balance-of-payments deficit, and an inadequate rate of growth. To achieve full employment with price stability, balance-of-payments equilibrium, and an acceptable growth rate, four policy instruments are generally required.

Expansionary fiscal policy would serve to increase the level of employment; however, this policy must be coupled with a policy of wage–price guidelines to prevent prices from rising. But expansionary fiscal policy would tend to worsen the balance-of-payments deficit, and consequently, a tight money policy might be used to attract capital from abroad. Such a tight money policy, however, would serve to dampen the rate of domestic investment, to the detriment of the growth rate and full-employment goals, and by reducing the rate of growth of labor productivity, it would render more difficult the implementation of wage–price guidelines. Consequently, the tight money policy would have to be accompanied by a program of liberalized depreciation allowances or an investment tax credit to compensate for the impact on the level of domestic investment.

Not only must there be an adequate number of instruments to achieve the policy targets, but these instruments must be effective. Thus, an easy money policy for stimulating employment in a recession may have no impact at all on the level of investment and, consequently, should not be counted in the set of useful policy instruments. Given that some policy instruments are not always effective and given the multiplicity and frequent inconsistency of the economic goals of a modern economy, it is important that policy planners have as many policy instruments at their disposal as are consistent with the values and institutions of the economic system of which they are a part.

14-3 Economic Policy and the Federal Budget

There has always been considerable misunderstanding concerning the impact of a federal budget deficit or surplus on the economy. In addition, many people voice concern over a growing national debt arising from federal budget deficits. In this section we shall consider the relationship between the budget deficit and the level of economic activity.

BUDGET DEFICITS AND THE FULL-EMPLOYMENT SURPLUS

We have seen that the way in which a fiscal operation is financed will influence its impact on aggregate demand. Deficit spending is always more expansionary than if the spending were financed by taxes. This observation has sometimes led to the erroneous inference that when the budget is in deficit, fiscal policy is more expansionary than if the budget were balanced or in surplus.

The budget deficit is determined by federal expenditures minus receipts. Suppose a given level of discretionary expenditures and tax rates is planned for a particular period. The size of the deficit at any time will depend not only upon that planned fiscal package but also upon the level of economic activity. The lower the level of national income, the smaller are the personal and corporate tax receipts and the greater are the transfer payments such as unemployment compensation and welfare payments. Thus, for any given fiscal package, the deficit will be greater, the lower the level of economic activity.

Figure 14-1 shows the relationship between the budgetary surplus and the level of economic activity for two alternative budget packages. If national income were 95 percent of full-employment income, budget A would be balanced while budget B would show a deficit of $3 billion. Clearly, budget B would be more expansionary than budget A.

Suppose, however, the more expansionary fiscal package B causes national income to rise to 98 percent of full-employment income, while fiscal package A retards growth and causes income to fall to 94 percent of full employment. Now budget B will be balanced while budget A shows a deficit of $1 billion. Does the deficit budget A reflect a more expansionary fiscal policy than the balanced budget B? Of course not, since the deficit in A

Figure 14-1   Budgetary Surplus and the Level of Economic Activity

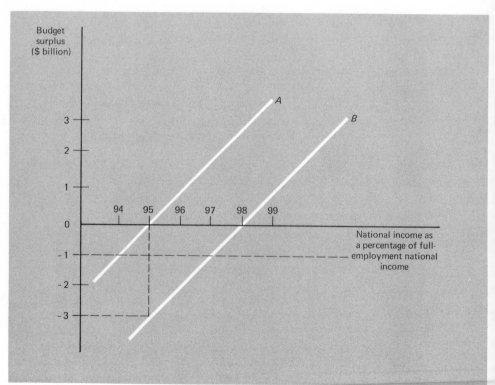

is induced by a decline in national income, due perhaps to the fact that the fiscal package in A is not sufficiently expansionary.

A comparison of the impact of alternative budgets should be made for some specified level of income. Note that at a full-employment level of income, both budgets would be in surplus. In recent years in the United States, the federal budget has been designed to produce a surplus if national income is at the full-employment level.[7] This means that the overall impact of the budget has represented a drag on the economy. To reach full employment, private investment would have to exceed private saving to offset the government saving represented by the budget surplus.

Recall that income earned can be consumed, saved, or paid to the government in taxes. Thus

$$Y = C + S + T$$

Ignoring the foreign sector, aggregate demand is the sum of consumption, investment, and government spending, or

$$D = C + I + G$$

National income equilibrium occurs when aggregate demand is equal to total income; that is,

$$Y = D$$

or

$$S + T = I + G$$

Rearranging terms, national income equilibrium occurs where

$$S - I = G - T$$

For equilibrium to occur at the full-employment level of income, the budget deficit, $G - T$, must be equal to the difference between private saving and private investment. If the budget is in surplus, that is, if

$$G - T < 0$$

then private investment must exceed private saving at full employment if national income equilibrium is to occur there.

[7] See the *Economic Report of the President* (Washington, D.C.: U.S. Government Printing Office, January, 1964), pp. 41–43.

Paradoxically, continuing budget deficits at less than full employment indicate that the budget is not expansionary enough. If the budget is designed to be in surplus at full employment, a budget deficit indicates that income is below full employment and a greater deficit is called for. Reducing the full-employment surplus by discretionary action would help to achieve the goal of full-employment while at the same time reducing the actual budget deficit.

THE NATIONAL DEBT

If budgetary surpluses do not match deficits over the cycle, the national debt will increase. Despite the fact that the U.S. budget has been designed to be in surplus at full employment, the budget is not cyclically balanced, being more frequently in deficit than surplus.[8] This is because the economy is rarely at full employment. Figure 14-2 shows the actual budget deficits which

[8]This situation is ironic since the ostensible purpose of the full-employment surplus is to retire the national debt. (See *Economic Report of the President, op. cit.*, p. 54.) Yet the fiscal drag caused by the full-employment surplus keeps the economy below full employment and the budget, on balance, in deficit.

Figure 14-2 Actual and Full Employment Estimates of the Federal Surplus or Deficit

Source: *Economic Report of the President* (Washington, D.C.: U.S. Government Printing Office, January, 1965), p. 64.

were experienced between 1960 and 1964 in relation to the projected full-employment surplus.

If the federal budget is not to be a fiscal drag, it is likely that the full-employment surplus will have to be eliminated. Conceivably, the budget may have to be slightly in deficit at full employment if full employment is, in fact, to be maintained. What will be the consequences for the national economy of piling up an ever-increasing debt, with little hope of retiring it?

It is clear that government debt is different from private debt in that governments have unlimited resources for debt service. Even if holders of government debt demand that it be retired, government can raise money through taxation to repay that debt. In an extreme circumstance, the government has the power to print money to meet its obligations. Since the government quite certainly cannot go bankrupt, it is unlikely that its debt would ever be recalled, and the only requirement or "burden" of the debt is to meet interest payments.

The public debt does not, as is sometimes believed, shift the burden of payment for today's expenditures to future generations. If there is unemployment, the government is using today's resources which would otherwise have remained unemployed today. Assuming that there is some benefit transmitted to future generations by the government spending program, the issuing of debt provides them a benefit they would not otherwise have enjoyed. Even if the economy is at full employment, deficit spending merely shifts today's resources from the private to the public sector. The burden on future generations can be measured only by the loss in private output weighed against the gain in public goods and services.

While future generations are saddled with paying interest on the debt, they are also recipients of interest payments, so that the transactions merely represent an intragenerational transfer. While this transfer represents a redistribution which may be slightly regressive with respect to income, the effect is generally considered to be negligible by most economists. Only when debt is held by citizens of other nations does debt service represent a drain on the resources of future generations.

Since World War II the size of the national debt relative to GNP has actually declined. Furthermore, interest payments on the debt have decreased as a percentage of national income. This means that the growth of the economy has exceeded the growth of the debt, and the tax *rate* required for debt service has declined.

If resources are not fully employed, deficit spending utilizes resources that would not be used otherwise, and there is no burden on future generations. If resources are scarce, however, they must be drawn from other sectors of the economy. To the extent that public spending is not as socially productive as the foregone private spending, then there will be a burden on future generations. The same could be said for tax finance, however. Suppose the federal government raises corporate income taxes to finance a war. This may cause a decline in the rate of private investment and a reduction in the potential rate of growth of the capital stock. On the other hand, the war may not represent any benefit at all to future generations. The burden on future generations does not necessarily depend upon the method of finance but is represented by the cost of the war in terms of the increases in capital stock foregone because of it.

The method of finance may, however, determine the way in which resources are drawn from the private sector and, hence, may determine the extent to which future generations will be affected by an increase in public spending. If debt finance tends to draw more resources from current investment relative to current consumption than tax finance, then debt finance will affect future generations more than tax finance. Whether a "burden" is actually involved, however, depends upon the benefits accruing to future generations from the expenditure program. From the viewpoint of intergenerational equity, a program whose benefits are expected to be realized over a long time horizon should be financed like any long-term private investment project, by the issuance of long-term debt, not by current revenues.

14-4 Economic Policy and the Keynesian Revolution

After 35 years, economic policy is still very much influenced by the ideas of Keynes, yet it is gradually abandoning some of the basic principles of Keynesian economic policy. Policy makers have come to recognize that no one model or set of rules is applicable to all situations, all the time. It is clear that our macroeconomic policy objectives cannot always be achieved merely by manipulating aggregate demand.

It took many years, a revolution in economic thought, and a chronic economic upheaval to convince society that government intervention is necessary in a free-enterprise economy. Keynes pointed out one way in which government can influence economic conditions, that is, by controlling aggregate demand. But it is a mistake to assume that controlling demand is a sufficient means of meeting all the national policy objectives. The institutional and behavioral structure of a modern economy is far more complex than that outlined in *The General Theory*, and much more work must be done if we are to understand the relationships underlying it. Improved specification of our macroeconomic models is a vital and challenging task.

Since economic policy must be based on such models, the more accurate the model, the more effective will be the macroeconomic policy we can design.

Questions for Study and Review

1. Keynesian economics suggests that macroeconomic policy objectives can be achieved by manipulating aggregate demand if we know enough about the structure of the economy. Do you agree? Illustrate your position with specific examples.

2. How do the traditional macroeconomic policy instruments—public spending, tax policy, and monetary policy—compare as measures for achieving full employment and growth with stable prices?

3. "Since a federal budget deficit means that the government is spending more than it receives from the private sector, the overall effect on demand must be positive. Therefore, a budget deficit means that economic policy is expansionary." Discuss.

4. "A full-employment surplus in the federal budget is good, because it means we can gradually retire the federal debt and reduce the burden of our past wars for future generations." Comment on all aspects of the quoted statement.

Additional Reading

"Budget Policy, 1958–63," *Economic Report of the President.* Washington, D.C.: U.S. Government Printing Office, January, 1962, pp. 77–84.

Domar, Evsey D., "The Burden of the Debt and National Income," *The American Economic Review,* XXXIV (December, 1944), 798–827.

Friedman, Milton, "The Case for Flexible Exchange Rates," in *Essays in Positive Economics.* Chicago: The University of Chicago Press, 1953.

Heller, Walter W., *New Dimensions of Political Economy.* New York: W. W. Norton and Company, 1967.

Miller, H. Lawrence, Jr., "The New and the Old in Public Debt Theory," *The Quarterly Review of Economics and Business* (Winter, 1966), pp. 65–74.

Okun, Arthur M., *The Political Economy of Prosperity.* New York: W. W. Norton and Company, 1969.

A

Appendix:
Econometric Models
for Designing
Macroeconomic Policy

If a Keynesian model is to be used for designing macroeconomic policy, the parameters of the model must be specified numerically. Furthermore, if the model is to be used for policy planning, estimates of the required values of the policy instruments must be obtained when the targets are known. If the model is to be used for forecasting or simulation, estimates of the targets must be obtained when values of the policy instruments are known. Since the number of unknowns cannot exceed the number of equations in the model, the policy planner must select certain variables as exogenous, or predetermined. In addition, numerical values for the predetermined values must be provided.

An econometric model consists of a set of relationships formulated in algebraic terms. The parameters of the model are *estimated*, that is, specified numerically from empirical data using techniques of statistical inference. In some cases values for the predetermined variables in the model are also found inferentially; sometimes these values are known with certainty.

If such a model is consistent, it can be solved for the unknown or endogenous variables. In a forecasting model the target variables are unknown and the policy instruments are predetermined; in a policy-planning model the target variables are predetermined and the policy instruments required to effectuate these targets are unknown.

In this text we have developed a macroeconomic model in algebraic terms. Given numerical specification, we have seen how such a model can be used for policy planning and forecasting. In this appendix, we shall review the basic aspects of model building from a theoretical framework, and consider some of the techniques of statistical inference most commonly used for parameter estimation in macroeconomic models. In addition, we shall examine some of the models of the U.S. economy which have been developed in recent years for actual policy planning and forecasting. Finally, some extensions of the analysis presented in the text will be presented with particular reference to their implications for forecasting.

A-1 Elements of a Macroeconomic Model

To solve for the endogenous variables of a model, there must be as many equations as there are unknowns. If this criterion is not met, then more equations must be added to the model or more variables must be given predetermined values.

The first step in constructing a model is *specification*. This involves determining the number of equations, the variables to be contained in each equation, the functional form of the equation, and whether or not the variables should be treated as predetermined or endogenous. Specification of a model presupposes an understanding of the system which the model describes, since it is essentially the translation of theory into mathematical form. Once the model is specified and the parameters are estimated by statistical techniques, then forecasting and policy planning on the basis of the model is relatively straightforward. It is the specification process that entails the most intimate acquaintance with the theoretical framework of the system.

EXACT VERSUS STOCHASTIC RELATIONSHIPS

The equations in a macroeconomic model can be either exact or stochastic. A *stochastic* relationship contains one or more variables whose value is not known with certainty, but which has a known probability distribution. Behavioral relationships such as the consumption function or investment function as well as technological relationships such as the aggregate production function are generally assumed to be stochastic. Thus, a consumption function may be specified as follows,

$$C_t = b_0 + b_1 Y_t + b_2 C_{t-1} + b_3 i_t + u_t$$

where

C_t = consumption in period t
Y_t = disposable income in period t
i_t = interest rate in period t
u_t = stochastic error term in period t

The stochastic error term, u_t, represents that consumption in period t not accounted for by the explanatory variables, Y_t, C_{t-1}, i_t, and the constant term, b_0, of the equation. The error term is generally assumed to have a probability distribution with a mean (expected) value of zero and a finite variance. There are several reasons for expecting some unexplained (stochastic) variation in consumption.

First, while a large part of the variation in consumption can be explained by variation in disposable income, lagged consumption, and the rate of interest, there are also other influences on consumption behavior. Since there are many such influences, they cannot all be accounted for in the model. Furthermore, taken together they should behave in a random manner, represented by the stochastic variable. The smaller the proportion of the variance in consumption which can be explained by the independent variables in the equation, the greater will be the proportion of the variance attributable to the error term.

A second reason for including a stochastic variable in behavioral equations is that human behavior often depends in part upon random influences and cannot always be explained, regardless of the number of variables included in the equation. In addition, misspecification of the functional form of the equation, that is, treating a nonlinear relationship as linear, will render an otherwise exact relationship inexact, requiring an error term to account for the difference.

Finally, random errors in measuring the dependent variable, consumption, can also be treated as a stochastic explanatory variable. Suppose the relationship

$$C = b_0 + b_1 Y$$

is exact. However, there is a random error in the data which measure consumption; that is,

$$\Gamma = C + \gamma$$

where Γ is measured consumption and γ is the measurement error. Then the equation, estimated statistically on the basis of these data, using Γ as a proxy for C, should contain a stochastic component, since

$$\Gamma = C + \gamma = b_0 + b_1 Y + \gamma$$

The error term in a stochastic relationship is assumed to have a zero mean, or expectation. This implies that it has no systematic influence on the dependent variable; that is, the most probable effect of the stochastic variable on consumption is zero.

Consider the simple relationship

$$C_t = b_0 + b_1 Y_t + u_t$$

where u_t is a random variable with zero mean. Since the most probable value of u_t is zero, that is,

$$E(u_t) = 0$$

where $E(u_t)$ is the expected value of u_t, then the most probable value of C_t is

$$E(C_t) = b_0 + b_1 Y_t + E(u_t)$$
$$= b_0 + b_1 Y_t$$

356

As seen in Figure A-1, the actual value of C_t may lie on either side of the line represented by the equation

$$C_t = b_0 + b_1 Y_t$$

In general, the larger the standard deviation of u_t, the greater the actual values of C_t will deviate from the (C_t, Y_t) line.

THE VARIABLES OF THE MODEL

Specification involves selecting the number of equations for the model, determining their functional form, and deciding whether the equations should be exact or stochastic. A second aspect of specification involves

Figure A-1   Graphical Representation of a Linear Consumption Function with a Stochastic Error Term

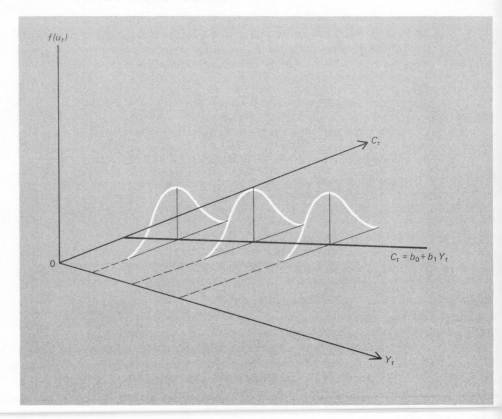

selecting the variables to be included in each equation, deciding whether they should be treated as endogenous or predetermined in each case, and selecting the appropriate statistical series for measuring them.

Since the number of endogenous variables in the model cannot exceed the number of equations, the endogenous set must be small in relation to the total number of variables which determine economic behavior. The choice of variables represents a trade-off between completeness of specification and manageability. An additional limitation to including a large number of variables is that these variables are often so closely interrelated that it is impossible to separate their influence. This interdependence of variables in economic relationships, known as *multicollinearity*, allows the model builder to explain a high proportion of the variance of the dependent variables with a few variables. It does, however, pose a problem for testing conflicting hypotheses.

Consider the problem of specifying the equation which describes investment in plant and equipment. Two explanatory variables, retained earnings and changes in sales, might be included. Suppose, however, that retained earnings tended to rise and fall with changes in sales. If the correlation between these two variables were high, presumably investment in plant and equipment could be adequately explained or predicted by either variable, and it would not be necessary to include them both in the forecasting model. On the other hand, suppose the policy planner wants to predict the impact of liberalized depreciation allowances on investment. On the basis of the data, he has no way of isolating the impact of an increase in retained earnings independent of an increase in sales. If, in the past, investment has increased with retained earnings, the effect could be due to the rise in sales which historically has accompanied an improved internal funds position. In this example, there is no way to test the accelerator hypothesis versus the cost-of-capital hypothesis for investment, since there is no independent historical experience.

Multicollinearity may occur among any of the explanatory variables, endogenous or predetermined. It is the principal factor which limits the total number of variables used in economic models.

The number of endogenous variables is limited by the number of equations in the model. The remaining variables must be predetermined. Many variables which are treated as predetermined are not known with certainty, but are treated as such for lack of any known behavioral or technological relationships to explain them. One example of such a variable is government spending. In the absence of a theory of the process by which government spending decisions are made, this variable is generally treated by policy planners as predetermined, even though its actual value may be subject to a large degree of stochastic variation. Given the large size of the public sector, economic forecasting in the United States has been greatly hampered by the need to treat this variable as predetermined and then to estimate it by primitive techniques outside the structure of the model. Much care is given to accurate specification of the equations in the model and considerable attention is given to employing the most sophisticated techniques for estimating the parameters in the model. Yet if decisions in the public sector are unknown, the policy planner will not be able to make reliable forecasts of the target variables.

Economic forecasting with econometric models was the subject of some criticism in the last year of the Johnson administration, since the models consistently underestimated the level of demand and implied policy packages that turned out to be inflationary. The main reason for this, however, was the fact that the president consistently underestimated the level of public spending, particularly in the military sector. Apparently, his economic advisors received these low estimates and incorporated them into their forecasting models. Since there was a multiplier effect to the spending programs, the forecasts for the economy as a whole were wider of the mark than the original underestimate for the public sector.

The reliability of a model is greatly reduced when exogenous variables are not known with certainty. Some variables, which we have treated as predetermined in this text, can be made endogenous if an appropriate theoretical relationship (equation) can be developed. Money supply, for instance, is treated as endogenous in some econometric models.

The choice of variables is often limited by the availability of data. Unless the variables in the model have been measured, the validity of the relationships cannot be established. We shall consider the problem of obtaining appropriate statistics for estimation and prediction in Appendix B. It is clear, however, that theoreticians, policy planners, and statisticians must coordinate their efforts to develop reliable econometric models.

A-2   Methods of Statistical Estimation

Once the model has been specified, the parameters of the equations must be assigned numerical values. When numerical values for the constants of the equations are estimated, then the model can be solved for the endogenous variables. The endogenous variables of an econometric model are often called "estimates," since their values are determined by estimates of the parameters of the equations as well as by the predetermined variables of the model.

The reliability of the forecasts of any model will depend upon the accuracy of the theoretical specification, the amount of nonrandom behavior in the system, the reliability of estimates of the predetermined variables, and the technique used for parameter estimation. This text has been concerned primarily with theoretical specification of macroeconomic models. To the extent that behavior is not subject to systematic influences, the science of economics fails as a method of forecasting and influencing behavior. In many cases political constraints prevent reliable estimation of predetermined variables. However, much work is left to be done in this area. Finally, we shall consider the question of techniques for parameter estimation.

Parameter estimation is one major area of concern for econometricians. In recent years, highly sophisticated techniques for estimating parameters in simultaneous equation models have been developed.[1] One rather old-fashioned technique is still widely used and is relatively easy to understand. This is the method of *least-squares regression*. Suppose the policy planner wants estimates for the parameters b_0 and b_1 in the relationship

$$C_t = b_0 + b_1 Y_t + u_t$$

He has a collection of data for C_t and Y_t which consists of paired values for each variable, each pair measured at some point in time. Such data can be displayed in tabular form as shown in Table A-1. The same data can be shown graphically as a scatter of points in a two-dimensional plane, as shown in Figure A-2. If the hypothesis that C_t and Y_t are linearly related has any validity, the scatter should approximate a straight line. Deviations from linearity are accounted for by the stochastic error term, u_t, in the equation.

The least-squares regression technique locates a line through the scatter such that the vertical deviations of the data points from the line are minimized. Consider such a line:

$$\widehat{C}_t = \widehat{b}_0 + \widehat{b}_1 Y_t$$

where the symbol, $\widehat{}$, refers to an estimate of a parameter or variable. For any value of Y_t, the corresponding estimate, $\widehat{C}_t$, can be found from the line.

---

[1] For a survey of the literature in this area, see J. Johnston, *Econometric Methods* (New York: McGraw Hill Book Company, Inc., 1963), Chapters 9 and 10, or Franklin M. Fisher, "Dynamic Structure and Estimation in Economy-Wide Econometric Models," in J. S. Duesenberry, O. Eckstein, and G. Fromm, eds., *The Brookings Quarterly Econometric Model of the United States* (Skokie, Ill.: Rand McNally & Company, 1965), pp. 589–633.

Table A-1 Personal Consumption Expenditures and Disposable Income, 1950–1969 (in billions of 1958 dollars)*

Year	Personal Consumption (in billions of 1958 dollars)	Disposable Income (in billions of 1958 dollars)
1950	230.5	249.6
1951	232.8	255.7
1952	239.4	263.3
1953	250.8	275.4
1954	255.7	278.3
1955	274.2	296.7
1956	281.4	309.3
1957	288.2	315.8
1958	290.1	318.8
1959	307.3	333.0
1960	316.1	340.2
1961	322.5	350.7
1962	338.4	367.3
1963	353.3	381.3
1964	373.7	407.9
1965	397.7	435.0
1966	418.1	458.9
1967	430.3	477.7
1968	452.6	497.6
1969	466.0	509.4

*Least-squares regression line: $C_t = 3.854 + 0.904Y_t$.

Source: U.S. Department of Commerce, Office of Business Economics. *Survey of Current Business* (Washington, D.C.: U.S. Government Printing Office, 1950–1970). (Issued quarterly.)

Now, consider the actual value of C_t associated with Y_t. The difference between the actual and estimated values for C_t,

$$e_t = (C_t - \widehat{C}_t)$$

is the vertical distance from the regression line to the data point. The least-squares technique locates $\widehat{b}_0$ and $\widehat{b}_1$, that is, the slope and intercept of the line, in such a way that the value

$$\sum_{t=1}^{n} e_t^2 = \sum_{t=1}^{n} (C_t - \widehat{C}_t)^2$$

is minimized.

This technique has the property of minimum variance for the estimators as well as for the estimated value of the dependent variable, $\widehat{C}_t$. If

Figure A-2   Least Squares Regression Line Fitted to Scatter
of Consumption and Income Data

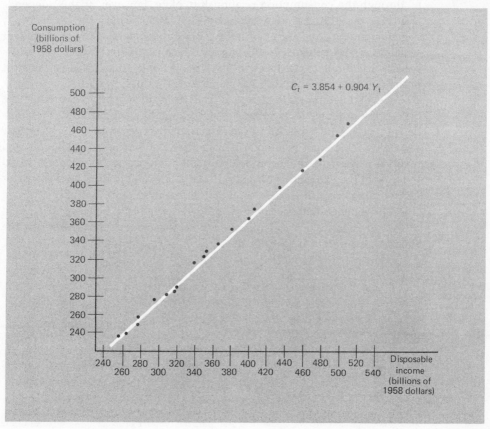

Source: Table A-1 of this volume.

the error terms have a zero mean and are independent of the explanatory variables of the equation, the most probable value of the estimators, $\widehat{b}_0$ and $\widehat{b}_1$, is the true value, b_0 and b_1. In statistical terminology, least-squares estimators are minimum variance unbiased for the true parameter values.

One problem with using least squares as an estimating technique for parameters in simultaneous equation models is that their unbiasedness depends upon the independence of the stochastic error term and the independent variables in the equation. This property does not apply for equations in simultaneous systems as can be seen in the following example.

Consider the simple macroeconomic model

$$Y_t = C_t + I_t$$
$$C_t = b_0 + b_1 Y_t + u_t$$

where I_t is predetermined. At any time, t, the value of C_t depends upon u_t, through the consumption relationship. Note, however, that Y_t depends upon C_t, through the national income equation. Thus, the value of Y_t depends upon u_t, and the error term is not independent of the independent variable in the consumption equation. This condition causes the least-squares technique to produce biased estimates of b_0 and b_1; that is, the most probable values of $\widehat{b}_0$ and $\widehat{b}_1$ are not the true values, b_0 and b_1.

Several estimating techniques have been developed to overcome the bias in the ordinary least-squares (OLS) estimators produced by the interdependence of the explanatory variables and the error terms in the stochastic equations. One such technique is called *indirect least squares*. This method involves expressing the dependent variable in the equation to be estimated in terms of the exogenous variables in the model and finding OLS estimates of the parameters in these *reduced-form* equations. These will be unbiased since the independent variables are predetermined and, hence, independent of the error term in the equation. Then, the original parameters of the equation are determined from the reduced-form parameters.[2]

Consider the model

$$Y_t = C_t + I_t$$
$$C_t = b_0 + b_1 Y_t + u_t$$

Expressing C_t in terms of the single exogenous variable in the model, I_t, the reduced-form consumption function is found to be

$$C_t = \frac{b_0}{1 - b_1} + \frac{b_1}{1 - b_1} I_t + \frac{u_t}{1 - b_1}$$

---

[2]This is only possible if the equation is exactly identified—that is, if the number of endogenous variables in the model less one, plus the number of exogenous variables in the equation, is exactly equal to the total number of exogenous variables in the model.

or

$$C_t = \beta_0 + \beta_1 I_t + v_t$$

where

$$\beta_0 = \frac{b_0}{1 - b_1} \tag{1}$$

$$\beta_1 = \frac{b_1}{1 - b_1} \tag{2}$$

$$v_t = \frac{u_t}{1 - b_1} \tag{3}$$

By the method of OSL, estimates of the reduced-form parameters, β_0 and β_1, can be found. Estimates of the structural parameters, b_0 and b_1, can be found from equations (1) and (2) above. Estimates of the structural parameters obtained by this method will not be unbiased for small sample sizes, although the bias disappears as the sample size grows. Furthermore, the method can be used only if it is possible to find the structural parameters from the reduced-form parameters. This implies there must be as many reduced-form parameters as structural parameters for the equation, a condition known as *identification*, and this is not true for all equations.

Other estimating techniques have been developed for equations that are not exactly identified. While most of these techniques still produce biased estimators for small sample sizes, many econometricians find them preferable to OLS because they have better large sample properties and because they tend to have a smaller sampling variance than OLS estimators.

Some econometricians have attempted to avoid the simultaneous equation bias by making their models *recursive* rather than simultaneous. A recursive model treats each equation as a step in a chain of events, with the dependent variable in the first equation becoming explanatory in the successive equations. The Duesenberry, Eckstein, and Fromm model is recursive.[3] In such a model, OLS estimators can be used.

SOURCES OF DATA

Data for estimating structural parameters can be historically generated, or they can be collected from a cross section at a single point in time. Historically generated, or *time series* data, are most commonly used for forecasting models, since the policy planner is most concerned with how behavior will

[3] J. S. Duesenberry, O. Eckstein, and G. Fromm, "A Simulation of the United States Economy in Recession," *Econometrica*, XXVIII (October, 1960), 749–809.

change over time in response to changes in the policy instruments. If he is interested in short-run reactions, such as behavior within a three-month time frame, then quarterly data should be used to estimate the model.[4]

Sometimes, however, time series data do not provide sufficient independent variation of the explanatory variables to estimate all the parameters in the equation. Suppose, for instance, that changes in sales and internal funds of corporations have tended to vary together over time. If both variables are included in an investment equation, it is doubtful that their respective influences on investment can be separated sufficiently to provide meaningful estimates for the least-squares regression coefficients. In this case an extraneous estimate of the influence of one of the variables on investment will have to be introduced. Such an estimate can be derived from a *cross-section* study of investment behavior.

A cross-section study involves examining firms of different size within a single time frame to determine the relationship between, for instance, the level of internal funds and investment. The parameter value for the estimated relationship can then be substituted into the time series equation, with the remaining systematic (nonrandom) variation in investment being attributed to the sales variable.

Cross-section estimates should be used with caution in time series relationships, however, since behavior in the cross section may be different from behavior over time. Consider an economy in a state of semirecession. Suppose one group of firms with internal funds of $200 million invests $150 million in plant and equipment, while another with internal funds of $300 million invests $200 million. Now suppose public policy initiates a recovery, and internal funds of the first group of firms rises to $300 million. A relationship based on a cross-section estimate will predict an increase in investment of $50 million. Actually, however, investment is likely to increase much more than this if a boom is initiated and the firms decide to invest beyond the limit represented by their internal funds position.

PREDICTION VERSUS STRUCTURAL ESTIMATION

Some economists argue that it is not necessary to isolate the separate influences of the explanatory variables in the model if the main interest of the policy planner is forecasting. That is, if the model predicts well, it does not really matter if we know whether changes in sales or internal funds are responsible for change in investment. Therefore, reliable estimates of the structural parameters are not important as long as all relevant explanatory variables are included in the model.

[4] Data for econometric models are generally not collected for time frames shorter than three months, since a quarter is assumed to be the shortest period within which reactions to changes in economic conditions take place.

Other economists argue that structural estimation is important for forecasting. The relationships which have been numerically estimated in the model are all based on past behavior and experience. The forecaster assumes that these same relationships will hold in the future. Suppose, however, the forecaster expects a change in behavior over the period of the forecast. For example, suppose firms anticipate a sharp increase in corporate taxes which will affect their internal funds position. If internal funds are an important determinant of investment, this will certainly have an impact. Firms will discount the importance of their internal funds position for investment planning. Therefore, it is important for the forecaster to have a knowledge of structural relationships if he is to take account of anticipated changes in these relationships.

A knowledge of structural relationships is also important for policy planning. Suppose the government wishes to restrict investment. Without a knowledge of the independent effects of changes in sales and internal funds on investment it would be impossible to determine whether or not an increase in corporate taxes would be an adequate measure or whether demand would have to be restricted as well.

While reliable forecasting is theoretically possible in the absence of reliable structural parameter estimates, most economists agree that a knowledge of structure is helpful when historical relationships are expected to change over time. Furthermore, econometric models are used for more than forecasting. Knowledge of structure is usually important for selecting appropriate policy instruments when models are used for policy planning as well as forecasting.

A-3 Econometric Models of the U.S. Economy

Beginning in the early 1950's, economists have developed empirical models of the U.S. economy. Although these models have been principally used for forecasting, they are also used for policy planning and simulation.[5]

THE KLEIN–GOLDBERGER MODEL

The Klein–Goldberger model[6] was first estimated in 1953 and has since been expanded, respecified, and reestimated. The most up-to-date version of the

---

[5] Simulation involves solving the model for values of the target variables under alternative assumptions about structure and for various specifications of the policy programs and values for the policy parameters.

[6] L. R. Klein and A. S. Goldberger, *An Econometric Model of the United States, 1929–1952* (Amsterdam: North-Holland Publishing Company, 1955).

model contains 20 equations and 20 endogenous variables which are listed below. The variables are expressed in the form of changes rather than absolute values. This reduces the problem of multicollinearity and improves the structural specification of the model. It will, however, increase the forecasting error in percentage terms, since changes in the policy targets are subject to a greater forecasting error than absolute values when the previous level of the variables is already known.

The equations for the Klein–Goldberger model, estimated from annual data for the period 1929–1964 (omitting 1942–1945) are given below.[7] Equations marked with an asterisk are identities and, hence, are exact. The remaining equations are stochastic, and the parameters are statistically estimated.

I. *National income identity*

$$*(1) \quad X = C_d + C_{ns} + I_p + I_h + \Delta I_i + G + F_e - F_i$$

II. *Consumption*[8]

$$(2) \quad C_d - 0.7C_{d-1} = 0.230(Y - 0.7Y_{-1}) - 0.105C_{d-1} - 4.51$$

$$(3) \quad C_{ns} = 0.228Y + 0.752C_{ns-1} - 1.468$$

III. *Investment*

$$(4) \quad I_p - 0.951_{p-1} = 0.0656(X - W_g)_{-1} - 2.11(i_L)_{-1} - 0.590I_{p-1} + 9.329$$

$$(5) \quad I_i = 0.137(X - \Delta I_i) + 0.396I_{i-1} - 24.702$$

$$(6) \quad I_h = 0.0517Y - 0.0402i_{s-1} + 0.335I_{h-1} - 1.853$$

IV. *Foreign sector*

$$(7) \quad F_i = 0.0284X - 10.14(p_i - p) + 0.463F_{i-1} - 0.942$$

V. *Factor share equations*

$$(8) \quad RE = 0.788(P_{cb} - T_c) - 0.667(P_{cb} - T_c - RE)_{-1} - 0.148$$

---

[7] From Michael K. Evans, *Macroeconomic Activity* (New York: Harper & Row, Publishers, 1969), pp. 498–499.

[8] Equations (2), (4), and (17) are estimated with the dependent variable in the form

$$X - \lambda X_{-1}$$

This is done to exclude capital stock variables which would be difficult to estimate statistically.

(9) $\quad D = 0.0492 \displaystyle\sum_{i=1}^{20} P_{-1}(I_p + I_h)_{-1} + 0.0856D_u + 1.411$

*(10) $\; p_{cb} = pX - D - T_i - W - RI - PB$

(11) $\; PB = 0.0107pX + 0.898(PB)_{-1} + 0.674$

(12) $\; RI = 0.0623p(I_p + I_h) - 0.0230\,\Delta i_L + 0.938(RI_{-1}) + 0.394$

*(13) $\; pY = pX - D - T_i - RE - T_c - T$

*(14) $\; W = whN_w$

VI. *Labor market*

(15) $\; h = -0.450\,\Delta w - 1.996(N_L - N_w - N_s) + 1.157$

(16) $\dfrac{W - Wg}{p} = 0.413\left(X - \dfrac{Wg}{p}\right)$

$\qquad + 0.282\left(\dfrac{W - Wg}{p}\right)_{-1} - 10.607$

(17) $\left(X - \dfrac{Wg}{p}\right) - 0.95\left(X - \dfrac{Wg}{p}\right)_{-1} = 0.364(I_p + I_h)$

$\qquad + 3.532(N_w - N_g + N_s) - 0.95(N_w - N_g - N_s)_{-1}$
$\qquad + 1.335(h - 0.95h_{-1}) - 6.483$

(18) $\; \Delta w = -1.697(N_L - N_w - N_s) + 1.116(\Delta p)_{-1} + 0.184$

VII. *Interest rate*

(19) $\; i_L = 0.157i_s + 0.835(i_L)_{-1} + 0.335$

(20) $\; i_s = 1.145i_d - 0.815RR_{-1} + 0.533Du - 0.511$

where ** indicates the variable is predetermined for this model and

$\quad C_d$ = consumption of durables, in billions of 1954 dollars
$\quad C_{ns}$ = consumption of nondurables and services, in billions of 1954
$\qquad\qquad$ dollars
$\quad\; D$ = capital consumption allowances, in billions of 1954 dollars
**Du = dummy variable: 0 for 1929–1946, 1 for 1947–1962
**F_e = exports, in billions of 1954 dollars
$\quad\; F_i$ = imports, in billions of 1954 dollars
**G = government purchases of goods and services, in billions of
$\qquad\qquad$ 1954 dollars

h = index of hours worked per week, in 1954 = 1.00

**i_d = average discount rate at all Federal Reserve banks, in percent

I_h = residential construction, in billions of 1954 dollars

I_i = stock of inventories, in billions of 1954 dollars

i_L = average yield on corporate bonds (Moody's), in percent

I_p = investment in plant and equipment, in billions of 1954 dollars

i_s = yield on prime commercial paper, four to six months, in percent

** N_g = government employees, in millions

** N_L = total labor force, in millions

**N_s = self-employed workers, in millions

N_w = wage and salary workers, in millions

p = implicit GNP deflator, in 1954 = 1.00

PB = proprietors' income, in billions of current dollars

P_{cb} = corporate profits including inventory valuation adjustment, in billions of current dollars

**p_i = implicit price deflator for imports, in 1954 = 1.00

RE = retained earnings including inventory valuation adjustment, in billions of current dollars

RI = rental and net interest income, in billions of current dollars

**RR = year-end ratio of member banks' excess to required reserves

T = personal taxes + contributions for social insurance—government and business transfer payments to individuals—interest on government debt, in billions of current dollars

T_c = corporate profits taxes, in billions of current dollars[9]

**T_i = reconciling item between net national product and national income, in billions of current dollars

W = wages and salaries and supplements, in billions of current dollars

w = annual wage rate of all employees, in thousands of dollars per year

**W_g = wage bill of government employees, in billions of current dollars

X = GNP, in billions of 1954 dollars

Y = personal disposable income, in billions of 1954 dollars

THE SUITS MODEL

A model similar to the Klein–Goldberger model was developed by the Research Seminar in Quantitative Economics at the University of Michigan

[9]The variables T and T_c are endogenous. Functions are not given for these variables because of frequent changes in the tax laws. Including these functions, there are 22 equations in the model.

under the direction of Daniel Suits.[10] This model contains about 40 equations and, like the Klein–Goldberger model, is estimated from annual data in terms of changes in the variables. The Michigan research seminar has been making annual forecasts of the endogenous variables since 1953. The model has been reestimated each year and is occasionally respecified.

An adaptation of the Suits model was estimated with quarterly data in the late 1960's, and a version of that model was used by the President's Council of Economic Advisors in the last years of the Johnson administration.

THE BROOKINGS MODEL

A more disaggregated model of the U.S. economy has been developed by a group of economists working at the Brookings Institution.[11] This model consists of nearly 200 equations, estimated from quarterly data. The model is broken down into seven sectors: durable manufacturing, nondurable manufacturing, trade, the regulated sector, construction, farming, and residual industries (primarily services). There is some debate among economists concerning whether such a highly disaggregated model is necessary to obtain accurate predictions. The forecasting record of the Brookings model has not been significantly better than that of smaller, more aggregated models. However, the model is still in the developmental stage and the forecasting record is rather limited.

THE OFFICE
OF BUSINESS ECONOMICS MODEL

The Office of Business Economics (OBE) of the Commerce Department maintains a model which is essentially an adaptation of the Klein–Goldberger model. This model contains 36 behavioral and technological equations and 13 identities. It is estimated with quarterly data and is used primarily for short-run forecasting.

THE WHARTON MODEL

The Wharton model is the most recent adaptation of the original Klein–Goldberger model.[12] This model uses quarterly data and generates short-run

---

[10] For a description of this model, see Daniel B. Suits, "Forecasting and Analysis with an Econometric Model," *The American Economic Review*, LII (March, 1962), 104–132.

[11] For a description of this model, see J. S. Duesenberry, G. Fromm, L. R. Klein, and E. Kuh, eds., *The Brookings Quarterly Econometric Model of the United States Economy* (Skokie, Ill.: Rand McNally & Company, 1965).

[12] For a description, see M. K. Evans and L. R. Klein, *The Wharton Econometric Forecasting Model* (Philadelphia: University of Pennsylvania, 1968).

forecasts for each quarter, up to two years in advance on a quarterly basis. This model is more disaggregated than the original Klein–Goldberger model, yet it is smaller than the Brookings model. It contains 47 stochastic equations and 29 identities, with 76 endogenous variables. The developers of the Wharton model claim that it is the largest and most detailed model of the U.S. economy that is continuously being updated.[13] While the Brookings model is larger, it is still being developed, is not continuously updated, and has not been used as much for actual forecasting and policy planning as the Wharton model.

DISCUSSION OF THE MODELS

The econometric models of the U.S. economy developed in the 1950's were highly aggregated and based on annual data. These models have been used to make annual forecasts and have a forecasting record of about 15 years. The models developed in the 1960's have been larger and more disaggregated and have been estimated with quarterly data. The largest model to date, the Brookings model, is still being specified, and most of the forecasting attempted with this model has been in the nature of simulation, where the actual values of the variables to be forecast (the endogenous variables) are already known. The Wharton model is smaller than the Brookings model, but more disaggregated than the OBE model. It has a forecasting record of about five years.

THE FORECASTING RECORD

A comparison of the actual forecasts and forecast errors made by the various models is shown in Tables A-2 through A-5. Table A-2 compares the short-run (quarterly) forecast record for the Wharton model and the more highly aggregated OBE model.

Both the OBE and Wharton projections were made in the fourth quarter of each year, from 1952–1964, from one to four quarters in advance. The table shows the average forecast error for each quarter over the 13 year period. In most cases, the OBE results are better than those of the Wharton model.

Table A-3 compares the mean absolute percentage errors in the Wharton and Brookings models, based on simulations for 38 sample quarters, 1953(3)–1962(4). Except for business investment, the Brookings model performed slightly better than the Wharton model.

[13] See Michael Evans and Lawrence Klein, "Experience with Econometric Analysis of the U.S. 'Konjunktur' Position," in *Is the Business Cycle Obsolete?*, ed. by Martin Brofenbrenner (New York: John Wiley & Sons, Inc., 1969), pp. 384–385.

Table A-2   Comparison of Short-Run Forecast Errors
for the Wharton Model and OBE Model

	Wharton	OBE	Wharton	OBE
	GNP (in billions of current dollars)		GNP (in billions of 1958 dollars)	
1Q	3.5	2.5	3.7	2.9
2Q	6.2	2.6	5.7	2.6
3Q	6.9	4.1	7.7	3.7
4Q	6.5	3.7	7.3	3.4

	Wharton	OBE	Wharton	OBE
	Consumption (in billions of current dollars)		Investment in Plant and Equipment (in billions of current dollars)	
1Q	2.1	1.9	0.7	0.6
2Q	2.4	2.0	1.2	0.6
3Q	3.7	3.0	1.4	0.7
4Q	3.5	3.6	1.4	0.8

	Wharton	OBE	Wharton	OBE	Wharton	OBE
	Residential Investment (in billions of current dollars)		GNP Deflator (1958 = 100)		Disposable Income (in billions of current dollars)	
1Q	0.9	0.7	0.2	0.3	2.1	1.4
2Q	1.1	0.6	0.4	0.3	1.5	1.5
3Q	1.0	0.8	0.5	0.5	2.6	3.0
4Q	0.9	0.8	0.6	0.7	3.1	3.3

Source: Michael Evans and Lawrence Klein, "Experience With Econometric Analysis of the U.S. 'Konjunktur' Position," in *Is the Business Cycle Obsolete?*, ed. by Martin Bronfenbrenner (New York: John Wiley & Sons, Inc., 1969), p. 381.

Table A-3   Mean Absolute Percentage Errors in the Wharton and Brookings Models (in percent)

	Wharton	Brookings
GNP (in constant dollars)	2.32	2.03
GNP (in current dollars)	2.79	2.70
GNP deflator	1.56	1.46
Aggregate business investment*	6.28	8.49
Aggregate consumption*	3.19	1.55
Disposable income (in current dollars)	2.90	1.75

*Wharton model data in current prices; Brookings model data in constant prices.

Source: Michael Evans and Lawrence Klein, *op. cit.*, p. 385.

Table A-4   Comparison of GNP Forecasts in the Michigan and Wharton Models (in billions of current dollars)

Year	Actual GNP	Michigan Forecast	Error	Wharton Forecast	Error
1959	483	464	−19		
1960	503	493	−10		
1961	519	521	2		
1962	556	560	4		
1963	584	578	−6	585	1
1964	623	619	−4	625	2
1965	666	652	−14	662	−4
1966	732	725	−7	728	−4
1967	781	794	13	784	3
Average absolute					
error: 1959–1967			8.8		
1963–1967			8.8		2.8

Source: Michael Evans, *Macroeconomic Activity* (New York: Harper & Row, Publishers, 1969), pp. 516–517.

Table A-5 Actual and Predicted U.S. GNP, Annual Rates
by Quarters 1952(3)–1964(2) in the Wharton Model
(in billions of current dollars)

Quarter	Actual	Predicted	Error	Error (in percent)
1952(3)	345.4	352.9	−7.5	−2.2
(4)	357.9	358.8	−0.9	−0.3
1953(1)	356.4	365.5	−0.1	−0.03
(2)	367.7	361.6	6.1	1.6
(3)	365.9	359.0	6.9	1.9
(4)	361.1	355.5	5.6	1.6
1954(1)	360.5	354.5	6.0	1.7
(2)	359.8	353.2	6.6	1.8
(3)	364.8	358.8	6.0	1.7
(4)	372.9	360.6	12.3	3.3
1955(1)	388.2	372.3	15.9	4.1
(2)	392.7	377.6	15.1	3.8
(3)	402.4	383.5	18.9	4.7
(4)	410.0	386.6	23.4	5.7
1956(1)	410.7	384.8	25.9	6.3
(2)	416.7	392.9	23.8	5.7
(3)	420.6	398.4	22.2	5.3
(4)	429.9	406.2	23.7	5.5
1957(1)	436.9	416.4	20.5	4.7
(2)	439.9	421.8	18.1	4.1
(3)	446.3	427.7	18.6	4.2
(4)	441.1	431.6	9.5	2.2
1958(1)	434.5	437.6	−3.1	−0.7
(2)	438.4	443.9	−5.5	−1.3
(3)	450.5	456.2	−5.7	−1.3
(4)	464.8	468.3	−3.5	−0.7
1959(1)	473.8	467.7	6.1	1.3
(2)	486.9	470.6	16.3	3.3
(3)	484.0	460.7	23.3	4.8
(4)	488.1	470.6	17.5	3.6
1960(1)	503.0	475.5	27.5	5.5
(2)	504.3	473.6	30.7	6.1
(3)	504.2	479.6	24.6	4.9
(4)	502.8	488.0	14.8	3.0
1961(1)	503.5	497.0	6.5	1.3
(2)	515.2	508.1	7.1	1.4
(3)	524.3	518.4	5.9	1.1
(4)	537.9	529.1	8.8	1.6
1962(1)	547.3	538.1	9.2	1.7
(2)	557.2	549.2	8.0	1.4
(3)	564.4	556.2	8.2	1.5
(4)	572.0	563.2	8.8	1.5
1963(1)	577.0	566.7	10.3	1.8
(2)	583.2	569.8	13.4	2.3
(3)	593.0	578.4	14.6	2.5
(4)	603.6	589.3	14.3	2.4
1964(1)	613.7	597.3	16.4	2.7
(2)	624.5	611.4	13.1	2.1

Source: Michael Evans and Lawrence Klein, *op. cit.,* p. 387.

Table A-4 compares annual GNP forecasts for the Michigan and Wharton models. Clearly, the Wharton forecasts are superior.

Although the models developed in the 1960's have a better forecasting record than the older, annual models, it is not clear that the highly disaggregated models (Wharton and Brookings) will perform better than a smaller model (OBE). Smaller models have the advantage of fewer data requirements, fewer equations to respecify and reestimate, as well as a certain simplicity which makes them easier to work with. A model such as the Brookings model with 200 equations is so complicated that no one individual can really be held responsible for it. At this writing, it has been in the development stage for 10 years and its forecasting record in simulation has not been as good as that of the OBE model.

Table A-5 shows the forecasting errors for predicting current dollar GNP in the Wharton model. These quarterly predictions for the period 1952(3)–1964(2) were obtained by simulation in which the actual values of GNP were known, but not used in the sample from which the structural parameters were estimated. Note that the model generally underestimates the true values of GNP.

A-4 Some Additional Problems of Specification

In the text we developed the multiplier analysis for forecasting policy targets for known values of the policy instruments, and for policy planning, that is, finding required values for the policy instruments when the targets are known. In this section we shall consider some additional multiplier problems. The foreign sector will be ignored for simplicity.

INCOME SHARES AND THE MULTIPLIER

As was demonstrated in Chapters 3 and 4, the value of the national income multiplier depends upon the marginal propensity to spend out of national income by consumers, business, and government. Recalling the aggregate demand identity and the national income equilibrium condition,

$$Y = D \equiv C + I + G$$

and expressing spending in each sector in terms of the autonomous and induced components,

$$C = a + bY$$
$$I = h + dY$$
$$G = G_0$$

the national income equilibrium condition is expressed as

$$Y = a + h + G_0 + (b + d)Y$$

and the national income multiplier is found to be

$$\frac{\Delta Y}{\Delta D} = \frac{1}{1 - b - d}$$

where ΔD is an autonomous change in spending from any sector.

In specifying the relationships in a macroeconomic model, consumption is generally assumed to be a function of disposable personal income, and business investment is a function business income. Thus, in an econometric model, the parameters to be estimated are typically the marginal propensity to consume out of disposable income (the regression coefficient for disposable income in the consumption function) and the marginal propensity to invest out of business income (the regression coefficient for the business profits variable in the investment equation). How can these parameters estimated from the behavioral relationships be used to formulate a national income multiplier which requires estimates of the marginal propensity to consume and invest out of national income?

National income can be broken down into the shares going to each sector:

$$Y \equiv Y_D + Y_B + Y_G$$

where

Y = national income
Y_D = disposable personal income
Y_B = business income net of taxes
Y_G = government income (tax receipts)

Suppose the distribution of income going to households, business, and government is known, and that

$$Y_D = kY$$
$$Y_B = lY$$
$$Y_G = mY$$

where

$$k + l + m = 1$$

and k, l, and m represent the percentage share of national income going to households, business, and government, respectively.

Suppose the behavioral equations, the consumption and investment functions, have been numerically specified, and that

$$C = \hat{\alpha} + \hat{\beta}Y_D$$

and

$$I = \hat{\gamma} + \hat{\delta}Y_B$$

Substituting the income shares equations into these equations, the relationships between consumption and investment and national income are found:

$$C = \hat{\alpha} + \hat{\beta}kY$$
$$I = \hat{\gamma} + \hat{\delta}lY$$

where $\hat{\beta}k$ is the marginal propensity to consume from national income and $\hat{\delta}l$ is the marginal propensity to invest from national income.

Suppose

$$\hat{\beta} = 0.9$$

and

$$\hat{\delta} = 1.2$$

with households receiving 60 percent of national income and business receiving 20 percent. Then the marginal propensity to consume from national income is

$$b = k\hat{\beta} = 0.6(0.9) = 0.54$$

and the marginal propensity to invest from national income is

$$d = l\hat{\delta} = 0.2(1.2) = 0.24$$

Therefore,

$$\frac{\Delta Y}{\Delta D} = \frac{1}{1 - b - d} = \frac{1}{1 - 0.54 - 0.24} = 4.545$$

Suppose the share going to households rises to 70 percent and that going to business falls to 15 percent. Then, if $\hat{\beta}$ and $\hat{\delta}$ are unaffected by the change in income distribution

$$b = 0.7(0.9) = 0.63$$

and

$$d = 0.15(1.2) = 0.18$$

and the multiplier becomes

$$\frac{\Delta Y}{\Delta D} = \frac{1}{1 - b - d} = \frac{1}{1 - 0.63 - 0.18} = 5.263$$

Thus, from a knowledge of relative income shares and the numerical parameter estimates of the consumption and investment functions, an estimate of the national income multiplier can be obtained.

DYNAMIC INSTABILITY
IN A MULTIPLIER MODEL

If the denominator of the multiplier becomes zero, its value becomes infinite, while if it is negative, the analysis is meaningless.[14] This implies the restriction that

$$b + d < 1$$

That is, the sum of the marginal induced effects be less than unity. Since

$$b + s = 1$$

where s is the marginal propensity to save from national income, this implies that the marginal propensity to invest must be less than the marginal propensity to save; that is,

$$s > d$$

if the multiplier analysis is to produce meaningful results.
   Suppose

$$s < d$$

so that a change in income will induce a greater change in investment than saving. If the economy were previously in equilibrium, then after the change,

$$I > S$$

That is, investment would exceed saving. Presumably interest rates would have to rise to discourage investment and stimulate saving.
   In this case the IS curve would have a positive slope, since at higher

[14]The analysis is meaningless in that it predicts that an autonomous increase in spending ultimately reduces the level of total spending which, as we shall see, does not occur.

levels of income, higher interest rates would be required to maintain national income equilibrium with saving equal to investment. A positively sloped IS curve may cause the national income equilibrium to be unstable. As demonstrated in Chapter 12, whether or not an equilibrium will be unstable depends upon the shape of the functional relationships in the model. It also depends upon the specific assumptions about behavior in the system, that is, the dynamic adjustment process.

Consider a system described by the IS–LM model of Chapter 8, with a product market lag and no lag in the money market. This implies that the interest rate adjusts instantaneously to a displacement of the general equilibrium so as to maintain continual equilibrium in the money market while the equilibrium between saving and investment is achieved only after the passage of time. Given these assumptions, the system will adjust along the LM curve, representing positions of money market equilibrium.

Suppose the economy is in general equilibrium. An increase in the money supply will cause the LM curve to shift rightward, displacing the old equilibrium.

If the IS curve is negatively sloped, the system will adjust to a new general equilibrium, as shown in case I in Figure A-3. Originally, the LM curve is LM_1, with income, Y_1, and the interest rate, i_1. An increase in the money supply causes the LM curve to shift to LM_2. The interest rate adjusts instantaneously to restore money market equilibrium, falling to i_1'. After a lag, income gradually increases in response to the reduction in the interest rate, and the interest rate rises with income as the transactions demand for money increases. The process of adjustment continues until equilibrium is attained in the product market at Y_2 and the rate of interest is i_2.

In case II of Figure A-3, the adjustment process is similar. Initially, the LM curve is LM_1 and income and the interest rate are Y_1 and i_1, respectively. An increase in the money supply causes the LM curve to shift to LM_2 and the interest rate declines to i_1', to maintain money market equilibrium. The decline in the interest rate stimulates investment and causes income to increase. Notice, however, that since the IS curve is positively sloped, the change in income will induce more investment than saving, since the marginal propensity to invest is greater than the marginal propensity to save. Other things being equal, once an initial increase in income takes place, increases in investment will exceed increases in saving, income will increase indefinitely, and a new equilibrium will never be reached. In this example, however, increases in income cause the transactions demand for money to increase and the interest rate to rise. In case II, the interest rate rises rapidly enough in response to increases in income to dampen investment causing it to be equated with saving and restoring a new equilibrium at Y_2 and i_2.

In case III, however, increases in the interest rate are not sufficient to restore equilibrium in the product market. The interest rate does not rise

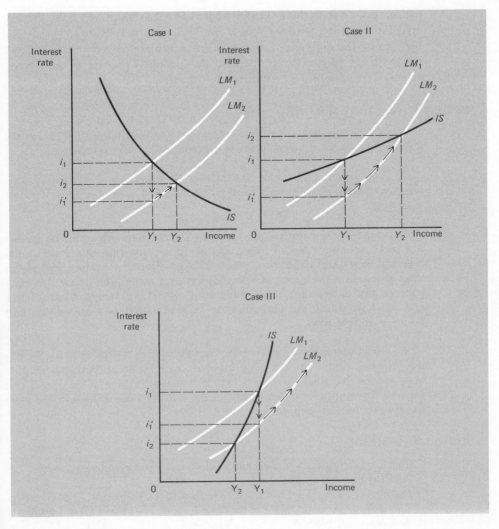

Figure A-3   Dynamic Adjustment in the IS–LM Model
with a Product Market Lag

rapidly enough in response to the increased demand for transactions balances to dampen investment to the level required to restore the saving–investment equality. While an equilibrium consistent with LM_2 is defined at Y_2 and i_2, it will never be attained (it is technically unstable), and income will increase indefinitely unless restrained by measures external to the model.

Given a positively sloped IS curve, implying that the marginal propensity to invest exceeds the marginal propensity to save, the adjustment

380

process described in this example will restore equilibrium only if the *IS* curve is flatter than the *LM* curve. A new equilibrium is most likely to be restored the smaller the difference is between the marginal propensity to invest and the marginal propensity to save and the greater is the rise in the interest rate associated with a given increase in income.

Questions for Study and Review

1. Why is specification such an important part of building an econometric model? How does the specification process differ from estimation?

2. Econometric models are stochastic rather than exact. What does this mean, and what does it imply for their usefulness for forecasting and policy planning?

3. Suppose you were asked to specify and estimate one of the equations in a macroeconomic model. Select one of the relationships discussed in this text and explain in detail how you would go about the project. Include in your discussion problems of specification and estimation as well as data sources and definitions. What difficulties would you expect to encounter and what would be the limitations of your equation as a forecasting and policy-planning tool?

4. The government is considering two alternative tax schemes for financing an expenditure project. One involves an increase in personal income taxes, while the other involves a tax on business income. How would you forecast the multiplier effect, if any, of the two projects? Which would have the greater impact, and why?

Additional Reading

Christ, Carl, "Aggregate Econometric Models," *The American Economic Review*, XLVI (June, 1956), 385–408.

Duesenberry, J. S., G. Fromm, L. Klein, and E. Kuh, eds., *The Brookings Quarterly Econometric Model of the United States*. Skokie, Ill.: Rand McNally & Company, 1965.

Evans, Michael, and Lawrence Klein, "Experience with Econometric Analysis of the U.S. 'Konjunktur' Position," in *Is the Business Cycle Obsolete?* ed. by Martin Bronfenbrenner. New York: John Wiley & Sons, Inc., 1969, pp. 359–388.

Hickman, Bert, ed., *Quantitative Planning of Economic Policy*. Washington, D.C.: The Brookings Institution, 1965.

Klein, L. R., and A. S. Goldberger, *An Econometric Model of the United States, 1929–1952*. Amsterdam: North-Holland Publishing Company, 1955.

Suits, Daniel B., "Forecasting and Analysis with an Econometric Model," *The American Economic Review*, LII (March, 1962), 104–132.

B

Appendix:
Sources
and Definition
of the Data—
The National Accounts

National income models would be useless for policy planning without data for evaluating the performance of the economy and measuring the impact of public policy. Furthermore, data are required for testing the validity of the structural hypotheses—the behavioral and technological relationships—of the model and for estimating the parameters of these relationships.

Although statistical measurement is a prerequisite for policy planning, there is no point in collecting data unless they have a useful meaning in terms of the economic model. Consequently, an understanding of the theoretical basis of the planning model must precede the discussion of the techniques of national income accounting and the conceptual problems associated with collecting meaningful data. For this reason we have departed from the traditional textbook format and have placed the treatment of national accounting at the end of this book.

We have seen how macroeconomic theory can be adapted into a model for policy planning and forecasting. Before concluding our study of the design of macroeconomic policy, it remains to consider whether or not the data of the national accounts provide a close empirical approximation to the theoretical structure of the model.

B-1 The National Accounts and the Design of Macroeconomic Policy

The data of the national accounts are used for several purposes. As we have seen, they are necessary for the construction of macroeconomic policy models, both for estimating parameters in the equations of the models as well as forecasting on the basis of these relationships.

National accounts data are also used as criteria for evaluating the performance of the economy and measuring the impact of public policy. Thus, a decline in GNP, as measured by the national accounts statistics, indicates a decline in the level of economic activity and suggests a need for remedial action. If government increases spending and GNP rises, this response may be viewed as indicative of the success of the policy.

Other implications, often of dubious validity, are sometimes drawn from national accounts data. National income statistics are often viewed as measures of welfare. This is particularly true when an international or intertemporal comparison is made. Thus, since per capita GNP in the United States in 1969 was $4242 while in Sweden it was $2859, then the assumption can be made that the "standard of living" in the United states is higher than that in Sweden. Alternatively, per capita GNP in the United States in 1963 was $2878. Does this imply that Americans are better off today than in 1963? Was the standard of living in Sweden in 1969 comparable to that of the United States in 1963? Since many people believe that an increase in real GNP or national income implies an improvement in economic welfare, understanding of the sources and definitions of the data is important for evaluating these statistics in these terms.

NATIONAL ACCOUNTING
AND THE KEYNESIAN REVOLUTION

Most of our data measuring national income aggregates and other variables which comprise the macroeconomic models are of post-World War II vintage. It is not surprising that national accounting developed after the Keynesian revolution, since before that time policy planning was not based on econometric models, and consequently, data were not required. Furthermore, national income and employment were not viewed as policy targets, and hence, measures of these aggregates were not required for policy design and evaluation.

Some pre-Keynesian economists, such as Simon Kuznets and Colin Clark, developed data series for national income or product because of their interest in the historical process of economic growth and development. While these data have provided a basis for statistical investigations of the prewar period, the interest of the compilers was primarily historical and descriptive. There was no serious attempt to incorporate the data into an economic model or to use them for policy planning. Consequently, the definitions employed in this early research are often quite different from those required for the theoretical analysis. Furthermore, differences in definitions often rendered the work of different compilers incomparable.

Just as Keynesian economic theory led to the development of macroeconomic planning models, so did the development of these models result in the establishment of the theory and practice of national income accounting. In many respects, practical policy planning is limited by the feasibility of measuring the variables in the model. For instance, suppose the policy planner decides to incorporate Friedman's permanent income hypothesis about consumption in his model. The essential explanatory variable, permanent income, cannot be measured. Consequently, a measurable proxy variable for permanent income must be found if the hypothesis is to be tested statistically and used for forecasting. The reliability of the model now will depend upon the reliability of the proxy for explaining permanent income as well as the reliability of the permanent income hypothesis for explaining consumption.

Not only are data required to make theory operational for policy planning, but national accounting must be done within a theoretical framework if it is to be useful for economic analysis. For example, for a Keynesian model, business expenditure (investment) must be separated from expenditures of households. Furthermore, business expenditure must be broken down into inventory accumulation and investment in plant and equipment. On the other hand, there is no point in collecting data for expenditures of people weighing more than or less than 200 pounds since there is no theoretical model to which these data can be applied.

As we shall see, national accounting is not merely a process of data collection, but involves many complex conceptual problems. This is due to the requirement that the data of the national accounts measure meaningful activities and phenomena from the viewpoint of economic theory. Before turning to these problems, however, we shall examine some of the definitions and approaches of national accounting.

B-2 Definitions and Approaches

The U.S. Department of Commerce computes income and expenditure accounts for the individual sectors of the economy—households, business, government, and foreign sector. It also compiles national income and product aggregates for the economy as a whole. The sector approach is useful for Keynesian analysis. The national income and product approach is useful for evaluating the overall performance of the economy and the impact of public policy. It is from the aggregated accounts that welfare implications are typically drawn.

THE AGGREGATED ACCOUNTS

Before turning to the sector accounts, it is useful to consider the definitions of the items which comprise the aggregated accounts. The accounting framework which shows the relationship between the various measures of economic activity is shown in Table B-1, with data provided for 1969.

Gross national product measures the value of the total output of goods and services during the accounting period, including consumption goods, capital goods, and exports. Only the value of final products (i.e., those goods not used up in the production of other goods during the accounting period) is included in this measure. Thus, while bread is considered a final good, the wheat from which the bread is made is an intermediate good. Since the value of the wheat is included in the price of the bread, it will be double counting to include both the wheat and the total bread value in the measure of GNP.

It may be difficult to determine which products are final products and

Table B-1   National Income and Product, 1969
(in billions of dollars)

Gross national product		932.3
less: Capital consumption	77.9	
Net national product		854.4
plus: Subsidies less surplus of government enterprises	1.1	
less: Indirect business taxes	86.6	
Business transfer payments	3.6	
Statistical error	−6.2	
National income		771.5
less: Corporate profits and inventory adjustment valuation	88.7	
Contributions for social insurance	54.4	
plus: Net interest paid by government and consumers	28.7	
Government transfers to persons	61.9	
Business transfers	3.6	
Dividends	24.6	
Personal income		747.1
less: Personal tax payments	117.5	
Disposable income		629.6
less: Personal consumption expenditures	576.0	
Interest paid by consumers	15.3	
Personal transfers to foreigners	0.7	
Personal saving		6.0

Source: U.S. Department of Commerce, Office of Business Economics. *Survey of Current Business* (Washington, D.C.: U.S. Government Printing Office; 1970).

which are intermediate. Suppose the wheat is made into flour. If the flour is used by a commercial baker who sells bread, then it is an intermediate product. On the other hand, if it is sold to a housewife who makes the bread herself, it is a final product, since a housewife's services are not counted as part of the nation's GNP.[1]

One way out of the dilemma is to use the value-added approach for measuring total output. This approach was outlined in Chapter 2. If the value of all intermediate products is subtracted from the value of output at each

[1] This omission may be due primarily to measurement problems rather than to the legitimacy of categorizing housework as economic activity.

stage of production, then the result, value added, is exactly equal to the value of the final product.

Table B-2 shows value added for each stage in the production of a loaf of bread. At each stage, the value of the goods in the previous stage is subtracted from receipts to obtain value added. Total value added in each stage is exactly equal to the retail price of bread, 20 cents.

The value-added approach is used in national accounting both because of its conceptual simplicity and because firms maintain records in terms of value added for tax purposes. As we saw in Chapter 2, value added is composed of wages, profits, interest and rent, that is, total income earned in the production process. Since this income is subject to tax, firms record it in their individual accounts. Accounts of business establishments are the principal source of data for the national accounts.

Net national product (NNP) measures the total output of goods and services after allowance is made for equipment that is worn out or rendered obsolete during the accounting period. Since some goods are used up in the production process, their value should be deducted from total output to obtain a true picture of the total performance of the economy. Since capital consumption cannot be exactly pinpointed, there is a large factor of inexact measurement in NNP. Capital consumption (depreciation) allowances are used as a measure of the value of worn-out or obsolete equipment. However, these may overstate actual depreciation since they are calculated for tax purposes. Firms will generally take the largest depreciation allowance permissible since depreciation is deducted from taxable income.

National income measures the total payments to factors of production in the form of wages, profits, interest, and rent. Conceptually, national

Table B-2 Value Added in the Production of Bread

Stage of Production	Receipts (in cents per unit)	Cost of Intermediate Goods (in cents per unit)	Value Added (in cents per unit)
Wheat	4	0	4
Flour	6	4	2
Bread (wholesale)	12	6	6
Bread (retail)	20	12	8
Total value added (in cents per unit)			20

income is exactly equal to net national product or to GNP when depreciation is included in corporate income. Within the national accounting framework, national income differs from NNP only by a few minor items which are essentially transfer payments. It is important to exclude income transfers from income actually earned in the production process. The difference between NNP and national income is definitional, however, and not theoretical.

Personal income, income received by individuals, is obtained by subtracting corporate income from national income. Transfer payments to individuals by corporations and government are included in personal income. *Disposable income* is obtained by subtracting personal tax payments from personal income.

THE SECTOR ACCOUNTS

For macroeconomic analysis with a Keynesian model, it is important that the data are broken down by sector. The Commerce Department classifies income receipt and expenditure by major economic groups—households, business, government, and foreign sector. Thus, total GNP can be viewed as the sum of the expenditures of each of these groups,

$$GNP = C + I + G + X_n$$

and national income is the total of incomes earned by each group. National income can also be broken down by type of income, that is, wages, profits, interest, and rent.[2]

Table B-3 shows receipts and expenditures for each sector. The excess of receipts over expenditures is net saving for that group. Notice that, for the economy as a whole, net saving equals zero. Table B-4 shows total saving for each sector. For the economy as a whole, saving equals investment. The absence of net saving in the aggregate or, equivalently, the saving–investment equality does not imply that the economy is in equilibrium, but merely that expenditure and investment as measured in the national accounts are *ex post* rather than *ex ante* concepts. Thus, unintended inventory accumulation is included in the measures of business expenditures and gross private domestic investment; and the sectoral accounts reflect the identities,

Income earned $\equiv$ Value of output $\equiv$ *Ex post* (actual) expenditure
Saving $\equiv$ *Ex post* (actual) investment

---

[2]While the Commerce Department also provides data for GNP by sector of origin, this categorization is not particularly relevant for macroeconomic analysis since practically all GNP originates in the business and government sectors. The breakdown is useful, however, for an indication of the proportion of GNP provided by the public sector.

Table B-3   Receipts and Expenditures of Major Economic Groups, 1969 (in billions of dollars)

	Receipts	Expenditures	Saving or Dissaving
Persons			
Disposable income less interest and transfers paid to foreigners	613.6		37.6
Consumption		576.0	
Business			
Gross retained earnings	98.6		
Gross private domestic investment		139.6	−41.0
Government			
Receipts minus transfer payments	223.7		
Purchases of goods and services		214.7	9.0
International			
Foreign net transfers by persons and government	2.6		
Net exports		2.0	0.6
Statistical error	−6.2		−6.2
Total	932.3	932.3	0

Source: U.S. Department of Commerce, Office of Business Economics. *Survey of Current Business* (Washington, D.C.: U.S. Government Printing Office, 1970).

Table B-5 shows national income categorized by type of income. This breakdown is useful for models which incorporate changes in income distribution as a variable. Suppose that the marginal propensity to consume (*MPC*) from rental or farm income is different from the *MPC* from wages and salaries. If this is the case, then the aggregate *MPC* will depend upon the distribution of personal income between the various sources. Data on distributive shares are required for parameter estimation and forecasting from this model.

Many events which affect the economy have an impact on income distribution. Furthermore, as the structure of the economy changes over time, distributional shares are affected. Not only do these changes affect overall spending decisions, but they have implications for economic welfare as well. Furthermore, a breakdown by type of income earned is indicative to policy makers of the distributional impact of their programs.

Table B-4   Saving and Investment, 1969
(in billions of dollars)

Personal saving		37.6
Business saving		98.6
Government saving		9.0
Federal	9.7	
State and local	−0.7	
Total saving		145.2
Gross private domestic investment		139.6
Net foreign investment		−0.6
Total investment		139.0
Statistical error		−6.2

Source: U.S. Department of Commerce, Office of Business Economics. *Survey of Current Business* (Washington, D.C.: U.S. Government Printing Office, 1970).

B-3   Conceptual and Theoretical Problems of National Accounting

Because the measurements of the national accounts must conform to the requirements of the theoretical model, national accounting involves far more than mere data collection and compilation (a massive undertaking in itself). In many cases, theoretical considerations pose conceptual difficulties for

Table B-5   National Income by Type of Income, 1969 (in billions of dollars)

Compensation of employees		564.2
Wages and salaries	509.8	
Supplements	54.4	
Business and professional income (unincorporated enterprises)		50.2
Corporate profits		88.7
Farm income		16.1
Rental income of persons		21.6
Net interest		30.6
Total national income		771.5

Source: U.S. Department of Commerce, Office of Business Economics. *Survey of Current Business* (Washington, D.C.: U.S. Government Printing Office, 1970).

measurement that are insurmountable unless somewhat arbitrary guidelines are followed. The Commerce Department has developed certain definitions for the accounting aggregates which, while imperfect, at least contribute to a standardized system of accounts which is comparable from year to year. It is, however, important to know exactly what is included in and excluded from the various measures of economic activity which appear in the national accounts, particularly when they are used as indicators of the performance of the economy and the success or failure of economic policy or as measures of economic welfare. We shall consider some of these conceptual problems in turn.

PARTICULAR PROBLEMS
OF MEASUREMENT AND DEFINITION

Depreciation. To obtain a measure of net national product, capital consumption or depreciation must be estimated. Suppose a machine wears out in five years. Two problems arise. First, how should depreciation be allocated on an annual basis? Does the useful service of the machine decline by one-fifth each year or does it remain equally efficient each year until it is replaced? Second, should the total depreciation reflect the original cost of the machine or the cost of replacing it?

In addition, there is the problem of obsolescence. A machine may be scrapped before the end of its useful life because technological change has made it obsolete. While firms will fully depreciate a machine when it has become obsolete, it is questionable whether or not obsolescence actually represents a cost of production from a theoretical point of view.

The practice of the Commerce Department is to use business estimates of depreciation as a measure of capital consumption. Because firms will select that measure which gives them the greatest tax benefit, depreciation is likely to be overestimated in the national accounts, and therefore, NNP and national income will be understated. This may affect the comparability of these measures over time if there is a change in the tax laws concerning allowable methods of depreciation.

Inventory Valuation. Changes in inventories represent an increase in output and should be included in any measure of the national product. The measurement of inventory change poses a problem when prices change over the accounting period. A firm may experience windfall capital gains from the sale of inventory when prices rise, but these gains do not represent an increase in real output.

Firms generally record inventory in terms of value rather than volume. Furthermore, the value of inventory is generally recorded at original cost. If prices are rising over the period, units sold will have a higher value than their original cost. Consequently, a measure of inventory change in value terms will overstate the actual physical change that occurred.

If prices are changing at different rates in different industries, it will be impossible to account for real inventory change by using aggregative measures. Standard national accounting practice is to incorporate an *inventory valuation adjustment,* which is negative when prices are rising and capital gains are being realized from holding inventories and positive when prices are falling and firms are experiencing capital losses from holding inventories.

Government Transactions. The value imputed to most goods and services produced is their market price which includes production costs— wages, rent, and interest—as well as profits. Public goods and government services are not always sold on the market, however, and therefore, these goods and services must be valued at their cost of production with no provision for profits or losses. Since demand is not taken into consideration, this method may understate or overstate the value of government transactions relative to transactions in the private sector.

Transfer Payments and Capital Gains. Some market transactions should be excluded from GNP since they do not correspond to output of goods and services. Transfer payments such as unemployment compensation and welfare payments as well as private gifts and charitable contributions are excluded. Interest on the national debt is excluded in the U.S. accounts with the rationale that the debt largely reflects the costs of our major wars and does not reflect a return on assets.

Transfers of real property such as land and second-hand goods are also excluded. For instance, if a car is sold and repurchased, the only entry in the national accounts is the salesman's commission or service charge. If the deal is privately made, it will not show up in the national accounts at all, although theoretically a charge should be imputed for the owner's effort in finding a buyer and making the transaction.

Capital gains and losses reflect changes in value not attributable to changes in real output. These are also excluded from the GNP.

Nonmonetary Transactions. One of the most difficult problems of national accounting is to estimate the output of goods and services not traded in markets. A good bit of arbitrariness is introduced into the national accounts at this point, because only those nonmarket transactions are included for which a method has been found to impute value.

Suppose a farmer raises cows, slaughters them, and consumes the meat at home over the winter. A neighbor raises cows, sells them to the slaughterhouse, and then purchases the meat for home consumption. If nonmonetary transactions are excluded from the national accounts, then in the first instance the raising and slaughtering of cattle contributes nothing to GNP, while in the second case GNP is increased by the full retail value of the beef. Similarly, GNP would be increased if all dwellings were rented rather than owner occupied, if banks charged a service charge for checking accounts and then paid interest on the money held in them, and if housewives hired themselves out as domestic workers and employed other women in their own homes. In all the cases cited, the real output of goods and services would be substantially unaffected.

The Commerce Department has devised methods of imputing value to farm products consumed on farms, rental from owner-occupied houses, and service charges and interest on checking accounts. There has been no attempt to impute a value to a housewife's services, however. This omission may be due to the conceptual difficulties involved or it may reflect a belief that a housewife's duties do not constitute legitimate economic activity.

Definition of Economic Activity. The national accounts are designed to measure the level of economic activity. Economic activity implies the use of scarce resources to satisfy human wants. However, there is always some controversy concerning what is appropriately designated economic activity.

War involves the use of scarce resources, yet many observers feel this activity does not satisfy human wants. The production of square wheels, unsafe automobiles, and electric toothbrushes again utilize scarce resources but are of dubious utility to society. However, all of these activities, when undertaken, are included in the national accounts.

Other excluded items are family activities such as the services of women as housewives and of men as householders. Illegal activities, such as gambling, bootlegging, trafficking in narcotics, and prostitution are also excluded.

The enjoyment of leisure is also excluded from the accounting definition of economic activity. While the earnings of a professional golfer are included in national income, the efforts of a weekend duffer are not accounted for. Whether or not the resources used in the enjoyment of leisure are scarce is a matter of debate. The exclusion of leisure, household, and illegal activities and the inclusion of wasteful activities is of concern when the national accounting aggregates are treated as measures of welfare.

B-4 Accounting Aggregates as Measures of Welfare

Changes in GNP, NNP, and national, personal, and disposable income over time are sometimes considered to be indicative of changes in economic welfare as well as of the performance of the economy. Thus, a growth rate of 5 percent is said to be better than a rate of 2 percent. The increase in GNP from $87 billion in 1920 to $932 billion in 1969 is taken to mean that the quality of life has improved markedly over the period.

Comparisons are also made between countries. If per capita GNP in Uganda is $400, then it is assumed that living standards there are low and that people are better off in a country such as the United States with a per capita GNP of $4600. In general, the interpretation of the national accounts aggregates in terms of welfare is erroneous, and it will be useful to consider the limitations of the national accounting aggregates from this point of view.

INTERTEMPORAL COMPARISONS
OF THE NATIONAL ACCOUNTS AGGREGATES

Intertemporal comparisons of the national aggregates, that is, over time, can be misleading for a number of reasons. Changes in statistical coverage and definitions can bias the comparison, usually favoring the later years. The main change in coverage over time is the increasing proportion of transactions occurring in the monetary sector. This is particularly true for a developing country moving from a traditional agricultural economy where most goods are produced at home and trade takes the form of barter, to a modern economy with a large monetary sector. High rates of GNP growth in these countries may reflect, in part, growth of measured transactions rather than an increase in the level of economic activity for the country as a whole.

In advanced countries, with a relatively stable proportion of total activity in the monetary economy, refinements in statistical technique will result in more extensive computation of nonmonetary transactions. Thus, the inclusion of an imputation for rental of owner-occupied homes increases GNP for that year. Estimates for previous years are no longer comparable once the scope of statistical coverage has changed.

Structural changes in the economy may produce changes in the national accounts aggregates which do not reflect changes in real output. As more and more household tasks are performed by professional service agencies, the measured GNP will increase even though the level of economic activity remains substantially unchanged. Also, the structure of output may change. Gross national product, for instance, increased quite substantially in the United States during World War II. This was due to an increase in the production of war materials and a rationing of consumer goods. Few people considered this period to be one of increased economic welfare, although it did reflect an increase in economic activity. Structural changes, unlike changes in statistical coverage, however, do not necessarily impart a steady upward bias to the measures of economic performance over time.

The introduction of new goods presents a conceptual problem for comparing national income aggregates over time. New inventions in medicine, household conveniences, and transportation may serve to render the quality of modern life incomparable to that of the past century. New goods do not necessarily represent improved living standards, however. Life with the atomic bomb, air pollution, color television, and electric toothbrushes may in some respects be inferior to that of an earlier era.

If the national aggregates are to be used as indicators of economic welfare, price changes must be separated from changes in real output. If GNP rises by 10 percent and prices increase by 5 percent over the same period, then the real increase in GNP is only 5 percent. Using a price index to calculate the change in real GNP presupposes that all prices are rising at about the same rate. Over time, however, relative prices are likely to fluctuate with changes in demand and relative cost conditions, presenting an *index number problem.*

The index number problem consists of finding an index of price change when prices are changing at different rates. Suppose the price of automobiles rises by 2 percent while the price of peanuts increases by 50 percent. If automobiles represent a larger component of GNP than peanuts, the 2 percent increase in automobile prices should be weighted more heavily than the 50 percent rise in peanut prices.

Consider an economy producing just two goods, automobiles and peanuts. Suppose automobile production accounts for 75 percent of GNP, while peanut production accounts for 25 percent. Suppose the money value of GNP increases by 10 percent, while automobile prices rise by 2 percent and peanut prices rise by 50 percent. What is the real change in GNP?

A price index is a weighted average of the price changes for the two goods, where the weights are determined by the importance of that good in total output. Thus, an index of price change for this economy is

$$\frac{\Delta p}{p} = 0.02(0.75) + 0.50(0.25) = 0.14$$

That is, the average increase in prices is 14 percent. If money GNP rose by 10 percent, real GNP has declined by 4 percent, the change in money GNP less the change in prices.

Suppose, however, that the rise in peanut prices has caused the demand for peanuts to decline relative to that of automobiles, so that at the end of the period, peanut production is 10 percent of GNP and automobile production is 90 percent. Using quantity weights from the end of the period,

$$\frac{\Delta p}{p} = 0.02(0.9) + 0.50(0.1) = 0.068$$

the average increase in prices is 6.8 percent, and real GNP has actually increased by 3.2 percent. Notice that, in this example, the change in prices for each good did not vary. The only change was the relative importance of the two goods in total output.

Suppose that during the process of economic growth, the prices of goods and services in the fastest-growing sectors are actually falling relative to prices in the slower-growing sectors. If quantity weights from the earlier years are used, the index of price change will be much greater than if current year quantity weights are employed. Thus, by using current year quantity weights, the real rate of growth will be greater than if base year quantity weights are used.[3]

An index using base year weights is a Laspeyres index; one using current year weights is a Paasche index. The longer the period under examination, the greater the discrepancy between the Paasche and Laspeyres indices is likely to be. Theoretically, either index is a legitimate measure of price (or quantity) change.

One way around the index number problem is to use an average of the Paasche and Laspeyres indices. Another is to recompute the Paasche index for each accounting period and calculate the real change in GNP each time. This is the method actually practiced by the Commerce Department. However, for historical studies in which short-period data are not always available, the problem still exists. In this case it is important to determine which type of index is being used to compute a measure of real income change.

National income aggregates provide no indication of the distribution of the product between individuals. Any measure of welfare must take this into account, however. A decline in real income might actually reflect an improvement in social welfare if the product is more equitably distributed.

Finally, using any measure of economic performance as a measure of welfare implies that an increase in economic activity is synonymous with an improvement in welfare. Whether or not more automobiles, bombs, beer cans, and skyscrapers represent an improvement is questionable. Furthermore, the national accounts place no value on leisure. Presumably, if the workday were to increase to 12 hours, GNP would increase, but the loss in leisure would undoubtedly represent a decline in welfare.

In sum, the aggregate measures of the national accounts are very poor measures of welfare change over time. Even as measures of the intertemporal change in economic activity, narrowly defined, they must be viewed with caution because of changes in statistical coverage, definitions, economic structure, and the index number problem.

[3] Equivalently, price weights can be used to formulate an index of quantity change. Notice that in the example above, base year price weights will overstate the real rate of quantity increase relative to an index using current year price weights.

INTERNATIONAL COMPARISONS

International comparisons of national income and GNP are subject to some of the same difficulties as intertemporal comparisons. The most obvious, of course, are differences in coverage due to international differences in the percentage of total transactions made outside the household or barter unit. Per capita GNP in Uganda may be $400, but this does not imply that the value of the goods consumed by each person is only $400. It merely suggests that measured per capita transactions (usually in money) are $400. Perhaps a more comparable measure of Ugandan GNP with that of the United States is to measure GNP per person living in urban areas. However, it is clear that welfare comparisons between tribal life in Uganda and life in the United States are largely a matter of individual values and cannot be measured by national accounting techniques, no matter how perfect and extensive the coverage.

National accounting in different countries often uses different definitions and measures things in different ways. Most of the developed non-communist countries have attempted to standardize accounting techniques to make the aggregates as comparable as possible. Accounting practice in the USSR, however, is so different from that in the United States that Soviet measures must be revised by experts before they can be compared with those in the United States. For instance, the Soviets count intermediate as well as final goods in their measure of GNP, thus greatly overestimating total output, relative to value added.

Because of differences in demand and cost conditions, different countries have different product mixes and price structures. Since market prices are used to value goods and services, this may pose problems for comparability. Furthermore, these differences may reflect differences in value systems which should be taken into account when welfare is being compared. A country which values leisure and dislikes the trappings of modern technology may be better off with a much lower GNP than its neighbors.

Differences in price structures pose further problems for comparability since prices must be converted from one currency to another. The problem of international conversion of currency when price structures differ is equivalent to the index number problem over time. For practical purposes, the Commerce Department uses foreign exchange rates for currency conversion; however, these rates only reflect price ratios in the foreign sector and may not be indicative of international price relationships for the rest of the economy. This is particularly true for less-developed countries in which the foreign sector is often quite independent of the domestic economy. Furthermore, if a country experiences persistent balance-of-payments deficits or surpluses, foreign exchange rates do not adequately reflect relative prices even for the foreign sector.

Finally, international differences in the distribution of income must be taken into account. Some countries, such as Kuwait, have relatively high levels of per capita GNP, but the income distribution is so inequitable that the median income is far below the average or per capita level. A country with a lower level of per capita GNP, distributed more equitably, may provide a higher standard of living for most of its citizens.

Unless all of these limitations are taken into account, data from the national accounts are not a valid basis for making international comparisons of economic welfare. Even as a comparative measure of economic activity, avoiding the necessity for making the value judgments inherent in welfare comparisons, data from the national accounts should be used with caution. The more similar the countries with respect to level of development, income distribution, tastes, and product mix, the more valid the comparison is likely to be.

Questions for Study and Review

1. What is the significance of macroeconomic theory for national accounting and of national accounting for economic theory?

2. How would the following transactions appear in the national accounts?

(a) Unemployment compensation is increased by $1000 which is financed by a payroll tax of $1000.

(b) An exporter buys $500 of shirts from a manufacturer and sells them abroad for $600.

(c) An investor purchases a bond for $95 and earns 5 percent interest.

(d) An automobile manufacturer purchases $5000 of steel from a manufacturer and produces and sells a $6000 automobile.

(e) Suppose the steel in part (d) came from inventories accumulated in the previous period.

3. Discuss some of the practical and conceptual problems associated with making intertemporal and international comparisons of welfare based on data from the national accounts.

Additional Reading

Gilbert, Milton, and Kravis, Irving, *An International Comparison of National Products and the Purchasing Power of Currencies*. Paris: Organization for European Economic Cooperation, 1954.

Kuznets, Simon, "National Income: A New Version," *The Review of Economics and Statistics*, XXX (1948), 151–179.

————, *National Income and Its Composition, 1919–1938*. Vol. I. New York: National Bureau of Economic Research, 1941, Chapter 1.

Mishan, Ezra J., *The Costs of Economic Growth*. New York: Frederick A. Praeger, Inc., 1967.

National Bureau of Economic Research, *A Critique of the United States Income and Product Accounts. Studies in Income and Wealth*. Vol. XXII. Princeton, N.J.: Princeton University Press, 1958.

U.S. Department of Commerce, Office of Business Economics, "The National Income and Product Accounts of the United States, 1929–1965, Statistical Tables," supplement to *The Survey of Current Business* (August, 1966). Washington: U.S. Government Printing Office, 1966.

————, "National Income Supplement, 1954," supplement to *The Survey of Current Business* (November, 1954). Washington, D.C.: U.S. Government Printing Office, 1954.

————, "U.S. Income and Output," supplement to *The Survey of Current Business* (November, 1958). Washington, D.C.: U.S. Government Printing Office, 1958.

Index

402